More praise for *They Were Her Property*

"Stunning."
REBECCA ONION, *Slate*

"Deeply researched, fast-paced."
San Francisco Chronicle, Recommended Reading

"Compelling."
RENÉE GRAHAM, *Boston Globe*

"Ought to dispel the myth of the Southern belle for good."
SORAYA McDONALD, TheUndefeated.com

"One of the most significant books on the history of women and slavery."
EDWARD E. BAPTIST, author of *The Half Has Never Been Told:
Slavery and the Making of American Capitalism*

"This is an important work that changes the way scholars and the public
will view the role of white women during antebellum slavery. This book
challenges the notion of southern white women as silent beneficiaries of
the peculiar institution and suggests that they played a more dominant
role in shaping the social and economic structures of plantation life."
LONNIE G. BUNCH III, founding director, National Museum of African
American History and Culture, Evoke.org

"This is a deeply researched and powerfully argued book that
completely overturns romanticized notions of the plantation mistresses
and resistant southern white women. Stephanie Jones-Rogers reveals
how deeply complicit slaveholding white women were in upholding
the everyday cruelties and barbarity of racial slavery."
MANISHA SINHA, author of *The Slave's Cause: A History of Abolition*

THEY WERE HER PROPERTY

THEY WERE
HER PROPERTY

White Women as Slave Owners in the American South

Stephanie E. Jones-Rogers

Yale
UNIVERSITY
PRESS
New Haven & London

Yale University Press books may be purchased in quantity for educational, business, or promotional use. For information, please e-mail sales.press@yale.edu (U.S. office) or sales@yaleup.co.uk (U.K. office).

Set in PostScript Electra type by IDS Infotech Limited, Chandigarh, India.
Printed in the United States of America.

Library of Congress Control Number: 2018953991
ISBN 978-0-300-21866-4 (hardcover : alk. paper)
ISBN 978-0-300-25183-8 (paperback)

A catalogue record for this book is available from the British Library.

10 9 8 7 6

For my foremothers, Isabella, Quessie, and Arthalia

CONTENTS

INTRODUCTION: MISTRESSES OF THE MARKET

In 1859, after touring the antebellum South, the journalist and *New York Tribune* editor James Redpath attempted to explain for his readers why white southern women opposed emancipation. He believed that their sentiments were tied to a lifetime of indoctrination, "reared," as they were, "under the shadow of the peculiar institution." Slavery was "incessantly praised and defended" virtually everywhere they went, by everyone they knew, and in most of the publications they read. Their consciences, "thus early perverted," were "never afterwards appealed to," with the result that they saw no reason to change their views.[1]

Redpath assumed that white southern women did not know "negro slavery as it is" because their society shielded them from the institution's horrific realities. Insulated by southern patriarchs, white women seldom saw slavery's "most obnoxious features"; they "never attend auctions; never witness 'examinations;' seldom, if ever, see the negroes lashed." More profoundly, they did not know that "the inter-State trade in slaves" was "a gigantic commerce." Southern men revealed only "the South-Side View of slavery," and if the women of the South "knew slavery as it is," he was convinced, they would join in the protests against it.[2]

Redpath's assumptions represented a commonly held patriarchal view. Yet narrative sources, legal and financial documents, and military and government correspondence make it clear that white southern women knew the "most obnoxious features" of slavery all too well. Slave-owning women not only witnessed the most brutal features of slavery, they took part in them, profited from them, and defended them.

Martha Gibbs was one of those women.

Litt Young, one of Gibbs's former slaves, was interviewed as part of the Federal Writers' Project (FWP) of the Works Progress Administration (WPA), established by the Roosevelt administration in 1935. According to Young, Gibbs was a "big, rich Irishwoman" who "warn't scared of no man." She owned and operated a large steam sawmill on the Warner Bayou in Vicksburg, where it emptied into the Mississippi River. She also owned a significant number of slaves—so many, in fact, that she had to build two sets of "white washed" quarters with "glass windows" to house them all. She also built "a nice church with glass windows and a brass cupalo" for their worship. She fed them well, but she worked them hard, too.[3]

In step with other slave owners throughout the South, Gibbs employed an overseer to make sure that the people she kept enslaved performed the tasks delegated to them, but she also oversaw her overseer. Almost every morning, she "buckled on two guns and come out to the place" to personally ensure that

Litt Young (Federal Writers' Project, United States Works Progress Administration, Library of Congress, Manuscript Division)

things were running smoothly, and "she out-cussed a man when things didn't go right."[4]

Twice married and once widowed, Gibbs would not permit either of her husbands to interfere with her financial affairs, including the management of her slaves. Even though her second husband was a reputable physician in Vicksburg, he had little influence over her or the slave-related activities on their plantation. Litt Young remembered Gibbs's husband addressing her after witnessing the brutal whippings her overseer inflicted upon her slaves. He softly interjected, "Darling, you ought not to whip them poor black fo'ks so hard, they is going to be free jest like us sometimes." Unfazed, she snapped, "Shut up, sometime I believe you is a Yankee anyway." She was right. During the Civil War, he served the Union forces by treating injured soldiers.[5]

After the Confederates surrendered, and for reasons that remain unclear, local Union officers arrested Martha Gibbs and "locked her up in the black fo'ks church," where they kept her under constant guard for three days, "fed her hard-tack and water," and then released her. After the soldiers set her free, Gibbs freed her slaves, but only temporarily. One day, when her husband had gone to buy corn for his livestock, she gathered up some of her slaves, "ten, six-mule wagons," and "one ox-cook wagon," and set off with them. They walked about 215 miles, from Vicksburg, Mississippi, to " 'bout three miles from Marshall," Texas. She hired "Irishmen guards, with rifles," to make sure that none of her "freed slaves" ran away during the journey, and when they stopped to rest, the guards tied the men to trees. Then, on June 19, 1866, one year after these legally free but still enslaved people "made her first crop in Texas," Martha Gibbs finally let them go.[6]

Married slave-owning women like Martha Gibbs have received scant attention in historical scholarship. Historians have acknowledged that some southern women owned slaves, but they usually focus on the wealthiest single or widowed women. When they do encounter married slave-owning women in nineteenth-century records, they generally assume that the women's legal status as wives prevented them from owning slaves in their own right. Historians rarely differentiate between married women who owned enslaved people in their own right and married women who merely lived in households in which they engaged with, managed, and benefited from the labor of the enslaved people that others owned. Historians rarely consider why slave ownership might have mattered to the women in question, to the enslaved people they owned, to slaveholding communities, to the institution of slavery, or, more broadly, to the region. Historians have neglected these women because their behaviors toward, and relationships with, their slaves do not conform to prevailing ideas about white women and slave mastery.

While it has long been recognized that southern slave owners were in the minority and that they were by no means a homogenous group, so much of what scholars know about women in the slaveholding South draws upon the diaries or letters of the most elite—those living in households that owned more than ten enslaved people. Historians have chronicled these lives, producing microhistories about an extremely small subset of an already small group of white southerners. Such studies should not be used to make generalizations about the majority of women in slaveholding communities at large; records indicate that the majority of slave owners owned ten enslaved people or less.[7]

Scholars who examine the authority that women held over their slaves frequently focus on the women's obligatory, rather than voluntary or self-initiated, management and discipline of enslaved people. They argue that women could not be true "masters" of slaves. Rather, they were "fictive masters." Even when they possessed the skills and the gall to manage their slaves, these historians argue, they typically did not relish their power: they did not view their activities as "slave mastery," and neither did southern laws and courts. This was especially true when it came to violent forms of discipline. White women might punish enslaved people; they might even be brutal and sadistic, but they fell short of wielding a "master's" power. In sum, these scholars argue that slave-owning women's acts of violence differed from those of slave-owning men.[8]

By extension, many of these scholars flatly reject the idea that white married women could adeptly manage enslaved people without the assistance of men, be they white or black, or that, aside from a few exceptional women, they could possess the acumen to do so while also effectively running plantations. Married women, they argue, begrudgingly assumed roles as "deputy husbands" and "fictive widows" when their husbands were away. When their men were present, these women happily and enthusiastically relinquished such responsibilities and exhorted their men to handle what one historian has called a "man's business."[9] And in the view of more than a few historians of American slavery and the domestic slave trade, this was especially the case when it came to the business of buying, selling, and even hiring enslaved people. These scholars claim that the nasty and unseemly business of transacting for human beings was considered ill-suited to white ladies.[10]

In *They Were Her Property* I build upon these earlier studies, but I also depart from them in significant ways. I focus specifically on women who owned enslaved people in their own right and, in particular, on the experiences of married slave-owning women. In addition, I understand these women's fundamental relationship to slavery as a relation of property, a relation that was, above all, economic at its foundation. I am not suggesting that this was these women's *only* relationship to the institution or that the economic dimension of their relations overrode other aspects of their connections to slavery; rather, I argue that pecuniary ties formed one of slave-owning women's primary relations to African American bondage.

The story of these women's economic investments in slavery, I shall argue, tells us much about their economic roles in the institution and the process of nation-making that historians did not know (or want to know) about before. The economic historian Sven Beckert has argued that "slavery was a key part of American capitalism" and that "slave plantations, not railroads, were in fact America's first 'big business.'" If we examine women's economic investments in slavery, rather than simply their ideological and sentimental connections to the system, we can uncover hitherto hidden relationships among gender, slavery, and capitalism.[11] The products of these women's economic investment—the people they owned—including the wages enslaved people earned when hired out to others, the cash crops they cultivated, picked, and packed for shipment, and the babies they nursed, were fundamental to the nation's economic growth and to American capitalism.

Historians who explore slavery's relationship to capitalism generally focus on the roles that men played in the development of both.[12] But if we considered the very real possibility that some of the enslaved people these men compelled to work in southern cotton fields actually belonged to their wives, the narrative about American slavery and capitalism would be strikingly different. And when we consider that the enslaved people women owned before they married or acquired afterward helped make the nineteenth-century scale of southern cotton cultivation possible, the narrative of slavery, nineteenth-century markets, and capitalism as the domain of men becomes untenable.

Adam Smith, the preeminent eighteenth-century economist, argued that a married woman's financial dependence upon her husband bound her "to be faithfull and constant" to her spouse.[13] In line with Smith's thinking, we tend to imagine marriage as a colonial or nineteenth-century woman's primary, if not her only, avenue to financial stability, and for many women this was true. But circumstances existed in which white *men* were economically dependent upon, even indebted to, the women they married, and this was a widely recognized fact, even in the North. Abigail Adams, the second First Lady of the United States, advised her son John Quincy to postpone marriage until he had accumulated enough property to ensure that he would not be wholly dependent upon the wealth his future wife might bring into their household. When John

Quincy hinted at the possibility that he might indeed marry for money, Abigail firmly advised him never to "form connextions" until he saw "a prospect of supporting a Family." In his response, John Quincy assured his mother that he would never be "indebted to his wife for his property."[14]

In the South, slave-owning women possessed the kind of wealth that prospective suitors and planters in training hoped to acquire or have at their disposal. Why else would John Moore crassly tell his cousins Mary and Richard that "girls . . . bait their hooks with niggers and the more they can stick on the better success" they would have in securing a worthy husband? According to John Moore, even young women outside the ranks of the most elite slaveholders, who typically owned twenty or more slaves, could increase their chances of marrying well if they owned a few. He told his cousins that "the girl that has but one or two will get a few nibbles and occasionally catch a trout, but not until he has tried and failed at the larger hooks."[15] As this correspondence suggests, some men entered their marriages with little or no wealth, and their unions with propertied women became *their* primary avenue to financial independence.

A white man's pecuniary circumstances could change drastically upon marriage because state and local laws generally gave husbands control over the property their wives brought to the marriage. Simply by marrying a woman with property, even if she maintained control of it, a man could improve his position: husbands often borrowed money from their wives and used the enslaved people their wives inherited to cultivate the lands they bought with those loans. Legal petitions are on record in which women describe themselves as their husbands' creditors and financiers. Many of these women did not accept the loss of their legal claims to the property they brought into their marriages. In fact, many married female petitioners described their slaves as property they still owned and controlled, considering their husbands' control temporary—and as we shall see, the courts often agreed with them. Enslaved people also testified to the ways such ideas shaped marital relations in white households. Thus, in many respects, married women, their slaves, and their other assets made their husbands' commercial endeavors possible and enabled slavery to thrive in ways it might not have without those women's economic investments in the institution.

I call the women in this book "mistresses of the market." But what exactly does that mean? Scholars such as Jennifer Lynn Gross argue that nineteenth-century southern "mistresses" assumed roles that were restricted to the "dependent positions of daughter, wife, and mother," and that "daughters relied completely on their fathers for their public identities, and this dependence transferred to their husbands upon marriage."[16] Because of these constraints, historians contend, white southern women had little to do with enslaved people beyond the household. They generally did not personally own slaves, and when they did, their husbands exercised control over them. Southern mistresses were not adept at slave or plantation management unless extenuating circumstances, such as a husband's prolonged absence or death, compelled them to be. Even then, such women typically complained about having to take on "masculine" responsibilities. When it came to legal and financial matters, the nineteenth-century southern "mistress" resembled the colonial "gentlewoman" who was "less likely to know about, or assist in, the management of her husband's affairs or to be involved in trade or business of any sort."[17] These women tended to defer to their spouses and male kin in legal and financial matters, and if they did not want to, scholars maintain, law and custom forced them to do so. In virtu-ally every dimension of life, then, southern mistresses were held to be at the mercy of white men.[18]

In this book I employ the term *mistress* in a radically different way, one that aligns more closely with its original meaning. In Western Europe, a mistress was "a woman who govern[ed]; correlative to [a] *subject* or to [a] servant." She was "a woman who ha[d] something in [her] possession," and according to the his-torian Amy Louise Erickson, that something was capital. A mistress also exer-cised "dominion, rule, or power."[19] The term *mistress* did not signify a married woman's subservient legal position or a woman's subordinate status to that of a master. By definition and in fact, the mistress was the master's equivalent. Thus, when South Carolina legislators declared that "every master, mistress or over-seer, shall and may have liberty to whip any strange negro or other slave coming to his or their plantation with a ticket" (the pass an enslaved person had to carry when he or she left the master's estate), they were not imbuing mistresses with subordinate powers or power in their husbands' stead; they were recognizing the comparable powers and authority that these women possessed.[20] The term used to describe women's control of subordinates was not *mastery* but *mistress-ship*. Moreover, when formerly enslaved people talked about the control that their masters and mistresses exercised over them, they often accorded equal power to men and women. Robert Falls recalled that when his "Old Marster and Old Mistress would say, 'Do this!' . . . we don' it. And they say 'Come here!' and if we didn't come to them, they come to us. And they brought the bunch of switches with them."[21] Slave-owning women may not have referred to their management of enslaved people as "slave mastery," but they used the same strategies and techniques that male planters described in the "Management of Negroes" col-umns that appeared in the pages of agricultural periodicals throughout the South. When we listen to what enslaved people had to say about white women and slave mastery, we find that they articulated quite clearly their belief that slave-owning women governed their slaves in the same ways that white men did; sometimes they were more effective at slave management or they used more brutal methods of discipline than their husbands did.

The Western European *mistress* was defined in another important way that is relevant to the women I discuss in this book and the central argument I make. A mistress was a woman who was "skilled in anything," and when it came to the nineteenth-century market in slaves, southern women were savvy and skilled indeed. They studied the slave market and evaluated its fluctuations. They blended into the crowds that surrounded public auction blocks and courthouse steps as enslaved people were exposed for sale. They glided past local slave markets and walked along the streets where slaves were openly displayed. They sat in the front rows of the more aesthetically pleasing slave-auction venues dressed in luxurious silks, satins, and jewels. They stood side by side with other women at public auctions to watch traders and auctioneers sell enslaved people to the highest bidders. But these women did more than observe the procession of black bodies placed before prospective buyers on sale days.

White southern women conducted transactions with slave traders, who bought slaves from and sold slaves to them as they lounged comfortably within the confines of their homes. And they were not meek in their bargaining: traders often wrote to one another with tales of slave-owning women who harassed them about pending transactions. Other men described women who entered slave markets to see what kind of "merchandise" slave traders had for sale. They recalled how these women would interrogate and inspect the slaves who piqued their interest, and they commented on women who bought and took enslaved people home. Slave-owning women brought legal suits against individuals, both male and female, who jeopardized their claims to human property, and others sued them in kind. They bought and sold slaves for a profit, and, on rare occasions, they owned slave yards.

As the historian James Oakes has pointed out, some African-descended people, indigenous people, and women were viable and active members of the master class.[22] Race and gender, however, created unique constraints that these groups had to endure, adapt to, or circumvent. The experience of slave ownership *was* different for married women. The legal doctrine that placed their persons and their goods under their husbands' control compelled them to take extra steps to secure their separate ownership and management of enslaved people, processes that were not required of men. Their legal subordination to their husbands also meant that women could potentially find themselves in court when spouses, kin, and community members jeopardized or violated their property rights or attempted to exploit them. These special contingencies could prove to be insurmountable impediments for southern women who might hold or want to hold legal title to enslaved people and who might want to exercise control over the enslaved people they owned or came to possess. But the women discussed in this book were not dismayed or deterred by the legal challenges. They and their families took the steps necessary to own and maintain control over the enslaved people given to them by loved ones or bought or acquired upon, during, and after marriage. Such steps were neither simple nor easy. That women decided to take them to secure slave property for their own use and benefit reveals their deep economic interest and investment in the system of American slavery. Their willingness to do these things suggests that they were more, not less, invested in slavery and its growth than some men were.

The historian Susan O'Donovan has argued that the South was a region "where the slaveries were many" and where "freedom often assumed numerous and differently gendered shapes."[23] Although she was speaking about the experiences of enslaved people in particular, her conceptualization of many freedoms is also useful for understanding the circumstances that the white women discussed in this book confronted and created. For them, slavery was their freedom. They created freedom for themselves by actively engaging and investing in the economy of slavery and keeping African Americans in captivity. Their decisions to invest in the economy of slavery, and the actions that followed those decisions, were not part of a grand scheme to secure women's rights or gender equality. Nevertheless, slave ownership allowed southern women to mitigate some of the harshest elements of the common law regime as it operated in their daily lives. Women's economic investments in slavery, especially when they used legal loopholes to circumvent legal constraints, allowed them to interact with the state and their communities differently. And these women's actions challenge current understandings of white male dominance within southern households and communities in the antebellum era.

In countless ways, then, slave-owning women invested in, and profited from their financial ties to, American slavery and its marketplace. Yet they rarely documented those economic connections. Others, however—white men and enslaved people themselves—did make note of and speak about their activities, which the Civil War made tenuous and to which abolition eventually put an end.

When FWP employees traveled through the South searching out glimpses of the past through their interviews with formerly enslaved African Americans, individuals like Litt Young discussed and identified their female owners. Serving as the metaphorical flies on the walls of southern households, formerly enslaved people talked about some of the most violent, traumatic, and intimate dimensions of life for those who were bound and those who were free. They heard and saw things that typically remained obscured from view, details that white slave-owning couples often left out of personal correspondence or public communications— that is, when they were able to write at all. Many of the slave-owning women I discuss in this book contended with some form of illiteracy; they either were unable to read and write or possessed the ability to do one but not the other.[24] Enslaved and formerly enslaved people's recollections about their female owners thus serve as some of the only archival records about these women to survive.

The nature of slavery all but guaranteed that formerly enslaved people would relocate many times, be compelled to work in different regions of the South, and possibly cultivate different crops in different climates over the course of their lives. The government employees who interviewed them worked from a questionnaire that did not include any questions about whether and how their experiences of enslavement changed as they moved across the South. While some formerly enslaved people did offer details "off script," others simply chose to answer the questions posed.[25]

Some historians caution scholars against relying upon the testimonies of formerly enslaved people gathered in the mid-twentieth century. They contend that formerly enslaved people could not possibly have understood what slavery entailed because, after all, most of them were only children when slavery thrived in the South. Furthermore, they suggest that even if the survivors were old enough to have experienced their bondage in all its dimensions, it was unlikely that they remembered details clearly after such a long period of time; some seventy years had intervened between emancipation and the interviews. Moreover, most of the interviewers were southern whites, many the descendants of slave owners, and in the face of such people formerly enslaved interviewees probably felt intimidated and confused, and were less likely to offer candid accounts of what they endured in bondage or the people who kept them enslaved.[26]

That many of the people interviewed in the 1930s were children during their bondage was certainly the case, but it was not true of all of them. Some women, like Delia Garlic, "wuz growed up when de war come" and "wuz a mother befo' it closed." She was a centenarian when Margaret Fowler interviewed her in 1937. Similarly, Willis Bennefield believed that he was "35 years old when freedom [was] declared." The WPA interviewers talked to many others like them.[27]

Additionally, although some formerly enslaved people were young when they were freed, it is unlikely that they could forget what psychologists and gerontologists call "salient life events": pivotal experiences such as marriages, births, deaths, and, in the context of slavery, brutal beatings, sexual assaults, or familial separations that occurred after the sale or relocation of loved ones. Delicia

Patterson, for example, was fifteen when her owner brought her "to the court-house," and "put [her] up on the auction block to be sold." When Anne Maddox was thirteen, she was part of a speculator's drove that traveled from Virginia to Alabama. Tom McGruder, "one of the oldest living ex-slaves in Pulaski County," was "eighteen or twenty" when he "was sold for $1250." These formerly enslaved people could not forget such events or the slave owners who initiated them and were ultimately responsible for the trauma that followed. Moreover, remembering certain details about their bondage could mean the difference between life and death for such people both during and after slavery. As enslaved and formerly enslaved people navigated the southern landscape, their safety, and sometimes their very lives, often depended upon their ability to produce passes ("tickets") which accurately identified their owners, among other things.[28] And their continued ties to the white families that previously owned them could spare them some of the racial violence that characterized Reconstruction in the South.

Formerly enslaved people may have found their interviews tense and uncomfortable, but many of them spoke openly of the tragedies and traumas of slavery nonetheless. Despite the possibility of provoking a violent reaction, formerly enslaved people spoke with their white interviewers about matters as intimate as cross-racial sexual violence, white paternity of enslaved children, and incest, and as horrifying as torture inflicted by their masters and mistresses or former owners who murdered enslaved people. They argued that these were things, along with the constant threat of sales that would remove them from their homes and families, that they could never forget, regardless of how much time had elapsed.[29]

Furthermore, the interviewees did not always give their testimony in isolation. Family, friends, and individuals who came by to assist some elderly formerly enslaved people with daily tasks were often present during their interviews. When the FWP employee Zoe Posey visited Mary Harris to interview her about slavery for a second time, she was confronted by Harris's angry son, who initially prevented her from continuing her queries. He interrogated her about her intentions and proclaimed, "Slavery! Why are you concerned about such stuff? It's bad enough for it to have existed, and when we can't forget it, there is no need of rehashing it." At such an outburst, *Posey* may have been the one who was intimidated during the encounter, not her interview subject.[30] To be sure, formerly enslaved people often responded to questions about their enslavement with silence because they did not always want to remember or talk about their experiences. But thousands chose to do so despite their reservations. They told their stories in an atmosphere of intense racial hostility and in a region where simply refusing to step off the sidewalk when a white person passed by could result in their deaths. They believed that telling their stories was worth these risks. I honor their courage, heed their words, and foreground their testimony and remembrances in this book.

As I wrote, I grappled with whether to include terms like *nigger* that might be offensive to my readers and seem disparaging to my African American subjects. Ultimately, I decided to include the language used in these interviews because they are the best sources we have for understanding how enslaved people understood their lives and their worlds. In addition, making any changes to the text presented its own problems. Such revisions would sanitize the experiences of these formerly enslaved people and make it difficult for readers to understand how they perceived what had happened to them. They did not have to tell their stories, and they received little or nothing in recompense for their interviews. Nevertheless, they did tell their stories, and in the ways they felt most comfortable. In this book they speak in their own words.

Slave-owning women rarely talked about their economic investments in slavery, and they wrote about them even less. Their silence did not reflect their aversion to slavery or human trafficking. Many of them simply did not have the time or the skill to put their thoughts on paper, while those who did probably saw their pecuniary investments in slavery as commonplace and unworthy of note. This is their story.

No group spoke about these women's investments in slavery more often, or more powerfully, than the enslaved people subjected to their ownership and control. They were the people whose lives were forever changed when a mistress sold someone just so she could buy a new dress. They were best equipped to describe the agony that shook their bodies and souls when they returned from their errands to discover that their children were gone and their mistresses were counting piles of money they had received from the slave traders who bought them. Only enslaved people could speak about their female owners' profound economic contributions to their continued enslavement with such astonishing precision. This is their story, too.

THEY WERE HER PROPERTY

MISTRESSES IN THE MAKING

Lizzie Anna Burwell was like many other white girls growing up in slave-holding households in the Lynesville, North Carolina, area in 1847. She loved flowers and often strolled through her parents' garden with Fanny, the enslaved woman charged with her care. After spending so much time with Fanny, Lizzie Anna developed an intense bond with her, but one day Lizzie Anna became "vexed" with Fanny, so she went to her father and demanded that he "cut Fanny's ears off" and get her, Lizzie Anna, "a new maid from Clarksville." Lizzie Anna was three years old.[1]

Although young children commonly express displeasure in extravagant, even violent language, the terms they use reflect their environment, and Lizzie Anna's complaint tells us something crucial about hers: During those walks through the garden, and perhaps while observing her parents interact with the enslaved people around them, Lizzie Anna was learning how to be a slave owner. She was coming to understand the "obscene logic" that made it perfectly acceptable to enjoy the company of her enslaved caretaker in one moment and threaten to mutilate her or buy another slave to take her place the next.[2] In the comfort of her home, she was recognizing that she possessed the power to command others to do as she wished. And her father did little to discourage her from that belief. In fact, he relayed the incident to his sister with an air of convivial amusement, which suggests that Lizzie Anna's aunt also accepted the justification for her niece's behavior: Lizzie Anna was a mistress in the making. The people around her were crucial to her development as such.

White southern girls like Lizzie Anna learned how to be mistresses and slave owners through an instructional process that spanned their childhood and

adolescence. Over the course of these formative years, white girls practiced techniques of slave discipline and management, made mistakes and learned from
them, modified their behavior to meet various conditions, and ultimately decided
what kind of slave owners they wanted to become. It should come as no surprise
that many of them wanted to be profitable ones.

Slave-owning parents were critical to this learning process in two important
ways. They gave enslaved men, women, and children to their young daughters
as gifts on special occasions like baptisms, birthdays (especially twenty-first
birthdays), holidays, and marriage, or for no reason at all.[3] They also bequeathed
enslaved people to their daughters in their wills. And when human property was
transferred to them, these young women came to value the crucial ties between
slave ownership and autonomous, stable financial futures. Parents also offered
their daughters vicarious lessons in how to own and control enslaved people
through their own words and deeds. As young girls watched their parents manage the enslaved people around them, they observed different models of slave
mastery and through a process of trial and error developed styles of their own.

White southern girls grew up alongside the slaves their parents gave them.
They cultivated relationships of control and, sometimes, love.[4] The promise of
slave ownership became an important element of their identities, something
that would shape their relationships with their husbands and communities once
they reached adulthood.

In the colonial period, primogeniture—the practice of leaving all the family
property to the eldest son—helped parents determine the size and nature of each
child's inheritance or whether a child would inherit at all. During and after the
Revolution, however, Americans looked upon primogeniture unfavorably, not
only because it disadvantaged many young men and women, but because it was
the means by which British aristocrats secured their power and ensured that it
remained within their ancestral lines.[5] The newly declared states moved to abolish primogeniture: South Carolina and Delaware abolished it in 1776, Virginia
did so in 1785, and every state except Massachusetts and Rhode Island had abolished the practice by 1786. "By the end of the century," the historian C. Ray Keim
observed, "equal portions for all children was generally the rule of inheritance."
But even before the abolition of primogeniture in these states, individuals could
circumvent it by writing their wills in ways that allowed them to bequeath their
property however they chose.[6] Slave-owning parents thought very carefully about
the kinds of property they would give their daughters at various points in their
lives, and one of their most critical considerations was the amount of control their
daughters, or their daughters' husbands, would have over these gifts after marriage.[7] Frequently, parents were more inclined to give their daughters slaves than

land, and they often gave them in the expectation that their daughters would take charge of them.

Enslaved people often knew that they would be given to their owners' daughters well before the transfer of ownership took place. Bacchus White recalled that his owners "alwa's sed" that he "wus to belon' to Miss Kathie." Agnes James's master chose her as a gift for his daughter Janie Little, because, as James remembered, "He give all his daughters one of us to have a care for dem."[8] Just as enslaved people came to anticipate the transition from one owner to the next, young white girls did, too.

As they planned their daughters' futures, some slave-owning parents preferred to give their daughters female slaves, and they began doing so when their children were only infants. In 1836, when Mary Fuller Knight was eight months old, her father executed a deed of gift that gave her an enslaved female named Rose as well as any children Rose might have in the future. When the slave owner and future abolitionist Sarah Grimké was a child, her parents gave her a "little girl," whom they "bought out of a slave-ship." Filmore Hancock's grandmother "was given to missus, as her own de day she [the grandmother] was born." Remarkably, Hancock recalled, "Old missus was only a year old den."[9]

Multiple generations of slave owners adhered to this inheritance practice. Charity Bowery's first mistress "made it a point to give one of [Bowery's] mother's children to each of hers." Charity eventually belonged to her mistress's second daughter, Elizabeth. Mrs. William Keller owned Sarah Thompson Chavis, and she and Chavis gave birth to daughters around the same time. When Mrs. Keller's daughter Julia was still a young girl, Mrs. Keller gave her Chavis's daughter Amy as a "daily gift."[10] These kinds of property transfers continued into the daughters' adolescence.

Slave owners occasionally gave their female family members human property in ritualized affairs that helped mold their young daughters' development as slave owners from early on. The elders would join the hands of young heiresses together with those of the slaves they were receiving and tell them that the enslaved people in question were their property forever.[11] Occasionally, the wills of slave-owning parents and kin divided their property equally among their heirs but did not specifically allocate certain enslaved people to the individual family members who were entitled to portions of their estates. The wills would include statements such as "share and share alike" and would leave decisions about equitable distribution up to the executor. Under these circumstances, estate administrators would arrange "drawing" ceremonies. One formerly enslaved person described how the drawings worked: "When my old mistress died she had four children. . . . When Christmas come we had to be divided out, and straws were drawn with our names on them. The first straw was drawn, you would get that darkey. . . . Miss Betsey drawed mother and drawed me. Everyone drawed two darkeis [*sic*] and so much money."[12]

The records that slave owners left behind corroborate this narrator's reflections. In the fall of 1844, John Devereux's executors held a drawing during which they portioned out Devereux's slaves to his widow, daughter, and two sons. The groups of enslaved people that each of the heirs drew were documented in the records. It is noteworthy that Devereux's married daughter Frances received the largest portion of his estate.[13] For reasons that remain unclear, these kinds of estate divisions also occurred when slave owners were still alive. Sallie Crane did not understand why her master's property was being divided because "he wasn't dead nor nothin'," but nonetheless she "fell to Miss Evelyn," his daughter.[14]

These affairs were not simply for show; the property transfers and acquisitions that took place were significant events in white girls' lives, and even at very early ages these young women assumed partial responsibility for managing the enslaved people their parents and kinfolks had given them. As soon as the transfer was complete, the enslaved men, women, and children would take care of their new owners in whatever way was necessary. When Jennie Fitts was just a girl, her owner gave her to his daughter Annie: "Ise can membah whens de Marster takes me to Missy Annie and sez, 'Ise gibin you to Missy, You jest do what she tells you to.'" Taking her master's charge seriously, Fitts attended to her young mistress's every need and want: "Ise wid Missy Annie alls de time and 'tend to her. Ise wid her night and day, Ise sleeps at de foot ob her bed. Ise keeps de flies off her wid de fan, gets her drink and sich, goes places fo' to get things fo' her. When she am ready to go to sleep, eber night, Ise rub her feet." From Annie's head to her toes, Fitts "sho tend to Missy."[15]

Jennie Fitts undoubtedly had to learn how to complete many of the tasks that her mistress asked her to perform, but Annie had to develop some important skills, too. She had to learn how to be a mistress, and she thought self-consciously about what kind of slave owner she would be. Fitts often heard her young mistress say, "Ise sho am goin' to take care ob my nigger." And by Fitts's measure, "She sho did."[16]

Ownership and control went hand in hand, and for white girls who had slaves, developing techniques of management and discipline was an important aspect of their early training. For those who were newly inducted into slave-owning communities, "the plantation was a school" where they learned how to be propertied women.[17] According to the historian Joan Cashin, "Young white men learned the fundamental lessons in exercising power from older white men," but white girls learned these lessons, too.[18] Slave-owning parents allowed their daughters to assume the roles of instructor and disciplinarian early on. White parents also taught their daughters the basic principles of slave ownership through naming practices and by requiring enslaved people to use salutations that conferred respect when addressing them and their children.

As the historian Ann Paton Malone observed, "Some owners forbade slaves to name their own children," and in a not-so-subtle way, slave-owning adults indicated future ownership when they named enslaved infants after their own children or even allowed their children to name enslaved infants, as Daniel and Cornelia Johnson allowed their daughters to do. Betty and Mary Johnson named Betty Curlett and her sister Mary after themselves. On one occasion, when Betty's young mistress was trying to teach her the alphabet, Betty became distracted. Her mistress expressed disappointment in Betty's behavior because she thought it was an indication of Betty's lack of intelligence. She regretted the fact that Betty was her namesake and declared to her mother, "If she goin' to be mine I want her to be smart." When Betty began to crochet skillfully, her young mistress's pride was restored.[19]

Slave-owning parents also forced enslaved adults and children to use the salutations "Master" and "Mistress" when referring to their children from the moment the infants were born. Louise Martin, an FWP interviewer, claimed that enslaved people had to call white boys and girls "Master" and "Mistress" only after they reached the age of twelve, but some slave owners required enslaved people to greet white infants and toddlers in this way.[20]

The objective in requiring such deference was simple. Slave owners wanted enslaved people to recognize the power that white children possessed over them, even at the time of their birth. George Womble asserted that his owner wanted the slaves he owned to hold "him and his family in awe"; he compelled them to "go and pay their respects to the newly born white children on the day after their birth. They were required to get in line, and one by one, they went through the room and bowed their heads as they passed the bed and uttered 'Young Marster,' or if the baby was a girl they said: 'Young Mistress.'"[21]

Enslaved people paid a high cost if they failed to use these salutations. Rebecca Jane Grant would not call her mistress's young son "Marster." One day, her mistress wrote a note and asked her to deliver it to a local store clerk. The clerk prepared a package in accordance with the note's instructions and gave it to Grant to deliver to her mistress. When she returned, she quickly learned what was inside: "a cowhide strap about two feet long." Her mistress immediately pulled the whip out of the package and began to beat Grant with it. She did not know why her mistress was beating her until she exclaimed, "You can't say 'Marster Henry,' Miss?" Grant quickly responded, "Yes'm. Yes'm. I can say 'Marster Henry!'" She bitterly remarked to her interviewer: "Marster Henry was just a little boy about three or four years old. . . . Wanted me to say 'Marster' to him—a baby!"[22] When another formerly enslaved woman forgot to refer to her mistress's eight- or nine-month-old daughter as "Miss," her mistress put her "in a stock and beat" her. While she was in the stocks, the woman twisted her leg until it broke, and even then continued to beat her until she was satisfied her point had been made.[23]

Sometimes, the punishment went farther. One enslaved woman recalled that "when you called your marster's chillum by their names, they would strip you and let the child beat you. It didn't matter whether the child was large or small, they always beat you 'til the blood ran down."[24] Teaching enslaved children to call their owner's offspring "Master" or "Mistress" also served to educate white slave-owning children about their difference from and superiority to all African Americans, regardless of age, and the deference that all African Americans had to show them. Beyond this, compelling and permitting white children to reinforce their superiority through bloodletting discipline allowed the children to practice the more brutal manifestations of mastery that might prove useful later in their lives when they came to own their own slaves.

As they were growing up, slave owners' daughters generally thought of and treated enslaved children as playmates and companions; but these future slave owners eventually came to realize that the African American children were far more. Enslaved children were their property, and they treated them as such.

At age three, newly arrived in Georgia after having spent her earlier years in Britain, Sarah Butler quickly grasped the distinction between slavery and freedom and some of the privileges accorded to those who were not in bondage. Sarah was the daughter of Pierce Mease Butler, the scion of a wealthy Georgia family, and the famed actress and writer Frances Anne (Fanny) Kemble. In a letter to her friend Elizabeth Sedgwick, Frances Kemble recorded an exchange between the young Sarah and Mary, an enslaved chambermaid who was charged with her care. During their exchange, Sarah told Mary that "some persons are free and some are not." Sarah established her own unbound status by telling Mary that she, Sarah, was "a free person." Then she paused and waited for a reply. When she did not get one, Sarah repeated her assertion: "I say, I am a free person, Mary—do you know that?" Finally, her chambermaid responded, "Yes, missis." And the little girl continued, "Some persons are free and some are not—do you know that, Mary?" And again Mary replied, but this time with her own understanding of the subject, "Yes, missis, *here* . . . I know it is so here, in this world." New to the plantation setting, Sarah was discovering a fundamental distinction between herself and the woman her father owned, and she sought to communicate and reinforce that difference. In this brief conversation, Sarah drew the line between free and unfree, between the powerful and the disempowered. She placed herself on one side of that line, ensured that Mary knew she was on the other, and implied that Mary must not cross it.[25] Despite, or perhaps because of, her early immersion in slaveholding culture, Sarah Butler rejected her father's proslavery views later in life.

Slave-owning girls also made it clear that they had the power to claim other human beings as their property when they selected specific enslaved children to serve them. When Betty Cofer was born, her master's daughter Ella was only a little girl, but she nevertheless "claimed" Cofer as her slave shortly after the child's birth. They "played together an' grew up together." Eventually, Cofer became Ella's personal servant, waiting on her, standing behind her chair during mealtimes, and sleeping beside her on the bedroom floor.[26] This selection process also happened in reverse. When Letitia M. Burwell and her sister visited the quarters where her family's one hundred slaves lived, she claimed to have heard the youngest slaves quarreling with each other about "who should be his or her mistress." In her will, Elizabeth Onion stipulated that the enslaved people she owned could choose which of her children they would serve after her death. Two of the enslaved people she owned chose to live with and serve her daughters.[27]

White girls also made claims of ownership in public and in conversations with enslaved people. Ella Washington's "'most grown'" mistress publicly asserted her ownership after she learned that her uncle-in-law was trying to sell Ella at auction.[28] A formerly enslaved woman named Melinda recalled that her young mistress would frequently tell her, "When I get big and get married to a prince, you come with me and 'tend all my chilens." When her mistress married Honoré Dufour, she took Melinda with her as part of their new household.[29] As southern girls, young white women thought about how enslaved people would fit into their lives, not just as playmates or companions, but as property. And when they were old enough, they turned their imaginings into reality.

Young white girls began to learn about and practice different management and disciplinary strategies, which helped them develop and refine the skills of slave mastery that they would need once they became mistresses of their own households. Fathers frequently imparted their wisdom about slave discipline to their daughters at second hand, but they also allowed them to participate in such brutality firsthand. In 1863, Solomon Bradley, who was formerly enslaved in South Carolina, told the American Freedmen's Inquiry Commission about a man named Mr. Farrarby who had committed violent acts against his enslaved cook in the presence of his daughters. This woman had burned the edges of his family's waffles, and upon discovering her "misdeed," he took her outside and whipped her. Each time she screamed too loudly, he kicked her in the mouth. After he finished whipping her, he lit a candle and poured the melted wax onto her wounds. Throughout the entire ordeal, Farrarby's "daughters were looking at all this from a window of the house through the blinds."[30] When a slave-owning parent's brutality caused the death of an enslaved person, evidence of what his or her daughters had witnessed and what they thought about the most violent forms of slave discipline might make its way into the courtroom. The testimony offered in the case *State of Georgia v. Green Martin* provides insight into how young girls in slaveholding households understood the relationships among slave mastery, discipline, and violence.

On May 9, 1857, Alfred, a twelve- or thirteen-year-old enslaved boy who was living in Washington County, Georgia, allegedly told Godfry Martin, the son of his master, Green Martin, to kiss his derriere. Over the course of three hours, Green and Godfry Martin beat Alfred to death. On at least two occasions, Green Martin straddled Alfred, choked him, and threw him to the floor. Godfry poured water on Alfred to prevent him from fainting. Then, after Green was done, Godfry fetched a saddle, commanded Alfred to kneel on all fours, placed the saddle on his back, and sat on him for "a quarter of an hour." After doing so, he beat him with a stick, kicked him and threw him on the ground, and finally dragged him about the yard. Although most southern states had laws that allowed slave owners to punish their slaves with impunity, even if such discipline led to death, such legislation often barred slaveholders from punishing enslaved people with "malice." Many of these laws also delineated in minute detail the instruments slaveholders could lawfully use to punish enslaved people. If they used methods or tools that did not meet the specifications outlined in these laws, they could be punished themselves. Someone in Green Martin's slaveholding community must have considered his actions abhorrent enough to report him to local authorities because Martin soon found himself charged with Alfred's murder.[31] Martin was convicted and sentenced to execution by hanging, but he appealed to the Georgia Supreme Court and the justices agreed to review his case.

Green Martin's three daughters, at least two of whom were minors, had witnessed much of the violence their father committed and testified about what they saw in court. Mary Martin, who was sixteen at the time of her deposition, saw her father and brother choking, kicking, and whipping the boy, punishment that she said was "continually kept up until the boy's death." Her sister Sarah also saw them abuse Alfred while she was sitting on the piazza and as she "passed frequently from the yard into the house." The eldest daughter, Catherine, saw the beating too. The Martin sisters did not know how Alfred died; they just knew that an hour before sunset he was dead, lying face down and naked in their yard. The sisters also corroborated the claim that Godfry and Green had beaten Alfred because of his alleged words to their brother.[32]

We might think that such brutality, which led to the death of an enslaved boy whom they probably grew up with, would have disturbed the Martin sisters or compelled them to intervene. But according to Catherine, "No one attempted to interfere during the events." She further testified that she "did not go to the boy, but saw him while passing [and] he was naked." Why did the Martin girls choose to keep out of the affair? Was it fear of the Martin men? Not necessarily. Catherine and Sarah said they were a *bit* afraid of their father and brother, but the court clearly did not find them convincing. Judge J. Lumpkin, who delivered the majority opinion, which reversed the lower court's guilty ruling, stated that the Martin sisters "were the unwilling," but "not . . . affrighted witnesses to this murder." Mary Martin claimed that she "was not particularly afraid of" her father or her brother and chose not to "pester either because she did not want" to, and because she "knew she was not able to do any good." This sixteen-year-old girl, who was not much older than Alfred at the time of his death, knew that the boy was probably going to die; her father told her so. But even this was not enough to sway her. Ironically, another witness, a fifteen-year-old white boy named John A. Bedgood, who was visiting the Martin estate at the time of Alfred's beating, was so frightened by what he saw that he went to a neighboring plantation to avoid seeing any more. Clearly, not all white southern boys were acculturated to the violence of slavery, but both boys and girls were receiving instruction in it.[33]

When the court asked the Martin sisters why they had not intervened, they offered two reasons that had nothing to do with fear: they believed that Alfred deserved the beating and the Martin men were behaving in ways they deemed normal and unexceptional. When asked to describe Alfred's general conduct prior to his death, Catherine said that he "was very saucy and uncontrollable," even though, as she added, "the boy was kindly treated, and was a pet negro." She also stated that the punishment was "no[t] uncommon violence," and her sister Sarah claimed that the Martin men "acted as they usually did."[34]

While many slaveholding parents tried to shield their children from the brutality they and members of their communities perpetrated against enslaved people, many others, like Green Martin, saw no need to do so. After years of exposure to such violence, the Martin sisters were apparently immune to it. They sat on their piazza and went about their daily routines, which frequently took them through the yard where their brother and father were torturing Alfred to death. They spoke of seeing the sunset and eating supper as Alfred lay in their yard battered, naked, and dying. The Martin sisters' conduct suggests that this sort of violence was part of their daily lives. And they exhibited a level of indifference to Alfred's suffering that many slave owners and their employees found necessary in their interactions with and control of enslaved people.

When slave-owning girls witnessed scenes of this kind, they could respond in a number of ways. While it was happening, they could interfere, or they could choose inaction (as the Martin sisters did). Later, they might reject violence altogether or adopt less brutal techniques toward their own slaves, or they might embrace their fathers' (and brothers') styles of slave discipline. Young women like James Curry's mistress chose to do the latter.

James Curry's mother had nurtured her master's children for much of their young lives. One evening, she and one of the master's daughters had a disagreement about dinner. The master's daughter struck Curry's mother, and she retaliated by pushing the girl, who fell to the floor. When Curry's master came home, the daughter told him what had happened. The master called Curry's mother outside, beat her fifteen or twenty times with a hickory rod, and "then called his daughter and told her to take her satisfaction of her, and she did beat her until she was satisfied."[35]

This young white girl and the enslaved woman who had cared for her learned at least two important lessons that day. They came to understand that there was no inherent chasm between violence and ladyhood in everyday life, even in the eyes of white patriarchs. They also learned that the intimacies that might have been forged between them over the years made no difference to the power that their society accorded to this young white girl over her racial "inferiors." In fact, it was that power that made such cross-racial intimacies possible in the first place.

As mothers, white slave-owning women were ideally positioned to teach their children about different methods of slave management and discipline, and they offered their daughters, and their sons, lessons on how to interact with and control enslaved people. Tines Kendricks's mistress owned both the slaves and the land on which they lived, and she was determined to manage her estate without her husband's interference. As a consequence, Kendricks said that her mistress's husband, Arch, "didn't have much to say 'bout de runnin' of de place or de' handlin' of de niggers." Kendricks's mistress enlisted her son's help instead, and she taught him everything he knew about operating a large estate profitably and managing the slaves who worked it. Kendricks recalled that the son "got all he meanness from old mis' an' he sure got plenty of it too." In a striking role reversal, Lewis Cartwright's master asked his own mother to whip

Cartwright when he refused to be beaten without a fight. While the master's decision might have been guided by the idea that most enslaved men would not dare hit a white woman, it is also possible that his mother was a more effective master, and her ability to command obedience from Cartwright and other slaves reflected that.[36]

On occasion, slave-owning mothers and daughters disciplined enslaved people together. When Henrietta King was about eight or nine years old, she was responsible for emptying her owners' chamber pots. When she went to collect the pot in her mistress's room each morning, she noticed that a piece of candy would be left on the washstand. She knew that her mistress had left it there as a test to see whether she would take it, and at first she resisted. But after several days, King yielded to temptation. (Her mistress, King claimed, kept the people who labored in her home in a state of near starvation.) King's mistress noticed that the candy was gone and questioned her. When she denied stealing the candy, her mistress began to whip her. King refused to remain still, so her mistress grabbed her by the legs and pinned her head under the rocker of her chair while her young daughter whipped her. For approximately an hour, averred King, her mistress rocked back and forth on her head while her daughter beat her with a cowhide. The constant pressure from the rocking chair crushed the bones in the left side of King's jaw. After the beating she could not open her mouth and the left side constantly slid sideways to the right. Her mistress called a doctor, but after examining her, he determined that nothing could be done; her face was irreparably mutilated. Her mistress never brutalized King again, but her disfigurement was disquieting, and the mistress was so disturbed by it that the family decided to give King to a female cousin, who King claimed treated her kindly.[37]

This one act of brutality affected the rest of Henrietta King's life. She could not chew, so she was forced to consume "liquid, stews, an' soup." The teeth on the left side of her face never grew back. When children saw her disfigured face, they either laughed or cried. Adults would stare at her "wonderin' what debbil got in an' made me born dis way." King also had to contend with encounters with her mistress's children and grandchildren, who apparently knew what happened. On one occasion, when King crossed paths with her former mistress's granddaughter in town, she got the feeling that the young woman was so ashamed that she crossed the street and pretended that she did not see her.[38]

It's clear that this event affected the rest of King's life, but what about her mistress's daughter? If the testimony of formerly enslaved people offers any evidence, we can be assured that in one way or another, this experience affected the way she treated the slaves who came under her control later in life.

Not all slave-owning mothers taught their daughters to use brutality when dealing with their slaves. As young girls began learning how to manage enslaved people, their mothers occasionally reprimanded them for employing brutal tactics. When Elsie Cottrell saw her daughter Martha abusing an enslaved adolescent, she interrupted her and said, according to her former slave Henry Gibbs, "Don't you know you will never have a nigger with any sense if you bump der heads against de wall?" Looking back, Gibbs believed that his mistress's daughter engaged in this practice because "she was young and didn't know no better." But Elsie wanted Martha to hone her methods of slave mastery in ways that would preserve these enslaved people's usefulness in the long run.[39]

White mothers often found their children to be willing pupils who easily absorbed their lessons in slave mastery, but some children clashed with their mothers over the best way to deal with slaves. Mary Armstrong's mother belonged to a couple whom she described as "the meanest two white folks what ever lived." In Armstrong's estimation, her mother's mistress was particularly cruel. She thought that "Old Polly" was the "devil if there ever was one," and one incident in particular brought her to this conclusion. Polly beat Armstrong's nine-month-old sister to death because she would not stop crying. Years later, Polly's daughter Olivia eventually came to own Mary Armstrong. During one visit to Olivia's marital home, Polly tried to beat the ten-year-old. Armstrong retaliated by picking up "a rock 'bout as big as half your fist an' hit[ting] her right in the eye." She "busted [Polly's] eyeball an' told her that was for whippin' [her] baby sister to death." When Armstrong told her young mistress what she had done, Olivia said, "Well, I guess mamma has learnt her lesson at last." After years of watching her mother abuse and in at least one case murder the family's slaves, Olivia had chosen a different approach to managing the people she owned as an adult. While Mary Armstrong described Olivia's parents as mean and cruel, she characterized Olivia in a starkly different way: "She was kind to everyone, an' everyone jes' love her." Despite her presumed training, Olivia allowed her slave to defend herself against her own mother; clearly she was making her own decisions about what kind of slave owner she wanted to be.[40]

Of course, not all young slave-owning women diverged so significantly from the methods that had worked for their mothers. Some employed the same tactics, only milder in intensity. As Jennie Brown prepared for her upcoming marriage, her parents gave her a pick of their slaves. Elizabeth Sparks was among them. As Sparks and several other enslaved women helped their young mistress get dressed for the day, she remembered her mistress asking them, "Which of yer niggers think I'm gonna git [you] when I git married?" They all responded, "I doan know." Then, suddenly, she turned and looked at Sparks, pointed her finger at her, and said, "yer!" Sparks was deeply relieved when Brown selected her because Brown was "a good woman" who would "slap an' beat yer once in a while but she warn't no woman fur fighting fussin' an' beatin' yer all day lak some I know. She was too young when da war ended fur that." Although Brown was prone to inflict physical violence when she deemed it necessary, her mother was far more severe in the forms of punishment she used, beating her slaves "with a broom or a leather strap or anythin' she'd git her hands on," without any legitimate cause. Brown's mother would also manufacture reasons to beat her slaves. She would make Sparks's aunt Caroline knit all day and well into the night, and if she dozed off, Brown's mother would "come down across her haid with a switch." Sparks remembered that "she'd give the cook jes' so much meal to make bread fum an' effen she burnt it, she'd be scared to death cause they'd whup her . . . Yessir! Beat the devil out 'er if she burn dat bread." Although Sparks made a distinction between the intensity of punishments that Jennie Brown and her mother chose to inflict, she also suggested that her mistress might have come to follow her mother's methods of slave management if the Civil War had not resulted in the legal end of slavery.[41]

The lessons of slaveholding parents were only one means by which daughters could learn about proper slave-management techniques. The *Rose Bud*, a weekly juvenile newspaper edited by Caroline Gilman and published through the 1830s, was another. Gilman created the *Rose Bud* "during a moment of growing tension over the slavery question," and she compiled the content in the newspaper with her own children in mind. She later expanded her vision to include a broader readership. The stories Gilman published in the *Rose Bud* were directed toward male and female readers, though the historian Gale Kenny argues that "the education of girls in the *Rose Bud* focused mostly on housework [while] lessons for boys centered around balancing filial obedience and white mastery." Regardless of Gilman's intentions, nothing stopped girls from reading the entire issue. A female reader named Julia submitted a letter to the editor describing how much she loved the magazine and mentioning that her female classmates tried to take it from her so they could read it too.[42]

Children who read the *Rose Bud* acquired extraordinary insight into the daily practice of slave ownership. They learned about the conduct that defined the character of ideal masters, were offered examples of proper and improper slave management, and were assured that the ideal plantations were "regulated with almost military like precision." Young female readers came to understand that "a planter's daughter fear[ed] none but white men." They also came to know what forms of deference they should expect from enslaved people and were taught that white people referred to enslaved men as "boys." They were advised on proper forms of religious instruction for enslaved people as well as the kinds of funerals and weddings slave owners might permit enslaved people to have. They learned about the pass system, which required enslaved people going from place to place to carry documentation that identified their owners and detailed their travels. And through Gilman's critique of abolitionist litera-ture, her readers even learned how to respond to public assaults upon slavery.[43]

   In 1835, the abolitionist Catharine Sedgwick wrote a three-volume novel, set during the American Revolution, whose protagonists were the Linwoods, a slaveholding New England family. They owned a woman named Rose who was very close to her owner's daughter, Isabella. One day, Isabella asked Rose if she was happy, and Rose replied that she was not because she was a slave. Isabella recounted her parents' kindness toward Rose and remarked how much she and her brother loved her. Rose replied that slavery was a "yoke, and it gall[ed]" her that she could be "bought and sold like cattle"; she would "die to-morrow to be free to-day." Seeing Rose's pain, Isabella promised the enslaved woman that she would be free and asked her father to manumit her. He refused her request, but through a bit of trickery, Isabella was able to keep her promise to Rose.[44]

   In response, Caroline Gilman wrote an op-ed in the *Southern Rose*, the new name of the *Rose Bud*, that refuted Sedgwick's description of slavery and charac-terization of enslaved people as embodied by Rose. She argued that "it is not true that African slaves pine for 'free breath;' they are the most careless, light-hearted creatures in the world." Without reservation, she believed that "the great mass 'enjoy the service they render,'" and that Sedgwick did not understand their character. She also questioned why Sedgwick and other northern women would "waste their sympathy on a subject so distant from their sphere of observation." She encouraged these women to come to the South, where southern ladies would "show them happy black faces enough, particularly on plantations."[45]

   Gilman failed to acknowledge that she, like Sedgwick, was northern born. She also ignored the North's long history of slavery, as well as the fact that, even as Sedgwick was writing *The Linwoods*, and when she herself critiqued it, she could have found African Americans in the North laboring under forms of bondage that resembled enslavement. Gilman also did not seem to realize that Sedgwick was referring to the North's history of slavery in her book or that Sedgwick did know at least one enslaved person's "character" quite intimately. In 1781, Catharine's father, Theodore, a prominent Massachusetts lawyer and politi-cian, offered to represent Elizabeth Freeman, an African-descended enslaved woman known as "Mum Bet." In *Brom and Bett v. Ashley*, Theodore Sedgwick successfully   challenged   Freeman's   enslavement   under   Massachusetts's

1780 constitution, which proclaimed that all men were born free and equal. After Freeman won her case, she served the Sedgwick family for the rest of her life and cared for Catharine during her girlhood. The many parallels between Rose's and Freeman's enslavement and eventual manumission suggest that Freeman served as Catharine's inspiration for the Rose character in *The Linwoods*. Gilman's op-ed, which also criticized Lydia Maria Child's 1833 publication *An Appeal in Favor of That Class of Americans Called Africans*, was undoubtedly responding to the surge of abolitionist literature written by women. But more important, she was providing her young readers with a ready response to abolitionist attacks on southern slavery.[46]

Enhancing the knowledge gained from slaveholding parents with the lessons they might have acquired by reading the *Southern Rose/Rose Bud*, young white girls learned how to be efficient and effective mistresses. Such guidance equipped young white girls to teach enslaved people the skills necessary to be the kind of servants they would need later on. When Ellen Thomas and her mistress Cornelia Kimball were young girls, Kimball taught Thomas "the arts of good housekeeping, including fine sewing." Her training also involved being "blindfolded and then [being] told to go through the motions of serving" so that she could "learn to do so without disturbing anything on the table."[47] Nancy Thomas (no relation to Ellen) recalled that she "was de special little girl fo' Mistress Harriett's daughter" Palonia. "Even durin' dem days I would sew and knit," Nancy Thomas recalled. She went on: "I had a little three-legged stool and I'd set it between Palony's legs, while she was settin' down. Den she'd watch me when I knitted. If I done somethin' wrong, she'd pinch my ear a little and say, 'Yo' dropped a stitch, Nannie.'"[48] As Ellen and Nancy Thomas's testimony shows, Cornelia Kimball and Palonia Smith were mistresses in the making, responsible for overseeing the production of the enslaved girls they would come to own and disciplining them when it did not meet their requirements. We can also imagine that Kimball and Smith were themselves being subjected to a certain kind of discipline; however, the "discipline" to which they were subjected paled in comparison to the kinds of discipline these enslaved girls might have endured. I am not suggesting that white parents did not inflict corporal punishment on their children but rather that, in these two cases, Kimball's and Smith's behavior conformed to that of other slave-owning women. Their mothers would be more likely to encourage them to continue such behavior than to punish them for it.[49]

It is important to note that young white southerners, by virtue of their skin color, were empowered by law and custom to exercise control over any enslaved person they crossed paths with, even those they did not own. The landscape

architect Frederick Law Olmsted published an account of his travels throughout the region that included an encounter he had with a southern girl and an
elderly enslaved man:

> I have seen a girl, twelve years old in a district where, in ten miles, the slave
> population was fifty to one of the free, stop an old man on the public road,
> demand to know where he was going, and by what authority, order him to
> face about and return to his plantation, and enforce her command with tur-
> bulent anger, when he hesitated, by threatening that she would have him
> well whipped if he did not instantly obey. The man quailed like a spaniel,
> and she instantly resumed the manner of a lovely child with me, no more
> apprehending that she had acted unbecomingly, than that her character had
> been influenced by the slave's submission to her caprice of supremacy; no
> more conscious that she had increased the security of her life by strengthen-
> ing the habit of the slave to the master race, than is the sleeping seaman that
> he tightens his clutch of the rigging as the ship meets each new billow.[50]

When interacting with enslaved people in this way, girls like the one Olmsted
encountered learned important lessons about the power of whiteness and its
pricelessness.

White girls learned one lesson about the value set on different groups of
human beings; enslaved people learned quite another. The historian Daina
Ramey Berry describes the ways enslaved children first learned about and reck-
oned with their bound and unfree status. She argues that the "visual cues, including coffles . . . heading to auctions," the separation of kin and loved ones, and the
slave auctions themselves quickly taught enslaved children where they stood in
the southern hierarchy.[51] White girls also learned about their place in the hierarchy and the inestimable value of their white skins when they witnessed these
spectacles. They were present when enslaved families were torn apart in their
parents' fields, and they saw slave coffles pass by their homes. They attended slave
auctions with their families on court days or sale days: they watched the bidding
process unfold, and they heard the wails of the enslaved as they were separated
from their loved ones. All around them, white girls found evidence of their difference from and superiority to enslaved people, as well as of the many privileges
their whiteness brought them. They recognized who was and who was not
chained to others in slave coffles; who was and who was not shrieking and reach-
ing for a child torn from a family's arms. They noticed who was and who was
not missing from the fields and the household, and whose absences the remaining enslaved people mourned. All these observations enabled them to understand the chasm between the free and enslaved, between those seen as human

merchandise and those seen as human beings, and ultimately, to acknowledge the security their whiteness afforded them.

Although it might be deeply problematic and should be approached with caution, some evidence does suggest that enslaved people sometimes developed caring and, perhaps, loving relationships with their young owners. But no matter how affectionate relations between white girls and enslaved people might have been, these young slave owners frequently articulated and exercised their power over their enslaved companions as mistresses in the making. Some girls and young women enthusiastically assumed their roles as mistresses early on, in their daily interactions with enslaved people; some also exhibited signs that they might evolve into brutal ones. A formerly enslaved woman recounted the cruelties that she suffered at the hands of all the white women in her household, but she dwelt in particular on her encounters with "the meanest" of her mistress's daughters. Her young mistress, she recalled, would whip her and then make her "kiss the switch" that she used to beat her.[52]

When parents gave their daughters enslaved people, those daughters assumed a new identity: they became slave owners. Over the course of their lives, they learned valuable lessons about the importance of property and how to be effective slave owners. They also learned how to determine when, if, and in what ways to allow other people to interfere with any aspect of their wealth in slaves.

When these young women married, they put all their knowledge, training, and experience to good use. Frequently their parents and others would give them additional slaves to mark the occasion. Formerly enslaved people related that they considered this kind of gift giving common, and married women's accounts corroborate their assertions.[53] Enslaved people also remembered slave-owning *women* giving their children human property, which contradicts historians' claims that bequests and gifting of enslaved people were practices in which only slave-owning men engaged. As Julia Casey recalled, her "Missis's mammy . . . gib me, mah mammy, mah sister Violet, mah two br'ers Andrew en Alfred ter Miss Jennie fer a wed'un gif." Similarly, Anna R. Ellis gave an enslaved mother and her child to her daughter Rhoda as a wedding present when Rhoda married. No matter whether they were mothers, grandmothers, aunts, or sisters, slave-owning women gave enslaved people to their female relatives, and ensured that they would possess them in their own right.[54]

For reasons that could have been related to incompatible personalities or economic inefficiency, a slave-owning woman might not approve of the enslaved people her parents gave her when she married. When Adeline Blakely was five years old, her master gave her to his daughter Elizabeth as a wedding gift. After settling into her new home, Elizabeth decided that the girl "was too little and not enough help to her"; she would make another mouth to feed without being economically productive. So she sent Blakely back. Even though Blakely remained in her master's home for another two years, Elizabeth still owned her because her father had "made a bill of sale for [Blakely] to his daughter, in order to keep account of all settlements, so when he died and the estate [was] settled each child would know how he stood."[55] Blakely eventually returned to Elizabeth's home and was responsible for the care of her mistress's children. When Elizabeth's daughter married H. M. Hudgens, Elizabeth gave Blakely to the daughter as a gift, just as her father had given Blakely to her years earlier.[56]

Some young women were able to avoid situations like this because their parents permitted them to choose the slaves they wanted to take with them to their new homes. James Winchester of Nashville, Tennessee, wrote to his daughter Maria Breedlove informing her that she could "have her choice of [his] negresses to wait upon you." When he did not receive a reply, he followed up with another letter asking her to let him know which one she wanted. He cautioned her against choosing the "two which your mother might not like to part with," although he believed that his wife would probably "yield to accommodate" Breedlove if she did choose one of her mother's personal favorites.[57]

Elite members of the planter class presented their children with enslaved people at elaborate events following their wedding processions. The formerly enslaved Bill Homer provided a remarkable account of how grand these ceremonies could be. When his mistress Mary Homer married William Johnson, her father gave her fifty slaves, and Bill Homer was one of them. Bill recalled that on Mary's wedding day, her father ordered the fifty enslaved people to line up, and he presented them to Mary by saying, "Fo' to give my lovin' daughter de staht, I's give you dese 50 niggers." Mary's new father-in-law presented his son with fifty enslaved people as well, with just as much ceremony.

These affairs also underscored the economic relationship between slaves and young white women's coming of age because white parents often sold enslaved people in order to help finance their daughters' weddings. Ben Johnson's master, for example, sold Ben's brother Jim in order to pay for his daughter's wedding dress.[58] Transactions such as these served as a brutal lesson for the other enslaved people in Ben Johnson's community, and an equally important one for the new bride: she could always sell one of her slaves, separating him or her from everything and everyone he or she knew and loved, if a more pressing need, like the purchase of a dress, arose.

Even after marriage, white slave-owning parents and other kin offered their daughters and female family members enslaved people as gifts. When Kittie

Stanford was ten, her female owner Mrs. Lindsay transported her to her daughter Etta's house and gave her to Etta so that she could care for Etta's baby. Stanford remembered Mrs. Lindsay saying to Etta: "I brought you a little nigger gal to rock de cradle." In her account, Stanford said nothing about whether her own mother came with her to Etta's home, so she probably did not. But Stanford's old mistress seemed unconcerned about the distress that *Kittie's* separation from her own mother would bring.[59]

Slave-owning mothers' deeds of gift, like the one devised by Ann V. Hicks of Marlborough District, South Carolina, on August 17, 1831, not only offer more concrete support for enslaved people's claims that their owners gave them to married daughters; they also show that these property transfers preserved their daughters' legal titles to these slaves as well. Hicks drew up a deed of gift that conveyed six enslaved people and their future children to her three married daughters. It stipulated that she gave these enslaved people to them "without any right in the husbands which they now have or may hereafter have, to exercise any control over said property, or in any manner to intermeddle therewith." The deed also expressed Hicks's intention to "convey a separate and exclusive interest in the said negroes to [her] daughters . . . and their children, without subjecting them in any manner to liability on account of any contracts of their husbands."[60]

Hicks envisioned a certain kind of life for her daughters, one that did not leave them subject to whatever financial blunders their husbands might make. She also sought to grant them a measure of economic stability that might extend beyond their first marriages and into any subsequent marriages. Other parents, such as Theodorick Bland of Virginia, took similar precautions. In 1784, after his daughter Frances married St. George Tucker, he drew up a deed of gift that indicated that he had given several enslaved people to Frances. It was a "parol" or oral gift, however, and not a written property transferal. In order to ensure its legality, he devised a formal written deed of gift that confirmed his earlier gift to Frances and granted the slaves to her for her "sole and separate use and benefit."[61]

When family and kin gave women slaves for their "sole and separate use and control," they often had specific ideas about how they wanted them to use that property, but women like Catharine V. Phillips frequently had plans of their own. When Phillips gave birth to her first child, her brother James Anthony gave her a twelve-year-old enslaved girl named Charlotte by deed of gift, "for her sole and separate use" during her lifetime. He did this to "relieve her in part from the drudgery to which, in her situation [motherhood], she was subjected to." He placed Charlotte and any children she might have in a separate trust for Phillips. Her family continued to grow, and to help her perform her maternal and household duties, her brother-in-law Weldon Phillips also gave her a sixteen-year-old enslaved girl named Louisa for her "sole and separate use," and he directed that Louisa should be "free from the direction or control of [Catharine's] husband, and under no event to become liable for [his] debts or contracts." This he did even (or especially) though her husband "was then somewhat embarrassed."[62]

Catharine Phillips did not use her slaves as her donors imagined she would. She established a boardinghouse with funds she brought into her marriage, and instead of having Charlotte and Louisa assist her in household and maternal duties, she set them to work in her new business and used them to sell her poultry and dairy products. Her business activities, along with Charlotte and Louisa's earnings, brought Catharine enough profit to buy a forty-five-year-old enslaved man named Handy from one A. M. Clanton. She paid Clanton two hundred dollars up front, and "after full consultation with her and under her instructions," Catharine's husband delivered the balance of what she owed from funds she provided to him. When Clanton drew up the bill of sale, it reserved Handy in trust for Catharine's sole and separate use.[63]

While parents presented their daughters with both enslaved males and females as inheritances upon marriage, they more frequently gave them female slaves. From a logical perspective, their decision to do so might seem motivated by the rationale that enslaved women and girls would be more useful to daughters, who bore the bulk of the domestic responsibilities in and management of their households, and sometimes this was the case. But they also gave enslaved girls and women (especially those of childbearing age) to their daughters, because females possessed the reproductive capacity to add to their daughters' labor force.

Of course, slaveholders in the colonial period did not value enslaved females' reproduction in the ways that their counterparts would in the nineteenth century. In the colonial period, especially before the abolition of the African slave trade to America in 1808, many slave owners discouraged enslaved women from reproducing. They considered enslaved infants to be time-consuming financial burdens who prevented their mothers from devoting all of their attention to their white households. Slave owners often sold such women simply because they *were* conceiving and delivering children too frequently. After 1808, however, when slave owners could no longer depend upon a steady supply of newly imported African captives, they had to rely on a domestic supply of enslaved laborers, and they became invested in the "natural" reproduction of the enslaved labor force. Hence, they increasingly sought women who could reproduce and had already given birth to healthy children.[64] By the third and fourth decades of the nineteenth century, slave owners prized enslaved females of childbearing age, affixed higher values to them because of their ability to bear children, and came to see them as sound investments that would augment their wealth with little effort or additional expense.

A parent's decisions to give a daughter a female, as opposed to a male, slave, however, could also be made because the parent was more concerned about the daughter's well-being than her husband's. When Mary Lindsay's mistress married Bill Merrick, her father would not give her any enslaved men or boys as part of her inheritance, and Lindsay wondered why. When she asked her mistress about her father's decision, her mistress speculated that her father had given her female slaves "because he didn't want to help her husband out none, but just wanted to help her. If he give her a man her husband [would] have him working in the blacksmith shop."[65]

Pragmatism and parental concern were only two reasons why slave-owning parents tended to give their daughters female slaves; there were legal and financial justifications, too. By the 1660s, colonies such as Virginia and Maryland enacted laws that ensured that children inherited the bound or free condition of their mothers. Other colonies followed suit in law or in custom. They further provided that whoever owned an enslaved woman also owned her offspring, regardless of who owned the father of the children she bore. Exceptions were sometimes made, however, if both owners were willing.[66]

Slave-owning parents knew about the legal and pecuniary benefits of owning enslaved women, and so did their daughters.[67] Enslaved men, particularly those in their most productive years, possessed a higher value in slave markets because they were strong, skilled laborers, and in this sense, they were exceptional financial investments in the short term.[68] But over the long term, enslaved women, because of the children they would potentially produce over the course of their lives, were far more valuable. If slave owners were patient, "producing children was a cheap alternative to purchasing them at the market."[69] Henrietta Butler's mistress Emily Haidee clearly knew the value that enslaved women possessed, and she developed two long-term financial strategies to maximize their worth. She not only forced Butler's mother to engage in nonconsensual sex with enslaved men so she could "have babies all de time," she made Butler do the same. When the coerced sexual liaisons that Haidee orchestrated produced offspring, she was known for "sellin' the boys and keepin' the gals."[70]

Multiple generations of women could benefit from their elders' decisions to keep enslaved women and girls. Three generations of enslaved women in the Linier family served as nurses to Aaron and Francis Hudson Haynie's female descendants. Lucy Linier nursed Aaron and Francis's daughter Ann. Lucy's daughter Patsy in turn nursed Ann's children. And Patsy's daughter Emma nursed the children of Ann's daughter Fanny.[71] Generation after generation, slave-owning women benefited from the reproductive and maternal labor of the enslaved women they owned.

A woman's interest in the reproduction of the enslaved women she owned could manifest in calculated and methodical ways. In their letters, diaries, and family Bibles, mistresses tabulated gains and losses in the wealth that was bound up in the bodies of the infants and children they owned.[72] And when these mistresses died, the pecuniary advantage of owning enslaved women emerged in their wills and estate inventories, documents that reveal the "natural increase" of their slaveholdings. Rachel O'Connor was a large-scale Louisiana slave owner and planter, and between 1826 and 1844 she offered an often joyful and proud accounting of the enslaved infants born on her plantation on twenty separate occasions. In most of these passages, she merely identified which women gave birth and indicated whether the infants were born healthy or otherwise. But several of her notations made it clear why she was so meticulous in her tabulations: these infants were future laborers and they increased her wealth.[73] During this time O'Connor owned almost twice as many enslaved women and girls (fifty-three) as she did men and boys (twenty-eight). Twenty-five of the enslaved females O'Connor owned were identified as "women" age fifteen years and older, while the remaining were identified as "girls" age two to thirteen years. According to the family pairings noted in the inventory, half of the eighty-one people O'Connor owned were the offspring of the enslaved women on her plantation. When O'Connor died, her estate was valued at over $30,000; her slaves were worth 84 percent of her total wealth ($27,875). Other women, such as the Louisiana divorcée Jane Kemp, also left no doubt about the importance of these women and their reproductive capabilities when they compiled lists of the slaves they owned. Kemp emphasized their value by creating a separate list of "women with families."[74]

White women's prideful exclamations about the offspring that enslaved women produced frequently took on a more ritualistic aspect when they put enslaved children on display for their guests. Whenever Ryer Emmanuel's mistress Miss Ross entertained visitors, she would gather together all the enslaved children she owned so her guests could admire them. According to Emmanuel, her mistress would then turn to her guests and ask, "Ain't I got a pretty crop of little niggers coming on?" Emmanuel remembered that there were so many enslaved children that "de yard would be black wid all different sizes." Her mistress chose a rather crass manner of expressing her pride in her growing group of laborers, but she was one of many slave-owning women who routinely told their friends and family about the births and maturation of enslaved children on their estates.[75]

Enslaved people grew to recognize white women's interest in their reproduction and the value they placed upon it. One formerly enslaved woman remembered overhearing her mistress tell a prospective buyer that she "wouldn't sell her for nothing" and "wouldn't take two thousand for her" because she was her "little breeder."[76] In another community, a white traveler named Eli West remembered one enslaved woman who simply could not, or would not, conceive. After she continually failed to become pregnant, her mistress had her stripped naked and whipped her severely. When this brutality proved ineffectual in remedying the problem, her mistress sold the woman to slave traders.[77]

Medical innovations have made us more knowledgeable about reproduction than those who lived in the nineteenth century could ever be. We now know that a host of environmental and physiological factors could have interfered with an enslaved woman's capacity to reproduce. Despite the fact that this was widely assumed in the case of white women, slave owners acted as though enslaved females' ability to carry their pregnancies to full term and deliver healthy infants was a certainty. In spite of copious evidence to the contrary, slave owners counted on the probability that these things would happen. As the historian Jennifer Morgan has demonstrated for the colonial period, slave owners' preoccupation with enslaved women's "issue and increase" persisted in the face of data showing high rates of infant mortality and infertility and low rates of childbirth among women of childbearing age. The historian Richard Follett's examination of fertility rates on Louisiana sugar plantations in the nineteenth century supports Morgan's findings. He found that the labor required to cultivate sugar had deleterious effects upon enslaved women's quality of life, their life expectancy, and, most especially, their capacity to reproduce. Frances Ann Kemble described similar reproductive difficulties among the enslaved women who worked the lands that her husband owned in Georgia.[78]

In addition to physical ailments and arduous labor conditions, nutritional deprivation affected the fertility of enslaved women, as has been shown by the historians Edward Baptist and Walter Johnson. Baptist tracked the brutal intensification of labor that slave owners required of enslaved people in the West, and Johnson determined that enslaved people barely received the calories necessary to perform a fraction of the work demanded of them on a daily basis, let alone facilitate conception and sustain the unborn.[79] This was undoubtedly why some enslaved women, such as the one Eli West described, failed to conceive. West stayed with the mistress who owned this woman for a year and remarked on the near starvation, beatings, and unceasing labor on her plantation.

White slave-owning women did not want to leave enslaved reproduction or infant health to chance. They tried to create more favorable working and living conditions for enslaved women that might enable them to carry their pregnancies to term and give birth to viable infants.[80] They also took great care to nurture enslaved infants and children and keep them healthy. As enslaved people told it, these mistresses often had profit in mind.

White slave-owning women further underscored their investments in the children enslaved women bore when they made efforts to provide for their nutritional and physical needs. While such actions might seem benevolent or "maternalistic," the economic advantages of caring for the children they enslaved often motivated these women's choices, and frequently these mistresses had their eyes on the slave market. Sallie Paul reasoned that slave owners in her community fed enslaved children well in large part because they wanted to "make dem hurry en grow cause dey would want to hurry en increase dey property."[81] John Brown's experience gives credence to her assertion. Brown's mistress Betty Moore would summon all the enslaved children to the "big house" each morning and give each of them a dose of garlic and rue, a medicinal plant used to treat a variety of ailments. To keep them physically fit, she would order them to "run round a great sycamore tree in the yard." When the children did not run fast enough to suit her, she would crack a cowhide whip at them, a disciplinary tool she kept by her side at all times. Brown said that she did this to keep them "wholesome," and to make them "grow likely for market."[82]

2

"I Belong to de Mistis"

In July 1847, Sarah Ann Davis married a widower named John C. Bethea in Marion County, South Carolina. She was twenty-nine, and he was twenty years her senior. According to the legal doctrine of coverture, the change in Sarah Davis's marital status made her a "feme covert." As such, her "very being" and "legal existence" were no longer hers; they had been subsumed into her husband's. The English jurist William Blackstone, who penned one of the most oft-cited explications of the legal doctrine of coverture, reasoned that the newly wed woman no longer needed an independent identity because, likening the husband to a bird, her groom offered her "cover" under his wing.[1]

From Sarah Davis's perspective, this wrenching of her rights and the legal denial of her independent existence probably appeared altogether different. Coverture would be particularly onerous for a woman like Davis because she received a number of slaves from her father, Francis Davis, upon his death and inherited more from her aunt, Elizabeth McWhite, when McWhite passed away several years later.[2] According to the doctrine of coverture, the enslaved people that her father and aunt bequeathed to Sarah became her husband's once they married. He had the right to sell them, benefit from their labor, collect the revenue they produced, and dispose of them as he deemed fit. Since Sarah was a feme covert, and she no longer owned or controlled her property, she had no right to sell her slaves, either. The legal doctrine forbade her from engaging in commercial endeavors in her own name and without her husband's permission. If someone wronged her, she could not sue that person in court unless her husband joined in her petition and put forth the bill of complaint on her behalf. When Sarah made the choice to marry John, it was the last decision that she would freely make about her own life, at least until John died. Legally

John "controlled her body and her property," and "there were relatively few constraints on what he could do with either."[3]

Assuming that Sarah and John adhered to the doctrine of coverture to the letter, this is how events were supposed to unfold on the Bethea plantation after they wed: Sarah would hand over control of her slaves to John, who would employ, discipline, and even sell them at his own discretion. But Hester Hunter, a formerly enslaved woman whom Sarah owned, did not remember things this way. According to Hunter, Sarah "had her niggers" and John "had his niggers," and anyone who saw them could easily differentiate between the two groups. Hunter vividly recalled that if a person visited the Bethea plantation, he or she "could go through dere en spot de Sara Davis niggers from de Bethea niggers" as soon as "you see dem."[4]

This was no accident. Sarah's slaves were looked after "in de right way." She cared for them when they were ill, made sure they ate well, and had their healthy meals prepared. In contrast to some slave owners in the South, Sarah made sure that the breakfast served to her slaves always contained meat. She also ensured that their clothes were well made and that they had a "nice clean place to sleep." She never allowed her slaves "to lay down in rags." She did not compel them to work on Sunday, and she made sure that they took care of personal chores, like washing and ironing, on Saturday, so they did not have to do them on the Sabbath. She did not permit the enslaved children she owned to work at all, or at least in their early years, and Hunter remembered playing with her dolls in the backyard "aw de time I wanna." When asked about who handled, managed, and cared for the people Sarah owned, Hunter reinforced the fact that Sarah "see 'bout aw dis she self."[5]

The distinctions between Sarah's and John's slaves extended to their accommodations. According to Hunter, the quarters where the couple's slaves slept were divided into two long rows; one housed "de Davis niggers," and the homes of the "Bethea niggers" formed the other. Hunter assessed the homes of Sarah's slaves and compared them with those of her husband's, which she considered inferior. Clearly, at least one member of this slave-owning couple wanted to demarcate the division of property even if it meant reconfiguring the architectural landscape of the plantation to do so.[6]

Sarah's desire to protect her investment in slaves went farther still. Hunter recalled that her mistress never had the enslaved people she owned "cut up en slashed up no time"; she "wouldn' allow no slashin round bout whe' she was," and she made sure that her husband refrained from punishing her slaves as well. One day when John set his mind to whipping one of Sarah's slaves, she stopped him and said, "John C., you let my nigger alone." He abided by her wishes. Sarah's decision to refrain from inflicting certain kinds of punishment preserved the value of her property and ensured that her slaves were healthy enough to work the way she needed and wanted them to.[7]

The arrangements that Sarah and John made that Hunter described were neither rare nor exceptional.[8] The enslaved people that women owned routinely described similar circumstances in their interviews with FWP writers. Yet these and other dimensions of life within slaveholding households, including agreements like Sarah and John's, have remained obscure because they occurred away from the public gaze. Even so, during slavery and long after it ended, the enslaved people that white women owned talked about their mistresses and how these women challenged their male kinfolks' alleged power to control their property, human and otherwise. Formerly enslaved people like Hester Hunter also make clear that while their female owners' humane treatment toward their slaves might appear to be motivated by benevolence or to spare them abuse, their grounds for contesting their husbands' authority were in fact predicated upon their position as slave owners who possessed the right and power to control their own property as they saw fit. Formerly enslaved people also described how their female owners' propertied status often formed the basis of marital conflicts and how these women's economic ties to slavery, their legal titles to enslaved people, and the juridical protection of their property rights configured the internal order of their households and influenced their interactions with individuals beyond them.

Many of these women had inherited enslaved people, some when they themselves were infants and girls. Slave-owning kin gave brides-to-be enslaved people as wedding gifts, which served to augment their economic investments in slavery at a time when historians contend that married women endured "civil death" and had no other choice but to resign themselves to their fate.[9] Countless studies have chronicled the lives of married women in the slaveholding South who were indeed constrained by the legal doctrine of coverture. But some wives found ways to circumvent the constraints that coverture imposed. For them, relinquishing the control they had cultivated since girlhood was not something they were willing to do without a fight. Marriage did not constitute civil death for these women. It marked another important life transition that allowed them to put the strategies of slave management and discipline that they learned as girls into practice and to increase their control over enslaved people.

The recollections of formerly enslaved people include descriptions of how slave-owning women sought to protect their human property within and near their households, and lay bare the confrontations and conflicts that ensued as a consequence. Yet people within and far beyond southern households routinely acknowledged that women in slaveholding households could in fact be slave owners in their own right who had the authority to control and dispose of the enslaved people they owned as they deemed appropriate. The actions of community members and representatives of the state also reveal that individuals outside the household acknowledged the legal title that even married women had to their slaves.

Slave catchers captured runaway slaves for female owners and took them to local jailors, who subsequently called upon these women, not their husbands, to retrieve their property. Newspapers routinely included women's advertisements concerning runaways, which identified them as lawful owners of those enslaved people and offered rewards for their capture and return. Women were counted among the slave owners enumerated in the Schedule of Slave Inhabitants, which contained data collected as part of the 1850 and 1860 U.S. federal censuses. When the state charged enslaved people with participating in insurrections or conspiracies, executed them, or sentenced them to sale outside state lines, court officials identified female owners in their judgments. Special committees often awarded these same women compensation for the loss of their human property, and if the amount proved disappointing, slave-owning women would petition the courts for more. Judges issued legal orders calling on women to have their slaves report to court in order to testify in cases against other enslaved people. Municipal officials compensated slave-owning women for the labor of enslaved people who assisted with public works. Other authorities issued receipts to women who remitted payment for taxes levied upon the slaves they owned.[10] And when husbands and others jeopardized slave-owning women's property rights, those women went to court, where judges routinely acknowledged their legal title to the enslaved people in question.

Given the standard view of coverture in the nineteenth century, much of this seems implausible. But truth be told, the doctrine of coverture was a legal fiction, and an imperfect one at that, and legislators and court officials seemed to know it. As the historian Marylynn Salmon has aptly observed, it was premised upon the ideal marriage in which "men always acted wisely and fairly" and assumed the role of patriarch and household head with almost perfect precision. Legal cases made it clear that ideal marriages were rarely achieved, and propertied women often found themselves in dire circumstances as a consequence of their husbands' poor judgment, misdeeds, and misfortunes.[11]

Jurists, the historian Hendrik Hartog asserts, came to know that "coverture alone offered little in the way of real protection for a wife." This was especially true during and after the economic panics of 1819 and 1837, financial catastrophes that left many southern men insolvent.[12] Under common law, when married men failed in their commercial and agricultural ventures, their creditors could seize their wives' estates to satisfy their debts, and many women lost their inheritances and the property they had acquired through their own industry in this way. Courts began to require that married women be accorded private or "privy" examinations whenever they received requests to sell their property. These examinations served to confirm their decisions to sell and ensure that their choices were not a result of their husbands' coercion. In many cases, however, husbands forced their wives to say that the decision to sell was their own and thereby defeated the intent of such examinations. Courts also mandated "women's signatures on land deeds," and they supported husbands and wives having separate estates.[13] Additionally, in the mid-nineteenth century states began to pass married women's property acts that granted women some control over their property. Although none of these protections was infallible, they signaled that legislators were attuned to the problems inherent in endowing husbands with unlimited power over their wives' property.[14]

But long before the widespread legislative acknowledgment of the shortcomings of coverture and the passage of these protective laws, slave-owning kin took steps to reduce the risks associated with granting husbands absolute power over the property of soon-to-be or already married women. Such protections proved to be especially important in the first decades of the nineteenth century, when many young couples were trekking to the West and Deep South. Male suitors from long-standing communities could be vetted, and their boasts of wealth and excellent pedigree verified. But when they moved to the West, they could reinvent themselves and misrepresent their financial circumstances to the women they courted. Emily Camster Green's owners, for example, gave her to their daughter Janie when she married. Before Janie and her prospective husband said their vows, he had convinced her that he "had a big plantation an lots o' money" in Mississippi. Later, Janie was devastated to discover that the plantation he claimed to own actually belonged to one Joe Moore and that Moore employed her husband as an overseer. She had been courted by many suitors, but, sadly, Green remarked, Janie "jes took de wrong one."[15]

Men like Janie's husband lied in order to attract propertied and well-to-do women in hopes of securing their estates or, as one woman claimed, "to make property in a way more easy than to work for it."[16] Slave-owning women frequently alerted each other to the risks that dubious suitors presented. They also wrote about the woes of property-owning women they knew who seemed blinded by love and oblivious to the dangers unscrupulous men posed to their economic security.[17] Sharing such knowledge could reduce some of the financial risks associated with choosing the wrong mate, but not all of them. It was essential for families to protect their female kin's financial well-being in whatever ways they could. Parents frequently gave their daughters less "real" property—land—than they gave sons. They also imposed limits upon the amount of time their female kin could hold property, usually granting them "life estates" that accorded them ownership for their lifetimes, after which the estates passed on to their children.

Historians tend to interpret parental decisions to limit their daughters' control over property in this way as an indicator of filial gender bias, particularly among fathers, and paternal favoritism shown to sons. However, slave-owning fathers as well as mothers left their daughters *and* sons life estates. On November 15, 1836, for example, Nancy Boulware drew up her will, in which she granted each of her two sons and her three daughters life estates comprised primarily of the slaves she owned. When Nancy's son Thomas drew up *his* will, he elected to bequeath enslaved people to his sons and daughters for their lifetimes as well, in emulation of his mother's vision of property distribution.[18]

Some slave owners consulted with family members about their preferences before writing their wills, and their legatees responded in ways that reflected their own interests. If the bequests involved property, legatees often made requests based on their ability to manage the property in question, sometimes suggesting that the land or slaves they were set to inherit be sold so that they could receive the proceeds from such sales. Sarah E. Devereux's mother-in-law consulted with her about what kind of bequest she preferred to receive on behalf of her young daughters. Devereux thought "it would be far better to have their money than land and Negroes," because if she received land and enslaved people she would have to depend upon her brother-in-law for assistance. She and her daughters lived in New Haven, Connecticut, where slavery had long been abolished, and state law prohibited her from holding individuals in bondage. She had no intention of moving south and preferred to manage her daughters' legacies herself.[19]

Sarah Devereux knew firsthand how troublesome such arrangements could be. Although she and her daughters lived in Connecticut, she still maintained a plantation and cultivated cotton in North Carolina. She had to rely on an overseer, local factors (brokers), and her deceased husband's family for help in managing the estate, selling the cotton, and preparing it for shipment. They would send Devereux updates, but she also kept herself informed about the cotton market and drew upon the knowledge she gained when she wrote to her brother-in-law regarding her concerns about the current price of cotton in the overseas market. So when considering her daughters' inheritances, she hoped to avoid similar cross-regional endeavors if she could.

These scenarios suggest that when elders devised their wills, many consider-ations influenced their bequests, such as whether slavery existed in the states where their heirs resided or how best to frame bequests that involved minor children. Testators, then, could decide to bequeath their property in ways that had little or nothing to do with a bias against heiresses or ideas about female ineptitude.

Among the most important steps a woman and her family could take to cir-cumvent the constraints of coverture were devising an antenuptial or marriage contract, which resembled a modern-day prenuptial agreement, or drawing up deeds of gift, deeds of trust, and wills that granted her control over all property she already owned or would acquire during her marriage. Although the histo-rian Michael B. Dougan claims that antenuptial agreements were "legally valid but not practically useful [and] of little use to young couples just starting out," and another historian, Woody Holton, argues that trust estates did not grant women separate property at all, both of these proved to be true only under cer-tain conditions.[20] Looking closely at the language of such agreements we can see that women and their families constructed them in ways that forbade their present and future husbands from having any control over their property. A husband could not dispose of it, and the property was not liable to seizure for his debts.[21] Some trust deeds went even farther, requiring trustees to consult with the female beneficiary before they made any changes to the estate and to obtain her consent before altering the trust in any way. Others added language that granted the woman all the income the property in the trust produced, as well as the power to control the property, dispose of it, or mortgage it, or to buy more property, as she saw fit, even though she had a trustee.[22]

The people drawing up such documents were as specific as possible when itemizing the property and assets involved, because they understood that omis-sions could lead to the seizure of any property not explicitly included. Such documents might also indicate that a married woman was entitled to the wages her slaves earned when they were hired out to others and that she possessed the crops that her slaves cultivated. Furthermore, when a woman owned enslaved females, she and her family made sure to secure her legal title to the "future issue" or "increase" of those slaves as well. Such a contingency secured property that could amount to thousands of dollars in the future. As a formerly enslaved woman named Mary Jane Jones observed, the gift of an enslaved female served "as a kind of nest egg" that parents gave to their children. Jones's own mother was a gift from father to son, and the intent of this gift was to enable Jones's mother to "breed slaves for him." After Jones's master took her mother home "he bought a slave husband fur her," and "children came to both families thick and fast." As Walter Johnson contends, "Slaveholders articulated their own family lines—their worldly legacies—through the reproduction of their slaves," and slave-owning women also benefited from this kind of calculus. The woman who owned F. H. Brown's family, for example, "got her start off of the slaves her parents gave her." She owned Brown's grandmother, who bore twenty-six children during her lifetime. Before freedom came, Brown's mistress owned seventy-five slaves in her own right.[23]

Close examination of the stipulations and clauses included in these documents reveals how practically useful these contracts could be for slave-owning women and the preservation of their property rights after marriage. Sarah Welsh's marriage agreement with her husband, Dennis, not only protected her property, it established her legal right to own, control, sell, and bequeath it in any way that she considered appropriate. At the time of her marriage to Dennis Welsh, she was "sole and unmarried" and owned "tenements, lots, houses, parcels, tracts of land in Mobile, Alabama," twenty-seven slaves who were considered her "personal property," and ten stock shares in the Planter's and Merchants' Bank of Mobile, as well as other personal property. She devised a marriage agreement that reserved it all for her "sole, entire and exclusive use, benefit and enjoyment." The agreement empowered her to "have, take, use, enjoy, receive all the rents, issues, and profits of all said above described real estate, all the hire and personal services and labours of said Negro slaves and of said horses, [and] all the dividends and interest on said ten shares of stock in the Planters and Merchants Bank of Mobile." It also specified that she should "in no [manner] be interrupted . . . in her full sole and exclusive use and enjoyment, management and control, and disposition of the same." She appointed Richard Redwood as her trustee and granted him the authority to sell, rent, hire, or otherwise dispose of her property, but only as she "may think proper . . . and may direct." Additionally, she specified that he could do so only with her "written request fully given in the presence of six reputable persons and in the absence of the said Dennis." She reserved her right to draw up a will and to "give, devide [*sic*] and bequeath to any person or persons all of any part of [her property] . . . as she . . . may think proper." To ensure that her husband did not "defeat, obstruct or impede . . . the true intent and meaning" of her will, she required that it be "duly signed, sealed and executed, published and declared in [his] absence . . . and in the presence of four reputable persons, one of whom shall be a clergyman." Dennis agreed to all the terms and signed the contract.[24]

The months and days preceding the wedding ceremony were critical for a slave-owning woman because she had to decide whether she trusted her prospective husband's professions of love, sobriety, financial security, and strong ethics enough to enter into marriage without a contract like Sarah Welsh's, or whether to err on the side of caution and insist on a settlement that protected her interests. Such decisions were not easy in part because prospective husbands could be reluctant or outright opposed to such provisions. A woman who confronted a recalcitrant fiancé could issue an ultimatum making the marriage conditional upon his acceptance of the marital settlement. A marriage settlement was especially important when a woman did not know the details of her future husband's past. Mary Williams, for example, had inherited a considerable estate from her deceased parents that she possessed in her own right. When William Williams proposed marriage, he was a widower with a large family and a sizable amount of debt. Knowing this, and not wanting to risk her own financial stability, Mary had "utterly refused" to accept William's proposal unless he agreed to "a marriage contract or settlement" that would reserve to her "for her own benefit her property of every description and money and choses in action [personal property] of every description . . . in short all that was hers in her own right." She also insisted that their contract emancipate her two slaves upon her death. Her goal was not merely to ensure that she had complete control over her property while she was living but also to ensure that it would not be subsumed into William's estate if he were to die before her, as the law required.[25]

Slave-owning widows who considered remarrying were especially keen to approach these decisions cautiously and sought to protect their property from possible misjudgments.[26] They often made their second, and third, marriages contingent upon antenuptial agreements. Eliza Strickland was a widow who owned land, slaves, and "other personal property ample for her respectable and comfortable support and maintenance." She was engaged to Barnabas Strickland and described him, when she later hauled him into court, as "a stranger recently from the State of Georgia [who] was introduced to her as a churchman of the Baptist denomination . . . a man of specious manners and respectable appearance and a minister of the gospel." Yet because she was "ignorant of [his financial] circumstances," she "consented to marry him only on condition that, by an ante-nuptial contract, her property should settle upon her absolutely as her sole and separate estate." This, she contended, was "an act of precaution." Her apprehensions proved justified when she learned that Barnabas was heavily indebted to people in his home state.[27] Women who failed to protect their property during their first marriage generally recognized their mistake and took care not to make it again. Others hoped that their second husbands would be more adept at managing their property than their first had been. But if their second husband dashed those hopes and squandered their property, some women set out to prevent more waste by petitioning courts for permission to establish *postnuptial* agreements, which granted them the right to create separate estates after their marriages began. The married women who sought these postnuptial agreements did not wish to be separated or divorced from their husbands; they merely sought to protect their property from their husbands' financial blunders.[28]

Once kin and couples had drawn up a marriage settlement, states like North Carolina required them to authenticate or prove it in the same manner they did other deeds. Couples needed to put the settlement in writing, sign it in the presence of "one credible subscribing witness," and register the agreement "in the office of the public register of the county where the donee reside[d]." They needed to complete this process within "one year after the execution" of the settlement.[29] Clerks in local county courts then recorded the settlement in a deed book.

As women left their home states in the Southeast and moved farther west with their husbands, they would file authenticated copies of these documents in the courts of their new residences.[30] Even in cases when they were not mandated to do so, women would often record the contracts or petition for recognition just to ensure that their local courts would recognize and protect their legal title to the enslaved people they brought with them as they migrated. In November 1841, while still a resident of Mississippi, Susan Hunter purchased eighteen enslaved people on three separate occasions. She later moved to Kentucky, and shortly after her arrival, she went to court to have her legal title to these slaves recognized. She had been advised that Kentucky law granted "a married woman . . . the right to purchase slaves or other property and hold the same to her own 'separate use,'" and she asked the court to recognize her right to hold these slaves for "her sole and separate use" in the state.[31] The court acknowledged Hunter's ownership of the slaves she named in her petition.

When Spanish Florida became an American territory, slave-owning women living there acquired a new opportunity to reassert their property rights. Although their property rights had been accorded under the Spanish regime, they took their cases to American courts to establish them in the common (and equity) law systems that prevailed in the United States. In 1831, Victoria Le Sassier entered the Escambia County Courthouse in Pensacola to inform the court that she had no intention of relinquishing her property rights. In her petition to the Superior Court of West Florida, she stated that "by the laws of the Spanish Monarchy subsisting and in force in the Province of West Florida prior to the year one thousand eight hundred and twenty two," she was "entitled to her separate property independent of the control and disposition" of her husband and this "right had

in no wise been changed by the transfer of the Province to the United States."
She also told the court that the "said property was secured to her by the treaty of
cession and by an act of the Legislative Council in the year one thousand eight
hundred and twenty four." The court recognized and upheld her right to hold
separate property, which included twenty enslaved men, women, and children.[32]

In Louisiana, where civil law prevailed, the state's system of property law also
allowed married women to hold certain kinds of property in their own names,
to control it, and to dispose of it without special provisions.[33] Even so, women in
the state often insisted on signing antenuptial contracts with their future husbands, and they also sometimes sued their husbands for a "separation of property" after they married. A separation of property was a provision that allowed a
married woman to legally separate her property from that of her husband, but
she could do so only under specific circumstances. Louisiana courts required
married women who sought a separation of property to prove that their husbands' pecuniary affairs, fiscal mismanagement, or economic circumstances
jeopardized their own property and economic well-being. One such form of
evidence was a husband's indebtedness to his wife or his misuse of her "para-
phernal" (separate) or her "dotal" (dower) property, which she would continue
to own after marriage, but would have placed under his management.

When courts granted such requests, these women were legally empowered
to control their "movable" property and administer it as they saw fit. Although
the law did not immediately grant them the right to do this with their "immovable" property, it contained a contingency clause that allowed them to do so
with their husbands' consent or with the court's permission if their husbands
refused. It might seem logical to assume that enslaved people would fit the
definition of movable property, but in fact they were considered "attached" to
the land, and thereby legally immovable.[34] Women who lived in Louisiana thus
had to complete extra steps to secure and maintain control over the slaves they
owned, and many did so.

Once a married Louisiana woman had legally separated her property from
her husband's, the court required her to publish a notice of the separation, in
English and French, at least three times, in two local newspapers. These notices
included the date of the judgment, the names of the plaintiff (wife) and defendant (husband), the case or docket number, a statement about the nature of the
suit, the amount of money the wife sought to recover from her husband (to
repay his debt to her), the nature of the judgment, the judge's name, and the
verification by the Deputy Clerk.[35]

Separation of property notices published in local newspapers were critical
because they served to alert the couple's community and their creditors about

THE STATE OF LOUISIANA—First Judicial District Court.—I hereby certify, that on the day of the date hereof, judgment was entered in this Court against T. B. Cabos, at the suit of M. E. H. Dupland his wife, in the words and figures following; to wit:

M. E. H. Dupland, wife of T. B. Cabos,
vs.
T. B. Cabos, her husband.

No. 7112

On motion of C. A. Canon, Esq, of counsel for the plaintiff, the court after hearing the testimony oral and written, produced by said plaintiff, and being satisfied that the allegations of her petition are

Judgment recorded in judgment, Docket page 265, Br.
Amount of judgment...$1500 00
Amount of costs.......... 25 87½
                          ————
                          $1525 87½
Signed, Joshua Lewis,
Countersigned J. L. Lewis, clk.

sufficiently proved, order that the judgment by default taken in this case on the 30th day of May last, be now confirmed, and it is further ordered, adjudged and decreed that a separation of property take place between the plaintiff and defendant, her husband, and that she recover of the said defendant the sum of fifteen hundred dollars, and costs of suit to be taxed.—10th of June, 1826—Which costs amount to the sum of twenty-five dollars and 87½ cents, exclusive of the Sheriff's fees.

In testimony whereof, I have hereunto set my hand and affixed the Seal of the said court, at the City of New Orleans, on this twenty-second day of February, in the year of our Lord one thousand eight hundred and twenty-seven, and in the fifty first year of the Independence of the U. States.

feb 24—3t in 10d]   JOHN L. LEWIS, *Clerk.*

Separation of property notice documenting the outcome of *M. E. H. Dupland v. T. B. Cabos, Louisiana Advertiser*, February 27, 1827 (Nineteenth-Century U.S. Newspapers database, Cengage/Gale)

the change in the wife's legal status and her newly expanded control over her property. It was imperative for a married woman to make sure the notice was published because doing so reduced the likelihood that her husband's creditors would challenge the legitimacy of her separate property status and seize her assets to pay her husband's debts, something that happened frequently. When creditors seized what they thought was Walter Turnbull's property to satisfy an outstanding debt, his wife, Matilda, filed an injunction preventing them from taking further action because she—rightfully—claimed the property belonged to her. Walter Turnbull's creditors rejected her assertion and stated that her separation of property was null and void because she had not published a notice of the court's judgment in local newspapers as the law required. The lower court agreed with the creditors, and Matilda appealed. Her counsel presented all the evidence reviewed by the Sixth District Court to the Louisiana Supreme Court, which ruled that while she *should* have published the notice in a timely manner, the "judgment of separation, unattended by publication [was] not *ipso facto* void," and the court thereby "annulled, avoided and reversed" the lower court's ruling. Matilda's separation of property was upheld and her injunction reinstated. Some other women were not so lucky.[36]

Separation of property notices publicized husbands' indebtedness to their dependents for friends and foes to see. Long-time citizens of Louisiana would probably know that a separation of property case had been filed because the wife believed that her husband's finances and commercial behavior threatened her economic stability. The notices signified a husband's irresponsibility and assaulted the sanctity of patriarchal households by unveiling typically private marital and financial affairs. Yet southern women filed them regardless. Rulings on separations of property and the subsequent publication of the notices undoubtedly delivered a severe blow to many a husband's ego. Charles N. Rowley was so appalled by the court's decision to grant his wife, Jane, a separation of property that he challenged the judge to a duel and killed him.[37]

Throughout the antebellum period, married women consistently asserted their rights to own and control human property without their husbands' interference, and they exercised those rights as well. Enslaved people witnessed altercations and overheard arguments between married slave-owning couples, and they and their fellow bondsmen were often the subjects of those disputes. Married women reinforced their property claims in conversations with or in the presence of their slaves, and formerly enslaved people later paraphrased these conversations, such as the one Morris Sheppard remembered. He told his interviewer, "Old mistress . . . inherit about half a dozen slaves, and say dey was her own and old Master can't sell one unless she give him leave to do it."[38] These spousal confrontations over property do not conform to historians' usual claims about the legal doctrine of coverture. Nor do they seem to reflect the gendered, hierarchical organization of nineteenth-century households that most historians describe. To justify their arguments, some historians argue that enslaved people were not in a position to know about their masters' and mistresses' "property rights" and "the law."

In truth, enslaved men, women, and children knew far more about white women's property and the law than they often disclosed, especially when they were the "property." The case of a wrongfully enslaved woman named Winney offers an example. On February 19, 1844, in Jefferson County, Kentucky, Winney sued the heirs of her deceased owner, Elizabeth Stout Whitehead. During her years of service to Whitehead, Winney had learned that before her marriage to William Whitehead, her mistress had signed a marital contract that "expressly agreed that each party should retain to him and herself the entire and exclusive right to the property owned by each before the marriage with the right to dispose of the same in such a way, as they should respectively choose to do." Winney had also learned that the contract included a provision that stipulated she was to receive her freedom upon Elizabeth's death. She knew that Elizabeth and her husband had not filed the contract with the court but had given it to the Reverend William Stout for safekeeping. Winney petitioned the court for her freedom and challenged her deceased owner's heirs, who were claiming her as a slave. Elizabeth's marriage contract had been lost or mislaid, but Winney submitted a letter from the minister that corroborated her account of the facts. In his remarkable answer to Winney's petition, William Whitehead's son John, who was also the administrator of his deceased father's estate, said that he had witnessed the marital contract described in Winney's petition "at the request of his step mother Elizabeth Whitehead." He also stated that he knew from his stepmother's "repeated declarations before her death, that she had an earnest desire" to emancipate Winney. Furthermore, he had "often heard that there was a marriage contract between his father and Mrs. Elizabeth Stout before their marriage." Based on his recollections, and after receiving Reverend Stout's letter confirming the existence of the contract, he told the court that he "cannot and he will not gainsay [Winney's] right to her freedom." He asked that "justice be done." Winney won her freedom.[39]

Although Winney achieved a positive outcome to her petition, John's admissions in his answer to her legal suit highlight how the heirs of women like Elizabeth Whitehead could be privy to these women's wishes with regard to the slaves they owned yet refuse to respect them. Well before John Whitehead became his father's administrator, he knew that the marital contract between William and Elizabeth existed, and he possessed firsthand knowledge of his stepmother's desire to free Winney after her death. And yet when he drafted the inventory of his father's estate, he listed Winney as a slave and made no subsequent arrangements to free her. John Whitehead's initial decision to ignore his stepmother's wishes illustrates a common obstacle that enslaved people such as Winney had to overcome. It also compels us to reconsider his seemingly benevolent response to Winney's legal complaint and approach similar declarations with caution.

Winney was one of many enslaved individuals who petitioned the courts for freedom based on their understanding of the terms set forth in their deceased owners' wills or marital agreements.[40] But even more enslaved and formerly enslaved people who never entered southern courts were aware that their female owners had protected their ownership rights with similar legal instruments. The reflections and remembrances of these individuals reveal that enslaved people knew a great deal about women's property rights and the law.

As the fugitive slave and later abolitionist James W. C. Pennington noted, every change in the financial, social, and personal affairs of a slave owner and his or her children could have traumatic consequences for enslaved people. An enslaved person's familial and community stability was inextricably linked to his or her owners' solvency and decisions about the disposal of their wealth. Out of necessity, African Americans came to understand critical features of southern law. When slave owners became insolvent and creditors sued them to recover debts that remained outstanding or when slave owners died and their estates were distributed according to their wills or in the absence of them, enslaved people were among the most affected. If they hoped to purchase their freedom or the liberty of loved ones, they needed to know how a basic contract worked. As commodities that could be bequeathed, seized, exchanged, hired, bought, and sold, they became intimately acquainted with the values their owners affixed to them. They also came to understand slave owners' inheritance practices, debts, loans, sublets, renting practices, installments and time payments, and mortgages. Enslaved people were knowledgeable about property and legal claims to it, both as chattel and as property owners in their own right.[41] Furthermore, they listened to their female owners' conversations about how they wanted the slaves they owned to be treated and used, and they understood that these women's assertions were grounded in what they considered to be their personal legal rights.

Abundant evidence from publicly available documents such as court records and newspapers supports enslaved people's claims that community members and representatives of the state recognized women's legal titles to human property. When an enslaved person ran away from his or her female owner, for example, runaway notices alerted the community to the owner's title to the fugitive. A woman would identify herself as the enslaved fugitive's legal owner and place ads in newspapers offering a reward for the slave's capture and return. Elizabeth Humphreyville's 1846 advertisement is an example. She operated a boardinghouse in Mobile, Alabama, and through her earnings was able to purchase two enslaved females named Polly and Ann. When Ann was "pretty far advanced in pregnancy," she ran away, and someone told Humphreyville that Ann had probably fled to a plantation located four miles from Pensacola, Florida. Based on this tip, Humphreyville placed an advertisement in the *Pensacola Gazette* offering a fifty-dollar reward to anyone who seized Ann and confined her in the guardhouse in Mobile until Humphreyville could claim her. Although Elizabeth Humphreyville deemed it likely that Ann had run away, she also considered it possible that her husband, Joseph, had stolen the woman. She accused him of pretending to be Ann's owner, and she cautioned the public "not to trade for her as the titles to [Ann rested] in me *alone*."[42]

Slave owners frequently identified slave-owning women as the owners of a runaway's relatives in their advertisements because they presumed that fugitives might return to these women's estates in hopes of reuniting with their loved ones.[43]

When individuals captured runaways, local jailors often held them until their owners could come fetch them. If they could not find the owners immediately, they posted "Committed to Jail" or "Brought to Jail" notices. One C. Tippett placed a notice in the Washington, D.C., *Daily National Intelligencer* stating that Edward Clarke had identified Mrs. Deborah Ray as the person who owned him. Clarke further specified the town and county where Ray lived. Tippett called upon Ray to come to the jail, establish legal title, and take Clarke back.[44]

$50 Reward.

Ranaway or was stolen from me on Saturday before Christmas last, a negro woman named **Ann,** of black complexion, about 19 years old, pretty far advanced in pregnancy. I have been informed that she is at or near the plantation of Mr. Jordan, 4 miles from Pensacola on the stage road. Any person who will deliver her to the Guard House in Mobile shall receive the above reward of $50. I have been informed that J. D. Humphyville took her away from my residence, and pretends is he her owner.— The public are cautioned not to trade for her as the titles to said woman is in me *alone*.

ELIZABETH HUMPHYVILLE.
March 8, 1846–49–3w

Elizabeth Humphreyville's (misspelled Humphyville) runaway advertisement for Ann, *Pensacola Gazette*, March 8, 1846 (Nineteenth-Century U.S. Newspapers database, Cengage/Gale)

NOTICE.

WAS committed to the Jail of Washington County, D. C. on the 1st day of February, as a runaway, a Negro Boy, by the name of EDWARD CLARKE; he is five feet one inch high, about 16 years of age; had on, when committed, old hat, kersey jacket and trowsers, coarse linen shirt, and coarse shoes; says that he belongs to Mrs. Deborah Ray, living near Unity, Montgomery County, Md. The owner of the above described negro boy is requested to come and prove him and take him away, or he will be sold for his jail fees, and other expenses, as the law directs.

C. TIPPETT, for

feb 11—w3w   T. RINGGOLD, Marshal.

C. Tippett's "Committed to Jail" notice in the *Daily National Intelligencer*, March 4, 1825 (Nineteenth-Century U.S. Newspapers database, Cengage/Gale)

The total number of women who pursued their slaves by placing ads might be higher than can be judged from the newspapers because editors often printed advertisements that did not identify owners by name, telling subscribers to "Apply to the Printer." Female owners might also be underrepresented in such advertisements because the names of their male agents might appear as the contact persons. But these documents nonetheless support formerly enslaved people's recollections of having female owners, illustrating the ways slave-owning women made their propertied status known to others and showing communal recognition of that status.

Municipal officials also publicly recognized women's legal claims to enslaved people. In fact, sometimes two women might claim to own the same enslaved person, and when that happened, these officials faced the same kind of legal hassle that often arose in their attempts to determine rightful ownership when male disputants presented them with competing claims. In 1841, James C. Norris was master of the Charleston, South Carolina, workhouse, an establishment where slave owners often sent their slaves to be confined and punished. (Local courts also sent enslaved people to the workhouse if they were convicted of committing crimes.) On February 28, on what was shaping up to be an ordinary Sunday for Norris, he agreed to confine an enslaved woman named Martha. Henry W. Schroder had lodged Martha in the workhouse "as the property of his wife Mrs. A. E. [Ann] Schroder." He left Norris with "positive instructions" not to give the woman "to any person whatsoever other than him" or "his wife . . . A. E. Schroder." A few days later, "Miss Ann Bell of Charleston caused a demand to be made, and did afterwards make a demand" that Norris give Martha to her because she claimed the enslaved woman "as her own absolute property." She, too, instructed Norris not to give Martha to anyone but her. When Ann Bell returned to the workhouse to retrieve Martha, Norris refused to give the enslaved female to her, and Bell sued him in the Court of Common Pleas for Charleston, entering a writ of trover (the wrongful taking of property) against him for "converting and disposing of [her] goods and chattels," and asking the court to award her one thousand dollars.[45]

Norris went to Schroder and told him about Bell's claim and her suit. Schroder insisted that Norris adhere to the instructions he had given and threatened to sue Norris if he disobeyed or refused to give Martha to him or his wife when they asked for her. He told Norris that Martha rightfully belonged to his wife via a bill of sale issued to her father, Charles C. Chitty. At the time of Martha's purchase, Ann Schroder was still a minor, and because of this, Charles Chitty had created a trust, which included Martha, and secured the property to his daughter for her "sole use . . . until she should arrive at the age of twenty-one years." At that time Martha would belong to her "absolutely" and be "discharged from the trust."[46]

All of this presented Norris with a costly dilemma. As the master of the workhouse, he was legally and financially responsible for the loss of any enslaved people confined within the establishment, and if he handed Martha over to either woman, while both claimed her as their "bonafide property," the other could sue him for Martha's value. In fact, the court record reveals that Ann Bell had already sued him, so his fears were well founded. To spare himself further trouble, he refused to give Martha to either woman and petitioned the court for assistance in determining which of them rightfully possessed legal title to the woman. He asked the court to make the Schroders and Bell interplead and "settle their rights to . . . Martha." Once a decision had been handed down, he would be "ready and willing to deliver up [Martha] to whom the same shall appear of right to belong." Although the petition does not disclose the outcome of the case, other documents show that H. W. Schroder was telling Norris the truth. On March 30, 1830, Catherine Roulain sold Martha and her six-year-old daughter Mary to Charles Chitty for $350, and the bill of sale indicates that Charles Chitty bought Martha and Mary for his daughter Ann Chitty (later Ann Schroder) in his capacity as her trustee. It also states that he bought them "for the sole use and behoof of his daughter until she shall arrive at the age of twenty-one," at which time the trust would cease, and the two would belong "to her and her heirs forever." In addition, the 1830 U.S. census shows that although Ann Bell owned two enslaved females, she did not own a six-year-old girl. Nor are there any documents indicating that Ann Schroder or her husband had sold Martha to Bell.[47]

Norris's petition, and others like it, show that not only did public officials recognize women's legal titles to enslaved people, these women's husbands did, too. Norris's petition also demonstrates that husbands might be the people who informed public officials about their wives' slave ownership in the first place. Schroder might have been involved in many of the encounters described in Norris's bill, but he consistently identified his wife, and not himself, as Martha's rightful owner. Furthermore, Martha and Mary's bill of sale revealed that not two women, but three claimed legal title to Martha at one time or another. Catherine Roulain was Martha's original owner, and her name appears on the bill that recorded the sale to Charles Chitty. A witness, James Kennedy, attested to being present when she signed the document, and John Ward recorded it on March 31, 1830. The original transaction between Catherine Roulain and Charles Chitty, along with Norris's case, offers powerful testimony of the broad recognition of women's legal ownership of enslaved people.

Between and within the lines of formulaic legal jargon, the legal petitions brought by married women repeatedly informed jurists that coverture was not working. Not only were many husbands not "covering" their wives under their wings in the ways that Blackstone indicated, they were robbing their wives, squandering their assets, and violating their property rights. Worse still, many of these men had come to their marriages impoverished and proved to be irresponsible and incapable of exercising the rights which coverture afforded them. Finally, their ineptitude paved the way for their creditors to further breach what should have been inviolable boundaries that protected their wives' separate property from seizure. Married women throughout the South called upon judges to step between them and their husbands, protect the property they claimed as their own, and prevent others from interfering with their enjoyment of the same. And when women's legal affairs were in proper order, and their cases were strong, judges routinely heeded their calls.

White women's petitions also document interfamilial conflicts over women's human property wherein mothers sued their sons, aunts sued their nephews, and daughters sued mothers and fathers. Wives sued husbands over property that they considered rightfully their own. The historian Laura Edwards argues that when wives went to court to petition or sue over matters related to property, "ownership, in the technical sense of state law, was not really the issue." In her estimation, wives were seeking the "restoration of the peace, not recognition of property rights." When they appealed to the courts, they were effectively able to do so because their cases were not about "competing property rights, which would have pitted wives' rights against those of their husbands."[48] Her analysis suggests that if women did indeed enter courts in an effort to secure legal recognition of their property rights or if their petitions pitted their rights against those of their husbands, they would have lost their suits. But white southern women *were* contesting other people's claims to ownership of their slaves, and they *were* attempting to establish and legitimate their property rights "against those of their husbands." Women appealed to courts when their husbands disposed of their property despite their directives not to do so. They also petitioned courts when their husbands' creditors attempted to seize their slaves to pay their husbands' debts. They routinely took action when their husbands overstepped the bounds of what they considered to be their rightful authority, thereby infringing upon their own property rights.

Feuding women and their family members were not the only people who found themselves hauled into court over married women's slaves. A community member might accuse a woman of stealing slaves and leaving the state with them. Business agents brought claims against women for selling slaves to prevent creditors from seizing them. Others demanded payment for services rendered when women had separate estates from which they could comfortably repay their debts.[49] Southern women answered these accusations, and their replies vividly demonstrate their willingness to appear in the most public realms of southern society to defend their property rights and challenge the power of anyone—including their husbands—to control the enslaved people they owned. Furthermore, the judges who adjudicated their cases often ruled in their favor.

Chancery courts, or "courts of equity," were critical to a woman's ability to control and manage her property and request legal intervention in maintaining it. Chancery courts as they came to exist in the United States developed in fourteenth-century England during the reign of Edward III. When British subjects could find no remedy for matters related to "trust, fraud, or accident" under the common law, they petitioned the king for relief and resolution of legal matters. He, in turn, created the Court of Chancery, appointing a member of his Council to serve as chancellor and assist him "in all cases in which natural justice, equity, and good conscience required his intervention." British subjects would apply to the Chancery Court when they "wanted a remedy for [a] right or redress for a wrong that had been done" to them. The chancellor and his court "exercised an authority especially in favor of the weak, for repressing disorderly obstructions to the course of the law, . . . and affording a civil remedy in cases of violence or outrage," which the common law could not address.[50]

In stark contrast to common law courts, jurists in nineteenth-century chancery courts treated married women as distinct persons, not as individuals joined in unity with their husbands.[51] If a married woman entered into a contract with her husband, whether before or after the marriage took place, chancery courts would enforce it. If a wife placed her separate property in her husband's hands as trustee or simply as manager, but the husband used or disposed of it in ways that she objected to, chancery courts would uphold her rights to that property and make her husband repay her for any property he had sold or squandered. Furthermore, if a husband incurred debts that he was unable to pay and his creditors seized his wife's separate property, she could sue him and his creditors in chancery court to reclaim that property. Chancery courts also protected married women's "pin-money," small funds used to purchase consumer goods. Chancery courts recognized and protected any separate property that might be willed to married women or given to them as gifts, even if the property came from their husbands. And most important, chancery courts recognized a married woman's right to possess and control a separate estate and dispose of it as the terms of the estate allowed.[52] "With a separate estate," Hendrik Hartog argues, "a wife gained a more separate self, a self not fully incorporated into the marriage, a self that an equity court could recognize as having choices and wishes, a self that could be revealed to have been coerced when a husband compelled certain outcomes."[53] Furthermore, when individuals gave women property through deeds of gift or trust that included protective clauses forbidding husbands from interfering with the property, chancery courts upheld and enforced these deeds.

Legal scholars and women's historians have argued that when nineteenth-century southern jurists protected women's interests they were acting as patriarchs. These men, they argue, stepped in to restore peace to households with faltering and fallible male household heads.[54] Yet women's bills of complaints make it clear that they had their own reasons for taking their cases to chancery courts and appealing to the judges who presided over them for remedy. They sought to protect, acquire, or reclaim property by any means necessary, and if that meant pandering to judges who considered themselves de facto patriarchs, they were willing to do so. No matter what southern jurists thought they were doing, court cases make it clear that the women who appeared, or were represented, before them used the courts for their own purposes. Women acquired and maintained legal ties to enslaved persons, and they were willing to bring spouses, kin, and others into chancery courts in order to protect their economic interests. These legal connections undergirded their economic relationships to the institution of slavery. Moreover, their legal title to enslaved people empowered white women within their households. They could determine who would be able to access their slaves and their slaves' labor and who could discipline and manage them. On more than a few occasions, slave-owning women denied these privileges to spouses, kin, and community members and exercised complete control over the enslaved people they owned. Court records also documented the experiences of typical, not simply elite, slave-owning women, litigants who owned fewer than ten slaves. The majority, in fact, owned only one or two.

As Cornelia Hughes Dayton discovered in her examination of women's experiences with courts in colonial New Haven, Connecticut, the records from southern chancery courts allow us to "hear women talking and being talked to" and to "see the extent to which they were recognized or ignored in the courtroom in a more tangible way than is possible in other public settings."[55] In their petitions to chancery courts, white women talked about their conflicts, problems, and concerns. But they also told judicial officials what their lives were like before the issues that brought them to court arose. They detailed routine household activities and interactions. And they talked about their slaves. They challenged those who claimed power over or ownership of the enslaved people they themselves owned. And when litigants claimed that they were lying about their legal titles to enslaved people, female petitioners presented court chancellors with evidence supporting their rights to the slaves in question. They documented chains of slave ownership that often led to and from slave markets. Although historians have asserted that wealthy women were the primary beneficiaries of separate estates, chancery court petitions show that most of the women who mentioned having slaves owned fewer than ten, making them average, rather than elite, slaveholders.

When women filed petitions in chancery courts, trustees or "next friends" frequently represented them and looked after their property interests. Female petitioners might have also sought legal assistance in drafting their complaints. The individuals who represented them and gave them advice were not always men; women also assumed these roles. And even when the people who assisted the petitioners were men, the experiences that shaped ordinary married slave-owning women's lives were set down in chancery court records and became part of the public record.[56]

Formerly enslaved people routinely spoke of female slave owners who ensured that their legal titles to human property remained viable. And nineteenth-century legal records verify what these formerly enslaved people said about their mistresses. Clear parallels can be drawn between what enslaved people remembered about their female owners' property claims and what these women said in their petitions. White women made the same kind of property claims within their households and communities as they did in the courtroom. Household-to-courtroom conflicts over enslaved property present critically important evidence that challenges historians' prevailing understanding of how the law functioned and affected the lives of slave-owning women in the Old South.

Husbands were not always pleased when their wives possessed separate property or decided to manage it themselves. Betty Jones's brother John, for example, purchased an enslaved woman named Nanny for her, and in the bill of sale he stipulated that Nanny and her offspring would belong to his sister and should be retained for her sole and separate use.[57] Betty later married Isaac Jones, and although Isaac owned at least two hundred slaves of his own, he was unhappy about the fact that his wife owned property that he could not sell—and he did not hide his feelings. Nanny's granddaughter Katie Rowe remembered that "Old Master [was] allus kind of techy 'bout old Mistress having niggers he can't trade or sell." On one occasion when he was entertaining family and guests, he brought them to the slave quarters. He called all the enslaved people together to stand before the visitors. He then made his wife's slaves—Nanny, Katie Rowe, and Rowe's mother—stand apart from the slaves he owned, and he proceeded to give his slaves a directive: "Dese niggers belong to my wife but you belong to me, and I'm de only one you is to call Master." In Rowe's recollection, "All de other white folks look kind of funny, and Old Mistress look 'shamed of old Master."[58]

Some men resorted to deception and coercion, including domestic violence, to gain control of their wives' property. They might refuse to give their wives copies of the contracts or even destroy the legal documents that granted their wives control over their slaves.[59] Such tactics did not always stop these women from establishing boundaries related to their slaves and making sure that their husbands did not cross them. Sally Nightingale owned Alice Marshall and her mother, and Marshall claimed that her mistress's husband, Jack, "ain' had nothin' to do wid me an' my mother" because they "belong to mistiss by law an' not har husband."[60]

If a woman's husband or her husband's creditors still attempted to interfere with or seize her property despite their having separate estates, she might, as Mary Massie Leake did, seek legal remedy in a chancery court. Mary's husband, Joseph S. Leake, had sold two of her slaves to John A. Dailey without her consent, though he had no legal right to do so. At the time of their marriage, Mary had appointed her mother, Susanna, as the trustee who would manage her separate property. Susanna ably assumed this role until her death. For reasons that remain unclear, Mary failed to appoint another trustee. Soon after her mother's death, Joseph began to dispose of Mary's property, some of it to Dailey, and she filed a bill of complaint against Dailey and named her husband as co-defendant. She asked the court to issue and deliver a subpoena to him, compelling him to "answer the allegations of said bill," and to appoint a new trustee so she would no longer have to be "at the mercy of her said husband and his rapacious creditors." She also asked the court to issue an injunction which would prohibit Dailey from disposing of her slaves or removing them from the state.[61]

Women like Mary Leake often delegated control and management of their separate property to trustees, and sometimes these were their husbands. Historians often interpret the decision to name a husband as trustee as an indication of a wife's lack of interest in property ownership and control; sometimes they attribute the choice to a husband's pressure or influence. But we should view these trusts and estates from another vantage point. First, a woman's choice to elect a particular individual as her trustee was a crucial decision; it determined the level of control this individual, and others, would have over her property. Choosing the right person for this role was critical to preserving her legal title to slaves and making sure that others did not violate her rights, so she took care to find someone she could trust. A formerly enslaved man named Shade said it best when he observed that "any sort o' man kin han'le his own money, but it takes er *hones'* man to han'le other folks money," and this is why so many women entrusted their slaves to family members.[62] This was especially true since women had to navigate many more obstacles than men in order to secure control over property. And although historians frequently assume that women delegated their authority only to men, the evidence shows that they also called upon mothers, sisters, and aunts to serve as their trustees.[63]

If a married woman did not appoint a trustee of her own choosing, the courts typically appointed her husband to serve in this capacity unless circumstances made it impractical or unwise to do so. From our vantage point, a husband-trustee might appear to be managing and disposing of his wife's property simply as husbands were entitled to do under coverture. But legally, this was not the case. When a husband acted as his wife's trustee, the doctrine of "marital unity" under coverture did not apply in the same way in the eyes of the law. If a husband-trustee squandered or mismanaged his wife's property in his capacity as such, she possessed the right to take her case to a chancery court and request that her husband be removed from the trusteeship and replaced. Take the case of Mary Ann Spears. When her father, John Goldsmith, died, he left all his children a portion of his estate, and when he specifically addressed the property he bequeathed to his daughters, he plainly indicated that he did not want their husbands to have any say in its management or disposal. Although her father's intentions were clear, his use of plain language rather than legalese posed a problem when the creditors of Mary Ann's husband, John, attempted to satisfy the debts he owed them by seizing her slaves. Mary Ann went to chancery court to ask for help in reclaiming them. She explained that her father "was a plain man with but a very limited use of Letters, and not at all acquainted with legal technicalities or the terms proper to use in the creation of separate estates of his daughters." According to Mary Ann, her father had intended and "often expressed his determination . . . to vest the property given to his daughters to their sole and separate use or to the separate use of his daughters and their children, and to . . . free the same from all liability to the debts of their husbands and to exclude the marshal right of [their] husband[s]."[64]

When Mary Ann Spears's father died and some of his property was conveyed to her, she appointed her husband as her trustee. Although he managed the property for her, she assured the court that he "again and again recognized said property as the separate estate of your oratrix." Mary Ann told the court about an incident that she believed demonstrated her husband's acceptance of this. While acting as her trustee, John decided to sell an enslaved boy she owned. She refused to "unite in a conveyance" or "ratify [the] sale or bargain" unless the proceeds arising from the sale could be "invested in another slave." After she and John came to an understanding about this contingency, and he agreed to her demand, she ratified the sale, and the proceeds "were in part reinvested in the purchase of a Negro woman Selah."[65]

As a consequence of his being "improvident and wasteful" and "very unfortunate," John Spears became mired in debt, and all his creditors successfully sued him for recompense. The sheriff seized his and Mary Ann's property, including the slaves who were supposed to be her sole and separate possession, and scheduled a date to sell them to the highest bidders. Mary Ann asked the court to remove John as trustee of her property because he was "not a suitable person to act as trustee for her in relation to said property." She also asked the court to enjoin John's creditors from selling or disposing of her slaves and return them to neutral parties. The court awarded the injunction and ruled that it "be made perpetual." The court also ruled that John's creditors would be "forever enjoined and restrained from selling or in any manner interfering with the slaves set forth and described in [Mary Ann Spears's] bill" and decreed that Mary Ann would hold the slaves she had inherited "as her separate estate." The creditors were ordered to pay the costs of her suit.[66]

It is important to acknowledge that not all husbands relished their roles as their wives' trustees. Mary Jane Taylor, who possessed a large estate consisting of eighteen enslaved people, 580 acres of land, twenty thousand dollars, "and other things," entered into a marriage agreement that appointed her husband, Thomas, as her trustee. After managing his wife's property for a short time, Thomas decided that he no longer wanted to do so. Mary Jane and Thomas asked the court to relieve him of his duties and appoint Warren D. Wood in his place. The court granted the couple's request.[67]

When husband-trustees proved themselves inept, women were not reticent about going to court to relieve them of these duties, removing their slaves from their husbands' control, placing them in another person's care, and recouping the profits that their property yielded. Elizabeth Duncan had no qualms about bringing her concerns to court. Petitions like hers offer a strong challenge to the view that southern households were monolithically patriarchal. Before Elizabeth's marriage to William Duncan, she possessed a personal estate that included a thirty-year-old enslaved woman named Mariah, along with Mariah's two young children, a twenty-year-old enslaved woman named Rany, an eighteen-year-old enslaved youth named Haden, and a sixteen-year-old enslaved youth named Williamson. Over the course of her marriage, her female slaves reproduced prolifically and increased her slaveholding from six to fifteen people. Her husband-to-be, on the other hand, was facing bleak pecuniary circumstances. According to Elizabeth, William was "not the owner of any negro property," was "poor and without any means," and already had a "large family on his hands to support." Despite knowing about William's financial troubles, Elizabeth still placed her slaves under his management in the hope that he would "increase the same by the purchase of other negroes and property." She soon discovered how wrong that decision was.[68]

William managed his wife's estate "in such a careless negligent and improvident manner" that he was "compelled to sell seven" of "the most valuable" slaves Elizabeth owned. She sued her husband and petitioned the court to remove him as trustee of her estate and appoint another to replace him. Her decision was largely motivated by her fear that William would "so mismanage" her property that he would "squander and waste away the whole of it," and she would be left destitute. She further requested that the judge divest "by a decree . . . the title to said negroes and their natural increase . . . out of said defendant," as trustee, that they "be invested in some suitable person" who would serve in this capacity, and that he declare the "issues and profits" of her property secure "for her support," "her sole and separate use," and her "absolute disposal." Upon her death, the property would revert to William and his heirs. In William's answer to Elizabeth's bill of complaint, he confirmed all his wife's assertions. He even acknowledged that he was "not a good manager" and that if his wife or "her trustee" could "manage the property better" than he had done, he was willing to relinquish his role. He admitted that it would in fact be "equitable" for a decree ordering his replacement to be made. The court granted Elizabeth's request.[69]

A husband's violation of his wife's property rights served as the catalyst for many a woman's decision to enter a chancery court and petition for relief. But it was just as common for married women to sue their husbands' creditors when these individuals seized enslaved people who rightfully belonged to them in order to pay their husbands' debts. Rachel Thompson's experience typifies the willingness of some married women to fight for their property. Her father, William Smith, had given her two slaves as a gift, and he specified that the title was to be vested "in her alone." He also stipulated that "her husband . . . would not thereby acquire any property therein," and that Rachel's slaves "would not be liable for any contracts entered into or thereafter to be entered into" by her husband, Samuel. He also forbade Samuel to have "any control or right . . . over said negroes." Smith drew up a deed confirming this, gave the document to Rachel, and "repeatedly stated to his friends" that he had given these enslaved people to his daughter as her own separate property in order to "prevent them from being sold" to pay Samuel's debts and to prevent Samuel "from disposing of them in any manner whatever." Samuel acquiesced in his father-in-law's wishes and routinely "disclaim[ed] having any right, title or claim" to Rachel's slaves; he frequently "represented [the] negroes to be the separate property" of his wife. Nonetheless, Samuel's creditors levied upon Rachel's property to satisfy the debts he owed them.

Rachel Thompson petitioned for a "trial of the right of property" and lost. Undeterred, she appealed, arguing that making her slaves "liable to be sold in satisfaction of [the] said judgment . . . would be contrary to Equity and good conscience." The lower court's verdict, she argued, rendered her "without remedy at law," and as a consequence she would "forever lose her just rights" unless she was "relieved by a Court of Equity where such matters are properly cognizable." She asked the judge to "inquire into the truth of the facts," and after assessing them issue "a perpetual injunction" restraining Samuel's creditors from selling her slaves and "staying all other and further proceedings" upon the judgment until he could make his ruling. On May 12, 1842, Rachel Thompson got her injunction, and she kept her slaves.[70]

Many of these petitioning women possessed an extraordinary command of the laws governing their property, much more than they were likely to have acquired in isolation, and their petitions sometimes documented their consultation with others who possessed a deeper understanding of the issues they sought to resolve. Many of these women decided to appeal to the courts only after they sought advice from their neighbors and friends. Some married women had the good fortune of knowing justices of the peace, and they drew upon these jurists' legal knowledge and the advice of their colleagues for help in working through the details of their cases. Others entrusted their legal affairs to their families, while still others may have consulted guides such as George Bishop's 1858 handbook, *Every Woman Her Own Lawyer: A Private Guide in All Matters of Law, of Essential Interest to Women, and by the Aid of Which Every Female May, in Whatever Situation, Understand Her Legal Course and Redress, and Be Her Own Legal Adviser.* But regardless of where they acquired their understanding of their "rights," petitioning women used this information to protect their slaves from their husbands and reclaim the property they deemed to be their own.[71]

The friends of betrothed women also played a vital role in helping them circumvent the possible pitfalls of marriage and develop ways of dealing with those that could not be avoided. As Margaret Witherspoon prepared to marry Edwin Mason, she consulted others about the match, and it was "by the advice of her friends" that she decided to devise a marriage contract. Before her marriage, Witherspoon was not "well acquainted" with Mason's "business capacity," and this ignorance probably goaded her to hammer out the legal details of her marriage arrangement in case he proved to be improvident. Witherspoon's "memorandum," as she called it, stipulated that she "retain the possession" of her property and have it "exclusively under her control." The contract protected her real estate, slaves, and other personal property from any debts her husband incurred. Margaret Witherspoon possessed property in her own right, derived in part from the estate of her first husband. Her friends probably underscored that she needed to secure that property before she married Mason. If she did not, her new husband might squander her wealth and leave her and her children destitute. Or he might be prejudiced against the children from her first marriage, deny them their rightful inheritances, and favor his own children. Historians often interpret marital contracts, separate estates, deeds, and trusts as legal instruments that family members used to protect their financial legacies. But Margaret Witherspoon's case demonstrates that friends and allies also played important roles in the decisions slave-owning women made about marital agreements. Once an affianced woman settled upon such protective measures, her advisers might have taken part in familial decisions to establish separate estates and deeds of gift, as well. These legal instruments, therefore, were not simply a reflection of familial financial self-interest; they were a product of collaborative efforts on the part of kin, friends, and the heiresses themselves.[72]

As these cases have shown, women who filed bills of complaint against their husbands and others in chancery court typically did so on the strength of legal documents that had been drawn up, duly recorded, and filed in a county courthouse. But some women who sought legal remedy had entered into oral or "parol" agreements with their husbands. Others conducted their business as though a legal agreement were in place, and when their husbands and communities acknowledged their ownership of separate property through tacit or explicit consent, courts upheld these kinds of "contracts" as well.[73]

When individuals did not attempt to infringe upon women's property rights, such oral agreements between spouses and agreements that parents failed to formalize before or after their daughters married probably remained out of the courthouses. The lack of documentation makes it difficult for us to determine with any degree of certainty how many women drew upon these protective measures and exercised the control that informal oral contracts afforded them. However, closer examination of those who did take their cases to court and the positive outcomes of the petitions explored here reveal that the impact of the common law upon the lives of married women, especially the legal doctrine of coverture, was not as absolute or as constraining as many historians have claimed.

Historians such as Sara Brooks Sundberg have contended that propertied women fought as hard as they did and in the ways that they did because they saw their property as part of a familial legacy that needed to be preserved for their children. Sundberg argues that women exercised their rights over property "because they shared their husbands' interests in protecting and advancing family property as a necessary component of their families' economic independence." This was certainly true for some female litigants. But the petitions of slave-owning women also reveal that their husbands' interests were often in direct conflict with their own. Furthermore, their children often proved to be the instigators of legal, yet underhanded, attempts to take these women's slaves from them. These women faced extraordinary challenges when they held legal title to property. In addition to husbands, married women's fathers, brothers, sons, and nephews often attempted to infringe upon their property rights. This was especially true for women who struggled with some form of illiteracy. Many women could only place a mark, instead of a signature, on the petitions and the documents they submitted as evidence of their legal title to enslaved people. Such women relied heavily upon family members to help them preserve their investments in slaves, and those same family members sometimes betrayed their trust and tried to steal their property.[74]

"Judicial patriarchy" could be the reason why a judge might rule in favor of a married woman. Yet court judgments show that rulings were based on legal codes, laws, precedent, and, most important, the evidence the plaintiffs put before the court. It was probably important that few husbands contested the facts laid out in their wives' petitions. Ordinarily, they were not the people who questioned the legitimacy of their wives' separate property; their creditors were. Creditors saw wives' separate estates as fraudulent and collusive arrangements between married couples designed to protect the husband's property by legally declaring it to belong to the wife and thus placing it beyond their own reach.[75] Creditors continually seized married women's property to satisfy their husbands' debts, and many of the women so robbed went to battle in the courtroom to get it back. The outcome of such a case would hinge largely upon the married woman's ability to offer evidence that substantiated her legal title, and generally the women who filed suit could produce such documentation.

When creditors contested the legitimacy of a married woman's separate estate, the burden of proof fell upon the woman. Women involved in such lawsuits brought a range of evidence into the court: bills of sale listing them as titleholders to slaves, wills, marriage contracts, deeds of trust, judgments granting them a separation of property, witness testimony. When a woman had come from another state, judges also evaluated the laws pertaining to married women's property in that state.

It is important to underscore that the majority of the women who filed lawsuits did not leave their husbands; they were not requesting "separations from bed and board"—that is, what we would consider a legal separation today—or a divorce. Of the 208 cases for separation of property that appear in the Westlaw Campus Research database for the period between 1800 and 1865, for example, only 28 of the women also requested separation from bed and board. Petitioning women stayed with their husbands during the legal proceedings and afterward. But despite their commitment to their marriages, by going to court these women exposed their households to intense public scrutiny, laying out their husbands' fiscal mismanagement, commercial failures, and insolvency for public view not only in the courtroom but in the local press. Word of their difficulties would naturally circulate among family and friends, and women who went to court had to contend with the negative consequences such exposure might have for them and their husbands. Yet still they persisted.

Petitioning women did not always win their suits. But their losses were often attributed to legal technicalities, not gender bias. Problems often arose when the donor of a property used vague or nonconventional legal language, especially when he or she neglected to articulate his or her intentions clearly and secure the donation for the sole use, control, and disposal of the female recipient. Another common problem arose when a lawyer did not include a detailed list in the contract of all the property that was being conveyed.[76] Some women lost their cases because they entrusted one or more steps in the legal process, such as filing and recording the marital contract in a county court, to a husband or trustee and then learned that it had not been done. Property was subject to seizure if the litigant did not complete the steps mandated by law within a stipulated time frame.[77] Sometimes, women won despite those problems; other times, procedural flaws caused judges to rule against them.[78]

Ironically, even married women's legal *losses* demonstrate the widespread recognition of their claims to separate property within southern communities and courts. Martin M. Crews and William C. Patrick, for example, filed separate legal suits against Charlotte Goodwin for debts she owed them. They claimed that she possessed a separate estate consisting of property that was more than sufficient to pay them what they were owed. The court agreed and ruled in their favor.[79]

The testimonies of formerly enslaved people concerning their married female owners and these women's relationships with their husbands, supported by runaway advertisements, jailors' notices, government and municipal documents, and propertied women's legal petitions, show that the doctrine of coverture did not operate in a monolithic way in antebellum southern households. Many slave-owning women continued to view their property as theirs alone, even after they married. They did not resign themselves to every aspect of their changed legal status. They did not accept the legal subsumption of their identities into their husbands'. They did not mourn the loss of their property, and they did not accept the "civil death" Elizabeth Cady Stanton described in the *Declaration of Rights and Sentiments* issued at the 1848 women's rights convocation in Seneca Falls, New York. Slave-owning women understood how their positions would change once they married, and they frequently rejected the legal and economic ramifications of marriage by devising instruments that protected their personal investments in chattel slavery. With documents in hand that legitimated their legal titles to enslaved people, and with the courts' acknowledgment of their ownership, women boldly articulated how they wanted their human property to be managed in their homes and communities.

Scholars of jurisprudence define ownership as a "bundle of rights" that an individual has to a thing. According to A. M. Honoré, that bundle includes "the right to possess, the right to use," the right to be secure in one's property, "the right to manage (which involves 'the right to decide how and by whom the thing owned shall be used'), the right to the income of a thing (which includes the 'fruits, rents, and profits') . . . the right to alienate the thing . . . during life or on death, by way of sale, mortgage, gift or other mode . . . and the liberty to consume, waste or destroy the whole or part of it." If someone infringed upon any of these rights, the owner could call upon "a battery of remedies in order to obtain, keep, and if necessary, get back the thing owned."[80] Honoré was not referencing slavery in his essay—or if he was, he did not mention it. But when applied to slavery, this definition describes the position of nineteenth-century southern slave owners. An owner's near-absolute right to discipline, maim, and even kill the enslaved people he or she owned and the power to delegate management and discipline to others were the cornerstones of the institution. Slave-owning women exercised all the rights included in the bundle, including the right to do what one formerly enslaved man referred to as their "own bossing."[81]

3

"MISSUS DONE HER OWN BOSSING"

In 1837, three years after Maria and Elisha Betts said their vows in Morgan County, Georgia, cotton fever swept over the state, catching up the couple. Like countless others, they moved west to try their hand at starting a plantation and established their new home in Macon County, Alabama. The honeymoon phase of their marriage had barely ended, however, when the Panic of 1837 caused Elisha's mercantile business to fail. He became heavily indebted and lost much of what he owned. Just when he was down on his luck and needed Maria's support the most, he saw a side of his wife that surprised him. As he reeled from his pecuniary losses, Maria "did not seem to sympathize with him as she should"; furthermore, she seemed unwilling to help him rebound financially.[1]

Over the next nine years of their marriage, the Bettses "never lived agreeably together," and by 1846 Maria and Elisha had reached a crisis. Much of the discord between them had to do with the fact that Maria owned slaves in her own right and possessed the legal authority to decide what to do with them. Almost a decade before Maria married Elisha, and while she was married to and separated from her first husband, Ambrose Nelson, her father, Moses Walker, had hired a lawyer to draw up a declaration of intention that stipulated three things. First, any property that Moses might give to Maria during his lifetime or at the time of his death was to be hers alone. This would be the case "whether [she was a feme] covert or not." Moses Walker also stipulated that all the property he conveyed to her must be completely "free from the marital right of her then present or future husband." Furthermore, the document empowered Maria to dispose of her property by will; if she died intestate, the property would descend to her children, rather than to her husband. At the same time he drew up the declaration of intention, Maria's father gave her three of his slaves;

he later gave her three more. As Maria prepared to marry Elisha on September 18, 1834, she told him about her father's declaration of intention; she made sure that he understood the limits it would place upon his marital rights, and he "agreed . . . that she might hold as her separate estate the property she then had or might afterwards get of her father." She even reiterated the terms of the legal document at their wedding reception.[2]

Elisha might have been willing to recognize Maria's property rights, but he still expected to take charge of her slaves. Maria would have none of that. She refused to let Elisha exercise mastery over them—at least, not the kind he had in mind. Once they settled into their new home in Alabama, Maria was rarely pleased with Elisha's treatment of her slaves. According to their neighbor Charles C. Mills, Elisha frequently complained about his wife and said that "much of their misunderstanding grew out of jealousy on her part of his treatment of the negroes given her by her father." Elisha confessed to Mills that "he could never chastise one of them without his wife's manifesting feeling and discontent." Elisha was putting it mildly.[3]

In his conversations with Mills, Elisha admitted that Maria was an excellent housekeeper, though she was "inclined to be self willed and not obedient to his wishes." In her own talks with Mills, Maria accepted her husband's characterization of her disposition and tacitly accepted his other statements about her but countered that Elisha "had always sought to controle her too much in her domestick concerns," even though she was perfectly capable of managing them for herself. By 1846, Elisha had decided that "nothing could induce him to return to his wife [or] to live with her again," and acting on those sentiments, he abandoned Maria and moved to Louisiana. In light of Elisha's abandonment, his looming debts, and the threats of his creditors, Maria filed suit against her husband and his creditors, requesting a divorce from Elisha, alimony for her support, and an injunction to prevent any of them from seizing and selling her separate property.[4]

Maria and Elisha had clearly approached their marriage with different ideas about how their relationship would work. But the most critical differences between them centered upon the way Maria expected Elisha and others to treat her slaves and what methods of slave discipline and management she would allow those individuals to employ. She envisioned a marriage in which her husband would grant her the liberty to express herself freely, to manage her household, and to determine how he and others would deal with the enslaved people she owned. And as Elisha's candid statements to his neighbor show, he entered the marriage anticipating the opposite. Their differing expectations, especially concerning the management and discipline of Maria's slaves, wreaked havoc in the Bettses' marriage and ultimately drove Elisha to abandon Maria. But despite the costs, Maria stood firm in her resolve.

Maria's views about marriage and her conduct toward Elisha were the likely outcome of being raised by parents, particularly a father, who nurtured her independence and ensured that she would continue to exercise a certain legal and economic autonomy during her marriage and throughout her lifetime. Although Moses Walker was a "plain farmer unversed in legal technicalities,"[5] he understood the power southern laws granted white men over their wives, and their wives' property, and he laid the legal groundwork that would ensure that Maria would not have to subject herself or her property to her husband's dominion. Even still, while Walker's declaration of intention and his subsequent deeds of gift gave Maria legal title to slaves, secured her separate property rights, and preserved her authority as a slave owner, Maria was ultimately responsible for deciding whether to exercise those rights and powers. It was her choice whether to delegate her powers to her husband or an overseer, to refuse to grant them any power at all, or to curtail or rescind any particular right of control at any time. When the men around her overstepped the bounds of what she considered their authority, she routinely intervened and reminded them that the power they exercised ultimately belonged to her and that this authority was grounded in her slave ownership. As Elisha's long-time acquaintance and former overseer, Abram Greeson, recalled, Maria "was very cross and disagreeable with me and meddled with the out door business [the fieldwork] too much."[6]

What Elisha described as Maria's "feeling and discontent," and what Abram Greeson called her "meddling," were really the manifestations of far more than moodiness. During those moments when she freely expressed her feelings about their conduct toward her slaves, she was making her husband and Greeson aware of her particular vision of slave mastery. Maria never described how she herself dealt with the slaves she owned, and the legal record gives no specific details about the kinds of "chastisement" Elisha used or how Abram treated Maria's slaves in the fields. But her response to their treatment makes it clear that she had conflicting ideas about proper methods of slave mastery, and as she observed and evaluated Elisha's and Greeson's disciplinary and management techniques, she determined that they were doing things the wrong way.

Despite their brief separation, Maria and Elisha Betts remained married and lived in the same household for more than two decades. During that time, Maria continued to own separate property, and her estate grew significantly. In 1850, Maria owned eight slaves, 100 acres of improved land, a farm worth $400, farming implements and machinery valued at $100, and livestock with an estimated value of $550. Ten years later, her personal estate was worth $16,000, her slaveholdings had doubled to sixteen, and she owned 320 acres of improved and unimproved land, and livestock worth $750. According to the censuses taken in these two decades, Elisha possessed no personal or real property to speak of. Had Maria relinquished control of her property to Elisha, he might well have treated the enslaved people she owned in ways that diminished their value and squandered her considerable assets. It would seem that her caution was well founded.[7]

The conflicts that arose between Maria and Elisha Betts over matters largely related to slave mastery bedeviled other households in the South. This was especially true in cases where husbands and wives each owned personal slaves or when women owned slaves over which their husbands had no legal authority. Formerly enslaved people routinely reflected upon encounters between slave-owning women, their spouses, their employees, and others. Although they rarely if ever used the term "master" to describe their female owners, formerly enslaved witnesses frequently characterized their mistresses as effective managers and disciplinarians and described their behavior with the same terms they used for slaveholding men. Harriet Collins spoke of her mistress as a "powerful manager" who "was sho' good . . . iffen you work and do like she tell you." Such a statement could be taken as referring simply to household management, but Collins also spoke of how her mistress managed her slaves beyond the household. Her mistress, recalled Collins, would "go round [the quarters] to see dat all was alright" each evening and was a "powerful good nuss" to boot. Collins's female owner, in fact, did *more* than a master; she assumed the responsibilities that mistresses, masters, and plantation overseers typically handled. Formerly enslaved people also remembered their female owners as powerful disciplinarians who used a variety of techniques that resembled those of male slave owners. Addy Gill was enslaved in Millburnie, North Carolina, and she recalled that her mistress Louise Krenshaw "done the whuppin on Mr. Krenshaw's plantation an she was mighty rough at times." As we shall see, other enslaved men and women recalled mistresses who meted out calculated, systematic, and rationalized violence and discipline, not as masters' subordinates and surrogates but as slave owners in their own right who possessed the authority to do so.[8]

But in their testimony formerly enslaved people emphasized that mastery did not always involve brute strength or physically violent methods of discipline. The (typically male) slaveholders who submitted commentary to the South's most widely circulating agricultural journals, such as *DeBow's Review* and the *Southern Planter*, generally agreed that the most skilled slave masters could command submission without resorting to brutality. By this argument, white women could also be masters of slaves without resorting to brutal methods of control.

Yet despite the recollections of formerly enslaved people concerning female owners who made sure they did their work, and despite contemporary recognition of white women as slave owners in their own right within southern communities and by courts, historians have contended that white women could not be true "masters" of slaves. They could be masters of household operations. They could be "fictive masters." They could be "masterful." But they did not possess the strength or power to make a servile class submit to their will. According to the historian Elizabeth Fox-Genovese, white women "could not exercise mastery of their own slaves, much less contribute to the control of the slaves in their communities" because "the law—not to mention the social emphasis placed on male governance of the household and its members—discouraged women from managing slaves." These social and legal impediments, she contends, "sharply limited the practical and psychological effectiveness of [slaveholding women's] discipline." Furthermore, enslaved people associated physical violence and punishment with white men, be they slave owners or overseers, a situation that undercut any attempts by white women to acquire mastery over their slaves. A white woman, even if she owned slaves, "was no 'massa.'" Yet Fox-Genovese admits that "as slaves would have been the first to insist, and as both male and female slaveholders well knew, mistresses could very well be the devil. A mean mistress stood second to no master in her cruelty, although her strength was less." This was particularly characteristic of white women's relationships with enslaved women in their household, for "on the grounds of physical strength they were less likely than men to kill them."[9]

Some historians contest the idea that women could not manage or discipline enslaved people effectively; however, they too differentiate between white women and white men's domination of enslaved people.[10] William Foster, for example, contends that slave-owning women developed and engaged in a uniquely female form of mastery, in which they interacted with and disciplined enslaved people as they would their own children.[11] But if we look carefully at slave-owning women's management styles, we find that these differed little from those used by slaveholding men—and they rarely treated enslaved people like their children.

Enslaved and formerly enslaved people recalled the ways their female owners exercised authority over them. They made it clear that white women did not subordinate their authority to white men nor did they confine themselves to operating at the "mid-levels of power," in Foster's phrase.[12] Their status as slave owners granted them access to a community that was predicated upon the ownership of human beings and afforded them rights they did not possess in other realms of their lives. White women embraced their role within this community, assumed positions of power over slaves within and outside their households, and challenged anyone who attempted to infringe upon that power. And local, state, and federal courts recognized, upheld, and protected them when they did so.

Mastery was an objective that male *and* female slave owners and their delegates aimed to acquire through techniques ranging from kindness to brutality. Their goal was to compel enslaved people to submit to their will and work efficiently and profitably. The system was malleable because it had to be; one strategy might be effective with one enslaved person yet ineffective with another. Even the specific circumstances under which an owner compelled an enslaved person to work—such as trying to force recently sold, relocated, and traumatized enslaved people to labor after being separated from their homes and loved ones—could affect the management and disciplinary techniques a slave owner used.[13]

Whether slave owners turned out to be effective managers of the enslaved people they owned depended on the broader communal, legislative, and judicial recognition of their power over the enslaved and a collective willingness to protect that power when it was called into question or when others threatened it. Southern communities, lawmakers, and courts recognized slave-owning women as individuals able to acquire and exercise mastery over enslaved people, as is evident from laws passed throughout the South. Laws dating back to the colonial period routinely recognized that mistresses owned enslaved people in their own right, and these same laws acknowledged the fact that these women were capable of exercising mastery over the enslaved people they owned.[14] In fact, southern laws held the mistresses accountable for their slaves' misconduct. For example, when an enslaved person in Louisiana was found "guilty of revolting, or of a plot to revolt against his or her . . . mistress . . . or of willfully and maliciously striking his or her . . . mistress, or the child or children of his or her . . . mistress, or any white overseer appointed by his or her owner to superintend said owner's slaves, so as to cause a contusion or shedding of blood," mistresses were required to report these acts to the state. If a mistress were to "wilfully and intentionally neglect to give information against, or refuse to give up . . . her slave or slaves . . . said . . . mistress shall, upon conviction thereof, forfeit and pay the sum of five hundred dollars, one half of which shall be given to the informer or informers, and the other half to and for the parish in which the offence shall have been committed, and imprisoned until the same is paid."[15] Furthermore, southern laws make it clear that legislators expected mistresses to discipline the enslaved people they owned, whether by proxy or by their own hand. In South Carolina, for example, if an enslaved person ran away for a period of twenty days or more, masters and mistresses were required to "publicly and severely" administer up to forty lashes with the whip for the first offense, and, if a slave owner failed to do so, the local constable would do it at the owner's expense. With each offense, the punishment became more brutal, eventually calling for branding, dismemberment, and, after the fifth offense, death. While legislators probably saw this intensified brutality as a deterrent for enslaved people who hoped to escape bondage, these punishments also served to compel slave owners to comply with state law. An enslaved person's value would diminish with each punishment, and paired with the state's decision to impose greater fines upon masters and mistresses for failing to punish their slaves after subsequent offenses, those owners had good reason to aquiesce.[16]

The "management of negroes" advice columns that appeared in agricultural journals such as *DeBow's Review* and the *Southern Planter* suggest that many southern white men coveted the role of slave master and yearned to rule over enslaved people, even those who were not their own. But this was not always the case. Rosalie Calvert found that her husband had no interest in being a master, and she had to assume the role herself. In 1818 and 1819, Calvert wrote several letters to her sister Isabelle complaining about her husband's laziness and indifference to all matters related to plantation operations and slave management. Exasperated by all the work she had to do, she told her sister that her husband conducted himself "as if he were not the master—not giving any instructions, not worrying about anything." As she became more heavily encumbered by the tasks that needed to be completed within and around her household, Calvert noticed how little her husband did. She confessed to Isabelle: "My husband takes care of nothing regarding the household or the servants. I must manage everything . . . all the arrangements fall on me."[17]

But men who conducted themselves like Calvert's husband occupied only one extreme on the behavioral spectrum. Far more frequently, spouses and overseers of slave-owning women, as well as public officials such as patrollers, gravitated toward the opposing end of this continuum. They often went too far when disciplining these women's slaves, and they challenged these women's authority to say how the enslaved people they owned would be managed or disciplined. In response, many women asserted their rights as property holders and used their legal authority as such to dictate how husbands and overseers might treat their slaves. They thereby protected the human beings they owned from the physical and psychic trauma brought about by the brutality of others and preserved the monetary value of the enslaved people they owned. Slave-owning women deemed it necessary to set parameters and establish rules for others, including their husbands, who might deal with their slaves. When these individuals did not appreciate or respect the boundaries slave-owning women set, these women found ways to enforce their decisions, and their examples offer unparalleled views of how married women understood, articulated, and asserted their power as slave owners and masters.

Shortly after Mary Homer married William Johnson, she made one thing clear: she would not tolerate him abusing the slaves who belonged to her, property that she had received from her father. According to her former slave Bill Homer, Mary insisted that "de treatment f'om de new Marster am jus' lak f'om de ol' Marster." Mary held a vision of slave ownership and management that differed from her husband's. Bill's memories suggest that her father's management style heavily influenced her own and helped determine the kind of relationship she would allow her husband to have toward her property. More important, her husband accepted and abided by her decisions when it came to her slaves. Mary's insistence that her husband refrain from abuse did not apply to the slaves *he* owned, however; Bill remembered Mary telling her husband, "If you mus' 'buse de nigger, 'buse your own."[18]

Long after they married, slave-owning women continued to demarcate and enforce, in word and in deed, the boundaries of their husbands' authority over their slaves. Generally they based their own authority on their ownership of the enslaved people in question. Frances Gray, a Scooba, Mississippi, woman who owned Lucy Galloway and her family, "didn't 'low nobody to mistreat her slaves" because they "wuz her property and her living and she want goin' to 'low nobody to whup'em." Sarah Davis Parnell went farther. She owned a number of slaves, including Henry and Priscilla Parnell, and her husband would often beat them unmercifully when he was drunk. Whenever she caught him doing it, she would "come right out there and stop him. She would say, 'I didn't come all the way here from North Carolina to have my niggers beat up for nothin.'" She might even grab her husband's whip mid-strike.[19] A woman's decision to intervene in a beating, even at the risk of her own safety, might have been an expression of her benevolence toward the enslaved people she owned. But it might equally have been an expression of her concern for her property interests and desire to preserve the value of her holdings.

Slave-owning women were equally adamant about making clear what constituted acceptable slave discipline to the men they employed as overseers. Ben Horry recalled that when "anybody steal rice and [the overseers] beat them," his owner Miss Bessie would "cry and say, 'Let 'em have rice! My rice—my nigger!'" One Carrydine, the overseer on the plantation where Rebecca Brown Hill grew up, was determined to whip her parents. When her mistress found out, she asked Carrydine to come see her so that they could "talk it over." At the conclusion of their meeting, she told Hill's parents to "give Mr. Carrydine his breakfast and let him go." Hill recalled that her parents "never got no whip-pings" after that talk.[20] The process of "talking it over" usually implies negotia-tion and compromise between equals. But Hill described this conversation as orders passed from employer to employee. Hill's mistress was in the position of power, and as her employee Carrydine was obliged to obey.

Notwithstanding such agreements, overseers constantly overstepped the bounds of their authority, and their female employers retaliated by firing them or filing a legal suit against them.[21] In 1826, James A. Williams served as Lucy Perrie's overseer on her plantation, Tunica, in West Feliciana, Louisiana. She was an absentee owner who lived on a plantation approximately twenty-five or thirty miles away. Perrie tasked Williams with managing her slaves and tending to the cultivation of her crops. In Perrie's estimation, Williams dramatically exceeded his authority: he and a neighbor, Arthur Adams, shot two of her slaves and "illegally, cruelly, unusually, and unnecessarily beat and whip[ped]" another. One of the men Williams shot eventually died of his wound, and the other two men sustained serious injuries. In addition Williams was reportedly so brutal toward Perrie's slaves that some of them ran away. Perrie not only fired Williams, she filed an order of trespass against him and Adams and sought com-pensation for the slave she lost. In Adams's answer to Perrie's allegations and suit, he called her mastery into question. He argued that all the charges she lodged against him stemmed from the fact that her slaves were "badly fed and provided for," and he suspected them of stealing and killing his cattle to augment their meager diets. A witness who testified on Perrie's behalf said that she had numerous hogs and cattle on her plantation, although he did not say that she gave any of the meat to her slaves. In the end, the court granted Perrie's request.[22]

Perhaps it goes without saying that white women acted within their purview when they determined how their employees would treat the enslaved people they owned. Whether through letters, termination of employment, or lawsuits to recoup the value of slaves lost at their overseers' hands, slave-owning women made it clear that the men in their employ merely exercised authority on their behalf and they, the mistresses, could rescind that power at any time. Mistresses also sought to establish the parameters of proper conduct for men whom the state empowered to punish their slaves. A woman named Mrs. Harris, for exam-ple, hired out an enslaved boy she owned to various men in her community. On one occasion, the boy clashed with the man who had hired him, and during their altercation the boy "knocked" his employer in the head. The injured man summoned the community squire and constable, the two men stripped the boy, and the squire whipped him. The boy began to make so much noise that Mrs. Harris heard him, "came out and told the squire to turn [him] loose." She threatened to kill the squire if he struck her slave one more time and "she showed him her gun." Appalled by her challenge to his authority, the squire reminded her that they were acting "within the law." Mrs. Harris retorted that she did not "care nothing about the law" and warned the squire not to hit her slave again. In the face of her defiance, the men saw no choice but to comply. They released the boy. This stand-off between the neighborhood squire and Mrs. Harris suggests that communal custom may have shaped the operation of law at the local level far more than the state did, a phenomenon that the historian Laura Edwards refers to as "legal localism." The larger community may have subscribed to certain forms of discipline that constrained the squire's power to inflict punishment under certain circumstances. Perhaps the squire overstepped those boundaries, and he recognized that Mrs. Harris's neighbors and friends would be more inclined to support her than him. No matter the underlying reason, he ultimately chose to respect her authority and her wishes.[23]

Not all slave-owning women sought to protect the enslaved people they owned from punishment. Some simply wanted to ensure that their delegates delivered the discipline they themselves thought was fair. Mrs. Rankin, the married woman who owned F. H. Brown's mother, also owned all the enslaved people in her household. According to Brown, she would not permit her overseer to discipline the enslaved females she owned, but she did allow him to whip her male slaves. Even then, he was permitted to do so only "in her presence, so that she could see that it wasn't brutal." Brown recalled that "When an overseer got rough, she would fire him." Peggy Sybert similarly fired the overseer who disobeyed her instructions about meting out discipline. Her slave, Arrie Binns, recounted how Sybert handled the patrollers who insisted upon whipping Binns's brother, whom they had captured after he left the plantation without a pass. Initially, Sybert angrily refused to allow the patrollers to beat him. After they insisted upon doing so, however, she stated that she would allow them to punish him only if she could watch and decide when they had punished him enough. They agreed to her terms. After they whipped Binns's brother three times, Sybert demanded that they stop, and they did.[24]

White men were not the only members of southern communities who challenged or attempted to ignore slave-owning women's power and control over their slaves. Other women did, too. When Ellen Campbell was fifteen, her mistress gave her to her daughter Eva, who subsequently hired her out to a woman who operated a local boardinghouse. While in this woman's employ, Campbell was tasked with transporting food from the kitchen into the main part of the establishment. One day she tripped, fell, and dropped the tray, scattering the food across the ground. The boardinghouse operator grabbed a butcher knife and struck Campbell in the head with the blade. Bloody, wounded, and distraught, Campbell ran back to her mistress. After seeing Campbell's condition, Eva wrote a letter to the woman notifying her that Campbell was her slave, whom she had inherited from her mother, that she would not tolerate Campbell's being brutally treated, and that therefore she would no longer permit Campbell to work for the boardinghouse keeper. The circumstances surrounding the brutal assault of Ellen Campbell forced Eva to assert her power as a slave owner. Both Eva and the female boardinghouse operator possessed and exercised control over Campbell, one as owner and the other as employer. But their systems of slave discipline and management were strikingly different. Campbell spoke highly of her mistress and her mistress's family, claiming that her mistress's father rarely mistreated his slaves and that her mistress adopted a similar system of slave management. She found herself in the middle of a conflict between her mistress and the boardinghouse operator, but ultimately her legal owner determined how she would be treated, who would control her, and what disciplinary methods they could reasonably employ.[25]

The term *possessed* might suggest that southern law accorded the powers of slave mastery equally to a slave owner and an individual who hired an enslaved person. However, "possession" and the power associated with it did not apply equally to both parties in the eyes of the law. Possession was only temporarily vested in slave hirers, and it ended as soon as the terms of hire did.[26] Furthermore, the contracts drawn up between the slave owner and the slave hirer might delineate acceptable forms of discipline and management, and if hirers violated the terms of those contracts, the owners of the enslaved people could terminate the agreement and take their slaves out of the hirers' possession. When enslaved people suffered injury or death due to hirers' actions, slave owners had legal recourse and could sue hirers and seek damages in court.

When a female slave owner hired white servants to work alongside the enslaved people she owned, her management style could take a surprising turn. When Joe High was a young boy, he strolled through a potato patch, dug a spud out of the ground, and asked the white woman who served as his mistress's cook to prepare it for him to eat. The woman marched the boy and the potato to his owner, Clara Griffin, and accused him of stealing it, telling Griffin, "Look here missus, Joe has been stealin' taters. Here is the tater he stole." She probably expected a different response from the one she received. Instead of punishing Joe High, Griffin replied, "Joe belongs to me, the tater belongs to me, take it back and cook it for him." In approaching her employer and accusing the boy of theft, this white servant was claiming a distinction between herself and the slaves who worked alongside her. Griffin's response to her actions suggests that Griffin may have thought the cook was placing herself on terms of equality with her mistress, and she found it necessary to reinforce the class and power distinctions between them. In the end, such differences tilted the outcome of the incident in Joe High's favor.[27]

The similarities between men and women's systems of management become clearer through the testimony of formerly enslaved people. According to Henry Watson, his "mistress had been brought up in Louisiana, and had witnessed punishment all her life, and had become hardened to it." He had seen her "perpetrate some of the most cruel acts that a human being could, yet I never saw her in a passion when she was inflicting punishment." Cecelia Chappel recalled that her mistress would give her slaves "sum wuk ter do, so she would kind ob git ober her mad spell 'fore she whup'd us." This was not feminine weakness; southern agricultural journals carried advice from slave-owning men to other slave-owning men urging them to avoid getting "overexcited," remain "dispassionate and detached," and ensure that they "never inflicted punishment on slaves in anger." One South Carolina planter went so far as to suggest that masters "allow 24 hours to elapse between the discovery of the offence and the punishment." Other men echoed his advice when they suggested that punishment should never be administered while "in a passion." And so far from indicating a womanly or ladylike gentleness, such calmness could accompany vicious cruelty: Henry Watson proclaimed of his mistress, "She seemed to take delight in torturing,—in fact, she made it a pastime; she inspired every one about her with terror." The practice of waiting to become calm before punishing a slave was not a matter of gender but of good slave management.[28]

Similarly, when slave-owning women delegated the task of discipline to others, typically men, it was not an indication of their discomfort as women with the brutality that so often characterized slave mastery, as some historians have claimed. According to the legal historian Ariela Gross, slave-owning men also "avoided administering whippings" themselves, leaving the task "to an overseer or to another. . . . Both owners and hirers sometimes sent slaves to the county jail, or to the Charleston Workhouse, for example, to be whipped for a fee rather than soiling themselves and their clothing with blood." But beyond their aversion to blood-stained clothing, slave-owning men tried to distance themselves from the violence of slavery in order to maintain a particular esteem among enslaved people. A slave-owning man from Georgia declared, "I rarely punish myself but make a driver"—typically an enslaved man who assumed the responsibilities of an overseer—"virtually an executive officer to inflict punishment [so] that I may remove from the mind of the servant who commits a fault the unfavorable impression too apt to be indulged in, that it is for pleasure rather than for the purpose of enforcing obedience and establishing good order that punishments are inflicted." By delegating brutal forms of mastery to subordinates, slave-owning men and women cleansed themselves of the dark taint that subsequently stained the men who carried out their orders. The alleged differences that scholars claim existed between men and women's punishment of the enslaved people they owned probably have more to do with these historians' own interpretations than with the evidence of the time.[29]

White women did face their share of resistance to their management of enslaved persons on plantation estates. After Letty Luke purchased an enslaved boy named Simon with the aid of her trustee, she found that she was "wholly unable to govern" him. Citing this as a reason to sell Simon, she petitioned the court for permission to buy an enslaved girl or woman to replace him, and the court granted her request. Letty Luke could easily have delegated Simon's "governance" to the white men around her, but she wanted to assume this responsibility herself. When she found herself unable to exercise her power over Simon in the ways that she thought appropriate, she sold him rather than relinquish control to the men she knew.[30]

Sometimes slave-owning women had good reason to delegate slave punishment to others, and their decision to do so aligned with the choices slave-owning men made in this regard. The white men in their families or those they hired generally proved to be willing participants. Yet slave-owning women also knew firsthand that slave management and discipline could pose difficulties that neither a master nor a mistress was capable of handling. Violent and resistant enslaved people might need more than the authority of a single man to keep them in line.[31] Pauline Howell's enslaved aunt, for example, killed two male overseers after she "grabbed [their] privates and pulled 'em out by the roots." Afterward, her aunt was sold, along with all of her children, to a man who lived in Mobile, Alabama.[32] A woman who could mutilate and kill two adult men in this way was not going to acknowledge the authority of a master because he was a man. And who knew what kind of damage she might inflict upon a mistress? Whether master or mistress, the owner was likely to seek reinforcement before attempting further punishment.

Enslaved people's modes of resistance compelled both women and men to develop a variety of tactics to maintain order, not simply because of their gender but because these African Americans challenged their owners' rights to their bodies and their labor. Sometimes owners found it easier to delegate the responsibility of slave discipline. It is also important to recognize that when men and women distanced themselves from violent forms of discipline, it allowed them to maintain their reputations as members of the southern gentility while preserving their authority as slave owners and employers of lower-class white southerners.

Yet some slave-owning men and women chose to handle slave discipline themselves. And when they did, men and women employed similar methods of control: some were careful of their slaves' welfare, and others, both men and women, were brutal toward them. Analiza Foster told her WPA interviewer that her "mammy belonged ter a Mr. Cash an' pappy belonged to Miss Betsy Woods. Both of dese owners wuz mean ter dere slaves an' dey ain't carin' much if'en dey kills one, case dey's got planty." Claiborne Moss described how the slave patrollers "didn't whip nobody" in the Arkansas community where he lived. He said that these white men "couldn't whip nobody on our place . . . on Jesse Mills' place . . . on Stephen Mills' place . . . on Betsy Geesley's place . . . on Nancy Mills' place . . . on Potter Duggins' place . . . Nobody run them peoples' plantations but theirselves."[33] Regardless of what the formal laws said about slave patrollers' rights to discipline slaves in their communities, and no matter how much authority the laws afforded to slave patrols, these slave owners—men and women alike—had created systems of management and control that denied power to these men. More important, Claiborne Moss's testimony indicates that the slave patrollers recognized the power of female slave owners on the same basis as that of their male counterparts.

The regime of slavery could not have been sustained if the power, authority, and violence that characterized it had belonged to elite white men alone. It required modes of flexible power. Those who owned enslaved people wielded extraordinary authority, but so did overseers and enslaved drivers, as well as employers who hired enslaved people from their owners. There were even occasions when enslaved people exercised power over the lives and deaths of free people and other enslaved persons. They could, for example, implicate an enslaved or free person in a plan for revolt, and thereby seal that person's fate. The hyper-surveillance the regime required was possible only if every white person—be it man, woman, child, slave owner, or non–slave owner—had the potential power to make an enslaved person obey him or her and submit to his or her will. And the law so empowered them. Such systems of shared power did not typically characterize hierarchical societies wherein white men sat at the apex; they existed in societies that could be considered "heterarchical" in nature.

Heterarchy allows power to be shared in a number of ways, not just vertically but also horizontally, and enslaved and formerly enslaved people spoke of slave-owning households that were structured in this way.[34] Although in most studies of slavery the underlying assumption is that only male heads of household exercised mastery over enslaved people, formerly enslaved people forthrightly challenged this view. Formerly enslaved people spoke about households in which slave-owning couples owned enslaved people independent of each other—that is, in their own right. They spoke of households in which slave-owning couples exercised "double mastery." Each spouse had his or her own style of slave management and discipline, styles that could be complementary or incompatible, and when their styles clashed, conflict was often the result. Some couples, for example, preferred one style of mastery for managing and disciplining their own slaves and another, perhaps more brutal, system to control those of their spouse. In other households slave-owning couples allocated discipline and management according to the enslaved person's sex. Millie Evans's master would "tend" to the enslaved men, and her mistress would tend to the women. Other couples, like Cecelia Chappel's master and mistress, delegated management and discipline according to where the enslaved people labored—in the house versus the field, for example. The couple shared the responsibility of punishing the slaves who worked in the house, while they employed overseers to discipline those who worked in the fields.[35]

Slave-owning couples also used different instruments to administer punishment, and this, too, was a reflection of their particular styles of achieving mastery and preserving the value of their human property. On the plantation where Anna Miller resided, her master punished the men with a cowhide whip and her mistress often whipped the women with nettleweed branches. At first glance, Miller's emphasis on the different instruments of discipline that her master and mistress used might imply that her mistress chose a milder method of punishment, a choice that could support the contention that white women were more concerned about their slaves' well-being. But this was not the case. When Miller's mistress whipped with the nettleweed, Miller remembered, "de licks ain'ts so bad, but de stingin' and de burnin' after am sho' misery. Dat jus' plum runs me crazy." The small hairs that cover the stems of the nettleweed, also known as "stinging nettle," probably caused the sensation Miller described. These small hairs contain several chemicals that cause intense pain when they come into contact with the skin. When the affected area was rubbed, the motion would push the hairs, and the pain-inducing chemicals, deeper into the skin, prolonging the pain and irritation. Miller's mistress's weapon of choice had a long-lasting, increasingly painful effect on the bodies of the enslaved females living within her household.[36]

Beyond achieving her disciplinary goals, this mistress's use of nettleweed branches might have been an economically sound choice as well. Cowhide whips were notorious for cutting open the flesh, causing debilitating injuries that could lead to an enslaved person's death; even when the victim lived, the whip left horrible scars that often decreased the price a prospective buyer was willing to pay for him or her. Slave owners who hoped to protect their slaves' potential value in the market used instruments that would allow them to inflict pain without leaving permanent marks. In typical cases involving contact with nettleweed, the sufferer developed a skin rash that healed on its own and generally left no marks. Thus, by using the nettleweed branch, Miller's mistress was able to punish her severely yet still preserve her value in the slave market.

Most commonly, when formerly enslaved people described households in which double mastery prevailed, they remarked upon a clear differentiation between the broader systems of management and discipline their masters and mistresses used, and frequently they reported that one of their owners would beat them while the other did not. While assumptions based on gender might suggest that women were the ones who refrained from beatings, this was not always the case. Husbands frequently disagreed with their wives' chosen disciplinary strategies because they were too brutal, and they were not always willing to dole out punishment on their wives' behalf. Julia Blanks recalled that her "marster was good" because "he wouldn't whip any of his slaves. But his wife wasn't good. If she got mad at the woman, when he would come home she would say: 'John, I want you to whip Liza. Or Martha.' And he would say, 'Them are your slaves, You whip them.'" In these cases, slave-owning women had little choice but to assume the role of disciplinarian or to delegate the task to others.[37] Slave-owning husbands sometimes found their wives' violence toward enslaved people so disturbing that they could not ignore it and felt compelled to intervene. Penny Thompson's master Calvin Ingram would fight with her mistress "lots of times 'bout de treatment" of the slaves they owned. He just "wouldn't let her 'buse" them. George G. King, who lived six miles northeast of Lexington, South Carolina, recalled that "Master talked hard words, but Mistress whipped." In fact, his mistress was "a great believer in the power of punishment," and she would "whip his mammy 'til she was just a piece of living raw meat." Even King, though only a child, frequently felt the cut of her lash. Her husband tried to intervene but was ultimately powerless to stop her. She was so cruel that her husband tried to sell George King to prevent his wife from abusing him further, but his mistress "owned the slaves and they couldn't be sold without her say-so." When King's mistress discovered her husband's plan, she prevented the sale and swiftly retaliated. As King and his master were forced to stand and watch, the mistress commanded the overseer to strip, bind, and whip his mother. The beating "left her laying, all a shiver, on the ground, like a wounded animal dying from the chase." King remembered his mistress walking away "laughing, while his Mammy screamed and groaned." His master had a remarkably different response; he stood there "looking sad and wretched, like he could feel the blows." One woman's violence toward her slaves was enough to drive her husband to abandon her. When he left, he took all the slaves he owned with him and left her with the three she had brought into their marriage.[38]

Beyond merely quarreling with their wives or surreptitiously selling their slaves, some white men felt the need to physically intervene on behalf of enslaved people when their wives acted brutally toward them. Jack Barbee would physically restrain his wife when her punishments became too much for him to bear. One woman who was enslaved by the couple remembered that Barbee "jerked her [mistress] off of [the slaves] many a time, and he'd say, 'Plague take you, you trying to kill that little baby.'" When he would find one of the cowhide whips his wife used to beat their slaves, he would cut it up so she could not use it. Without a cowhide whip at her disposal, Jack Barbee's wife resorted to beating her slaves with small, thorn-covered branches that pierced their skin with every strike. This, the formerly enslaved woman thought, was more brutal than the cowhide whips. Ria Sorrell claimed that her owner Elizabeth Sorrell "wus de pure debil" because "she jist joyed whuppin' Negroes." Elizabeth was so violent, in fact, that her husband would stop her from whipping her slaves in his presence; she would wait until he went into town to do so. She also refused to feed the slaves properly, and "when she had her way our food wus bad." Ria remembered Elizabeth saying that the "under-leaves of collards wus good enough for slaves." Her husband had other ideas; he "took feedin' in his hands an' fed us plenty at times." Ria Sorrell said that he did so because he believed "people couldn't work widout eatin'." Jack Barbee's wife held similar ideas to Elizabeth Sorrell's about the kind of food suitable for the enslaved people she and her husband owned. The enslaved children on their farm did not receive any meat because they did not work. Barbee's wife exploited this fact, and her slaves' near-starvation conditions, to develop a dastardly form of food-related torment. Her former slave remembered:

Once a man brought some old hog heads and pieces of fresh meat like that to old mistress in a barrel, to make soap with, and the things was just floating on top; and she got mad 'cause the grown folks (slaves) wouldn't eat it. She give it to us chillen, and 'course we was glad to get it, 'cause it was meat, and we eat it till it made us sick, and they couldn't give us any more. Mr. ___ (man who had given meat) came by and found out what she had done, and he said, "I just brought that meat here 'cause I thought you might want it to make soap. I didn't know you was going to make nobody eat it. I wouldn't give it to my dogs."[39]

Women's slave ownership influenced the character of their mastery as well as the methods of discipline they used to control their own slaves versus those their husbands owned. Silas Glenn remarked that his mistress "was good to the slaves that come into her from her daddy" but "was mean to some of the slaves that come from the Glenn side," her husband's family. Susan Merritt made the same distinction between her master's kindness and her mistress's meanness. On a number of occasions, her mistress would tie Merritt to "a stub in the yard and cowhide" her until she became too tired to continue. She would take a break, and after she was rested, resume her violence. Merritt believed that her mistress treated her this way because she was "massa nigger and she have her own niggers what come on her side" so "she never did like" her.[40]

A formerly enslaved woman's new mistress, who owned enslaved people in her own right, exhibited particular disdain for her husband's slaves. Once she moved into their conjugal home she removed her husband's female slave from the house, reassigned her to fieldwork, and replaced her with "one of the slaves her mother give her when she married." On another occasion, a calf found its way under the house and "made water." The mistress accused two young boys, who belonged to her husband, of relieving themselves under the house instead. She waited until her husband was away from the house, then bound the boys in the kitchen so they could not get away. She pulled up a chair, sat down, and ordered *her* slave to beat them. The beating became so brutal that "all of the slaves on the place was cryin'." One of the enslaved men ran to his master and told him what the mistress was doing. The master returned home as quickly as he could, but discovered that his wife had locked the door. He demanded that she open it, and she refused. He eventually had to break the door down. By that time, too much damage had been done. The boys were so traumatized that they "couldn't even cry when he got there." One boy died two days later, and the other died within a month.[41]

Slave "mastery" involved more than corporal discipline and the spectacular scenes that often accompanied such brutality. Mastery and slave discipline were embedded in what literary scholar Saidiya Hartman calls "the quotidian routines of slavery." Mastery and domination masqueraded as kindness and benevolence. Slave owners' indulgences, allowances for "free time," concern for preserving the integrity of enslaved couples and families, refusal to sell those they owned, and countless other behaviors and choices appeared to be acts of humanity but in reality were calculated decisions made to enforce submission or preserve an enslaved person's value in slave markets.[42] Underlying each of these choices was the implicit, looming danger of sale. Whether spoken or unspoken, threats of sale could sometimes be more effective than beatings. When enslaved people misbehaved, male and female slave owners would often threaten to "put them in their pockets"—sell them—recognizing that the mere threat of a sale could produce the submission they desired.

Formerly enslaved people did talk about kind and caring mistresses; but "kindness and caring" often meant that their female owners treated them like human beings and respected their dignity in basic ways: they did not starve the people they owned, did not sell them, compel them to bare their bodies in public for want of proper clothing, or flay their flesh for burning the biscuits. Enslaved people interpreted such acts of humanity as calculated choices along a spectrum of many others. They knew, for example, that a variety of reasons might explain why a slave owner decided not to sell them. Something as simple as the time of year could affect their value in the market and influence the owner's decisions to sell or keep them. If we wish to understand how a slave owner's behavior adversely affected the lives of enslaved people, even when their actions appear to be kind or benevolent, we must approach all these behaviors with a critical eye and take our cues from the enslaved people who described them.

Nonetheless, the advice, suggestions, and examples submitted to the "Management of Negroes" columns in agricultural journals like *DeBow's Review* and the *Southern Planter* make it clear that many members of the master class assumed that their compatriots *did* consider violence a tool that helped them achieve mastery over enslaved people. In many pieces it was assumed that readers used or knew others who used brutal forms of discipline on a consistent basis, and many slave-owning authors felt it necessary to caution subscribers and fellow slaveholders against using brutality too often. Writers advised their fellow slave owners to punish in moderation and not with "severity" and reminded them that "in the infliction of punishment it should ever be borne in mind that the object is correction." Such cautionary advice suggests that brutal discipline as such was not perceived to be the problem, but rather the unceasing use of such violence. These authors instructed subscribers to use brutality only when necessary; they did not advise them to refrain from it altogether.[43]

In the third installment of the 1843 issue of the *Southern Planter*, "Cecilia" published an article titled "Management of Servants." In her short essay, Cecilia offered guidance to women who might be experiencing trouble managing their slaves. Cecilia recognized that women were capable of possessing and exercising the power to make enslaved people submit to their will, and she instructed them to mete out punishment themselves. She advised, "Never scold when a servant neglects his duty, but *always* punish him, no matter how mildly, for mild treatment is the best; severity hardens them. Be firm in this, that no neglect go unpunished. Never let a servant say to you, '*I forgot it.*' . . . Finally, let regularity mark every action, and the consequence will be, that everything will be done in its right place and at its right time; and the comforts and happiness of the family will be secured." Cecilia not only advised her female readers to inflict punishment, she also recommended that they develop a system by which they could do so with "regularity." She advised them against impulsive and sporadic acts of violence and suggested inflicting discipline in a systematic and calculated way.[44]

Cecilia's article was somewhat unusual for two reasons: the author was a woman and she directed her advice to female readers, even though the periodical had a primarily male readership. If Cecilia wrote this article with a female readership in mind, it suggests that she assumed that such a readership existed.[45] Such an assumption also suggests that the similarities between the women's and men's systems of slave management and discipline could have been the result of women reading such periodicals.

Southern laws did not offer a clear or universal definition of what constituted cruelty in the context of slavery. Phillipe Toca, the justice of the peace for Saint Bernard Parish, Louisiana, argued that it was not possible to craft a single legal definition of what constituted cruelty in all cases. In *Walker v. Cucullu*, a case involving the rescission of a slave sale, Toca argued that "however severe the chastisement may appear to certain persons," it was acceptable if it "was done within the limits prescribed by law." Moreover, he opined, punishment "must necessarily depend on the circumstances of each case in particular," and if the case was "a grave one, the chastisement will probably be severe": for example, if "the slave is of a robust constitution, the chastisement may be increased in proportion to his strength compared with the gravity of his faults." "Everything depends upon circumstances," of which "the owner is the judge." The law alone "prescribes to him the instruments of punishment to be made use of, and forbids him the right to punish, so as to maim, mutilate, disable or put in jeopardy and peril his life; if the law was otherwise, the right of discipline would be illusory."[46]

Most states were in agreement. As long as the punishment did not maim, mutilate, or imperil the life of an enslaved person, brutality was legal. There were, however, exceptions that allowed whites to kill enslaved people with impunity. South Carolina declared it "lawful for any white person to beat, maim or assault" a black person, and "if such negro or slave cannot otherwise be taken, to kill him, who shall refuse to shew his ticket, or, by running away or resistance, shall endeavor to avoid being apprehended or taken."[47] When slave owners' methods of punishment *did* maim or kill, the laws in states like Mississippi and South Carolina included provisions that absolved them of wrongdoing. If Mississippi slave owners swore an oath that they had not intended to cause their slaves' deaths or claimed that a death was caused "by accident and misfortune, in lawfully correcting a . . . servant" or "in heat of passion, upon any sudden and sufficient provocation," courts would typically acquit them. If the slaves they owned inflicted punishment on their owners' behalf, they, too, would be acquitted.[48] The murder trial of Eliza Rowand and her husband's slave Richard offers a powerful example of how these laws condoned brutal acts that led to enslaved people's deaths and absolved their owners of responsibility, even when the owners were women.

In 1847, Eliza Rowand became the first woman in the state of South Carolina to be put on trial for the murder of a slave. She was accused of commanding her husband's slave, Richard, to strike an enslaved woman named Maria multiple times on the head with a block of wood, a beating that eventually led to Maria's death. South Carolina law stipulated that if a slave died as a result of a master's punishment and no other white persons were present to witness the incident, the slave owner could exculpate him- or herself by claiming that the violence had not been inflicted maliciously.[49] Eliza Rowand told the court that Maria had misbehaved that morning and she had ordered Richard to take her to "Mr. Rowand's" (her husband's) "house, to be corrected." She did this knowing that "Mr. Rowand was absent from the city." She also claimed that Richard never punished Maria on her command and that no beating took place in her chambers. In fact, Rowand claimed that she had no idea who inflicted the blows that killed Maria. Even so, she, "as law permits, by calling on God, exculpated herself." No white witnesses came forward to challenge her claims. Considering her oath alone to be good, the jury found her not guilty. Richard was tried around the same time as Rowand and was subsequently found not guilty as well. The freeholders who adjudicated the case exonerated Richard because he was "merely the instrument of his mistress's cruelty." In another case, the fugitive slave turned abolitionist William Wells Brown told a London audience that a "woman was recently tried for causing the death of a negro girl; she was acquitted, on the ground that it was her slave-woman who actually committed the deed. The slave-woman was afterwards tried and acquitted, on the ground that she committed the murder on the authority of her mistress!"[50]

Similar incidents went unnoticed by the southern press and have escaped scholarly attention for a number of reasons. The majority of these women's crimes against their slaves remained confined within their households, and more often than not enslaved people were the only witnesses. Since southern laws forbade them to testify against white people, their testimony was inadmissible.[51] In some court cases, a woman's violent action caused an enslaved person's death and served as the underlying cause of a legal suit, but the woman herself was never named as a defendant or punished for her crime. On January 1, 1824, Marshall Mann hired an enslaved girl named Fanny from Charles C. Trabue with the proviso that he could purchase her once the contract for her hire expired. When the time came to return Fanny or pay Trabue for her hire, Mann refused to do either because Fanny had died shortly after he hired her. Mann stood trial for Fanny's death, and the jury acquitted him. Undaunted by their decision, Trabue sued Mann for breach of contract. In his own defense, Mann told the court that he was not obligated to pay Trabue because, although Fanny died in his possession, her death was the consequence of an "act of God," something that dissolved Mann's liability. The court disagreed and ruled in Trabue's favor, and Mann appealed, citing his acquittal in the case of Fanny's death in the lower court. The Missouri Supreme Court dismissed Mann's appeal and upheld the lower court's ruling. One thing remained unsaid in all of Mann's cases; his wife was responsible for Fanny's death. Even members of their community knew it. One Missouri man recounted in precise detail how Mann's wife had brutalized Fanny, and claimed that the day after Mann's wife had tortured Fanny, she was found dead. Fanny was "silently and quickly buried, but rumor was not so easily stopped. . . . The murdered slave was disinterred, and an inquest held; her back was a mass of jellied muscle; and the coroner brought in a verdict of death by the 'six pound paddle.'" Mrs. Mann fled the district for a few months, but no action was taken against her.[52]

By some accounts, white slave owners concealed their most brutalized slaves from observers who might object to their violence, even going so far as to borrow healthy slaves from neighbors when they entertained visitors. When slave owners inflicted punishments that resulted in a slave's death, some rid themselves of the body or told inquisitive people that the slave in question had died of disease. Enslaved people's deaths were not complete financial losses to their owners. Medical schools across the nation bought the bodies of deceased enslaved people from southern slave owners for dissection and research and thereby offered slave owners a profitable way to make such bodies disappear.[53]

The brutality of some slave-owning women, especially when it led to disfigurement or death, might strike us as "irrational destruction" that was counterproductive, in large part because it seemed to be in direct conflict with their financial investment in the people they owned. After all, such violence impaired enslaved people's ability to work and decreased or obliterated their value in the market.[54] But a slave-owning woman's decisions to abuse, maim, or kill her slaves was simply an "extreme version" of her "right to exclude" others from reaping the benefits of having access to the slaves she herself abused or destroyed. Moreover, there were "benefits" that accrued from such actions, and they served an important purpose for slave-owning women and their communities. The abuse and murder of enslaved people had "expressive value" that affirmed a slave-owning woman's power.[55] It was also expressive because some slave-owning women enacted this violence in ritualized performances and forced enslaved men, women, and children to watch as a way of further convincing them of that power.

Broader social order was another important benefit. By evoking terror in enslaved populations, slave owners and their communities increased the likelihood that they could exact submission from enslaved people. When enslaved people fled beyond their owners' reach, southern laws endowed members of militias, community patrols, and ordinary white southerners with the power to destroy them and display their remains, such as the heads of decapitated rebels, in public.[56] A number of factors help explain different outcomes in cases involving slave abuse or homicide. First, a slave owner had to have a reason for killing a slave. An owner could not kill a slave "without cause" or out of cruelty, "wilfulness, wantoness, or bloody mindedness."[57] In reality, owners could easily manufacture justifications that satisfied the court and could not be disputed because enslaved witnesses were barred from testifying against them. Second, community norms could shape a court's decision to convict or acquit a slave owner who killed.[58] If white members of the community found a slave owner's abuse or murder of an enslaved person so reprehensible as to compel them to alert authorities and testify in subsequent legal cases, their disapproval might influence the court's judgment. Far more often, however, communities sought to sanction slave owners who refused to punish their slaves or who allowed their slaves too much freedom.[59] Finally, legislators did not impose legal constraints upon slave owners' powers to abuse, punish, and kill their slaves out of concern for enslaved people's well-being. They did so in order to preserve the interests of relatives who would inherit their estates and would suffer if the property was squandered. If abuse and destruction did not threaten to deprive heirs of their rightful inheritances, courts might acquit a slave owner who killed.[60]

Some of the cases discussed here might appear to suggest that when slave-owning women brutalized and killed enslaved people, southern judges and jurors exonerated them because of gendered ideas about women or an assumption that a woman's violence toward enslaved people was somehow different from a man's. But judges and juries were consistent in their leniency toward slave-owning men and women, and southern laws generally allowed most white southerners, *not just women,* who killed, dismembered, or maimed enslaved people (even those who did not belong to them) to do so with impunity. Most southern judges and members of southern juries were slave owners themselves and could sympathize with the defendants before them. Even if they did not, their decision to exonerate a defendant might have been influenced by the thought that they might eventually find themselves before a jury of their slave-owning peers, from whom they would hope for similar consideration. Judges and jurors generally adjudicated their cases according to precedent, building upon other decisions in cases involving an owner's murder of an enslaved person. With the exception of the most egregious cases, slave-owning and non-slaveholding white men and women were not held accountable for such crimes beyond a possible fine—say, the estimated value of the deceased slave if she or he belonged to someone else—though their actions would have been punishable by death if their victims had been free and white. White women were members of slave-owning communities built on a system of white supremacy and the subjugation of African-descended people. The laws governing these communities gave slave-owning women the right to make enslaved people submit to their will and they routinely exercised that right.

4

"She Thought She Could Find a Better Market"

Martha J. Jones was a young white girl living in the upper western region of Virginia when she acquired extensive knowledge about the slave market and trade. Her father's slave-dealing brother was her teacher, and his farm served as her school. Martha Jones not only knew through secondhand knowledge that her uncle, John C. Turner, would "buy, sell and trade" slaves "all the time"; she witnessed him engaging in these activities herself. During her childhood, she would visit her uncle and watch him "swap and buy slaves, just the same as he was buying any other stock for his farm." From her observations, Jones also learned about the slave-market economy. After seeing her uncle negotiate prices for enslaved people, Jones reasonably concluded that those who were "big and strong . . . would bring a good price, as they would be better workers for the fields."[1]

Martha Jones's parents did not think that exposing their daughter to her uncle's business would warp her sense of humanity or make her any less feminine, sensitive, or marriageable. Although in the WPA interview she gave in the 1930s she never says whether she visited a slave market or bought slaves herself, her reflections about her uncle reveal why she did not have to. She knew what the slave market was like because it was all around her.

The process of buying and selling slaves began long before individuals stepped into a slave market.[2] The market that Martha Jones remembered was not contained within the slave pens, yards, or auction blocks housed within the commercial center of her community, it was conducted at her uncle's home, and her memories mirror those of young white women throughout the South. Recent studies about the slave trade offer more expansive schemata of the southern slave market, which similarly push beyond the architectural boundaries of the commercial spaces associated with it. But the slaveholding household assumes a rather benign role within this broader framework. Formerly enslaved people's reflections about the entire slave-market system and the people responsible for buying and selling them are beginning to figure within current understandings of the slave marketplace and the process of sale.[3] Most commonly, historians see the slave market as a masculine place, a domain in which white women did not belong. When women wanted to buy or sell a slave, they "found ways to participate in the market without going to the marketplace" such as "through instructions given in a letter or arguments made in a parlor discussion." Typically, these historians assert, women asked the men in their lives to do the work of slave buying and selling for them.[4] If such were the case, the household and the slave market never met in tangible ways. But such a depiction of the slave market and of white women's alienation from it presents a characterization of the slave trade and the slave-owning household that belies the testimony of both formerly enslaved people *and* white women. For both groups, the slave market pervaded the household and in many instances the two were one and the same. And women took full advantage of this convergence.

Formerly enslaved people frequently spoke about this more expansive slave market. For them, the slave market was a mobile, spatially unbounded economic network that connected urban commercial districts to plantation estates and incorporated boardinghouses, rural pathways, urban streets, taverns, and coffee shops, as well as holding pens and auction houses. They also saw slaveholding households—their porches, kitchens, dining rooms, and bedrooms—and the fields and the quarters, along with the pathways and roads surrounding them, as fundamental parts of the slave market. In all these places, slave-owning women orchestrated the sale and purchase of enslaved people. Not only did slave-owning women participate in the public haggling over black bodies in the slave pen, the slave yard, and the auction block, they frequently subjected enslaved people to the terror of the slave market in the privacy of their homes. While slave traders, auctioneers, and brokers prepared enslaved people for sale by the sides of country roads, in southern auction houses, and in slave-trading establishments, white women talked with friends and family members about their labor needs and their desire to buy or sell enslaved men, women, and children. They were often able to fulfill that desire without visiting a brick-and-mortar marketplace because this process often took place—or at least began—in their homes.

Historians of the southern slave market view it as corrosive, corrupting, sexually charged, and brutal, and many claim that it was considered too abhorrent a place for white women to visit. But when women chose to hire, buy, or sell enslaved people in or near their homes and beyond the formal marketplace, they were not avoiding the "perceived sexual and social disorder" associated with these markets; the plantation landscape was itself marked by that disorder.[5]

On any given day, white women and girls could witness white men and women committing violent acts upon the nude and partially exposed bodies of enslaved people in their households and their fields. Lizzie Anna Burwell, the child who at age three wanted to replace her enslaved companion, lived in a household where her father, John A. Burwell, beat her mother, Lucy, and ran the "negroes about with guns & sticks," something he claimed to do "out of fun." He openly engaged in an extramarital affair with and quite likely sexually assaulted an enslaved woman who belonged to his wife. On one occasion, he told his wife that he had no intention of "sharing her bed that night; but would occupy a different room." Then, in the presence of his wife, his sons, and his daughters, including Lizzie Anna, who was not yet twelve, he summoned an enslaved female to his room, where he allegedly "required [her] attendance" and she "remained in the room with him during the night." This same enslaved female had "within a few years past been the mother of two children, the off-spring of a white father," and Lucy believed that John had fathered them.[6] Such incidents make it clear that the social and sexual disorder that characterized southern slave markets also pervaded slaveholding households.

The slaveholding household was a place of coerced production and reproduction, racial and sexual exploitation, and physical and psychological violence.[7] It was a place where white southern women grew accustomed to the violence of slavery, contemplated the sale and purchase of slaves, and used the bodies of the enslaved people they owned in ways that reinforced their pecuniary value. The household became an extension of the slave market, and white women capitalized upon their access to both. They not only "did the thinking about slave buying," taking stock of their labor needs and the kinds of workers who could meet them, they orchestrated the sale, purchase, and exchange of slaves in these domestic spaces.[8] When they were ready to finalize their decisions, they summoned slave traders to their homes to transact their business.[9] The argument that white southern women were alienated from slave markets and immune to the machinations of the trade seems far-fetched in the face of the ubiquity of slave traders and speculators and their business in urban and rural landscapes, as well as in private homes. White slave-owning women frequently did not need to go to the slave market because the slave market came to them.

Some women employed their husbands and male kin as agents and proxies who would conduct their business in slave marketplaces. This delegation of authority might seem to offer proof that men dominated the partnerships these women formed with them and that such delegation signified these women's relinquishment of control over their financial affairs. But this perspective simplifies the ways women used agents and proxies, and leaves out the fact that slave-owning women also employed other women to serve as their agents and attorneys-in-fact. Furthermore, even when women employed male agents to conduct some aspect of their business in southern slave markets, they also ventured into these markets or attended slave auctions themselves. Moreover, it is inaccurate to assume that the reliance on kin and friends as proxies was a uniquely female practice. It was not. Relying on proxies was a common practice among slave-owning men as well. After an enslaved seamstress named Tempe died suddenly of unknown causes, for example, her owner, John A. Burwell, asked his son to find a replacement. Some men, particularly those who did not own slaves, often asked slave-owning or slave-dealing men to accompany them when they went to markets to buy their first slaves. They wanted a seasoned slave owner to help them avoid making unsound purchases and buy the best enslaved people for their money. Men also appointed women who were not married to them as their agents and attorneys-in-fact.[10]

It was common for eighteenth-century sailors and merchants to appoint their wives as their attorneys-in-fact when their business required extended absences away from home. The historian Sarah Damiano argues that in these commercial contexts, "many financial activities were not coded as masculine or feminine," and "women who acted for their husbands demonstrated financial and legal skill as they negotiated with creditors and debtors, collected and paid debts, and safeguarded financial documents." Sometimes when husbands appointed their wives to act as their attorneys-in-fact, they delegated some of the more technical and complex responsibilities to men who worked in conjunction with their wives to ensure that business was taken care of.[11] While this may have been the case in reference to women acting on their spouses' behalf as "deputy husbands," such scenarios do not tell us about the arrangements that married slave-owning women made with male attorneys-in-fact, nor does it give us a sense of the constraints married women imposed upon these men's power to act on their behalf. Additionally the constraints and limitations that married women, who served as their husbands' attorneys-in-fact, confronted cannot, however, help us fully understand the arrangements these women made with and the powers they granted to *female* attorneys-in-fact.

While many white slave-owning men established business relationships with men whom they did not consider kin, friends, or even social equals, white slave-owning women's business relationships were generally with male kin and family friends. The relationships between factors and their male clients can help elucidate how these women's business arrangements functioned. Factors operated as proxies for their clients, and they were useful because planters often lived far from the commercial centers of the South. Hiring factors allowed a planter to "buy and sell, contract and pay his debts, and in general have his affairs cared for without being required to travel to town or to concern himself with problems of exchange, transfer of funds, discounts, and the like."[12] Factors also attended to personal requests for products and goods that had nothing to do with planting. More important, factors sometimes became close acquaintances with their clients, even developing long-standing friendships over the years, and establishing kinship ties through marriage.

Slave-owning women relied upon people they knew or individuals whom loved ones recommended to conduct their business, and these proxies served very practical purposes. Employing factors was risky because such business partnerships required planters to invest enormous amounts of trust in men they knew only cursorily—men who might take their crops and their money and abscond with them. White slave-owning women reduced their level of risk by employing family members and friends. Of course, family and friends were not always above betrayal. But relying on male friends and kin decreased the likelihood of it. Recall that Sarah Devereux, for example, lived in New Haven, Connecticut, but her plantation and slaves were located in North Carolina. As an absentee owner, she called upon her brother-in-law Thomas to serve as her agent and factor, in large part because he lived near her property holdings, and she was unable to travel across the Mason-Dixon line as often as she would have liked. They corresponded regularly about her land, slaves, and cotton, and when her slave Sally became troublesome, she began to contemplate selling her, along with, or without, Sally's children. Sarah asked Thomas for his opinion. She explained that it was difficult for her "to sell her and those children, or without them," and because of this, she was "perplexed" and was not sure what "her duty" was. Ultimately, she told Thomas that Sally had given her "trouble enough ever since she was grown," and if he thought it "best to make her an example," then he should sell her. Since Thomas had previously mentioned that he was planning to sell some of his own slaves, Sarah suggested that he sell Sally along with his.[13]

Sarah's hesitance about selling Sally was not grounded in her sense of inadequacy as a businesswoman. Rather, her letter suggests that prices might have been low at the time or that there might have been low local demand for enslaved persons with Sally's skills. Sarah does convey some emotional disease about the sale, but her letter to her brother-in-law suggests that she was not particularly interested in his "judgment" about a decision she had already made. Sarah seemed to want Thomas to confirm that she was right to sell Sally for misbehavior and, perhaps, grant her absolution from the moral implications of the sale. Had she been in North Carolina to manage her own estate and slaves, she might have excused her brother-in-law from his managerial role and felt more certain about her decision to sell Sally away from her home and family.

Elizabeth Guy also employed her brother-in-law John A. Burwell to help her with financial transactions involving the enslaved people she owned, and her decision was similarly grounded in matters of distance and proximity. She had relocated from Kentucky to New Orleans, and she had not yet made arrangements to transport the enslaved people she owned to her new residence. Burwell lived closer to where her slaves were, which made him better placed to conduct this business.[14] Their correspondence demonstrates that men generally took their responsibilities to their female kin seriously, and their relationships with these women were much like those between factors and clients who were not related by blood or marriage. In his report about her slaves' well-being and their earnings, Burwell wrote with businesslike formality, explaining every delay and possible discrepancy in Guy's financial affairs. In addition, he provided an itemized statement, which delineated every penny of Guy's that he had spent. Even though she was family, Burwell granted Guy the respect that an agent or factor would confer upon a client.[15]

When women hired agents not related to them to handle their business, they held these men to high standards of professionalism and were not afraid to call their decisions into question. Throughout the first half of the nineteenth century, Eliza Bowman Lyons, a large-scale Louisiana planter who lived near Bayou Sarah, employed multiple agents, factors, and commission merchants to sell her cotton. Burke, Watt, and Company, one of the agencies with which she steadily did business, routinely sent her detailed accounts of various sales and explained any discrepancies or shortfalls. On more than one occasion the company also bought enslaved people on her behalf. Glendy Burke was Lyons's agent in the purchase of an enslaved woman and her children in 1839, and Lyons asked another of the company's agents, Louis deSaulles, to "purchase a woman servant who [was] a good washer and ironer" in 1843. He informed her that he "had one for sale," and for a thousand dollars he would be willing to sell her to Lyons.[16] For the most part, Lyons maintained amicable professional relationships with these men. But the response of one of her factors, one Lallande, to a letter of December 5, 1850, leaves little doubt that Lyons had expressed her displeasure about the way he handled her business, calling his reputation and character into question, and rejecting what she considered his ill-conceived advice. The trouble between them began after Lallande learned that Lyons was "sending cotton to three or four commission merchants" and not solely to him. Although Lallande had assured Lyons that his agents "were fully competent to sell cotton or do anything else," she had "no confidence" in his employees. Lyons told Lallande that she had been "so fortunate for twenty-six years to have met *only with gentlemen*," and she was sorry that she and Lallande had "so far misunderstood each other's character." What seemed to bother Lyons most was her inability to pay two notes worth five thousand dollars each that had come due within a month of each other. Lyons had counted on the proceeds from the sale of her cotton to pay them but Lallande had advised her to "hold on your cotton" while he was on a trip in New York. As a consequence, she had "met with serious losses." For this, Lyons believed, she had "a right to complain," and so she did.[17]

Some women avoided these kinds of encounters by relying on networks made up of female kin and acquaintances to purchase the goods they wanted. Familial and friendship ties often provided women with the credit or money to finalize their transactions. If a woman was seeking goods in a distant market, she might entrust a friend or family member with whom she shared "a common sense of 'value'" and style with the purchase choice.[18] A woman's sale and purchase of enslaved people was handled in the same way as her sale and purchase of other goods. Slave sales were often collaborative efforts, involving a number of individuals bound to one another in some way or another. As the historian Ellen Hartigan-O'Connor has argued, "Power was a part of every transaction," and "the roles individuals played within those collaborations shaped the power they had over the transaction: Some held the purse strings. Others performed the leg work, balancing commands and judgment. Still others provided opinions—solicited and unsolicited—about goods, shops, and money."[19]

Slave-owning women frequently hired their slaves to or purchased them from neighbors and friends, and such arrangements may well have been executed in the home rather than in a slave market. Lelia Tucker wrote a letter to her husband in which she documented one female acquaintance's negotiations with three slave-owning women in their social circle. A woman she called "Mrs. P.," who had recently settled in their Virginia community, had not only "hired a houseservant" from one Mrs. Braxton, she had also hired or purchased a washerwoman who belonged to a Mrs. Charlton. Tucker told her husband that Mrs. P. expected "to take Mrs. Prentis's cook on trial, before she venture[d] to purchase her." Lelia Tucker mentioned no involvement by male kin, a proxy, or an agent in the agreements between Mrs. P. and the other women. Mrs. P. was likely to have learned about the available servants through local female networks and approached the slave owners herself. Such local sales and hires between friends and acquaintances could be the reason why these transactions remained out of slave traders' account books.[20]

Mrs. P.'s negotiations and transactions with Mrs. Braxton, Mrs. Charlton, and Mrs. Prentis offer further evidence of the integration of the home and the "insensitive and brutal" market in slaves. The slave market so thoroughly saturated the slaveholding household that a slave-owning home could never be a place characterized solely by "human relations unqualified by a price."[21] All four of these women incorporated currency and human commodities into their social network.

When African Americans characterized southern households as vital components of the slave marketplace, they rarely made a distinction between the "private" household and the "public" slave market, for good reason. According to their accounts, white women and girls were routinely exposed to the sale and purchase of enslaved people in their homes and around them. The men who plied their trade in human flesh were their husbands, fathers, brothers, friends, and neighbors, and they owned slaves, too. Slave dealers exposed their wives and daughters to the trade when they brought their work home with them. They passed by or visited white women's households and stayed in their homes while they were traveling to distant slave markets. They brought slave coffles to estates in hopes of selling some of the people in them. They also approached white women about selling the slaves they owned. In a variety of ways, enslaved people's testimony reveals that there was little separation between home and work for the men engaged in the slave trade.[22]

If the slave market and the trade had been considered unsuitable for women, white women could have simply avoided all talk of business when slave traders came around. But some mistresses were clearly taking part. Sallie McNeill, a slaveholding woman residing in Brazoria County, Texas, in the mid-nineteenth century, wrote in her diary about her grandfather's business negotiations with John Evans, a man who was involved in the slave trade. On June 21, 1859, McNeill recorded her concern because Evans "had been gone for negroes two months," taking ten thousand dollars of her grandfather's money with him; Evans had "suddenly disappeared from the horizon of our limited vision."[23] Evans eventually came back with the slaves he bought for McNeill's grandfather and a female neighbor. Her grandfather was apparently satisfied with the purchase because he sought out Evans's services on subsequent occasions.[24] While McNeill discusses her neighbors' suspicions about Evans's trustworthiness, her grandfather seemed relatively comfortable buying slaves from him.

Furthermore, from McNeill's diary entries, it seems that her grandfather made no attempt to shield her from his dealings with Evans. McNeill may not herself have purchased slaves from Evans, but she was privy to the transactions he secured for her grandfather, even going so far as to cite the amount of money her grandfather gave him, the number of slaves he purchased, and whom he purchased them for.

Whether connected by bloodline or nuptials, the wives and female kin of southern men involved in the business of buying and selling slaves (and their children) experienced the intersection of the slave market and the household firsthand because they knew about the work their spouses and male kin did, they understood the financial stakes involved, and they sometimes had to protect their property from those men.[25] Some slave traders relinquished their ties to the business once they married, a proceeding that one historian asserts was done in order to spare their wives from the trade's unsavory character. Isaac Franklin, a slave trader who was one of the richest Americans in the country before his death in 1839, quit the trade after he married Adelicia Hayes, but only after he had grown wealthy from buying and selling enslaved people.[26] Other traders could not afford to quit the business, however, and still more did not see any reason to do so.

It is also quite likely that some husbands quit the trade because the work involved long absences away from home, which could strain a marriage and lead to its dissolution. The North Carolina slave trader Isaac Jarratt entered the slave trade long after he said his vows, and when he was on the road, he, like other traders, kept his wife abreast of his whereabouts and details of his work. Beginning in the 1830s Isaac regularly wrote loving and affectionate letters to his wife, Harriet, when he was away from home buying and selling slaves, and he routinely updated her about his sales and business prospects. In a letter of December 7, 1834, he informed her that he and his partner had sold six enslaved people that day and he anticipated selling the remaining slaves a short time thereafter. But he warned her that he would not be able to return home until he had collected the money that was due after the sales had been finalized.[27] Wives like Harriet had to develop ways to contend with the uncertainties associated with their husbands' business. On one hand, Harriet endured Isaac's long absences and dealt with the comings and goings of his partners and associates because, in large part, her livelihood depended upon Isaac's line of work. But at the same time she was candid about her displeasure when he neglected her and his duties at home. In her response to a letter from Isaac on October 19, 1835, Harriet expressed her loneliness and her disappointment that he still had not come home. She further complained that although he was now a married man, he worked as hard at his business as his unmarried partner did: "I am affraid my Dear Husband that you and your friend [illegible] Carson will keep up negro trading as long as you can get a negro to trade on . . . but one good thing[,] Mr. Carson has no wife to leave behind when he is gone."[28]

The voices of women whose husbands bought and sold enslaved people for a living do not emerge often, but their actions speak volumes about how they felt about their husbands' work. Ebenezer Johnson's wife frequently accompanied her husband on slave trading—and kidnapping—excursions. Johnson was a member of a notorious group that operated on the Delaware-Maryland border, kidnapping indentured and free people of color from the North and selling them into slavery in the South. These men committed their crimes under the leadership of Patty Cannon and her son-in-law Joseph Johnson. Ebenezer was Joseph's brother. One of the gang members and Samuel Scomp, a fugitive slave from New Jersey who was one of Ebenezer's captive victims, testified to seeing Ebenezer's wife accompany him on several such ventures. Scomp even overheard Ebenezer telling his wife how much one of his male captives sold for.[29]

On the rare occasions when we do hear the voices of slave traders' wives, we find that these women exhibited far more concern about their husbands' long absences from home than the fact that their husbands sold human beings for a living. The absences and the uncertainties of the market proved to be more than some women could bear. They believed that slave trading had changed their husbands into men they hardly knew, and they sought to end their marriages to spouses who appeared as strangers to them. A Nash County, North Carolina, woman named Piety Tisdale sought to divorce her husband for this reason. According to her divorce petition, she and her husband had lived peaceably for fifteen years, until he decided to become a slave trader. Shortly after he entered the business, he became an alcoholic, gradually distanced himself from his family, and eventually abandoned them.[30] Mary Crosby confronted a similar situation; her experience also shows how men invested their wives' wealth in the slave market-economy whether they asked them to or not. Like the Tisdales, she and her husband, William, had enjoyed a comfortable life for several years, until he decided to go into the slave trade. Before their marriage, Mary had saved approximately six or seven hundred dollars, but these funds legally became William's when they married. Sometime after they married, William took Mary's money and began buying, trading, and speculating in slaves. William also began spending long periods of time away from home, though in the beginning he would return to care for his family as often as his work allowed. Gradually, he began spending more and more time in Alabama, where Mary claimed he possessed a sizable amount of property and, presumably, where he sold his slaves. She and her two children had only been able to survive in the six years after William took up the slave trade and left them because of the kindness his mother showed them.[31]

Women were equally concerned about the pecuniary threats that their husbands' slave trading posed to their own slaveholdings. Armstead Barrett's owner Ann was married to a slave speculator named Ben Walker, and she was determined to maintain her personal investments in slavery. She refused to let her husband sell Barrett and the other enslaved people she inherited from her father. Mattie Logan's mistress was also married to a slave trader, and she warned him not even to think about selling her slaves, especially the girls.[32] In another exasperated letter to her husband, Isaac, after his prolonged absence, Harriet Jarratt confessed her suspicions that when Isaac could no longer find enslaved people to buy and sell, he would "carry of[f] all" the slaves he could "pirade [pirate] at home." The enslaved people to whom Harriet referred were probably her own. In Isaac's response, he assured Harriet that he would never take the slaves unless *she* wished it, and as long as she was satisfied with them, he would try to be content with them as well. He also assured her that if *she* "wish[ed] them sold" he would "sell them and not till then."[33]

Some wives went beyond letter writing to protect their human property from their slave-dealing husbands. They flatly refused to let their husbands jeopardize or destroy their personal investments in the trade, and they took precautions to prevent their husbands from disposing of the slaves they owned. When a woman bought an enslaved person, she would make sure that the seller included a clause in the bill of sale that indicated that the slave was her "sole and separate property."

Women like Adelaide Vinot Hite of New Orleans might also petition the court for a separation of property to protect their slaves from their husbands' possible commercial blunders in the slave market. Adelaide married Samuel N. Hite when he was one of the most active slave traders in the New Orleans market. Throughout their marriage, Samuel continued to engage in the slave trade, and he exposed Adelaide to his business on a routine basis. He not only entertained slave traders in his home, he permitted them to stay with his family and keep the slaves they hoped to sell with them. James W. Boazman, for example, a prolific and prominent New Orleans slave trader, resided in the Hite household for a short time, and while there he worked as a "negro broker" and kept the slaves he had for sale on the premises with him. Yet despite Adelaide's marriage to this savvy speculator in human flesh—or perhaps because of it—she did not entrust him with the responsibility of executing and finalizing slave purchases and sales on her behalf. On December 5, 1844, after they had been married for a year or so, Adelaide sued Samuel for a separation of property. Her request included a claim against him for five thousand dollars, the amount of her dowry. According to John Tarbe, another slave trader, who testified on Adelaide's behalf, Samuel was supposed to invest her dowry in the slave trade and "make a good deal of money with it, by trading in negroes." Adelaide's legal action suggests that Samuel failed to do so, or that he made poor investments. She told the court that Samuel's financial affairs were in such disarray that she feared his creditors would seize her property to satisfy his debts. The judge granted her request for separation of property on April 4, 1845, and from that point forward, she had the court's permission to control her own property and purchase more in her own name.[34]

Almost immediately, Adelaide's name began to appear in New Orleans conveyance records buying and selling slaves on her own account. And while these documents often mention Samuel as her husband, they do not identify him as her agent or broker. When a married woman bought or sold property, the notarial record included the clause "duly authorized and assisted by her husband," or something similar. When he represented her during the transaction, the record clearly stated his role. In all Adelaide's transactions, only the language "duly authorized and assisted" or "duly assisted and authorized" by her husband appears, which means that Samuel merely gave his permission for her to act on her own behalf when she bought or sold property. While married to Samuel, Adelaide bought and sold slaves twenty-six times, and she continued to buy and sell slaves without his help well into the Civil War period, when she bought her last slave, Charles, on July 30, 1862.[35]

Slave traders and speculators were neighbors or members of the family, and they brought their trade into the homes of their friends and kin. Susan Merritt's owner lived on a plantation adjacent to one owned by a man who operated an establishment in the local slave market. Wade Dudley's owners Bill and Nancy Kidd had a slave-trading son. Alex Woods's master had a slave-trading brother, and Woods would often see him "bringin' slaves in chains to de plantation when he wus carryin' 'em to Richmond to put 'em on de auction block to be sold." Speculators also routinely stayed with people they knew while traveling into the lower South or passed through plantation estates to rest as they made their way to slave markets. W. L. Bost was just ten years old when slavery ended, but he could remember that "the speculators [would] come through Newton[, North Carolina,] with droves and slaves." There was a good reason for him to remember, too: "They always stay at our place." When Robert Glenn's owner put him up for auction, a slave trader by the name of Long bought him. After the sale, they set out for Long's home, and they "stopped for refreshments, at a plantation" along the way. Glenn recalled the white women he met while he was staying there. They knew that Long had just purchased Glenn and they also knew that Glenn had been separated from his mother and would probably never see her again.[36]

The itinerant traders did more than sleep and rest when they visited estates throughout the South; they bought and sold slaves from their hosts while they were there.[37] Enslaved people like Caleb Craig were frequently present when slave dealers and speculators came to their owners' plantations to ply their trade. Craig recalled that "slave drovers often came to de June place. . . . They buy, sell, and swap niggers, just like they buy, sell, and swap hosses, mules, and hogs."[38] Women, too, took advantage of the opportunities presented to them when traders visited their farms and estates. In April 1801, James Murrel came to Mary Craig's York County, South Carolina, plantation with a five- or six-year-old enslaved boy named Mike, whom he hoped to sell. Mary Craig negotiated with Murrel and purchased the enslaved boy from him. It is worth mentioning that Mary Craig was married to Henry Craig at the time of the sale, but she, not her husband, negotiated with Murrel. The purchase was not as successful as Mary might have hoped. A little over a year later, Mike became "sick with fever" and his illness progressed to "swellings and running sores." Mike died a short time thereafter, and Mary sued Murrel for breach of warranty.[39]

Speculators frequently enticed slave owners with proposals to buy their slaves, though some owners, like Liza Jones's mistress, refused their offers.[40] One white southerner commissioned a local slave trader to purchase a black-smith on his behalf, and claimed he was willing to pay any price for a good one. As the trader traveled through the countryside looking for an enslaved man who met his client's specifications, he heard about a wealthy but dying woman who owned exactly the kind of blacksmith he sought. He approached her and offered her a price she could not refuse. For a thousand dollars, the dying woman sold her blacksmith away from his wife and children, whom he probably never saw again.[41]

Slave traders and speculators sometimes conducted their business in the roads adjacent to plantations, and enslaved people would watch them along with white women who were attentive to and interested in the enslaved people they offered for sale or who wanted to sell their own.[42] As Charles Henderson's sister watched a slave trader and his coffle pass through her Danville, Kentucky, neighborhood, she spotted a crying and distraught enslaved girl among the group. She "sent word to her brother to buy [the] child at once for her." He tracked down the slave trader and bought the girl for his sister for seven hundred dollars. Charity Bowery's mistress sold her to a speculator who would pass by her estate. Unknown to her, Bowery had often served the man oysters from a food stand she operated, even when he was unable to pay. The slave trader remembered her kindness, and after he bought Bowery and several of her children, he set her and one of the children free as recompense.[43]

Slave-trading men brought southern households and slave markets together, allowing white women to execute transactions in the slave market and benefit from the trade without ever having to leave their farms or plantations. But formerly enslaved people also spoke of occasions when their owners sold them in slave markets of their own making and bid them off in venues they organized on their estates for that very purpose.

Saidiya Hartman has called the slave auction the "theatre of the marketplace" because enslaved people's captors forced them to "perform" roles that made them appear to be white southerners' ideal slaves. Under the threat of violence, they fabricated life stories and feigned fitness, pleasure, and contentment before an audience of prospective purchasers.[44] Although these kinds of performances are typically associated with sales in slave markets that were located in cities and towns, they also occurred in auctions on plantation estates and farms. Katie Rowe was raised on an estate where her owner's husband would sell slaves during auctions he held on his plantation. He had a tree stump fitted out for the purpose, placed it in his yard, and "made de niggers stand [on it] while dey was being sold." Rowe remembered that "white men from around dar come to bid, and some traders come." The slave traders who attended these sales brought along the droves of slaves they had purchased with hopes of reselling them, and they would "have 'em all strung out in a line going down de road." The master's wife, who owned Katie, her mother, and her grandmother, would not allow him to sell her slaves, but she undoubtedly witnessed these affairs.[45] Joe High, who was enslaved in North Carolina, remembered that slaves were sold on the block his mistress used to mount her horse: "There were two steps to it. . . . I remember seeing them [slaves] sold from this block."[46]

When asked about his mistress Annie Poore, Tom Hawkins explained that she "was all time sellin' [her slaves] for big prices atter she done trained 'em for to be cooks, housegals, houseboys, carriage drivers, and good wash 'omans." Hawkins also said that he saw "Old Miss sell de slaves what she trained. She made 'em stand up on a block, she kept in de back yard, whilst she was a-auctionin' 'em off."[47] Within the confines of her home and in the open spaces of her Georgia estate, Annie Poore trained the slaves she owned and sold them to the highest bidders. She was not married to a slave trader or speculator. She did not approach the men of the trade who walked past her estate so that she could buy one or more of the slaves in their coffles. Nor did she send male family members, friends, or business associates to the local market to buy or sell her slaves. She transformed her backyard into a slave market, with its own auction block to boot. From Hawkins's recollections, it would seem that the men who made their living selling and buying humans knew Poore's business well, for he remembered seeing slave traders all the time.

Annie Poore was a slave master, a slave trader, and an auctioneer, and by all measures, she was a mistress of the slave market. She knew that training enslaved African Americans to fulfill specific functions would augment their value, and she could command specific prices for them on those bases. She also knew that if she had slaves with these skills to sell, the buyers would come to her to bid upon them. And they did.

These kinds of details about slave-owning women and enslaved people's daily lives were what the abolitionist Angelina Grimké called the "minutiae of slavery."[48] For women like Annie Poore and Joe High's mistress, nothing connected with the business was strange or unfamiliar because they spent their lives immersed in slavery, even its most appalling details. Slave-owning women's lifelong exposure to every dimension of slavery made it possible for them to take advantage of the intersections between the market and the plantation, and allowed them to effortlessly navigate the slave-market economy that connected them.

Not all women engaged in such elaborate and orchestrated affairs when they wanted to buy or sell enslaved people. Far more women bought and sold slaves privately, and have therefore often escaped historians' notice. Their slave-market activities also remain relatively invisible because the sales took place among family members or among other women, and, most important, because the transactions occurred outside formal slave markets. George Womble's mistress, Mrs. Ridley, sold him to her brother Enoch Womble for five hundred dollars. Mrs. Ridley's brother was not completely at ease about the purchase, even though the seller was his sister. He took the same precautions that any purchaser would. He bought George only after three doctors examined him and gave him a clean bill of health.[49]

Slave sales involving women might also remain obscure if the sales were rescinded. Martha Organ's mistress "Missus Jones" sold her slave Alice to a female neighbor, but she questioned her decision when she learned of her neighbor's brutal conduct toward the enslaved girl. Whenever Alice became cold while performing her work, Missus Jones had permitted her to come inside and warm herself by the fire. Alice assumed that her new owner would allow her to do the same thing. But, according to Organ, Alice's new mistress "made her stand fore de fire till her legs burned so bad dat de skin cracked up an' some of it drapped off." When Missus Jones found out, "she give de 'oman back her money an' took Alice home wid her."[50] Smokey Eulenberg's slave-owning mistress tried to sell his mother and siblings to "a sassy old woman" named Mrs. Sheppard who lived in their community, but the sale fell through for reasons Eulenberg made readily apparent: "I rec'lect one time missus sold my mother and four children but it wasn't no trade. . . . She [the buyer] come into my mother's cabin and grabbed her and told her she [was] going to take her home. Mother jes' pushed her out de door and said she wouldn't go—and she told missus she wouldn't go—so dey had to call it off—it was no trade."[51] In this instance, two women came together to buy and sell slaves, and they deemed themselves capable of executing the sale on their own. However, neither of them seemed prepared for a determined and resistant enslaved woman who stood between them and the sale they hoped to finalize.

White men also transacted privately with women who hoped to sell their slaves. In a letter to his acquaintance St. George Tucker, Sir Peyton Skipwith wrote about a woman named Mrs. Dunbar who owned several "excellent servants." Skipwith believed that there was some probability that she might be moving from Virginia to Philadelphia or New York, and "she had determined to sell all of her black servants" if she did. Skipwith was especially interested in buying an enslaved man who served as her cook. The man who told Skipwith about Mrs. Dunbar's cook spoke of the enslaved man's "abilities & good condition," and since Skipwith was "in want" of a servant like him, he asked St. George Tucker to buy the cook on his behalf "upon the best terms" possible. He was willing to pay Mrs. Dunbar 150 pounds for him.[52] Skipwith was writing to Tucker from his plantation in Clarksville, Virginia, so he was probably too far away from Mrs. Dunbar to handle the transaction himself. But he knew that he could entrust the deal to a local friend. Whether male or female, none of the participants in these sales needed to go to a slave market because through networks of family and friends and via written and verbal communication they learned about a slave owner's willingness to dispose of the enslaved people he or she owned.

White slave-owning women also negotiated with enslaved people who hoped to buy their freedom or the liberty of their loved ones, sales that constituted another aspect of slave-market activities. These transactions reveal how white women used their slave-market savvy to bargain with enslaved people while profiting from the transactions that took place in their households and on their estates.

Formerly enslaved people offered countless examples of mistresses who bargained with them for their freedom or the liberty of loved ones. These transactions offered slave-owning women and enslaved people opportunities to acquire detailed knowledge about the slave-market economy and the region's financial structure more generally, and they may have served as preparation for more sophisticated fiscal dealings later. Historians who acknowledge that some white slave-owning women were astute in financial and commercial matters often contend that these women developed these skills out of necessity and they rarely suggest that transactions with enslaved people might have been instrumental in helping women acquire those skills.[53] Faced with the death of a husband or father, a fiscally inept spouse, war, or destitution, white slave-owning women quickly learned how to protect their assets and their families' financial well-being.

It is crucial to recognize that, as human property that was exchanged, bought, sold, hired, and parceled out among white southerners, enslaved people were not simply objects of sale or potential liquidation; they took an active interest in the market processes to which they were subjected and acquired extensive financial knowledge as a consequence. The slave market in all its aspects was a pervasive feature of enslaved African Americans' daily lives, and their direct and indirect encounters with three dimensions of the slave-market economy—slave auctions and sales, inheritance or debt collection, and self-purchase—offered opportunities to learn about credit, debt, and contracts; allowed them to engage in financial negotiations; and taught them to develop strategies for fiscal management. They calculated their own value, established the price for their freedom, decided terms of payment, and worked until they reached their financial goal. These financial calculations and dealings challenge us to rethink the intellectual and economic relationships between slavery and freedom for African Americans in the nineteenth century and the roles white slave-owning women played in the process.

While most southern states prohibited enslaved people from entering into legally binding contracts, enslaved people consistently struck financial deals with their mistresses and potential allies in hope of purchasing their freedom. Although slave-owning women were not bound by law in most southern states to honor the particularities of these negotiations, their transactions were contractual by definition, with important exceptions. In French colonial Louisiana, slaves were forbidden to enter into contracts, but Louisiana's Code Noir recognized that, despite this prohibition, slave owners continued to strike bargains with slaves who wanted to buy their freedom. Fearing that slaves might attempt to secure the funds to buy their freedom through dishonest means, the Code Noir required slave owners to obtain a "decree of permission" allowing the slaves to buy themselves. The Code Noir thus legitimated these agreements.

And through a system called *coartación*, Spanish colonial Louisiana also pro-vided enslaved people with a legal means by which to contract for and buy their freedom, even if their owners refused to let them. Enslaved people clearly took advantage of the opportunities such laws and systems presented because, as noted by historian Jennifer Spear, the slaves who became free via the system of coartación "accounted for half of all manumissions in Spanish New Orleans."[54] This also means that enslaved people's male and female owners had to at least be cursorily familiar with these laws, too.

Enslaved people who decided to purchase their freedom understood how their status as property shaped the ways in which they could expect to rely upon the state, or local courts, to protect their financial interests as they worked to secure the funds with which to do so. Lunsford Lane knew exactly what risks he faced when he negotiated with his mistress to purchase his liberty because he was her property by law: "*Legally*, my money belonged to my mistress; and she could have taken it and refused to grant me my freedom." Lane's experience with his mistress explicitly reveals the ways the slave market might have helped him *and* his mistress determine his value and how the economy of the slave market permeated their negotiations:

> After paying my mistress for my time, and rendering such support as was necessary to my family, I found in the space of some six or eight years, that I had collected the sum of one thousand dollars. I kept my money hid, never venturing to put out a penny, and never let anybody but my wife know that I was making any. *The thousand dollars was what I supposed my mistress would ask for me, and so I determined now what I would do.* I went to my mistress and inquired what was her price for me. She said a thousand dollars. I then told her that I wanted to be free, and asked her if she would sell me to be made free. She said she would; and accordingly I arranged with her, and with the master of my wife, Mr. Smith . . . for the latter to take my money and buy of her my freedom, as I could not legally purchase it, and as the laws forbid emancipation, except for "meritorious services." [emphasis mine][55]

Lane was able to negotiate with his mistress for his freedom not simply because she was benevolent but because he offered her a competitive price, one that she could demand of any buyer if she had chosen to sell him in the slave market instead. The fact that his mistress settled upon the same sum he did implies that she too was attuned to the value of her slaves, and perhaps Lane became privy to this information when she sold her other slaves or while hired out to various individuals in his community. Enslaved people developed a keen understand-ing of their value in the market, and they sometimes used that information to facilitate their own sale. They conducted such negotiations to find and secure kind masters, or to keep their families intact. Enslaved people gleaned significant information about their own value, the particulars of the slave-buying process—especially the qualities, skills, and character slave buyers sought in the market—and details about local slaveholding cultures. While being coached by slave traders and examined by potential owners, they also assessed the character of the individuals who hoped to buy them and acquired the knowledge to "shape their own sale." Slave buyers paid particular attention to the sex of the slaves they hoped to purchase, and enslaved women possessed skills, qualities, and abilities that prospective buyers valued highly. Enslaved people recognized this fact, and they promoted those skills in their efforts to keep their families together, even in the slave market.[56]

Formerly enslaved people's testimony suggests that they developed their financial knowledge long before they reached the market, and they used that information to create a very different kind of slave-market transaction from the ones white southerners might have envisioned. They established and negotiated the terms upon which they could purchase and secure their freedom. Drawing upon the same information owners used to calculate the profits of a potential slave sale—skills, character, sex, and appraised market value—enslaved people bought themselves and their loved ones and thereby ensured that they would never have to enter the slave marketplace again.

These transactions did not always go the way enslaved people hoped, however. They came to realize that, despite considering every factor that might determine whether their female owners would accept their offers to purchase their liberty, their mistresses could renege on such agreements or reject their proposals outright. An enslaved man named Henry negotiated the terms upon which he would buy his freedom from his mistress, and paid nearly the full amount they agreed upon, but Henry's mistress sold him to a slave dealer anyway. When Dred Scott decided to purchase his freedom and that of his wife and children, he was unable to offer his mistress, Irene Emerson, full payment. He approached her and proposed to give her a down payment and pay the rest in installments. He even secured a reputable "co-signor," who vouched for him and was willing to ensure that Scott would fulfill his agreement. Emerson rejected his offer, and as the eventual consequence of her decision, the nation throughout 1856–1857 watched one of the most important U.S. Supreme Court cases defining the relationship between race and citizenship unfold.[57]

Charity Bowery, who resided on the Pembroke plantation, about three miles from Edenton, North Carolina, repeatedly tried to buy her children from her mistress. Her mistress not only rejected each of her offers, she later sold five of

Bowery's children to slave traders. In one instance, Bowery's mistress sent her on an errand that required her to remain away from home for an extensive time, and when she returned, her "mistress was counting a heap of bills in her lap." Bowery knew that something was wrong because she saw her daughter crying while she stood behind her mistress's chair as she "counted the money—ten dollars—twenty dollars—fifty dollars . . ." At first, she did not understand the reason for her daughter's tears, but her little girl eventually "pointed to mistress' lap, and said, 'Broder's money! Broder's money!'" When Bowery asked her mistress whether she had sold yet another one of her five children, her mistress proclaimed, "'Yes Charity; and I got a great price for him!'" By Bowery's estimation, her mistress was "a rich woman" who "rolled in gold"; she did not need to sell slaves to sustain her livelihood, nor did she urgently need the money that she gained from their sale.[58]

Within the confines of her household, Charity Bowery's mistress thought about selling, and finally did sell, her slaves to men who traded in human flesh. It was here, in the household, that Bowery approached her and attempted to negotiate a price at which to buy her children and establish the terms of payment for them. It was also here that this slave-owning woman calculated the value of those human beings and repeatedly rejected offers for their freedom because "she thought she could find a better market" in which to sell them. White women in the South understood the darkest dimensions of the market in people firsthand, and the transactions that took place in their own homes and among their friends and family equipped them to initiate and finalize their own within and outside formal slave marketplaces.

—————•—▪—•—————

5

"WET NURSE FOR SALE OR HIRE"

On a rather ordinary day, a woman named Mrs. Girardeau was strolling the streets of Charleston, South Carolina, when she suddenly came upon a "good natured healthy looking Negro woman . . . with an infant in her arms." Mrs. Girardeau happened to know of a friend who was in search of a woman to nurse her baby, so she approached the woman and asked if she "knew of a wet nurse to be hired." The enslaved woman immediately told Mrs. Girardeau that "she was one herself and was in the hands of a broker for sale." The enslaved woman also told her that she had given birth to "many children," and she was "therefore somewhat experienced in the care of them." Mrs. Girardeau relayed this information to her friend, and the new mother, her husband, and the couple's agents immediately arranged to purchase the enslaved mother and her infant.[1]

Through parlor talk, or perhaps by a passing mention in a letter from a friend, Mrs. Girardeau had learned that a mother was in need of an enslaved woman to suckle her baby, and she was able to assist in finding one. Everything that Mrs. Girardeau did that day—approaching and questioning the enslaved woman about her qualifications to perform a certain kind of labor, determining that she would be suitable for that purpose, and passing along the information that would facilitate the purchase—characterized the typical transactions that unfolded every day in slave marketplaces throughout the South. And like many of those sales and purchases, this transaction did not start in the brick-and-mortar slave market. It began in a southern household, moved into the street, was finalized in a slave trader's establishment, and ended with an enslaved woman moving to a new slaveholder's home to breastfeed a white child.

As this incident suggests, white women, especially mothers, were instrumental in these kinds of market transactions. They routinely sought out and procured enslaved wet nurses to suckle their children, creating a demand for the intimate labor that such nurses performed in southern homes. They were crucial to the further commodification of enslaved women's reproductive bodies, through the appropriation of their breast milk and the nutritive and maternal care they provided to white children. The demand among slave-owning women for enslaved wet nurses transformed the ability to suckle into a skilled form of labor, and created a largely invisible niche sector of the slave market that catered exclusively to white women.

The intersection between slave markets and southern households can shed light on the formal as well as informal markets through which enslaved mothers circulated. It also enables us to examine white women's investments in these markets and the roles they played in creating them. And such an exploration reveals details about southern slavery which challenge characterizations of skilled enslaved labor as largely performed by men.

The labor that enslaved wet nurses performed remains relatively invisible in historical studies of American slave markets and scholarship about southern motherhood. When scholars do address the issue, they discuss these women in ways that do not fully account for how they circulated within southern households, communities, and the slave market. Even though white mothers routinely sought out and procured enslaved wet nurses to suckle their children, scholars of the slave market and trade generally ignore the roles they played in the transaction. A recent study contends that it was white men who were largely responsible for converting enslaved women's breast milk into "capital."[2] The consensus among historians holds that white elite and middle-class mothers tended to use enslaved wet nurses only as a last resort, not because they were readily available.[3] Sally McMillen, for example, quantified infant feeding practices for the years 1800–1860 and found only seventy-three comments about the subject in her selected sources, which were primarily elite women's diaries and personal correspondence. She concluded that 20 percent of these women used wet nurses. She also argued that enslaved women rarely attested to serving as wet nurses, and she pointed to this as further evidence that white women rarely used them in this way.[4] Such a small sample of documents, however, particularly those that well-to-do, literate women left behind, does not tell us much about the practice among the non-elite white women who made up the female majority living in the South during this period. Many formerly enslaved people, not just enslaved women, remarked upon white mothers' use of enslaved wet nurses, and they used a range of terms—"nuss," "suckle," "titty"—to describe wet nursing in their testimony. They also used the term "breast" interchangeably or along with these terms. A more nuanced examination of their testimony that includes all the WPA interviews—rather than simply the interviews with women who personally served as wet nurses—and that bears their more complex terminology in mind, reveals that enslaved people talked about the practice of wet nursing far more often than McMillen claimed. Even when they described enslaved women serving as "nurses" to white infants, they made it clear to their interviewers that wet nursing was the kind of nursing about which they spoke.

It is equally important to acknowledge that the questionnaire that the WPA's National Advisor on Folklore and Folkways developed did not include any questions about slave owners' maternal or parenting practices, nor did it include specific questions about the practice of wet nursing. This might explain why a formerly enslaved person would neglect to mention the practice in an interview.[5] The alleged scarcity of such testimony might also be explained by the fact that the WPA writers interviewed only about 2 percent of the formerly enslaved people who were still alive in the 1930s.[6] It is likely that formerly enslaved people neglected to mention wet nurses or wet nursing during their interviews because the nature of the questions did not goad them to do so, and a larger sample of formerly enslaved interviewees would have produced more references to the practice if the writers had been able to locate these people and record their testimony.

In the nineteenth century, the use of enslaved African American wet nurses by white southern women was troubling to outsiders, and to some southerners as well.[7] However, their discomfort did not arise because wet nursing was an unusual practice. Mothers have placed their infants at the breasts of other women since antiquity.[8] Moreover, in her study of the cultural significance of nursing and infant caregiving in early modern England and British North America, Marylynn Salmon discovered that people of European descent used breast milk for a host of medicinal purposes because they believed that it "possessed a life-giving force."[9] In this way, the milk that mothers produced served a communal good. Whether this assumption characterized how Anglo-Americans understood *enslaved* women's breast milk in the eighteenth century is unclear. What is clear, however, is that by the nineteenth century, Anglo-Americans had grown increasingly concerned about the power of bodily fluids and a child's ability to imbibe moral and racial essences through a woman's breast milk. Fears of contamination served as the basis for stern warnings to new mothers about putting their babies at the breasts of strange women. Medical professionals and authors of maternal and infant advice literature strongly encouraged mothers to assume complete responsibility for nursing their own children. They cautioned them against delegating this task to other women or feeding their infants by bottle and other "unnatural" methods. And they summarily shamed mothers who chose not to take their advice.[10]

Such attitudes are particularly important when considering the matter of cross-racial and cross-ethnic wet nursing. In the nineteenth century, as the United States witnessed unparalleled waves of European immigration, and as nativist fears influenced the attitudes of American-born whites toward the people entering the country's major urban centers, male physicians and "scientists" embraced this problematic understanding of breast milk with renewed fervor. They cautioned American-born white mothers against sending their children to immigrant women to nurse because breast milk served as a means by which women passed their traits on to their infants.[11] The association between breast milk and moral and physiological contagion spread throughout the South and faced southerners with a peculiar paradox: if breast milk carried the racial and moral essence of the lactating mother, and African Americans were morally and biologically inferior beings, what would be the fate of the white children who suckled at the breasts of the enslaved? Many white southern women thought of their own fragile health, which prevented them from nursing or producing an adequate milk supply, and decided that using a wet nurse was essential, regardless of their repulsion. Other white southerners decided that the bound condition of enslaved wet nurses was the problem, not their race. A formerly enslaved man named John Van Hook claimed that in the part of Georgia where he resided, "It was considered a disgrace for a white child to feed at the breast of a slave woman, but it was all right if the darkey was a free woman." John's great-great-grandmother Sarah Angel earned her freedom because of this aversion. A member of the Angel family needed a wet nurse, and since Sarah Angel was nursing a child of her own, the family chose to use her. They did not want Sarah to sleep in the slave quarters while she was feeding the white baby, so they freed her.[12]

Most slave owners were not so generous. On some plantations, like the one where Peggy Sloan was raised, slave owners "had a woman to look after the little colored children, and they had one to look after the white children." Sloan's owners charged her enslaved mother with wet nursing the white infants, though despite the racial division in maternal care, her mother *was* permitted to suckle her along with her mistress's children. The owners did not free Sloan's mother so that she could perform this labor, however.[13]

White southern mothers grappled with the paradox of cross-racial wet nursing by prioritizing the health of their infants over all else and subordinating the needs of enslaved women and their children in the process. These white women were instrumental in creating a market for enslaved wet nurses' labor. In doing

so, they helped augment the potential value of enslaved women within southern slave markets more broadly.

    While white mothers routinely expressed a desire to nurse their own children,
many were ill or too weak following childbirth and could not nurse or could do
so only with great difficulty.[14] Newspapers targeted women who experienced
those difficulties with advertisements like the one captioned "Sore and Swelled
Breasts" that appeared in the *Ripley Advertiser*: "Since the invention of Bragg's
Arctic Liniment," the ad proclaimed, mothers no longer were obliged "to transfer
their infant children to the care of a wet nurse," if their own breasts "should be
sore or swollen": "All that is necessary, is to procure some of Bragg's Arctic
Liniment and rub the affected parts with it, gently, for a few times, and the evil is
remedied."[15] Esther Cox, a white South Carolina matron who frequently corresponded with her daughters after they gave birth, advised them on what to do
when their bouts of weakness, ailments affecting their breasts, or their infants'
seeming unwillingness to nurse made it difficult to breastfeed. She recommended
that her daughter Mary apply a salve to her hardened breasts, a treatment that
proved to be a "fine remedy" for another woman experiencing similar problems
nursing her infant. However, after a year, Mary still struggled to nurse her child.[16]
    Blocked milk ducts and breast infections could endanger the lives of nursing
mothers. Such complications could even require a surgical intervention that
involved removing portions of the breast.[17] Faced with these circumstances,
women often had little choice but to call upon other women, who were often
enslaved, to care for their infants, a practice referred to as "mercenary nursing"
in nineteenth-century Brazil.[18]
    Formerly enslaved people described the circumstances that would lead a
white mother to use an enslaved wet nurse for her children, and their recollections support the argument that some white women were too ill or physically
unable to nurse their infants following childbirth. As white mothers recovered
from the effects of childbirth, enslaved women provided nutritive care to their
infants.[19] Other white mothers could not nurse their own children because of
insufficient milk production or because their infants could not suckle.[20] But
maternal unfitness or fractious infants alone did not explain the prevalence of
enslaved wet nurses among white southern families.
    Formerly enslaved people such as Rachel Sullivan claimed that the use of
enslaved wet nurses for white infants was a widespread practice. According to
Sullivan, "All de white ladies had wet nusses un dem days." Betty Curlett
believed that other women used wet nurses for purely aesthetic reasons: "White
women wouldn't nurse their own babies cause it would make their breast fall."

Some white mothers, such as Jane Petigru, cited convenience: she had a "distaste for" breastfeeding her own infants because it made her "a slave" to her children.[21] Her reluctance becomes more understandable in light of the number of children southern mothers bore in the eighteenth and nineteenth centuries. Historians estimate that women in the Old South on average gave birth to between five and twelve living children during their lifetimes.[22] Formerly enslaved people described their own mothers being tasked with feeding all their mistresses' children even when nothing prevented their mistresses from doing so themselves. Mary Jane Jones claimed that her mother "would have a baby every time my mistress would have one so that my mother was always the wet nurse for my mistress." Eugenia Woodberry breastfed all of her mistress's children, too.[23] Mattie Logan recalled that her mother, Lucinda, "nursed all Miss Jennie's children because all of her young ones and my mammy's was born so close together." Logan thought this arrangement was "a pretty good idea for the Mistress, for it didn't keep her tied to the place and she could visit around with her friends most any time she wanted 'thout having to worry if the babies would be fed or not." In order to expedite this labor arrangement, Lucinda's mistress had a two-room cabin built behind the main house, away from the other slave quarters, for Lucinda and her family.[24]

The practice of using enslaved women as wet nurses placed increasing physical demands on them. Enslaved mothers were generally deprived of adequate food and nutrients to support and sustain their own health, much less that of two or three babies, and white mothers dealt with this difficulty as they might any other household problem. The slave owner Ella Gertrude Thomas used a number of enslaved wet nurses to feed her children, and when one woman could not produce enough milk for Thomas's infant and her own, she would replace her.[25]

As this testimony suggests, in some households, breastfeeding simply constituted another form of labor that slave owners required enslaved women to perform. For Warren Taylor's mother, nursing white children was one of her primary jobs. Nursing white children was the *only* work that Mary Kincheon Edwards performed during slavery.[26] These recollections make it clear that enslaved women were giving birth on a routine basis. But what often remains unexplored is what led to these constant conceptions. While enslaved women performed the most arduous forms of labor in their owners' fields and households, they also had to conceive, carry a pregnancy to full term, give birth, and lactate in order to be able to serve as wet nurses. Sources suggest that this is precisely what happened. Some of the enslaved women's children were undoubtedly conceived within relationships of love, but others were undoubtedly the result of sexual assault.

John Street was a married slave owner who also ran a business in which he held slaves and then sold them to slave dealers. Louisa Street, one of the enslaved women he owned, conceived three children by him: Amy Elizabeth Patterson and her twin sisters Fannie and Martha. Street's wife gave birth to an infant around the same time that Amy Elizabeth was born. In her interview, Patterson alluded to the fact that she was a child born of violence and that her mistress "knew the facts" surrounding her conception. Despite this knowledge, her mistress gave her white child to Louisa to nurse alongside Patterson, a decision that must have added to the psychological trauma Louisa Street suffered after the rape.[27]

Mary Kincheon Edwards, formerly enslaved woman who served as a wet nurse (*Born in Slavery: Slave Narratives from the Federal Writers' Project, 1936–1938*, Digital Collection, Library of Congress, Manuscript Division)

Similarly, Emily Haidee, a white Louisiana woman who owned Henrietta Butler, forced Butler to have sex with a man on her plantation. The assault perpetrated against Butler resulted in pregnancy, and she gave birth to the child, who died shortly thereafter. While she mourned the loss of her baby, Haidee made Butler suckle her own infant.[28] Violence, loss, and separation often characterized the experiences of enslaved mothers who were compelled to serve as wet nurses to their owners' children.

Many white southern mothers seized upon the chance to develop their maternal bond with their infants by nursing them. Others employed enslaved wet nurses routinely, not simply as a last resort, even though they knew that other white southerners were averse to, if tolerant of, the practice. Ellen Vaden's enslaved mother nursed both her and her mistress's infant son Tobe. But "when they had company, Miss Luisa was so modest she wouldn't let Tobe have 'titty.' He would come lead my mother behind the door and pull at her till she would take him and let him nurse." This incident lays bare some of the ways in which white children came to understand the social mores of slave-owning communities. Tobe was young enough to nurse, but old enough to understand that suckling at an enslaved woman's breast in public or in the presence of company was unacceptable.[29]

While some white mothers, like "Miss Luisa," hid their reliance upon enslaved wet nurses from their friends and neighbors because of modesty or communal mores, others were not so bashful. Rachel Sullivan's owners allowed a white mother visiting from Russia to use her aunt as a wet nurse while she stayed on their plantation. Sullivan knew about this firsthand because her owners made her serve as the dry nurse to her infant cousin in her aunt's absence.[30]

Formerly enslaved people's remembrances do more than merely affirm that white mothers used enslaved wet nurses or touch on the motives behind their decisions. It is no minor point that the children and grandchildren of enslaved wet nurses offered much of the testimony about the practice, for they were the individuals most deeply affected by these women's constant absences or, in some cases, complete separation from their children. The people who owned T. W. Cotton and his family, for example, compelled his mother to nurse their infant son Walter. Her work left Cotton in the care of his grandmother, who fed him animal milk or pap from a bottle, a dangerous practice that many physicians strongly discouraged at the time.[31] Formerly enslaved people spoke of the painful separations of nursing mothers from their enslaved kin, and although these severances did not occur in formal slave markets, the marketplace nevertheless shaped them.

Historians have also examined the commodification of maternal labor and the wet nurse marketplaces in the United States, but their studies focus primarily upon markets in the North rather than the South. Such studies are nonetheless useful for understanding the contours of the southern wet nurse marketplace and identifying key differences between the markets in these two regions. The historian Janet Golden describes an informal northern market in which white parents would seek out and procure wet nurses by word of mouth through familial and communal networks. She also uncovered an urban "marketplace": a labor network in the North in which free white women—often poor immigrants, single mothers, or "wayward" or "fallen" women—were the primary providers. This marketplace was particularly active from the 1850s to the 1870s. It depended upon medical referrals and employment recommendations and involved a number of public facilities, intelligence offices, and benevolent organizations that gradually institutionalized the use of wet nurses and offered these women's services to parents of all social classes. It was largely organized by "patterns of immigration, ethnic stereotypes, and racial prejudice, as well as medical thinking and local domestic practices."[32]

Golden argues that "the wet nurse marketplace . . . responded not only to the creation of new sources of supply but also to shifting levels of demand," and newspapers proved crucial to recruitment. In a review of northern newspaper advertisements, she identified a distinct vocabulary that characterized the wet nurse marketplace, one that served as a "kind of shorthand" and "combined the vernaculars of medicine and domestic service." It "emphasized four qualities: good health, upstanding character, plentiful milk, and milk that was fresh," and individuals incorporated such phrases when they placed ads for their ideal wet nurses.[33] Wet nurse advertisements "exposed the real economic value of mothers as producers" because "employment of a wet nurse provided needed income for poor mothers," while "for middle-class and elite families, the hiring of a wet nurse replaced the productivity of the mother."[34] In the South, the use of enslaved wet nurses' bodies and the circulation of these women through the region's slave markets present other ways to understand the economic dimensions of maternal labor in the nineteenth century.

In the context of slavery, the southern wet nurse marketplace operated differently from the northern one. The institution of slavery permitted slave owners, slave traders, and prospective hirers and buyers to manipulate and examine the bodies of enslaved women in ways that were unavailable to white parents in the North. Many laws regarding slavery allowed owners to ignore an enslaved mother's desire to nurse and raise her own children. And white southern women were among those who took full advantage of their access to enslaved women's bodies and labor. These women were instrumental in creating a market for enslaved wet nurses, determining how such women would be employed, and seeking them out within and beyond the walls of the slave yard.

Southern women constructed and participated in an informal market network of family and friends from within their own homes, and they relied on this network for information about enslaved wet nurses who might be available. The market was informal in the sense that it was contingent upon the circulation of wet nurses largely outside the brick-and-mortar slave market, and it did not usually involve the exchange of currency, although money did occasionally change hands. Rather, this informal market resembled other female-dominated systems of barter and exchange that characterized early American households.

It was common practice for women in the North and the South to support their families by bartering and exchanging home-produced goods and foodstuffs with other women in their communities, and in similar ways, white women routinely borrowed enslaved people from and lent them to one another.[35] They were in essence bartering and exchanging enslaved wet nurses as living goods, and in this context, enslaved mothers could be transferred from one person to another without diminishing their value in the formal slave market. Unlike other barter exchanges, these white women did not "produce" enslaved wet nurses through their own labor, but they did claim ownership of their bodies and the products of wet nurses' labor—their breast milk. The narratives of enslaved people and slave-owning women's personal letters and diaries attest to the existence of this informal market. And its informality has generally obscured it from historians' view.[36]

An advertisement that Sophia Young submitted to the *Federal Gazette & Baltimore Daily Advertiser* suggests another possible reason this market has escaped our attention. Young was a midwife who practiced her craft in the Baltimore, Maryland, area, and in her ad she notified potential clients that she had relocated. She also wanted them to know that "a good Wet Nurse [could] be heard of by applying to her." Midwives were the principal individuals involved in women's and infants' care during childbirth in the colonial era and much of the nineteenth century, and they offered their clients medical advice and passed on pertinent information about childcare. Young's aside about the availability of "a good Wet Nurse" suggests that this kind of information might have circulated among other midwives and the mothers they assisted, obviating the need to advertise for such help.[37]

The women who supplied enslaved wet nurses capitalized on their informal connections in order to procure other kinds of enslaved laborers, as we can see from a case involving two Saint Landry Parish, Louisiana, residents. During the summer of 1827, Elizabeth Patterson hired out an enslaved woman named Becky to George Jackson's wife as a wet nurse for her young son. Patterson initially offered Becky's services "gratuitously" because the enslaved woman "was of no use" to her. Patterson reasoned that by hiring Becky to the Jacksons, she would be spared the expense of caring for her. Mrs. Jackson apparently informed her husband about the proposal, but he "was unwilling to accept the services . . . without paying for them." Mrs. Jackson went to Patterson's plantation the following day, and Patterson once again proposed that she take the enslaved woman, whom she agreed to hire out "for six or seven dollars per month." Mrs. Jackson and her husband accepted the offer. After Patterson finalized the deal with the Jacksons, she in turn hired three enslaved men from them to work her sugar plantation during the 1827 and 1828 grinding seasons.[38] These negotiations illustrate how slave-related transactions might unfold outside the formal marketplace. They also highlight the roles white women, especially new mothers, played on both ends of these transactions. Moreover, they underscore the equivalence between field and maternal labor, two kinds of work that are often categorized quite differently, and the value slave owners placed on each. Here, we could say that the labor of one wet nurse was considered equivalent to that of three field hands.

There were parallels between the formal wet nurse marketplaces in the North and South, but there were also important divergences. Whereas the formal wet nurse marketplace of the North involved agencies and organizations that profited from the labor of free white women, advertisements posted in southern newspapers establish direct connections between the wet nurse marketplace and the slave market. As the historian Frederic Bancroft observed, the "slave wet nurse was a peculiar but not rare commodity," and "she could, if buxom, spare one ample breast for the profit of her owner." Furthermore, if she was "of good character and appearance, she was at a premium."[39]

Thousands of advertisements for wet nurses appeared in southern newspapers throughout the late eighteenth and the nineteenth centuries. In a sample of fifty-seven nineteenth-century newspapers published in Alabama, Washington, D.C., Maryland, Virginia, Louisiana, Kentucky, Georgia, South Carolina, North Carolina, Florida, Missouri, Mississippi, and Tennessee, individuals placed 1,322 advertisements for wet nurses between 1800 and 1865. In close to 300 of those advertisements, individuals placed "Wet Nurse Wanted" or "Wet Nurse Wanted Immediately" advertisements, wording which highlights the demand and often urgent need for these women's labor. In these ads slave owners and potential hirers actively sought out "colored," "negro," and enslaved women within slave-hiring markets throughout the South.

These advertisements also reveal the vibrant hiring market that white southerners created in order to fulfill the demand for enslaved women's maternal labor. Women were key to defining the contours of this market because they were ultimately responsible for deciding which wet nurses would best serve their infants' needs; they were the primary hirers and the only laborers. Yet many historians still describe the southern slave-hiring marketplace as a male purview.[40]

Women entered slave-hiring markets to obtain both enslaved wet nurses and other kinds of enslaved laborers. In the small town of Mount Sterling, Kentucky, the buying, selling, and hiring of enslaved people took place at ten o'clock in the morning on New Year's Day.[41] This was a highly public family and community affair in which the sale, purchase, and hire of enslaved people took place among "throngs" of men, women, and children. Such transactions were not confined to or bound within the slave yard; some took place in the streets. The people who "flocked from various parts of the country" represented every stratum of society, including African Americans, and attendees represented all age groups. As the author and educator William Henry Venable walked through the crowd, he overheard one enslaved woman express dismay about the white woman who had just agreed to hire her. She was crying because it had "fallen to her lot to serve a mistress whom she feared." Venable's account not only suggests that women were present at public events where enslaved people were hired and sold, it also reveals that they were active participants. What is more, this enslaved woman's lamentations indicate that her new mistress may have routinely hired enslaved people because she had acquired a reputation among slaves for being difficult to please, or even cruel, and they circulated this knowledge among themselves.[42]

While the southern market in enslaved wet nurses was primarily a hiring one, white mothers' demands for these women eventually led to the development of a niche sector of the slave market in which individuals offered wet nurses for sale. Men such as Robert Hill and firms like R. M. Montgomery and Company also sought out enslaved wet nurses to purchase for their families or on their clients' behalf. On two separate occasions, Brian Cape and Company offered enslaved women and their children for sale and noted the mothers' ability to serve as wet nurses. Even when the nation was in the throes of civil war, J. W. Jordan, Sr., of Renwick, Georgia, placed an advertisement in the *Macon Daily Telegraph* through which he sought to "buy or hire" a "young, healthy, and intelligent" enslaved wet nurse. Other advertisements informed interested subscribers that they could buy *or* hire the enslaved wet nurses mentioned.[43]

Slave traders were responsible for placing most of the advertisements related to selling, rather than hiring, enslaved wet nurses. The well-known New Orleans slave trader James W. Boazman placed an advertisement in the *Daily Crescent* in which he offered "a wet nurse, about nineteen years of age, with her second child" for sale. He planned to sell them both at a "low [price] for cash, fully guarantied"—that is, they were free of any ailments that might impair their function or value. Hundreds of miles away in Charleston, South Carolina, the slave-trading firm Capers and Heyward placed an advertisement in the *Mercury* in which they offered an enslaved wet nurse for private purchase.[44] Male slave traders may have dominated these advertisements as the purveyors of enslaved wet nurses, but they placed them with an eye toward a female clientele.

As in the northern marketplace, individuals in the southern market emphasized good health, upstanding character, and plentiful, fresh milk when they sought or offered the services of enslaved wet nurses. A typical advertisement, for example, would request "a healthy Negro woman, with a fresh breast of milk, to suckle and nurse an infant child."[45] But one important difference distinguished the language used in the southern marketplace from that in the North. Southern

FOR SALE—A Wet Nurse, about nineteen years of age, with her second child, six weeks old, will be sold low for cash, fully guarantied. Also—A first-rate Seamstress, who can cut out and fit well. Also—Several first-rate House Servants, Mechanics and Field Hands. Those who wish to purchase would do well to call on the undersigned before buying elsewhere.
d19 tw*   J. W. BOAZMAN, 157 Gravier st.

Wet nurse ad submitted by slave trader J. W. Boazman, *Daily Crescent*, December 21, 1850 (*Chronicling America: Historic American Newspapers*, Library of Congress)

Private Sales.

Healthy Young Wet Nurse.

Capers & Heyward

Offer at private sale, a young and healthy WET NURSE. For further particulars, apply at our office, SOUTH SIDE ADGERS' WHARF.
June 7   smw3

Capers and Heyward newspaper ad for private sale of enslaved wet nurse, *Charleston Mercury*, June 7, 1856 (Nineteenth-Century U.S. Newspapers database, Cengage/Gale)

advertisers not only used the vernaculars of medicine and domestic service to describe their "wares," they drew upon the lexicon of the slave market.

Terms such as "likely," "good," "excellent," and "superior," and phrases like "first rate" and "No. 1," allowed slave traders to assign value to the bodies of the individuals they advertised by placing these slaves within "saleable lots." They also enabled slave dealers to place enslaved people in racial categories, and the terms and phrases they used came to signify the ideal characteristics prospective buyers sought in enslaved people. Traders often emphasized that the enslaved people they hoped to sell were "sound" in mind and body and were thereby healthy and free from injury or disease. The characters and personal histories of enslaved people were equally important factors to those selecting them.[46]

When white southerners were in the market for enslaved wet nurses or when ordinary folks hoped to sell them they used the terminology of the slave market. Thomas Theiner, for example, placed an advertisement in the *Charleston Mercury* that offered "a likely COLORED WET NURSE, 17 years old" for hire. A Richmond area agent and collector named O. H. Chalkley announced that he had a "superior wet nurse" who was of "first rate character" on hand for anyone interested. Other southerners sought wet nurses who were "neat and sound in body and reputation."[47] None of these qualifiers or phrases would strike southerners as strange, especially in regard to buying or hiring enslaved laborers. The individuals who placed these ads also understood that white mothers would be equally familiar with these terms and phrases as well as with their coded meaning.

In the context of southern slave markets, enslaved mothers' breast milk was a commodity that could be bought and sold, and buyers and sellers recognized these women's ability to suckle as a form of largely invisible yet skilled labor. The conception of what constituted "skilled labor" in general use among scholars is far too narrow to account for the kind of work that enslaved women performed or the prices they commanded when exposed for sale. Furthermore, it does not take into account the computational logic white southerners used to assign value to certain types of labor or the ways gender shaped their appraisals. Georgia slave owners not only assigned significant value to the kinds of labor women performed every day—work that historians do not typically define as "skilled"—they differentiated among levels of skill in their routine tasks and appraised the value of enslaved women accordingly.[48] Wet nursing was a kind of work that only women could perform, and more often than not white mothers were the ones who assessed enslaved mothers' levels of skill and efficiency. As with other kinds of labor, breastfeeding required certain qualifications and skills: women had to be physically capable of nursing children, they had to learn how to breastfeed, and they needed to refine their skills over time. Some mothers could not nurse children, and some were more adept at it than others. This might prove especially true when we consider the impact of environmental factors such as diet, previous illness, or problems during pregnancy. All these factors could adversely impact an enslaved woman's long-term health, her ability to produce plentiful milk supplies and avoid medical conditions associated with nursing such as mastitis, and ultimately, her ability to be an effective wet nurse. Historians who view nursing a child as "natural" rather than a form of skilled labor ignore the view of the white mothers who sought the services of enslaved wet nurses, of the enslaved mothers themselves, and of the men and women who sold and hired out enslaved mothers for this purpose, all of whom most certainly saw it as such. Individuals in need of a wet nurse often sought enslaved women who had previous experience breastfeeding white children, and southerners who had such women to sell or hire made sure to remark upon their experience in their advertisements. In a number of such advertisements, owners indicated that the enslaved mothers they sought to hire out were "accustomed to attending to white children," were "well experienced in that line" of work, had served as wet nurses "in the most genteel families," or had previously "given suck to a white child."[19]

White southerners not only assessed enslaved women's level of skill by determining whether they possessed previous experience, they also evaluated and graded the quality of enslaved women's milk as "young," "good," "very good," "fine," and "excellent."[50] White mothers assessed the quality of enslaved wet nurses' milk using factors that included the age of the enslaved woman's current infant and the number of children she had previously borne. The younger her child, the fresher or "younger" the milk was presumed to be. Occasionally, the milk was labeled with the child's age, as when an individual in Savannah, Georgia, sought a wet nurse with "milk from six to seven months old."[51] Prospective buyers and vendors also judged the quality of the milk by determining whether the children the mother was nursing were thriving. An advertisement in the *City Gazette and Commercial Daily Advertiser* of Charleston stated that the enslaved mother on offer for hire had "given suck to a white child for a short time past, who is very healthy."[52] In her chance encounter with a wet nurse, Mrs. Girardeau had visually examined the "fine healthy looking infant" in the enslaved mother's arms as she conversed with her on the street. Based on the enslaved mother's previous experience and the conclusions Girardeau drew about the health of the woman's infant, Girardeau determined that the woman might suit the needs of her acquaintance, and she was right. Ella Gertrude Thomas, who had employed a number of wet nurses, also determined that

Georgianna, her enslaved wet nurse at the time, was suitable once her son "commenced to fatten."[53]

Prevailing scholarship that focuses on "skilled" enslaved labor does not attend to this particular kind of labor or the systems that southerners used to evaluate and grade it. In his global history of cotton and capitalism, Sven Beckert argued that "the logic of capital" was forced upon "the logic of nature," a process that changed "the way the cotton plant itself was seen." The same could be said about breast milk, which was, like cotton, a product of nature that enslaved people cultivated and produced and white southerners sold. Just as cotton growers created grading systems that informed interested parties about the quality of the cotton for sale, white southerners developed a system by which to inform potential buyers and hirers about the quality of enslaved women's breast milk.[54] Enslaved wet nurses nurtured white southern children who would grow up to serve critical roles in the expansion of slavery into the West and Deep South, as well as the exponential growth of southern cotton cultivation in these regions. Their intimate, skilled labor, and the products of that labor, are key to understanding the complicated history of cotton and capitalism.

On occasion, prospective hirers and buyers wanted enslaved wet nurses to do more than suckle white children, and the slave traders, brokers, and slave owners who had such women in their possession knew exactly how to appeal to them. Advertisers touted enslaved wet nurses' skills as seamstresses, washerwomen, house servants, and ironers or advised prospective hirers that an enslaved female laborer could double as a wet nurse if the need arose.[55] The firm Milliken, Primerose, and Company advertised a "valuable young negro wench, about 23 years of age" along with her son, whom they described as a "likely smart boy about 6 years old." The woman was a house servant but, promised the firm, she "would be valuable as a wet nurse," too. In the winter of 1820 the Charleston jeweler John Baptiste Duplat similarly advertised "a wench" who was "an excellent house servant, cook, washer and ironer, and a good wet nurse with her infant child" for sale.[56] Theodore A. Whitney, a broker and an auctioneer in the Charleston area, was more aggressive as he used bold capital letters to advertise a "wet nurse, seamstress, washer, ironer, and house servant . . . her child about six weeks old," and a "Boy to attend to it" in the *Southern Patriot*. He clarified that the woman could "be hired either as a wet nurse, or either of the above capacities," and he reassured interested individuals that she was "a complete seamstress, washer and ironer, and house servant"—the word *complete* signifying her ability to perform all of this work adeptly.[57]

On at least one occasion, an individual advertised an enslaved woman's ability to serve as a wet nurse before she even began to lactate. This advertiser informed prospective hirers that the enslaved woman was "used to attend[ing] in the house," but that she would also "answer as wet nurse in a few weeks," thereby suggesting that she was pregnant and had not yet delivered her child at the time when the ad was placed.[58]

Very few advertisements mentioned prices for enslaved wet nurses or the wages they earned when hired, and this omission makes it difficult to determine whether they were considered more or less valuable than other enslaved female laborers. Advertisements that do include this information, however, reveal that the labor enslaved women performed as wet nurses could be quite valuable to their owners and costly to those who hired them. In 1803, for example, one individual sought to sell an enslaved woman and her child for six hundred dollars. The advertisement alleged that she was "very fond of children" and "would answer for a wet nurse." Five years later, Thomas Screven of Hampstead, South Carolina, offered "a healthy young WENCH, with her child, about three weeks old" for sale. He claimed that she was "fond of children" and "expected [to] make a good Wet Nurse," thereby implying that she had not yet performed this particular labor. He wanted four hundred dollars cash for the two of them.[59] When white southerners hired out, rather than sold, enslaved wet nurses, the owners retained the value of their bodies and repeatedly reaped the pecuniary rewards of their maternal labor. In 1804, an individual who hoped to hire out an enslaved wet nurse indicated that he or she expected to receive ten dollars a month for her wages. Another expected to receive eight dollars a month.[60]

Concerns about the costs associated with procuring enslaved wet nurses also connote something about their value within the slave marketplace. One white woman, Kitty Harris, had trouble getting her son to nurse, and she suffered from an insufficient milk supply after he began to feed. Her mother hoped that she would persevere, despite the trouble she faced, because she worried that Harris's young family could not afford to hire or buy a wet nurse.[61] Like the Harrises, not all families could afford enslaved wet nurses, and this financial impediment not only presents another reason some women did not employ enslaved wet nurses, it also hints at the considerable value of enslaved mothers' nutritive labor in slave markets and the South more broadly. Some white southern women left little doubt that they valued the maternal labor that enslaved women performed. After a white slave-owning woman learned that her female slave had been accused of theft by the man to whom she was hired, she ordered him to whip the enslaved female for her crime, but she asked that he "spare her breasts, as she is giving suck to a very young child."[62] Whether this enslaved woman was nursing her own child or a white woman's is unclear. Nevertheless, her owner assigned immense value to her breasts and the milk that flowed from them.

Court records offer additional evidence of the respect white southerners accorded an enslaved woman's ability to nurse. Raphaël Toledano emancipated an enslaved woman, Delphine, in part because she had served as "the wet nurse of two of his children." Samuel Street similarly sought to emancipate an enslaved woman named Delia, because she was "a faithful & attentive nurse to his oldest son." Street told the court that it was "from her breast [that] his infancy was supported."[63] Other cases, such as one involving an enslaved mother named Mima, offer further clues about the value some white southerners placed on an enslaved woman's ability to suckle. Jane Gladney owned Mima, and when Gladney died, her will stipulated that Mima should go to her grandchildren. Since they were still minors, the executors of Gladney's will held Mima in trust until Gladney's heirs came of age. Gladney's will required her executors to hire Mima out and use her wages to create two twenty-five-dollar legacies for her grandchildren and to allow any of Mima's remaining wages to accrue until they reached their majority. After Gladney died Mima gave birth to a son named Isaac, and not long afterward Gladney's executors discovered that Mima suffered from a "disability of suckling," which they attributed to the fact that she was "badly burned in her breast" in her youth. As a consequence of this injury, Mima was "unable to give any sustenance or support to her children from the breast." The executors claimed that they were experiencing difficulty in hiring Mima out because few persons were "disposed to hire" or were "willing or in a situation to furnish milk or provide suitable attendance for raising the children." In light of these circumstances, Gladney's executors decided to sell Mima and sought legal permission to do so, and the court granted their request. They sold Mima and her child on January 1, 1838. It is important to note that the executors did not have to sell Mima because of her inability to suckle. Slave owners frequently compelled enslaved women to leave their infants in other enslaved women's care while they worked in the fields and limited the time they could spend nursing them. They also separated enslaved mothers from their children when they hired them out as wet nurses, a practice that also required enslaved women to nurse enslaved infants who were not their own. Gladney's executors had at their disposal a number of ways by which they could have solved this problem. Nevertheless, their decision to sell Mima because she could not suckle underscores how important lactation was in the financial calculations slave owners made when ascribing value to enslaved women.[64]

Wet nurse advertisements like the ones described above highlight a darker dimension of the slave market. Many of these ads reference the loss of an enslaved woman's child and separation from her newborn infant. In fact, many made it clear that an enslaved mother had recently lost her child or would be hired without the baby. On June 17, 1813, an advertisement appeared from someone who sought to hire out a wet nurse who had "just lost her first child" in the *City Gazette and Commercial Daily Advertiser*. Five months later, in the same newspaper, another subscriber advertised "a wet nurse" who was a "healthy, young, and sober wench, with a good breast of milk, having lost her child."[65] Far more frequently, those who offered enslaved women as wet nurses said nothing about their children, implying that these mothers had lost them through death, sale, or some other manner.[66]

There was an important reason individuals mentioned an enslaved mother's loss in these advertisements: their lack of children was a selling point. Individuals routinely placed advertisements that expressed the desire to hire or purchase a wet nurse without children or, in the common parlance, "without encumbrance."[67] Mrs. Dawson, a Charleston area resident, offered for hire a "healthy black wet nurse, without a child," and a woman named Mrs. Palmer sought a wet nurse without a child.[68] Prospective buyers and hirers recognized that enslaved wet nurses who were accompanied by their children would not be able to devote all their time and milk supply to white infants because they would need to attend to their own. They also realized that separating enslaved mothers from their children could present problems. These potential separations were a "constant point of tension and negotiation" between white families and the enslaved mothers they bought or hired.[69] Furthermore, as owners or hirers they would not only be responsible for the well-being of the enslaved mother, they would also have to provide for any children who accompanied her. Therefore, indicating that an enslaved wet nurse would be hired or sold without her children eliminated later confusion and assured interested parties that these women would be able to perform their duties with minimal interference. Conversely, notifying readers that children would accompany the wet nurses who were offered for sale or hire helped all parties "avoid trouble" and reduced the likelihood of miscommunication between them.[70]

Information about an enslaved woman's children was important to these market transactions for other reasons as well. Advertisers would routinely include information such as the birth order and ages of an enslaved wet nurse's children; these statistics served as shorthand for individuals who sought enslaved wet nurses "with young milk" or a "fresh breast of milk."[71] An enslaved child's birth order and age offered interested parties important details to help them determine whether the advertised laborer would suit their needs.

The testimony of formerly enslaved people and the language that individuals like Mrs. Dawson and Mrs. Palmer used when seeking to hire, sell, or purchase

enslaved wet nurses reveal the ways in which a white woman's decision to initiate and finalize such a transaction constituted an act of maternal violence.
Maternal violence is generally defined as a case in which a mother commits a
violent act against her own children. But here I offer another way of defining
maternal violence that takes slavery into account. White mothers treated
enslaved women's bodies, their labor, and the products of their labor as goods,
and in consequence were able to commit violence against these women, in
their role as mothers, that slavery and the slave market made possible.[72] In prioritizing their own infants' nutritional needs over those of their wet nurses' children, white mothers separated enslaved mothers from their children, often
prevented enslaved women from forming maternal bonds with their infants and
providing them with the nutrition they needed, and distanced them from the
communities and kinship networks that were integral to their survival. The
demands slave owners placed upon enslaved mothers as manual laborers and as
wet nurses gave rise to circumstances that could result not only in psychological
but also physical violence against these women and their children.[73] And yet,
white mothers like Ella Gertrude Thomas ignored or failed to acknowledge the
effect their choices would have upon the enslaved women who nursed their
white infants.

Thomas had experienced difficulty nursing because of an inadequate milk
supply, and after her unsuccessful attempts to bottle-feed her babies, she chose
to use at least four enslaved women to nurse her two infants. America and
Georgianna nursed her son, Jefferson, and Nancy and Emmeline suckled her
daughter, Cora Lou.[74] Ella Thomas borrowed America and Emmeline from
her father, who lived on a different plantation estate, thus separating them from
their community. In her journal she did not reveal why she used two enslaved
women to nurse her son. But several years later, when she used Nancy and
Emmeline, she did indicate why one would not suffice. Nancy served as her
daughter's first wet nurse, but Thomas was prepared to install Emmeline as her
replacement if Nancy's milk did not agree with her infant's palate. In her journal, Thomas never mentions how these enslaved women might have felt about
her decision to use them as wet nurses for her children or the ways they might
have supported each other through the experience. And Thomas seemed unin-
terested in the negative impact her choice had upon America, who had recently
lost a child and would have been in mourning.[75] What might enable a mother
to so easily ignore or neglect to note another mother's grief and pain?

In the eighteenth century, British men who bought female captives on the
west coast of Africa claimed that these women did not have the same emotional
attachments to their children that European women did.[76] Such assumptions

continued to shape how Anglo-Americans thought about enslaved women's relationships with their children in North America and might help explain why millions of slave owners were so willing to sever parental and kinship bonds and why, when faced with enslaved people's grief, trauma, and pain, they described it as something else. Ella Gertrude Thomas certainly subscribed to this idea when it came to people of African descent more generally. When the enslaved man who served as her driver informed her that he had been separated from his daughter and that his daughter had been separated from her children, Thomas remarked in her diary that they were fortunate because "the Negro is a cheerful being."[77] Such a view of African-descended people probably explains why Thomas failed to acknowledge the psychological distress her children's wet nurses endured. In her estimation, these enslaved women were "cheerful beings"; they were not distressed at all.

White southerners developed a special terminology to describe enslaved people's emotions, terms and phrases intended to render their pain, grief, trauma, and emotional loss invisible. The literary scholar Anne Anlin Cheng identifies a discourse common to both scholars and laypeople in discussions of race that views marginalized people's expressions of grief as pathological, while simultaneously defining white people's expressions of grief as healthy. Nineteenth-century white southerners employed their own version of this.[78] When confronted with enslaved women's emotional responses to losing or being separated from their children, white southerners construed their grief as "the sulks," or even a form of madness—"vices," flaws, or pathological conditions—that made such women less valuable and less desirable in the slave market.

An enslaved wet nurse with "the sulks" was one whom prospective buyers and hirers desperately sought to avoid. An advertisement in the *City Gazette and Commercial Daily Advertiser* on June 16, 1792, for example, requested a "black wet nurse" who would "if possible be free from the sulks" and "of good disposition." Yet their very desire to avoid confronting the mental anguish and psychic suffering of the enslaved mothers they hoped to acquire made the reality of that grief clear to anyone who read the advertisements. Scholars of slavery have elaborated upon the ways slave traders and slave owners compelled enslaved people to feign joy and contentment in the slave market precisely because their trauma and sorrow were palpable to buyers. White southerners also sought to disguise the maternal grief of enslaved women in their advertisements with claims that these mothers were "extremely fond of children" and possessed "cheerful" and "uncommon good" dispositions. The advertisers were, in essence, marketing a particular kind of maternal sentience along with enslaved women's maternal labor.[79]

Enslaved mothers' grief and white southerners' attempts to render it invisible stand in stark contrast to the simultaneous "culture of mourning" that allowed whites to openly express their sorrow after the loss of loved ones. During the nineteenth century, white women were encouraged to mourn for the dead, and their "private expressions of grief helped usher in new conventions that enabled women to more fully express their acute sense of loss." However, while "nineteenth-century [white] Americans were encouraged to openly mourn for the dead, especially for infants and young children," white southerners brutally denied enslaved mothers and fathers the right to do the same. In the face of these denials, the enslaved mothers whom slave owners compelled to serve as wet nurses, particularly those who had recently lost a child or who were forced to separate from him or her, could not, or would not, hide their sorrow and grief, and such emotional displays were disturbingly obvious to owners and potential buyers. While from today's perspective we might have assumed that the culture of mourning would inevitably lead white mothers to commiserate with enslaved women who lost their children or were separated from their infants, contemporary evidence makes it clear that women who employed wet nurses often chose to ignore enslaved women's expressions of maternal grief.[80]

Whether they recognized it or not, white southern mothers were ultimately responsible for the ordeals that many enslaved wet nurses endured in and out of the slave market. These women decided when enslaved wet nurses would best serve them and their children, and only they knew the motives underlying these decisions. White mothers determined whether they could withstand the physical toll breastfeeding imposed upon them and whether they would be able to produce an adequate supply of milk to feed their newborns. Consequently, they were the ones who decided whether to borrow, hire, or buy an enslaved wet nurse, even if a man might finalize the transactions in the slave market. Some men did influence their wives' decisions to charge other women with nursing their children.[81] But the politics of respectability that shaped white southern culture and domestic relations ensured that few men would dare violate white women's bodies in order to determine whether they were concocting reasons not to nurse, especially those of the elite and planter classes. Physicians, husbands, and other men had to take women at their word and allow them to make maternal decisions for themselves.[82] White women separated enslaved mothers from their children and placed their own infants at the breasts of these women. They compelled enslaved women to suckle their white children shortly after these mothers had lost their own. They denied enslaved women the right to publicly express their grief. In short, they perpetrated acts of maternal violence against these enslaved mothers, and the slave market made this violence possible.

6

"That 'Oman Took Delight in Sellin' Slaves"

In 1858, Elizabeth Childress decided that it was time to sell her only slave—a fifteen-year-old named Sally—and "convert her into money." Childress was not much older than Sally when she made up her mind to initiate the transaction; she was still under twenty-one. But it was her prerogative to dispose of Sally if she pleased, for she had "acquired her of her own right and exercised all the rights and authority of a person of full age." Rather than call upon her male relatives to broker the sale, Elizabeth Childress hired William Boyd, who was "a negro trader by occupation" and "kept a negro yard in the city of Nashville." She probably settled upon Boyd because, like many of the most successful men in the slave trade, he routinely "published as a general agent to hire, purchase, and sell negroes for all persons who might avail themselves of his experience and honesty in the business." Convinced that he was the right man for the task, Childress placed Sally in Boyd's "negro yard" and waited for him to sell her for "the best price he could get."[1]

A few days passed without any word, but Boyd soon informed Childress that he knew a man who would buy Sally for $1,000. Unfortunately for Childress, the sale fell through. A short time later, Childress walked into Boyd's office and asked him about the prospects for Sally's sale. This time he said he knew of someone who would be willing to buy Sally for $900. He assured her that this was all Sally "would command in the market," and "that that was a very high price," and he advised her to take it. "Trusting in his honesty and judgment as her agent," Childress agreed to accept the lower price. Boyd immediately sat down at his desk and drew up Sally's bill of sale. He identified William Whitworth and J. K. Taylor as Sally's purchasers and handed Childress $890, the amount he owed her once he deducted his $10 commission.[2]

Elizabeth Childress left Boyd's office that day with a sense of satisfaction, but her contentment was short-lived. She soon discovered that not long after Boyd sold Sally to Whitworth and Taylor, the two men sold the enslaved girl again— for $1,050. Moreover, she also suspected that one or both of the original "purchasers" were Boyd's partners in his slave-trading firm. Boyd, Whitworth, and Taylor had bamboozled her. Not only did Boyd sell Sally for more than he originally said she was worth, he made a $150 profit. Childress believed that Boyd had "never exerted himself to sell" Sally, and the reason was that he had planned to "cheat and defraud" her from the outset. She was so staunchly certain about this that on March 1, 1859, she filed a lawsuit against the three men to get the money that she held to be her due.[3]

In a typical courtroom maneuver, Childress told the judge that Boyd, Whitworth, and Taylor had been able to perpetrate their allegedly fraudulent sale because she was "very young and unexperienced in business" and easily "imposed upon." Contrary to her contention, however, her youth and inexperience had little to do with the profits Whitworth and Taylor made when they sold Sally. The circumstances that unfolded before, during, and after Sally's sale, especially Boyd, Whitworth, and Taylor's speculative practices, were systemic and fundamental dimensions of the domestic slave trade. The business ledgers slave traders maintained, and the trails of public, financial, and legal documents that followed every slave sale they initiated and finalized, routinely recorded similar transactions and profit margins. And Boyd, Whitworth, and Taylor's response to Elizabeth's allegations indicated as much.[4]

While Elizabeth Childress feigned youthful helplessness in court, Boyd argued that she had represented herself to be very much the lady when she came into his Nashville office. He told the court that she had never disclosed that she was under age and acted as though she had already reached her majority, when she would have the legal authority to dispose of Sally. Since she was a minor, he argued that the sale should be null and void because his title to Sally was invalid. Furthermore, Boyd denied Childress's accusations that he had already sold Sally for the higher price before finalizing the sale with her. He also dismissed her charge that he had formed a partnership with Whitworth and Taylor and colluded with them to defraud her.[5]

Boyd's answer to Childress's charges revealed more than he might have intended, however. Just as she had suspected, Whitworth and Taylor were indeed "engaged in buying and selling negroes, and were in the habit of keeping their purchases at . . . Boyd's establishment." Boyd admitted that he did "sometimes become interested with his co-defendants in some of their purchases, as he did with other negro-dealers," though he insisted that they maintained separate accounts. Whitworth and Taylor also claimed that when they purchased Sally they never expected to sell her for a profit in Nashville. They intended to sell her farther South, where they knew she would bring a higher purchase price. Before they could do so, a prospective buyer from Mississippi, James Lewellen, agreed to buy her. Thus, they argued, there was no collusion on the part of the three men. In fact, they charged Elizabeth Childress with deception and claimed that she knew that as a minor she did not possess the legal authority to sell Sally to them. They therefore asked the judge to declare the transaction null and void.[6]

In the end, the judge sided with Childress. He ruled that she was entitled to an additional $125. Thus, she received more than she had expected to get when she agreed to the sale. Despite being an underage female "unexperienced in business," Elizabeth Childress was still able to initiate and partially execute a sale in the Nashville slave market and later win her case in the Davidson County Chancery Court. And when confronted by three slave traders in court, Childress left as the victor. Of course, she had help, but the individuals who aided her did not offer their services to shield her from the Nashville slave market or the commerce that occurred there. None of the parties involved in the sale or lawsuit mentioned her sex as a reason why Boyd, Whitworth, and Taylor had taken advantage of her. Nor did anyone claim that the sale should be invalid because she was a woman. In fact, everyone involved—from Childress's friends, to the slave traders, to the judge—behaved as though it was perfectly natural for a woman to walk into a slave trader's office and hire him to sell her slave. When Elizabeth Childress settled upon William Boyd as her agent, and when she brought Sally to his establishment, she was conducting business in the commercial center of the second-largest slave market in the state of Tennessee.[7] None of these details deterred her.

Given what historians have said about white women and nineteenth-century southern slave markets, none of Elizabeth Childress's actions should have been possible. One historian's explanation for women's exclusion from southern slave markets was that "by law and by custom white women had little business being" there. Another scholar made a similar point when he emphasized that "a slave trader or speculator was a man." Yet in her examination of women and property in colonial South Carolina, the historian Cara Anzilotti found that white women "actively participated in the slave marketplace, buying and selling laborers, used them as a source of revenues by renting them out, and expected these slaves to further their relatives' economic welfare." She also contends that "many women managed the task of buying and selling slaves themselves."[8] This was also true of the nineteenth century.

Quantitative data analyses of the domestic slave trade have ignored female slave owners, be they single, married, or widowed. The economic historians Robert Fogel and Stanley Engerman collected data on 5,009 transactions completed in the New Orleans slave market between 1804 and 1862. Their findings have since become one of the most widely used data sets in studies of American slavery, yet they offer no specific data about white women's slave-market activities or buying and selling patterns. While Fogel and Engerman accounted for the sex, age, and color of the enslaved people who appeared in their data set, they did not collect similar information about the buyers and sellers of these individuals. Out of the forty-seven variables they gathered altogether, only two—initials and place of origin—pertained to buyers and sellers.[9] Thus, we can use these data to analyze gendered elements of enslaved people's experiences in the New Orleans slave market, but we cannot use them to determine how gender did or did not affect white southerners' slave market activities.

The masculinized story of slavery's nineteenth-century expansion and the rewards reaped from investing in that process through settlement on and cultivation of newly available lands serves to further marginalize white women and dismiss their economic contributions to slavery's growth. Historians chronicle the ways that slavery, white voluntary migration, and the forcible removal and dispersal of indigenous and enslaved people and their labor transformed the nation's political economy, as well as the global economy. But their narratives are built largely upon the stories of men. Women do appear in these histories, yet rarely does one find them among the ranks of "slavery's entrepreneurs." Instead, women often appear as mere tag-alongs.[10]

In some respects, the slave markets of the eighteenth and nineteenth centuries were different. In the wake of the Louisiana Purchase, the Adams-Onis Treaty, and the Treaty of Guadalupe Hidalgo, the nation doubled in size during the first half of the nineteenth century. The market economy grew along with it, shifting from separate regional consumer markets to a national one. The slave trade changed from a system of exchange consisting primarily of the sale of captives from the Caribbean and the west coast of Africa to a domestic market involving the purchase and sale of enslaved people born in the United States. It became more regimented and more formalized and drew upon technological and fiscal innovations to maximize efficiency and profit.[11] If women had access to the domestic marketplace in the colonial period, an era when the southern markets in slaves were disjointed, far from regional in scope, and rudimentary at best, then the developments that occurred during the nineteenth century probably brought more women into the slave market. Women responded enthusiastically to the development of a formalized, regimented, and regional slave marketplace, and they took advantage of the benefits that came with the transactions they initiated and finalized in those slave markets.

Travelers, slave traders, city officials, and enslaved people all attested to the presence of white women in nineteenth-century slave markets. White male and female sightseers visited slave markets and attended slave auctions during their excursions through the South, and they occasionally observed and wrote about the women they saw there. Although women rarely wrote about their exchanges with slave traders, the traders themselves routinely recorded their encounters with their female clientele who hoped to sell or buy the slaves they had in their possession, and they documented these women's purchases and sales in their account books. Most southern states required slave sales to be formally recorded, and bills of slave sale, which functioned like modern-day receipts, reveal how frequently women bought and sold enslaved people. Clerks and notary publics in states like South Carolina and Louisiana recorded each and every slave sale and maintained meticulously detailed records of their business. Women's names appear throughout these records as buyers and sellers of enslaved people. And in later interviews, formerly enslaved people repeatedly recalled the women who bought and sold them in the region's slave markets.

Southern slave markets, it would seem, were tourist attractions for white travelers. The Swedish writer and social reformer Fredrika Bremer described the New Orleans slave market as "one of the great sights of 'the gay city.'" For Bremer and travelers like her, these marketplaces were filled with striking scenes. For some, their encounters with white women in slave marketplaces and at slave auctions presented the most notable events they witnessed during their time in the South. Around 1859, Dr. John Theophilus Kramer attended a slave auction in the rotunda of the Saint Louis Hotel in the New Orleans French Quarter. Remarkably, at least to Kramer, he noticed "four ladies" who were "splendidly dressed in black silk and satin, and glittering with precious jewels" in attendance. These women were not standing discreetly on the outskirts of the festivities; they sat in close proximity to the platform upon which slaves would be sold. Kramer's description of their attire suggests that they may have been members of the upper class. Equally notable, these four women came to the slave auction together, without male escorts.[12]

As the auctioneer called off the slaves for sale, recorded Kramer, he addressed both the men and the women in the room as potential bidders: "Ladies and gentlemen," he said, "look here at this healthy child!" The four women did not participate in the auction proceedings, and Kramer offered a theory of why they did not. Although he deemed it plausible that the women already owned slaves and thus possessed the quintessential qualities that characterized slave owners as a group, their feminine sensibilities kept them from actually purchasing slaves themselves. Yet based on other historical evidence, it seems equally possible that they attended the auction to buy slaves with particular characteristics or skills, and the slaves exposed for sale did not meet their criteria, so they elected not to buy.[13]

The slave sale that Kramer attended and described does not conform to the kind of auction ordinarily associated with such transactions. Kramer describes an upscale, sanitized, and more palatable scene in striking contrast to the conventional image of a scantily clad slave up on an auction block in the center of a male audience of prospective buyers, usually in an auction house located in an obscure section of a city's commercial district. The Saint Louis Hotel was one of the finest establishments in the city, offering accommodation to hundreds of guests, including military and political officials, and providing entertainment for city residents as well.[14] The hotel's rotunda was a breathtaking structure made of marble and encircled by columns and offices where auctioneers and others conducted their business. Perhaps this was a slave marketplace suitable for "ladies."[15] To be sure, the grandiose spectacle that unfolded in the Rotunda on the day Kramer attended was not the only kind of auction that took place there. But nonetheless, white women of all classes could be found among the observers and prospective buyers.

The author and clergyman Joseph Holt Ingraham also encountered a white woman in the Natchez, Mississippi, slave market he visited, but she was no spectator. She had gone to buy slaves, and that is exactly what she did. Just as Ingraham was preparing to leave, an elderly woman drove up in a "handsome carriage." Accompanied by a young male, she entered the slave market and approached several enslaved females exposed for sale. She asked them questions in a "kind tone" before finally settling on an enslaved woman and her child. The young male who accompanied her appealed to her to purchase the enslaved woman's husband as well, which she elected to do. And she left with the mother and child sitting beside her in the carriage and the husband in the coach box with her driver.[16] Despite requiring the physical assistance of a companion, this elderly woman made a trip to the slave market to buy slaves on her own. Ingraham did not express the same surprise Kramer had about seeing a woman at the market, nor did he feel the need to rationalize her presence or her slave buying. He found her mode of transportation more remarkable than her actions.

Like Kramer and Ingraham, Fredrika Bremer was keenly interested in visiting slave auctions, markets, and yards during her forays into the South, and she wrote in detail about the women she met there. Accompanied by a male escort in New Orleans, Bremer walked "a short distance to the rail-road, on the other side of the river" and "passed through the slave market." There she saw "forty or fifty young persons of both sexes . . . walking up and down before the house in expectation of purchasers. They were singing; they seemed cheerful and thoughtless. The young slaves who were here offered for sale were from twelve to twenty years of age. There was one little boy, however, who was only six: he belonged to no one there. He attached himself to the slave-keeper."[17] Bremer had come face to face with the landscape of the New Orleans slave market; it encompassed more than the slave yards, depots, warehouses, and auction houses—it also included the city streets. The scene she described was not one that other white women could avoid unless they stayed away from commercial centers altogether. In fact, it was commonplace.

Joseph Peterson was a free man of color who grew up on Canal Street in nineteenth-century New Orleans, and he would rise early in the morning before commerce commenced to "watch them parading the folks up and down." The traders dressed the men in navy-blue suits and "stove-pipe hats," while the women wore "pink dresses, white aprons, an' red han'kerchefs on dey haids." Traders would compel these enslaved men and women to walk the lengths of the promenade "two by two" so that they "would attract attention from the eyes of prospective buyers, to say the least." These "parades," Peterson remembered, were a "gran' sight!"[18]

Fredrika Bremer was not content with simply visiting slave markets. She also traveled to the slave jails of Virginia, where enslaved people were held until their owners were ready to sell them, and to a slave pen in the District of Columbia.[19] Much of the District's slave trade occurred "in or near the taverns and small hotels, at the public market or the private jails and about the country markets" in the city; these were all places that women visited.[20] During Bremer's time in the District of Columbia, she spent many of her days in the Capitol listening to members of the Senate, and a male acquaintance, Dr. Hebbe, would frequently accompany her. Before going to the Capitol on July 21, 1850, he served as her escort to the slave market, and her "good hostess," a married woman named Mrs. Johnson, also accompanied her. Mrs. Johnson "wished to have a negro boy as a servant," and she hoped to purchase one. Although Dr. Hebbe escorted Bremer and Mrs. Johnson, he was not the person who bargained with the slave keeper: Mrs. Johnson took care of this business herself. She went to the slave pen with a precise idea of the kind of slave she wanted to buy, and she knew how much she wanted to pay for him. But this particular slave pen was a holding station in which enslaved children were "fattened" and prepared for sale before being shipped to slave markets in the lower South, so the slave keeper was unable to accommodate her.[21]

The women of Charleston could also visit their city's slave traders, or they could attend public slave auctions. The largest of these routinely occurred at ten o'clock in the morning, right "in front or just north" of the customhouse. The building also housed the post office and was near "City-Hall, the *Courier* and the *Mercury* [newspaper] buildings," and "nearly all the churches and banks," as well as the "offices of many lawyers, factors, brokers, commission merchants," and other commercial agents. The auctions were so large that the city passed an ordinance in 1856 forbidding such commerce because "the crowd often overflowed into the East Bay street and obstructed traffic" and "was sure to attract the attention and excite the condemnation of Northern and foreign travelers."[22]

This might have been where Harriet Martineau, a British sociologist, feminist, and traveler, encountered a public slave auction. Just as she arrived, the auctioneer was exposing "a woman, with two children, one at the breast, and another holding her apron" for sale. She surmised that the woman's "agony of shame and dread would have silenced the tongue of every spectator; but this was not so." According to Martineau "a lady chose at that moment to turn to me and say, with a cheerful air of complacency, 'You know my theory, that one race must be subservient to the other. I do not care which; and if the blacks should ever have the upper hand, I should not mind standing on that table, and being sold with two of my children.'"[23] The woman was not repulsed or disgusted at the sight of an enslaved mother being sold with her children, even though she was a mother herself. Her gender and motherhood did nothing to compel her to sympathize with the enslaved woman's plight. In fact, she seemed relatively comfortable with the idea of all human beings being sold to the highest bidder.[24]

It is critical to acknowledge that slave trading was not sequestered in urban vice districts because it was not considered a vice.[25] It was part of the fabric of southern communities and the region's economy. Slave traders often clustered in particular segments of commercial districts, and they marked their businesses to make them easier to find. Even a woman like the diarist Mary Boykin Chesnut, who belonged to a prominent South Carolinian slave-owning family and was married to a high-ranking political figure, would confront the peculiar institution's ugly underbelly during occasional strolls into town.[26]

As Ann Maria Davison and her acquaintance Mrs. Benton solicited New Orleans residents for donations to support the "Bible Cause," they "came in contact with four negro Traders Yards":

We stopped at the door of one of them not knowing its character. One of the most pleasant smiles sat upon the face of the odious trafficker as he advanced to the door and invited us in. . . . [T]rue to my earnest desire to see all I could of the traffick I said let us go in. The trader looked all delight! Here ladies, said he, is as fine a lot of young Negroes as you will find any where, and turning round to them who were all seated on benches round the large room with their newly purchased suit for the occasion—he gave this word of command in a very peremtory manner by saying Form the line. In an instant they all sprang to their feet making two long rows not one seemingly over twenty years old and truly were they a likely looking set of young men and women.[27]

As this encounter shows, slave traders and dealers did not consider female purchasers to be anomalous. Moreover, when white women entered slave traders' offices and slave dealers' establishments, the enslaved people waiting to be bought acknowledged them as property owners with the money, power, and authority to buy them.

Davison and Benton's inability to recognize a slave trader's establishment could be attributed to their lack of familiarity with the business, but it is far more likely that it was because the businesses of slave traders and other kinds of merchants were indistinguishable. As Fredrika Bremer observed, the "great slave-market" consisted of "several houses situated in a particular part of the city," which visitors would probably find unremarkable until they encountered "the groups of colored men and women, of all shades between black and light yellow, which stand or sit unemployed at the doors." Speaking directly against the notion that women avoided the sexual aspects of the slave market, Bremer remarked upon the enslaved men with "really athletic figures, . . . good countenances and remarkably good foreheads, broad and high." There was "one negro in particular" who captured her attention. He was valued at "two thousand dollars." Although Bremer was in the slave market to observe, she "took a great fancy" to this enslaved man, and "said aloud that she 'liked that boy'" and was sure that she and he "should be good friends." She was playing the role of slave buyer, but the enslaved man's response to her chatter revealed that he took her seriously.[28]

Women could examine enslaved people's bodies, take notice of their features, talk to them, and express a desire to buy them, all in public view. If what they saw piqued their interest, they could enter the trader's establishment and be assured that the proprietor would cater to their needs. Such evidence further refutes the argument that white southern women were repulsed by or alienated from slave markets and ignorant of the details of slave transactions.

Residential and business directories and censuses of merchants show that hundreds of women conducted business in the same places where slave traders plied their trade. They also reveal that the layout of commercial districts in nineteenth-century southern cities made it difficult for white women to avoid slave marketplaces or evade the business and economic community that flourished there. New Orleans city and business directories show that women worked on the same blocks as slave traders, and some of their businesses were only a few doors apart. A Madame Harriet, for example, established her oyster restaurant on the corner of Gravier and Philippa Streets, with the slave trader C. F. Hatcher located nearby on Gravier between Philippa and Baronne. Mrs. Mary Sweneua (or Brzarenne) operated a fancy retail shop on Baronne, Gravier, and Common Streets. The slave dealer Thomas Foster worked at 157 Common Street between Baronne and Carondelet. Foster's fellow slave dealers Frisby and Lamarque's establishment was located at 156 Common Street also between Baronne and Carondelet.[29] The directories also show that female merchants outnumbered individuals who identified themselves as slave traders in the commercial center of the city, thereby suggesting that these men were locating their businesses in proximity to the female merchants, not the other way around. For example, *Cohen's New Orleans and Lafayette City Directory* lists 427 female merchants or businesswomen operating in the city in 1849. This number jumps to 463 if the women who worked as teachers and principals and who ran schools and seminaries are included.[30] Yet only 20 male slave traders and dealers appear among them. Of course, many people involved in the slave trade did not call themselves traders, dealers, or auctioneers. They often identified themselves as "planters," "commission merchants," "factors," and "agents" because they often sold other commodities or conducted other types of business transactions in addition to slave sales.

It is important to recognize, too, that the commercial districts of cities like New Orleans were bustling with white women. The 1854 *Census of Merchants* offers evidence of women's commercial activity in the city. There were 330 *licensed* female merchants operating in the first, second, and third districts of the city. This number only hints at the actual number of working women in the area because the census only tracked individuals who were employed in professions that required licensure. Many of the most common occupations for women, such as seamstress work, laundering, baking, and confectionary work did not require a license, and the women who were employed in these kinds of labor were not counted.[31]

Female merchants and entrepreneurs who worked within public marketplaces provided the kinds of goods and services that could prove useful to slave traders. Their proximity to the slave trade's primary arbiters and the demand for what they had to offer made it feasible for slave traders and dealers to buy white women's goods and services, even if those "services" consisted of enslaved labor. The woman who owned Susan Boggs, for example, hired her out to a slave trader to work "in the trader's jail." Boggs's mistress was thus indirectly benefiting from the slave trade. The trader made a living buying and selling human beings, and Boggs's labor was directly tied to business that occurred in the "trader's jail." By extension, the wages Boggs gave her mistress and the benefit her mistress derived from those wages were made possible because of the sale of human beings.[32]

Single, married, and widowed women appear frequently in slave traders' correspondence and in legal documents that recorded the purchase and sale of slaves. The slave trader A. J. McElveen, for example, contracted with several women who wanted him to buy or sell slaves on their behalf, and he wrote letters to his partner Ziba Oakes about them. On August 10, 1853, McElveen notified Oakes that he had sent him a slave he purchased from a woman named Mrs. Pedrow while he was in Sumterville, South Carolina.[33] Nineteen days later, he wrote Oakes again, from the Darlington, South Carolina, courthouse, and in a postscript informed Oakes that he "saw the lady Mrs. Blackwell who wishes to Sell 4 or 5 negros. She has promised to waite until I Return from charleston before She sells."[34] Two years later, McElveen wrote to Oakes seeking advice on how to handle a matter arising from a sale involving his purchase of two enslaved men who belonged to a woman named Miss Fleming. In his January 13, 1855, letter, he told Oakes, "I have just Received a note from Miss Fleming, the lady I bought George & lefegett from. . . . She will take boath the boys as I could not Settle with them by Returning one." Three days later, he asked Oakes for assistance again: "Will you advise me the course to persue in this Case[?] Miss Fleming is not willing to take one boy without the other therefore I am at a lost to Settle the matter as She has my note and will not Give it up."[35] Although white women do not appear regularly in McElveen's letters, the instances in which they do reveal that they dealt with him on numerous occasions, entrusted him with their economic investments, bought slaves from him, and sold them to him as well. More important, McElveen never mentioned the involvement of male kin or proxies; nor did he express reservations about dealing directly with women or imply that these women had concerns about dealing with him. In fact, his letters show that his female clients were in control of the sales and purchases, and at least one of them exerted enough pressure on him that he felt compelled to write Oakes more than once about how to resolve the situation.

Bills of sale also reveal that slave traders throughout the South bought slaves from and sold slaves to women on a regular basis. On December 16, 1845, Harriet A. Heath purchased a twenty-three-year-old enslaved woman named Jane from Ziba Oakes, and on July 8, 1846, she came back to him for another purchase. This time she bought a twenty-eight-year-old enslaved woman named Dianna who was "warranted sound and healthy."[36] Elihu Creswell bought a slave from Marie Carraby; Miss Eleanor Hainline bought a slave from George Ann Botts, John Hagan sold a slave to Mrs. Mathilda Mascey; Margaret Flood sold a slave to John Rucker White; and William Talbott sold a slave to Mrs. Louise Marie Eugenie Bailly Blachard.[37] It is not clear whether these women went to their local slave market to buy or sell their slaves, but they certainly negotiated directly with slave traders and dealers and finalized the transactions with them.

Slave traders' account books and ledgers offer further evidence of transactions with women. The slave-trading partners Tyre Glen and Isaac Jarratt sold enslaved people to Clarissa H. Mabson, Elizabeth Nobles, and Nancy Capehart and bought one from Sally M. Craw. Between 1849 and 1859, John White bought and sold enslaved people to women on at least forty-eight occasions, and he recorded seven additional sales without dates. Several of White's transactions are worthy of note. In 1849, Madame Mollere bought five enslaved people — three women, one man, and one of unspecified sex — from White. She purchased another enslaved woman the following year. Three other women, Mrs. A. Cross, Mrs. Newman, and Mademoiselle Bersije, also bought enslaved women from White that year. While White's female customers overwhelmingly bought enslaved girls and women from him, some, especially those engaged in sugarcane cultivation and processing, spent their money on enslaved men. In September 1852, Madame Burke of Lafourche Parish bought two enslaved young men, a twenty-year-old named Jack Barnet and a seventeen-year-old named Wiley Shields, from White for twelve hundred dollars each. He made a thousand-dollar profit. All together, at least thirty-five women bought enslaved people from him.[38]

White women were not anomalies at local slave auctions, either, and no group could testify more powerfully to white women's presence at and involvement in slave auctions than the enslaved people who were there. Formerly enslaved people remembered these women as astute, sophisticated, and calculating slave-market consumers. One formerly enslaved person remembered several white women at the public sale of a mixed-race woman; when the woman was placed on the auction block, the white women in the crowd exclaimed, "I don't want that mulatto bitch here." It was common for white men to purchase mixed-race women as part of the "fancy trade," a sector of the slave trade that catered almost exclusively to white men who sought to purchase sexual slaves. The white women who objected to the sale of this mixed-race enslaved woman probably knew this.[39]

The women present at this auction seemed to be spectators rather than buyers, but enslaved people also described women who actively participated in the bidding at other auctions. When B. E. Rogers asked his formerly enslaved father whether he had ever seen a slave auction, he replied, "Yes, I saw one at Raleigh once. About half a dozen Negroes being sold, mostly to women."[40] Liza Larkin bought Ank Bishop's mother at a slave auction in Coke's Chapel, and in acquiring an enslaved woman of childbearing age who could perform household tasks, she made an economically sound choice. Bishop's mother cooked, washed, and milked Larkin's cows. She also gave birth to Ank and five other children, and with each infant, Larkin watched her initial investment increase.[41]

Occasionally formerly enslaved people also spoke of their female owners' unique slave-market selection processes and buying habits. Ike Thomas's owners sold his parents away from him when he was a child, but his mistress kept him so she could train him to be a carriage boy. As Ike spoke of his life on the Thomas plantation, he reflected upon his mistress's distinct way of determining which slave boys would be suitable for purchase. She paid particular attention to the way they wore their hats. If the enslaved boys set their hats "on the back of their heads," she believed that they would grow up to be "'high-minded,' but if they pulled them over their eyes, they'd grow up to be 'sneaky and steal.'"[42] When Rose Russell's mistress decided to sell her, she asked Russell which of her parents she loved the most. Russell contemplated the question for a few moments before saying she felt the most love for her father. The mistress sold Russell with her father and separated the young girl from her mother.[43]

Sometimes white women saw financial opportunities in the very situations that white men thought burdensome. Some men considered enslaved children not worth the costs associated with rearing them to working age. Thomas Jefferson claimed that "the estimated value of the new-born infant [was] so low, (say twelve dollars and fifty cents,) that it [the infant] would probably be yielded by the owner gratis." Jefferson hatched a plan to deal with such nuisances, and at least a few slave owners considered it a good one. In a letter to Jared Sparks dated February 4, 1824, Jefferson proposed emancipating the infants of enslaved women, compelling their unfree mothers to care for them until they were able to work, and then deporting them. Shortly after Nat Turner led his slave rebellion in Southampton County, Virginia, a group of concerned male citizens put forth a petition to implement Jefferson's plan.[44] That never came to pass, but some male slave owners and traders showed that they agreed with Jefferson's low valuations of enslaved infants when they gave enslaved infants and children away to white women. H. B. Holloway recalled that at some slave auctions, "a woman would have a child in her arms. A man would buy the mother and wouldn't want the child. And then sometimes a woman would holler out: 'Don't sell that pickaninny . . . I want that little pickaninny.' And the mother would go one way and the child would go another."[45] Infants could be especially trouble-some to itinerant slave traders transporting enslaved people to the Deep South. While William Wells Brown was enslaved, he worked for a slave trader who became so annoyed by an infant's incessant crying that when they stopped to rest at an acquaintance's house, he gave the enslaved newborn to the man's wife as a present. She, perhaps more market-savvy than the trader, thanked him.[46]

Children cost far less than enslaved adolescents or adults, and if a slave owner was willing to pay the lower purchase price and invest in the care of the child until he or she was old enough to work, the owner could see his or her investment grow exponentially over the enslaved child's lifetime, especially if the child was female. Some white women chose to acquire enslaved infants and children for free or at rock-bottom prices, a decision that would eventually pay off handsomely.

Besides benefiting from their personal transactions in slave markets, women also served as intermediaries, attorneys-in-fact, and agents for other women and men, including slave traders, who wanted to buy or sell slaves.[47] In the latter months of 1852, after the slave owners Elias and Mary Gumaer moved to Wisconsin, they hired Ann Young to sell their slave Letty and her son William in the District of Columbia. They stipulated that she not sell the two to slave traders or to any buyer who would remove them from their own community. Young kept her end of the bargain, going so far as to sell them for a much lower price than they were worth and rejecting higher offers from several local slave traders. But Peter Hevener, the man who bought the Gumaers' slaves, did not bind himself to the same terms. The Gumaers petitioned the court to prevent him from selling Letty and William out of state, and their case elucidates Ann Young's extraordinary slave-market activities, which might otherwise have gone unnoticed.

The Gumaers' petition suggests that they considered Young to be a compe-tent, astute, and trustworthy arbiter of the slave market. The slave traders and prospective buyers who approached her about buying Letty and her child prob-ably saw her in this light as well. She possessed important knowledge about the slave-market economy, and what she knew allowed her to negotiate with a host of prospective buyers. Perhaps the couple entrusted Young with the transaction because she was a family member or because Letty and William were in her possession already and the Gumaers saw her as the most logical person to sell them. But whatever the reason, if they had not believed that Ann Young could sell Letty and William while simultaneously abiding by their wishes and obtaining the best possible price, they had other options. Everything Young did as the Gumaers' agent defined her as a slave dealer. They may not have wanted her to sell Letty and William to slave traders, but in appointing her to sell them at all, the Gumaers essentially authorized Young to assume that title.[48]

The intricacies of this sale make it abundantly clear that women like Ann Young did engage in complex slave-market transactions, and this was the case even when spouses or male proxies were involved. While some married women entrusted their husbands with conducting portions of their business in the slave market, they often handled other aspects of these transactions themselves. Ruth Williams is an example. Her mother bequeathed an enslaved woman and her children to Williams and her sister, stipulating that the property should be for the women's "sole and exclusive use and benefit" and should not be seized to satisfy their husbands' debts. The sisters decided that Ruth would get the male child of the enslaved woman, "he then being about twelve or fourteen years of age," and her sister would take the enslaved woman and any remaining children she might have. Upon securing the enslaved boy, however, Ruth discovered that he was "a stubborn, bad boy" and "she found it very hard to control him." She feared "that when he grew up to be a man . . . she would not be able to keep him in proper subjection." Since Ruth was "in very feeble health, and standing greatly in need of a woman to assist her in her domestic . . . business of her house," she "instructed and requested" that her husband "dispose of" the enslaved boy for her, "either by exchanging him for a woman, or by selling him and purchasing for her a woman with the proceeds." Furthermore, she specifically told her husband to do one of two things: "exchange him for a woman owned by one of her acquaintances or . . . sell him for not less than six hundred dollars cash." If he could not do either, he was "to return her the boy." Her husband returned without the boy and placed $408 in Ruth's hand, claiming that the funds were only "part of the proceeds" from the sale and she would soon receive the rest. On January 1, 1853, she "heard that one Zachariah R. T. McGuire had in his possession a negro woman that he wished to sell." Despite her "very feeble health," Ruth Williams visited McGuire, "examined said woman . . . in person . . . and after seeing her she contracted with . . . McGuire for the said woman," named Nancy. The contract stipulated that Williams would take possession of Nancy and assess her disposition and the quality of her work for a trial period, and if she was "pleased after trying her," she would purchase her "at the price . . . of two hundred and fifty dollars." Williams found Nancy to be a suitable servant, and she decided to buy her. She asked her husband "to go and complete the purchase . . . and to have the bill of sale executed to her, as her separate property." Ruth Williams allegedly needed this enslaved woman because of physical ailments, not simply so she could escape domestic labor or ascend to ladyhood. Furthermore, Ruth Williams underscored the fact that "her . . . husband completed the trade" on her behalf and that he did so with money he "obtained by and through her, and not from [his] means or money."[49]

Even though men conducted some aspect of women's business in slave markets, women did venture into these markets or attend slave auctions themselves. When Jane Buie was seventeen years old, she decided to purchase an enslaved woman and her children. She had enough money, but "she was young and timid and did not like to come into the crowd." So she asked her father, Malcolm, to accompany her to the auction and bid upon the enslaved mother and child as her agent. Before the sale began, Malcolm pulled the commissioner of the auction aside and informed him that his daughter wished to bid. However, because of her apprehension about the crowd, he was going to bid on her behalf. The commissioner assented to this arrangement. Once Malcolm Buie secured the commissioner's assent, he then "made known" to the crowd of prospective buyers that he was bidding "not for himself" but for his daughter. Malcolm was the highest bidder, and he later delivered the bill of sale to Jane and accompanied her to Cumberland, North Carolina, where she retrieved her "property."[50]

Jane's decision to ask her father to bid was probably based on her lack of experience, and perhaps the anxiety of trying to bid in a crowd of individuals who might have participated more routinely in the frantic bidding that characterized these auctions. Since she trusted her father to handle the transaction adeptly, she did not have to attend the auction in person. But her decision to do so suggests that she might have wanted to observe the bidding process so as to gain a deeper understanding of how to bid successfully in the future. It is also important to recognize that her father did not use this as an opportunity to affirm his masculinity or role as paternal protector; rather, he let the auctioneer and the crowd know that his daughter was present and he was merely acting on her behalf.

It was common, however, for women to initiate and finalize transactions in the marketplace themselves. When a formerly enslaved woman named Sarah was "jus' de age when gals begin bringin' good money in de market," a slave trader stole her from her mother. After trying unsuccessfully to sell her in several slave markets in different states, the trader decided to try again in New Orleans. Once they arrived in the city, the trader placed Sarah in a "trader-house," where she remained for several days. When it was time for the auction to take place, he prepared Sarah for sale by cleaning her up and giving her a new dress to wear. Later, Sarah described what happened next. The trader placed her on the auction block and Sarah began to see "de white folks pass by." Soon, she noticed a "white lady stop an' look" at her. After giving Sarah a thorough once over, the woman approached the slave trader and spoke to him for a while. Then she mingled with members of the growing crowd and suddenly exclaimed, "I think dat nigger gal was stole!" The woman approached Sarah again and began to ask her a series of questions: "'Whar yo' live at, gal?' de lady ask." Sarah replied, "My home in South Car'lina, Ma'am." "Don' you want ter come live wid me?" the woman asked. Sarah responded, "Yas'um." Satisfied, the woman returned to the crowd of prospective buyers and waited for the bidding to commence. As the auctioneer called off the bids, the woman staked her claim to Sarah and called out her price: "I'll take dat little nigger," she said. "Bid hundred an' fifty dollars!" She won. "Sold!" the auctioneer said. "An' she pay him."[51]

Sarah's female owner attended a slave auction, saw an enslaved girl exposed for sale, questioned her, decided to buy her, and successfully bid for her. She was clearly familiar with the litany of questions prospective buyers should ask the enslaved person they hoped to purchase, and she asked them to find out what she wanted to know.[52] She also displayed a sophisticated knowledge about the intricacies of slave commerce. Something suggested to her that Sarah was in an unfamiliar place. While such a scenario was not unusual, given the stream of enslaved people whom slave traders purchased in the Upper South and sold in the Lower and Deep South, Sarah's new owner recognized a different kind of displacement. Perhaps Sarah's youth implied that she had been sold away from her mother, something that was strictly prohibited under Louisiana acts passed in 1806 and again on January 31, 1839.[53] These acts stipulated that individuals must sell enslaved children who were younger than ten with their mothers, unless they were orphans. The man who captured and later sold Sarah might have been taking advantage of the "orphan loophole" by stealing her, and others, and selling them in distant slave markets where owners could not find them and potential buyers could not trace their origins. Sarah's new owner might not have cared whether Sarah was in fact stolen. If she really had been concerned about Sarah being kidnapped, she could have refrained from bidding on her, as others sometimes did, or tried to find Sarah's rightful owner.[54] Instead, she used allegations of unlawful sale as a means of decreasing the number of people willing to bid, which kept the bidding price low. Confronting the slave trader and canvassing the crowd of prospective buyers to spread news of her suspicions, Sarah's owner exhibited her slave-market savvy and comfort within the slave-trading community.

Beyond street-side sales of this kind, women also attended auctions in places like Bank's Arcade, a New Orleans venue that was "situated in the very center of business," and was well known for its sales of enslaved people, for "mass meetings of . . . various political parties," and for being a "great resort for merchants and others."[55] On June 10, 1843, for example, Bedilia Gaynor Kellar attended a public auction there. That particular day, Richard Richardson called off the bids. Richardson was the business partner of Joseph A. Beard, a man who was considered "New Orleans' most prominent auctioneer" and "the largest slave-seller in New Orleans during the 'forties and 'fifties."[56] Upon seeing an enslaved woman named Aimé standing on the auction block, Kellar decided to place a bid. She continued to raise her offer until the auction closed and she was the "last and highest bidder." She took Aimé home for $530.[57]

Women sold and bought enslaved people, and just about everything else, from men like Richardson and Beard. Auctioneers advertised sales for slaves as well as for bonnets, fabrics, lace, women's dresses, and ladies' shoes. If she were in the market for one, a woman could also buy houses, lots, and plantations. Individuals in cities and towns throughout the South regularly held auctions just for women, at which they could bid upon a variety of items such as "bedsteads, bureaus, chairs, carpets, [and] mattresses," as well as "a splendid assortment of rich dress goods and trimmings, elegant silk . . . cloaks . . . wool blankets, counterpanes, quilts," and "housekeeping articles." G. W. Hanna called upon "all the ladies" to attend auctions he held "every morning and evening" just for them. E. Barinds and Company also held "ladies' auctions . . . every Tuesday and Friday from 2 to 5 o'clock during the month of December" in 1857.[58] "Ladies' auctions" took place in cities like Charleston, New Orleans, Iberville and Shreveport, Louisiana, Nashville, Memphis, Baltimore, Richmond, Hannibal and Glasgow, Missouri, and Raleigh, Fayetteville, and New Bern, North Carolina. These auctions were well attended; sometimes crowds of a hundred or more women would pack themselves into the auction rooms. It became so crowded at one of these venues that women had to stand on chairs to view the items put up for bid. The same men who held ladies' auctions also served as auctioneers "for the sale of real estate, slaves, successions and out-door business generally."[59] They often announced their ladies' auctions and the sales of enslaved people in newspaper advertisements that appeared side by side. Rapelye, Bennett, and Company, for example, promoted the auction of a "mulatto wench, with her child" as well as her eight-year-old brother, directly above a notice expressing their intention of having a "ladies' auction" the next day. Similarly, A. S. Levy advertised the sale of a "negro boy," who happened to be twenty-two years of age, directly above his ad for a Ladies' Auction he planned to hold the following Monday.[60]

"Negro Boy at Auction by A. S. Levy & Co." and
"Ladies' Auction. Fancy Dry Goods by A. S. Levy &
Co.," *Memphis Daily Appeal*, August 10, 1861
(*Chronicling America: Historic American Newspapers,*
Library of Congress)

Ladies' auctions taught women all they needed to know about bidding at auctions where enslaved people were the "goods" being sold. The auctioneers who orchestrated these events probably used the same chants they employed to auction off enslaved people, and allowed winning bidders to pay for their items with cash or on credit if the purchase prices exceeded a certain amount.[61] Although auctioneers did not sell enslaved people at ladies' auctions, their effective and voracious advertising ensured that women would know where to find such auctions, if they did want to buy them.

When women sold slaves in public markets, they sometimes did so because of familial responsibilities.[62] Yet even under the pretext of resolving family business, some women sold enslaved people for more selfish reasons. Charity A. Ramsey was acting as her husband's estate administrator when on "the first Tuesday in June 1857," she organized a sale in Campbell County, Georgia, at which she sold a seven-year-old enslaved girl named Martha to Zadock Blalock. Blalock soon discovered that Martha was afflicted with a "running off of the bowels," a malady that local residents attributed to her tendency to eat dirt. At least two physicians claimed that she suffered from typhoid "numonia" and typhoid fever. Whatever her affliction, Martha eventually died of it. Blalock accused Ramsey of selling him a sickly slave who she knew was ill and falsely warranting her as healthy and sound.[63] He was right. Ramsey had told two of her female neighbors that her decision to sell Martha and other slaves had nothing to do with repaying her husband's debts. She planned to sell them because they were sick and she feared "they might die and she would loose them."[64] Ramsey decided to sell these enslaved people because she did not want to lose their value.

Women also sold enslaved people because they were too old, because they were male instead of female, or because they found their temperaments disagreeable. Women like George White's mistress sold enslaved people so they could buy dresses with the proceeds. White recalled that his mistress "was a dressy woman," and her penchant for the latest fashion often led her to the slave market. He said that whenever "she wanted a dress, she would sell a slave." The desires that could be fulfilled through the slave market seemingly had no end, and whether a woman wanted servants who were younger, of a different sex, or better behaved—or even a new dress—the slave market helped satisfy her needs.[65]

Frequently, though, women unburdened themselves of laborers they deemed unworthy of their continued investment, and in most cases, they did not care about the lasting consequences such decisions had upon enslaved people's lives.[66] Sometimes, in fact, such traumas were part of their decisions. Leah Woods decided to sell her slave precisely because she knew that doing so would remove him from all he knew and loved. Woods considered her slave Buck, who was "young and very likely," and was "at that time worth twelve or fifteen hundred dollars," so "insolent and highly provoking . . . [that] she determined as a punishment to send him out of the state," "far off from his kindred and those with whom he was familiar."[67]

White women sometimes decided to sell enslaved people away from their loved ones and communities for darker reasons. Eliva Boles's first mistress sold her because Boles's master was her father.[68] Sarah Hill and Margarette J. Mason wanted to sell enslaved men because they were "too white to keep." Both men were so light in color that they could successfully pass as white. Hill and Mason were concerned that the men would run away and they would incur significant financial losses. Mason was able to finalize the sale of her slave in time, but Hill was not so lucky. Once Edmund, the mixed-race, nineteen-year-old enslaved man she hoped to sell in the New Orleans slave market, discovered her plan, he made his escape. Months later, after placing multiple runaway advertisements, she still had not found him.[69]

Another formerly enslaved woman spoke of being sold twice. Her first mistress sent her to a slave trader's office to be sold because she had violently resisted the sexual advances of her mistress's son. Her second mistress demanded that she be sold because she was a "half white nigger" whose presence disturbed the mistress so much that she gave her husband an ultimatum: if he "didn't get rid of [her] pretty quick she was goin' to leave." When a month passed and he still had not sold the enslaved woman, his wife left, just as she promised. The husband took the enslaved woman back to the same slave trader he had bought her from. These white women did not sell enslaved people out of necessity; they got rid of them because of shame, jealousy, and anger.[70]

On rare occasions, women sold slaves because it was a lucrative business. At the close of the American Revolution, Ann Robertson engaged in activities that could undoubtedly be characterized as slave trading. She attended slave auctions, sought out sickly slaves, and purchased them. She nursed them back to health and then sold them for a profit. Robertson recognized that such business strategies involved uncertainties that could prove ruinous. Even her husband, John, tried to warn her about her risky bidding behavior, but she "repelled his interference and said the money was her own [and] she would do as she pleased with it." He replied that this "was no reason she should ruin herself."[71] But Ann was willing to take her chances despite her husband's warning and the risks. She knew that sick slaves cost less than healthy ones, and she understood that there was no guarantee that they would recover. But she also knew that if their health did improve, she could sell them for much more than she paid for them.[72]

The kind of speculation that Ann Robertson engaged in required a sophisticated understanding of the vagaries of the slave market, a willingness to gamble on the physical uncertainties inherent in the bodies she exposed for sale, and an acceptance on the part of prospective buyers that they could trust the person presenting these bodies to them for purchase. Her gambles paid off. Through her slave trading and other commercial endeavors, Robertson amassed considerable wealth and a substantial amount of property in her own name. At the time of her death, she possessed an estate worth more than fifteen hundred pounds. Twenty-seven enslaved men, women, and children were listed among her most valuable possessions.[73]

Some white women partnered with others to trade in slaves for profit. One such woman was a widow named Mathilda Bushy. Because she did not keep a diary or write letters, much of her life remains cloaked in silence, but notarial and court records lay bare her extensive investments in the New Orleans slave market and trade as well as her relationship to Bernard Kendig, one of the wealthiest and most infamous slave traders in the city.[74] When Bushy decided to sell seven of her slaves, she hired Kendig to handle the sale and it became one of the many he transacted for her during his lucrative career.[75] For two years, Kendig acted as Bushy's agent and attorney-in-fact, and he bought and sold numerous slaves for her in this capacity. One historian has claimed that Bushy was merely an underwriter for Kendig's trade and that the slaves he bought and sold may not have been hers. Court testimony from an 1858 case filed against Kendig would seem to support this conclusion.[76] N. Folger and J. Folger sued Kendig for payment of a debt he owed them. Kendig refused to pay because he claimed that he was insolvent and could not jeopardize his livelihood and his family's well-being. The Folgers contested his claim, asserting that he possessed considerable wealth. Their legal counsel called upon Kendig's former business partner and fellow slave trader James W. Boazman to support their assertions. Boazman testified that Kendig conducted business in Mathilda Bushy's name in order to avoid paying his creditors. He also claimed that she had nothing to do with their slave-trading business because he himself had never seen her and did not personally know her.[77]

Boazman, however, did not tell the court the whole story. The Folgers' 1858 case, and other suits that preceded it, reveal that Bushy and Kendig were more than business associates. Moreover, these legal records show that she was more intricately involved in Kendig and Boazman's slave-dealing business than the latter wanted the court to believe. She was, in fact, Kendig's aunt, and the United States census identifies her as one of the individuals residing in his household in both 1850 and 1860. In the 1856 case that William H. Nixon filed against Boazman and Bushy for selling him a sickly slave, Kendig was compelled to testify. His testimony in this case makes it clear that he was actually Bushy's employee. When Nixon's counsel asked Kendig whether he had a personal stake in the outcome of the case, he claimed that he had no interest in the final judgment and qualified his financial disinterest by explaining his business relationship with Bushy.[78]

According to Kendig, Bushy gave him money to buy and sell slaves on her behalf. He would then retain a portion of the profits and give her the rest. Under cross-examination, Kendig stated that his compensation came from the commission he earned on each sale. The suit also contradicts the allegations Boazman put forth in his discrediting testimony in *Folger v. Kendig*. In the *Nixon* case, Boazman and Bushy were named as codefendants, and the court records reveal that the two were "partners in trade in buying and selling slaves." Kendig seemed to support this assertion; he testified that "Boazman negotiated the sale from Mrs. Bushy to Nixon." Surprisingly, Boazman did not deny this fact or qualify it at any time during the court proceedings. In fact, the lawyers who represented Boazman against Nixon also represented Mathilda Bushy in this case, and they confirmed the partnership between her and Boazman in their answer to Nixon's charges.[79] The *Nixon* case not only establishes Boazman and Bushy's business connections, it also calls Boazman's later denial of having known Bushy, and his dismissal of her slave-trading activities, into question. Furthermore, one witness testified that Boazman acted as Bushy's agent in the slave sale that lay at the heart of the legal suit. Boazman testified in this case as well, and claimed to have "bid off the negro Willis" for Bushy and that Willis was "bought to be resold."[80] Buying slaves at the behest of a business partner, with the express intention of reselling those slaves for profit, qualifies by any measure as speculation or trading in slaves.

Kendig made his aunt's economic investment in the New Orleans slave market abundantly clear when he was again called to testify in a suit that Edward Moore filed against her in 1857. He told the court that before buying and selling slaves for Bushy, he was a drayman and had much of his money invested in his drays and mules. Then he became interested in doing business with her, and she gave him the authority to use her money to buy groups of slaves and resell them on her behalf. As part of their agreement, Bushy allowed Kendig to retain half of the profits he earned when he resold the slaves, and he deposited her half in the bank.[81] Kendig's testimony also suggests that she was not new to the trade in human flesh; she was already profiting from the slave trade before he decided to take his chances on slave speculation. In fact, she had been buying and selling slaves without the aid of a proxy for years before Kendig became her agent and business partner. Bushy also appears in numerous court cases in which purchasers sued her for selling them diseased or otherwise "faulty" slaves. She also owned a slave yard.[82]

Bernard Kendig is well known to historians because he purchased enslaved people who were allegedly unsound in some way and knowingly resold them as healthy and sound, a shady practice that earned him a nasty reputation among fellow slave traders.[83] Mathilda Bushy's court records show that she, too, engaged in this practice. Was Kendig the mastermind behind this underhanded strategy to maximize profits in the slave market? Or did he learn from his aunt Mathilda? Was Mathilda Bushy a devoted aunt looking after her nephew's financial interests and well-being? Or was she a woman who sought to engage in and exploit the gains that could be had in the lucrative trade that her nephew practiced? Mathilda Bushy did not leave behind her own answers to these questions, but from the records that do exist, it is evident that she operated in many of the same ways as did other individuals engaged in the slave trade. In fact, Kendig and Bushy's partnership virtually mirrored an agreement which Boazman struck with Elisha Cannon in 1850: "Boazman was to receive 1/3rd the proceeds of buying and selling, and . . . Cannon was to furnish the capital."[84]

The familial ties that undergirded Kendig and Bushy's partnership resembled the ones that existed between male members of the notorious Woolfolk family, who used kinship ties to create a slave-trading network that operated in the most lucrative, geo-strategically positioned slave markets in the South. In addition to the Woolfolks, numerous cases exist of speculators forming similar partnerships with their kin.[85] Similar partnership agreements also reveal that Mathilda Bushy's decision to provide Bernard Kendig and James Boazman with the funds to purchase slaves, and her agreement to let them sell such slaves on her behalf, were not unusual either.[86] Individuals like Bushy and Kendig structured their slave-trading partnerships in a variety of ways intended to draw on the strengths of each partner and benefit all parties. When difficulties arose, they modified their arrangements accordingly.

The women who bought and sold enslaved people for personal use, sold enslaved people on behalf of others, engaged in slave speculation, and partnered with others to trade in slaves for profit were not the only women navigating southern slave markets. Slave-owning women who set enslaved women to work in their "negro brothels" also benefited from their engagement in slave-market activities, and their livelihoods brought the markets in slaves and sex together. Some historians have assumed that "white men's sexual access to slave women . . . lessened the market for black prostitutes," and other scholars who examine the fancy trade—the sector of the market that catered to white men who sought to purchase sexual slaves and concubines—position them as the only individuals who seized the economic opportunities that such a market presented. But this was not always the case, especially in cities like New Orleans.[87]

Nineteenth-century New Orleans was one of the most important port cities in the world. It also held the largest slave market in the South, and it had plenty of brothels and prostitutes.[88] Historians have studied the city's slave market and fancy trade, including slave traders' sales of these enslaved women to individuals who operated southern brothels, as well as the relationship between prostitution, city politics, and economic growth.[89] These discussions usually center on male actors. But even a cursory glance at newspaper reports of arrests for crimes related to prostitution and brothel keeping makes it clear that women constituted the majority of the accused. And stories about white women who benefited from their involvement in the city's markets in slaves and sex offer a dramatically different view of the ways white women exploited enslaved bodies for profit.

In what the New Orleans *Daily Picayune* described as a "disgusting affair," police arrested four "light colored" enslaved women on the charge of living in a "house of ill-fame." They belonged to Mathilda Raymond, the keeper of the house. According to the *Picayune*, these women were not simply Raymond's domestic servants; they were in her house for "the vilest purposes"—in other words, to engage in prostitution. Raymond's neighbor Thomas Lynch accused her of "keeping a disorderly house" that was "the resort and residence of lewd and abandoned women." He did not, however, mention that some of these so-called lewd and abandoned women were enslaved.[90]

Mary Taylor also operated what the local newspaper described as a "negro brothel" in New Orleans, and she owned at least four women who were employed there. In 1855, three of them—Margaret, Patsey, and Josephine—were arrested on the charge of keeping a disorderly brothel, which was probably Taylor's establishment. In 1858, they, along with another of Taylor's slaves named Theresa and several enslaved people who belonged to local residents, were brought before court officials for unlawful assembly and harboring runaway slaves in Taylor's brothel. And in 1862, two of her female slaves were charged with conspiring with Taylor to "rope in" and rob a man, probably a client. Taylor and her two female slaves were subsequently arrested, seized by the police, and placed in the local jail. While Taylor was incarcerated, police officers took her house keys and searched her home for the money that she and her slaves had allegedly stolen. She accused the officers of taking more than five thousand dollars' worth of gold, silver, and cash, a gold watch, a gold chain and locket, a set of diamonds and other jewelry, and a gold pen with an ivory holder. The stolen money and property would have the purchasing power of more than $160,000 today, part or all of which Taylor undoubtedly earned through the sexual labor of her slaves.[91]

It's difficult to say how many brothel-keeping women operated during these years. In the early- to mid-nineteenth-century South, courts charged many women with crimes *related* to prostitution, such as "keeping a disorderly house," but prostitution itself was not a crime. Thus, slave-owning women's sexual exploitation of enslaved women often remains invisible. In addition, the authorities often held slave-owning women's female *slaves* responsible for crimes such as brothel keeping, even though their owners were ultimately responsible for their engaging in such acts.[92] The assistant recorder of the First District of New Orleans, for example, ordered an enslaved woman named Sarah to be whipped for the crime of "keeping a house devoted to unlawful purposes" and imposed a twenty-five-dollar fine upon her owner, Mrs. Bonsigneur. There is no indication of whether court officials contemplated whether Sarah kept this brothel for or at the behest of Bonsigneur, or whether Bonsigneur compelled Sarah to engage in the work against her will.[93]

When slave-owning female brothel owners like Mathilda Raymond and Mary Taylor purchased enslaved women and compelled them to serve as prostitutes in their establishments, they were acting as slave traders of a different stripe. Their commerce condemned the enslaved women they owned to sexual violence, and they orchestrated every assault their male customers made upon their female slaves, acts that moved beyond the typical atrocities of the fancy trade. When white men sold fancy girls to men who sought sexual gratification, they generally profited from these transactions once. But slave-owning female brothel owners sold the most intimate parts of these enslaved women's bodies to their customers over and over again. The money enslaved women earned while enduring these violations was not theirs to keep; by law and by custom their wages belonged to their female owners. Some historians have argued that enslaved women *chose* to engage in prostitution because sexual labor paid more than other kinds of work. Perhaps this was the case for some enslaved women whose owners allowed them to hire themselves out in whatever way yielded the most profit. But the enslaved women whom white women compelled to engage in prostitution within southern brothels were not afforded the same pseudo-autonomy or opportunities to determine what kind of labor they would perform.

It is noteworthy that when historians discuss white *men's* involvement in the fancy trade, they do not frame the sale of enslaved women for the purpose of sexual labor, or the men's perpetration of sexual coercion and violence against these women, in the same way. Recent studies have focused on slave traders who raped "fancy girls" before their sale and then passed these women off to business acquaintances so that they could do the same. After they and their friends had raped these enslaved females repeatedly, their owners sold them to other men who wanted them for the same purpose. The white men who engaged in these behaviors never claimed that the enslaved women they sexually violated willingly participated in these sexual encounters. Nor do historians suggest that the enslaved females whom slave traders subjected to these violations wanted to be fancy girls, wanted to engage in sex with these slave traders, or agreed to be sold as sexual slaves.[94] The question then must be asked: If we do not assume that the enslaved women whom slave-trading men bought, owned, sexually violated, and sold as sexual slaves were "freely" engaged in sexual slavery, then why should we assume that the enslaved women and girls who belonged to white madams and brothel keepers chose or consented to the same kinds of sexual violation? Acting as brothel keepers, white women initiated the sexual violence against enslaved women, and acting as mistresses of the household they personally orchestrated acts of sexual violence against enslaved women and men in hopes that the women would produce children who would augment their wealth. The formerly enslaved women who recounted these ordeals unequivocally described their experiences as nonconsensual. As Sharon Block has made clear, "choice" or "consent" within coercive contexts such as slavery are impossible to judge, but in the end, enslaved women had no choice.[95]

The slave market offered a range of possibilities for white women, and until now these women have been among the slave trade's best-kept secrets. But white women's invisibility within southern slave markets has little to do with their avoidance of or aversion to the commerce that took place there. In fact, white women were ubiquitous in slave-market dealings. Regardless of how they might have felt about the system, their slave-market activities brought them wealth that they would not have accumulated otherwise. Most did not verbalize their innermost feelings about the morality and justness of slavery in the records they left behind. Yet every time a white woman chose to buy and sell slaves, provide a slave trader with goods or services, or prostitute the bodies of the enslaved females she owned, she contradicted the sentimental or maternal view of white women's relationships with slaves and the institution as a whole. Their decisions to buy and sell enslaved people helped sustain the institution of slavery and the domestic slave trade, severed relationships between enslaved family members, and broke emotional bonds that would never be mended. The slave-owning women who engaged in slave-market activities were far more than begrudgingly complicit bystanders on the margins of the peculiar institution. They had an immense economic stake in the continued enslavement of African Americans, and they struggled to find ways to preserve the system when the Civil War threatened to destroy the institution of slavery and their wealth along with it.

7

"Her Slaves Have Been Liberated and Lost to Her"

A year after Union forces began their occupation of New Orleans in the spring of 1862, Captain Tyler Read of the Eighth Division of the Third Massachusetts Calvary and his men made a discovery while they searched for "arms and munitions" on the estate of a French Creole woman named Madame Coutreil. They not only found contraband, they also uncovered a "small house, closed tightly . . . about nine or ten feet square." It was, according to Read, a "dark and loathsome dungeon, alive with the most sickening stench that can be imagined." Appalled, he exclaimed to Coutreil, "In Heaven's name, what have you here!" and to this she replied, "Oh, only a little girl." When Read ventured inside, he found "sitting at one end of the room upon a low stool, a girl about eighteen years of age." She was "nearly white" and had an "iron yoke," surmounted with three prongs "riveted about her neck, where it had rusted through the skin, and lay corroding apparently upon the flesh." She had been languishing in this place for three months, and was "almost insensible from emaciation, and immersion in the foul air of her dungeon." Her only "crime" was attempting to run away from her mistress, who, suspecting her of Yankee sympathies, hoped to keep her hidden away until the Confederate army had driven the Union soldiers away from the city. Madame Coutreil's action signaled her staunch determination to hold on to the young girl she considered her property, regardless of the circumstances that threatened her, and slave-owning women like her, with the loss of all they owned.[1]

Slave-owning women continued to buy, sell, and hire enslaved people even as the country—half-slave, half-free—moved steadily toward civil war. The days when they would be at liberty to do so, however, were waning. Men and women across the nation viewed the presidential election of Abraham Lincoln on November 6, 1860, as a sign that abolitionists had won. They believed that he and his administration planned to implement changes that would lead to slavery's dissolution. Many southern slaveholders immediately prepared to defend the institution at all costs. Within days of Lincoln's election, two South Carolina senators, James Chesnut and James Hammond, withdrew from their seats. Then, on December 20, 1860, citing the free states' persistent assaults upon slavery and the federal government's failure to protect the institution from such attacks, South Carolina seceded from the Union.[2] Congress moved quickly to stave off impending conflict. Members proposed a constitutional amendment that would have prevented the federal government from abolishing or interfering with slavery, but their efforts proved unsuccessful.[3] By June 1861, Mississippi, Florida, Alabama, Georgia, Louisiana, Texas, Virginia, Arkansas, North Carolina, and Tennessee had followed South Carolina's lead and seceded from the Union one by one. Delaware, Maryland, Kentucky, and Missouri (which, with West Virginia, formed in 1863, were known as the Border States) took a different course; they remained committed to the Union and by so doing, ensured that the federal government would uphold their right to keep enslaved people in subjugation.

On April 12, 1861, a month after Lincoln took office, South Carolina took the lead once again when the newly formed Confederate States Army attacked Fort Sumter, a federal garrison situated in the Charleston harbor, an act that launched the Civil War. Three days after this assault, Lincoln issued a proclamation which called forth "the militia of several States of the Union . . . to suppress" the growing rebellion in the South. He also commanded southern rebels "to disperse, and retire peaceably to their respective abodes within twenty days" of its issuance.[4] The rebel states ignored his command and continued their resistance. To the shock and dismay of many slaveholders, enslaved people responded to this conflict between brothers by intensifying their own rebellion against their owners and the institution they sought to preserve.

Enslaved people had long abandoned plantations in search of freedom, and they continued to do so as the conflict grew. But now they began to run toward federal military forces, rather than away from them. Initially they were unsure that Union soldiers sympathized with their plight, and they were right to be cautious. Enslaved people knew that they were taking enormous risks by leaving their homes and appealing to Union officers for help and protection within federal encampments. Throughout the war, many Union soldiers proved that they were no allies to the enslaved. Many northern soldiers were as prone as their southern counterparts to accept denigrating ideas about free and bound

African-descended people in their region, and these views affected their interactions with enslaved people in the South. Even in states that seceded, some slaveholders remained committed to the Union and joined federal military forces while staunchly defending slavery. For all the good Union officers often did for escaped slaves, others returned enslaved people to their owners, even after military policy forbade them to do so. Union soldiers and officers stole from enslaved people, raped and brutalized them, sold them and pocketed the profits, and kept enslaved people for themselves.[5] Complicating the situation, Abraham Lincoln and his administration gave enslaved people no indication that fleeing from their owners and crossing Union lines would result in their freedom. To the contrary, both before and after Lincoln became president, he emphatically expressed his commitment to upholding slave owners' property rights. Lincoln's speeches repeatedly assured slaveholders that he had no intention of interfering in their domestic affairs, and after he was elected president he reinforced this assurance in the opening passages of his First Inaugural Address: "Apprehension seems to exist among the people of the Southern States that by accession of a Republican administration their property and their peace and personal security are to be endangered. There has never been any reasonable cause for such apprehension. Indeed, the most ample evidence to the contrary has all the while existed and been open to their inspection." The Constitution protected American citizens' rights to hold people as property, and Lincoln routinely and publicly declared his intention of abiding by it. He also promised southern slaveholders that any "fugitives from service or labor"—the euphemism for enslaved people—would be returned to them.[6] However much of this most slaves might have been aware of, all knew that it was safer to venture into Union occupied regions cautiously, and if they did not face immediate rejection and learned of no plans to send them back, they communicated this information to other enslaved people who hoped to cross Union lines. Over the course of the war, enslaved people fled to Union-occupied territories and federal encampments by the thousands.

One of the earliest examples of this extraordinary exodus began in the spring of 1861 under the auspices of the Massachusetts lawyer, businessman, politician, and Union general Benjamin F. Butler, who oversaw Fort Monroe in Hampton, Virginia. As enslaved people found their way to Fort Monroe, Butler faced a dilemma that plagued other Union commanders as well: Should he allow these individuals to stay within Union lines, or should he return them to their alleged owners? Like many other Union officers, he wrote to his superior for advice. Up to this point general military policy aligned with the Fugitive Slave Act of 1850: Union soldiers were duty-bound to return enslaved people to those who claimed them. Risking censure, some Union officers and soldiers refused to do so. But Butler resolved his quandary in an ingenious way, one that allowed him to avoid reprimand. Versed in the laws of war, Butler knew that any property that rebels used to aid and abet an insurrection against the government could be seized as contraband. He reasoned that, because enslaved people were technically property under southern law, and Virginians were in a state of rebellion against the Union, enslaved people who came to Fort Monroe could be defined as contraband and thus liable to confiscation. He also reasoned that he and the soldiers under his command were not obligated to adhere to the Fugitive Slave Act because it applied only to states within the Union; since Virginia had seceded, the law was no longer applicable there.[7]

In spirit and intent, Butler's policy was not aimed at abolition or ensuring the freedom of escaped enslaved people; only a month before Butler implemented it, he wrote to the governor of Maryland reassuring him that he was "anxious to convince all classes of persons that the forces under my command are not in any way to interfere with or countenance interference with the laws of the State." To that end, he promised the governor that he was "ready to co-operate with your excellency in suppressing most promptly and effectively any insurrection against the laws of Maryland."[8] Defining enslaved people as contraband liable to federal seizure and use was a military policy designed to weaken southern resistance by compromising the slaveholders' ability to use the enslaved people they owned to support and sustain the rebellion. Despite Butler's intentions, however, his policy laid the groundwork for a series of congressional actions that did indeed have emancipatory effects.

General Butler's solution to the problem posed by enslaved people crossing Union lines proved a palatable one for Congress. On August 6, 1861, it passed "An Act to Confiscate Property Used for Insurrectionary Purposes," also known as the First Confiscation Act, which provided for the seizure of any property that individuals in rebellion against the Union used to support their insurrectionary efforts, including enslaved people. In quick succession the following year, Congress passed several acts of legislation that slowly but steadily weakened the institution of slavery throughout the Confederacy. In March 1862, Congress approved an additional article of war that forbade Union soldiers from returning enslaved people to slaveholders deemed to be in rebellion. In April, it passed a law that abolished slavery within the District of Columbia and compensated slaveholders for the financial losses associated with the emancipation of the enslaved people they owned. In June, a congressional act prohibited slavery in territories belonging to the United States and any territories that the government acquired in the future. The following month Congress passed the

Second Confiscation Act and the Militia Act. Together, these two acts freed all enslaved people who belonged to individuals residing in Confederate states, even slaves who were not compelled to aid the rebellion, barred Union officers from assessing the legitimacy of enslaved people's claims to be free or claims that disloyal slaveholders put forth with regard to the ownership of runaways, and permitted the president to "employ as many persons of African descent as he may deem necessary and proper for the suppression of this rebellion [and] organize and use them in such manner as he may judge best for the public welfare," including enlisting enslaved and free men of African descent in the Union armed forces. More powerfully, the Militia Act granted freedom to the family members of African-descended men who served in any military capacity within the Union.[9]

While this congressional activity was taking place, two Union generals— John C. Frémont, who commanded the Union Army of the West, and David Hunter, who served as Commander of the Department of the South—exceeded their military authority by issuing general orders regarding the emancipation of all enslaved people in the states of Missouri, Georgia, South Carolina, and Florida. Lincoln swiftly denounced and rescinded their orders, fearing that their unconstitutional assaults on the property rights of slaveholders, especially those who lived in Missouri, would compel the other three slaveholding states within the Union to secede.[10] Yet even with Lincoln's public renunciation, southerners across the region, not just in the Border States, understood Frémont and Hunter's emancipatory proclamations as part of a more systemic effort to abolish the institution.

In September 1862, Lincoln removed virtually all doubt about the institution's future when he issued the Preliminary Emancipation Proclamation. In it, he offered Confederate states the opportunity to rejoin the Union as long as they were willing to "voluntarily adopt, immediate or gradual abolishment of slavery within their respective limits." As further incentive, Lincoln also provided for slaveholder compensation for any slaves who might be freed by state-level abolition. He gave Confederate states a hundred days to decide whether to accept abolition and rejoin the Union. If they chose not to do so, all enslaved people within their states would be "then, thenceforward, and forever free," and Union military forces were ordered to recognize and protect that freedom. On January 1, 1863, finding that the Confederate states remained in rebellion (with the exception of Tennessee and a number of parishes in Louisiana and counties in Virginia which were under federal control) and unwilling to cede the institution of slavery willingly, Lincoln issued the final Emancipation Proclamation. It freed all enslaved people in Confederate states but stopped short of abolishing the institution of slavery entirely. Enslaved people who labored in Missouri, Maryland, Delaware, and Kentucky, the slaveholding states that remained loyal to the Union, remained in captivity.[11]

Taken together, the Union troops' arrival in southern communities, the flight of enslaved people toward federal forces, Congress's legislative actions, and Lincoln's proclamations signaled irreversible transformations in the institution of slavery. Slave-owning women were acutely aware of these actions, and historians have remarked upon the ways they dealt with the conflict, indulging in bouts of intense and prolific writing during the Civil War era. White southern women and girls wrote about cold and indifferent Union soldiers, the impact of prolonged food and supply shortages, the heartache and yearning they experienced because of loved ones' absences, the loss of the men and boys who had fallen in battle, the challenges of rural isolation, widowhood, and even the difficulty of making the transition from using enslaved to using free labor.[12] And interwoven within their diary passages and personal correspondence, slave-owning women also grappled with the economic impact the Civil War had and would have upon them as individuals who owned enslaved people in their own right.

After lifetimes shaped by slavery and persistent efforts to sustain it, the prospect of emancipation caused slave-owning women tremendous concern for reasons that rarely emerge in existing studies of their wartime experiences: it robbed them of their primary source of personal wealth by redefining enslaved African Americans as people, not property; placed them in positions of economic dependency; and forced them to establish restrictive relationships with those who still had financial resources, in order to survive. Slave-owning women also feared emancipation because it held the potential to destabilize and reallocate the power they exercised within their marriages and families, authority which was often vested in their ownership of property. The government's emancipation of enslaved people made it all but certain that such women, who commanded a level of respect and legal and economic autonomy within their households and wider communities from their status as slave owners, might lose that status. Throughout the war, women who owned enslaved people shouldered the tremendous burden of dealing with its consequences.

Often alone and isolated on plantations and farms scattered throughout the rural South, slave-owning women lived most days of the war surrounded by millions of enslaved people who embodied their fiscal loss and defeat. Slave-owning women often saw the Civil War as a personal battle, one they deemed worth fighting not just as southerners resisting the Union advance onto their land, or as "soldiers' wives" whom the government of the Confederate States of America (CSA) promised to care for in exchange for their menfolk's military service and sacrifices.[13] It was also a fight they vigilantly took on to ensure their own financial autonomy, economic stability, and survival. But like the Confederate soldiers who lay slain on the battlefields, slave-owning women lost their war—and most of their wealth along with it.

As slave-owning women observed the signs of slavery's dissolution all around them, they devised a multitude of strategies to protect their financial investments. At their best, slave-owning women freed their slaves and hired them to work their land for wages. One slave-owning woman "liberated all of her people . . . about three years before the Civil War [ended], and give them a home as long as they lived."[14] But at their worst, they perpetrated brutal acts of violence against the people they hoped to keep in bondage. The majority opted for methods that fell between the extremes. However, all their strategies were contingent upon local circumstances: the states in which they lived, the presence or absence of federal troops, and whether they could call upon individuals within the federal government or military forces to assist them. In their efforts to retain possession of their slaves white women traversed treacherous wartime terrain as well as seemingly peaceful countryside that might become a bloody battlefield at any time. When their slaves escaped to Union lines, slave-owning women who lived in the Border States appealed to members of their communities, the federal government, and high-ranking Union officials for protection of their investments in slavery, help in reclaiming their human property, or compensation for their losses. In Confederate states, as Union forces drew closer to slave-owning women's communities and homes, the federal military policies implemented in 1861 and 1862 allowed women who swore an oath that they were not in rebellion to claim and repossess any of their slaves who could be found within military camps. Slave-owning women who lived in areas that had not been infiltrated by Union forces still feared their arrival because they suspected that the enslaved people who remained in their possession would either run away, be confiscated by Union troops, or, if they themselves were secessionists, be emancipated.

To circumvent these threats, many slave-owning women packed up and moved themselves and their slaves out of the Union's reach, a process referred to as "running" or "refugeeing." Other women, like Madame Coutreil, imprisoned their slaves to prevent them from escaping and often intensified their brutality against them. As the federal government moved inexorably toward emancipation, some slave-owning women rightfully concluded that they could no longer hold on to the enslaved people they owned, so they sold them or relinquished their property rights in them and forced their former slaves off their lands. Eventually most slave-owning women came to terms with their financial losses and reconstructed their lives without slaves. But they did not let go easily or willingly.

As the Union forces occupied the South, enslaved people began to behave strangely, and began disappearing in greater numbers from their female owners. Such was the case for Eliza Ripley, who remarked upon the change in the behavior and comportment of an old enslaved woman she had known all her life: "Old 'Aunt Hannah' (that was my mother's laundress long before I was born . . .) stood in her little cabin-door as straight as an arrow; she always complained of *rheumatiz*, and I don't think I ever saw her straight before; but there she stood, with the air of one suddenly elevated to an exalted position, and waved me a 'Good-by, madam I b'ar you no malice.'"[15] Some slave-owning women found it hard to believe that their slaves would leave unless the Yankees had compelled them. Sarah Johnson Berliner assumed that her family's slaves "didn't want freedom." A "squad of Union soldiers," she maintained, had summarily forced "freedom on them" and "told them that the proper thing for them to do was to get out for themselves."[16] After the Union declared it legal in 1862 for federal troops to confiscate the property of those who served in rebel forces or aided and abetted the rebellion, women like Berliner saw the Union officers who were authorized to take their silver, furniture, food, and livestock as thieves, and they particularly resented the "theft" of their most valuable property, their slaves. It was one thing to take precious metals, household goods, victuals, and animals. It was quite another to take human beings who were doubly, and sometimes triply, valuable and whose bodies, production, and reproduction paid dividends. Union troops did sometimes seize enslaved people against their will, but over the course of the war it became clear that, even without Union troops' influence, enslaved people were more than willing to leave their female owners in search of freedom.

Some women interpreted the changes in their slaves' conduct, especially their flight to Union encampments and enlistment in the Union Army, as a personal affront. One formerly enslaved man joined the Union Army when he was seventeen, and he returned to his mistress's estate while on furlough. She asked him, "You remember when you were sick and I had to bring you to the house and nurse you?" He replied that he did, at which she exclaimed, "And now you are fighting me!" He explained that he was not fighting her personally but to secure his freedom.[17]

Their enslaved escapees' "ingratitude" was not all that grated. The women who remarked or reflected upon the actions of runaway slaves realized that as enslaved people fled, all the wealth bound up in their persons was lost. These were fears that many southerners shared. Mary Boykin Chesnut related a conversation she had with a physician as they watched a Confederate regiment conducting marching drills while their slaves stood by. The doctor told Chesnut that the enslaved people gathered there constituted "sixteen thousand dollars' worth of negro property which can go off on its own legs to the Yankees whenever it pleases." As a slave-owning woman, Chesnut would have been familiar with such estimations and the financial losses runaway slaves represented. Women like Chesnut were acutely aware of the tactics that slave owners were using "to keep the negroes from running off." Another southern slave owner, Catherine McRae, wrote about some of these strategies, but she also noted that despite such efforts, "a boy of Madame Dilmas' and of Mr. Ellison's made their escape the week previously." Southern women might not have wanted to face the fact that enslaved people did not need encouragement to leave them, but enslaved people's words, actions, and even body language often compelled them to do so.[18]

Even the youngest slave-owning females felt the economic impact of the war as the people they owned slipped away. Mary Elizabeth Woolfolk was only twelve or thirteen in 1862, but she already owned slaves, and that year they decided to "go off on [their] own legs to the Yankees." Over the course of the war, Woolfolk lost twenty-four men, women, and children. On April 1, 1862, only weeks after Congress passed the article of war forbidding Union soldiers and sailors from returning fugitives to their owners, four of the enslaved men Woolfolk owned left and allegedly allied themselves with the Union forces occupying Fredericksburg, Virginia. According to Woolfolk's trustees, Union soldiers visited the plantation where she and her slaves resided later that year, and on August 3, 1862, they "had a long conversation with the negroes." Shortly thereafter, another three of her male slaves left.[19]

Not long after Congress passed the First Confiscation Act in 1861, the Confederate Congress passed its own act in order "to perpetuate testimony in cases of slaves abducted or harbored by the enemy and of other property seized wasted or destroyed by them." Although the act never specified to what end this testimony would be put, its passage implied an eventual Confederate victory and alluded to the possibility that such documentation might be used to compel the Union to compensate slave owners after the secessionists won the war. In October 1862, in conformity with the Confederate act, Eldred Satterwhite, the Woolfolks' overseer; Jourdan and John W. Woolfolk, Mary's trustees; and William Woolfolk provided sworn affidavits to the Confederacy's Department of State attesting to the losses Mary suffered valuing these men at $9,300.[20] Two years later, on May 24, 1864, more of Woolfolk's slaves fled to the Union as federal forces passed through her community. This time, the women and children outnumbered the men who fled. One Robert Y. Henley captured this "family of negroes" belonging to Mary as they tried to "make their escape to the Yankees." He returned them to Mary and her trustees paid him $500 in compensation.[21]

Mary Woolfolk was lucky; she could call upon a number of male relatives and at least one family employee to help her apprehend her slaves when they ran away. But by 1862, many white southern women were not so lucky. Their fathers, uncles, brothers, husbands, and sons were fighting on battlefields throughout the South, and they were left behind with little to no male protection. Despite the dwindling numbers of white men still residing in southern towns and on rural estates, or perhaps because of their absence, slave-owning women called upon members of their communities to help them reclaim their human property. When Joe and Alfred Shipley fled from the men who hired them, their owner, Emily Mactaviah, posted a runaway advertisement in which she offered an award of fifty dollars for each. Ann L. Contee, a large-scale landowner from Laurel, Maryland, suffered the loss of three of her male slaves over the course of two months. She, too, posted an advertisement in the *Sun* on the same day that Emily Mactaviah did, and offered a fifty-dollar reward for each man to the individuals responsible for apprehending them. Seven months after her slave Lewis disappeared, Esther Baker placed an advertisement in the Macon, Georgia, *Daily Telegraph* requesting help in apprehending him as well. Almost a year after Eliza Sego's slave Hector escaped, she offered a twenty-dollar reward to the person who would take him to the local jail so that she could reclaim him there.[22]

These runaway-slave advertisements also underscore the ruptures in the families of enslaved people, separations that slave-owning women brought about, sustained, or exacerbated. When an enslaved man named Sam ran away from Mary Gilbert, she placed an advertisement in the Charleston *Courier* six months after he escaped. Although Gilbert lived in Cuthbert, Georgia, she advertised in the *Courier* because she believed that Sam would try to find his wife, who lived on Anna Rumph's estate in Walterboro, South Carolina.[23] In many of these advertisements, slave owners theorized that their slaves, especially the men, had fled toward Union forces or their encampments. Gilbert, however, believed that Sam's love for his wife had motivated his flight.

Although it remains unclear as to whether any of these specific women were able to reclaim the enslaved men they owned, some women seemed to have done so. Jailors' notices scattered throughout southern newspapers during this period suggest that members of slaveholding communities were still hunting white women's runaways, placing them in local jails, and possibly collecting the rewards that these women offered.[24]

While southern men talked valiantly of fighting to protect "hearth, home, and womanhood," the women they left behind demanded government and military protection for their households.[25] In the absence of southern men, white women called upon both Union and Confederate officers to respect their rights to such security.[26] But in many cases, the "protection" that *slave-owning* women sought was not predicated upon their fears that soldiers would do them bodily harm, but rather on their concern that these men would violate their rights to and possession of their slaves. When southern women requested that their menfolk be exempted from military service, for example, they often based their appeals upon the effect that these men's absence would have on their slaves. Without white men around, they argued, the enemy might persuade the enslaved people they owned to accompany them or run away. In a letter that Mrs. P. E. Collins penned to Alabama governor John Shorter, for example, she informed him that she wrote on behalf of a community of large-scale female (and male) slave owners who were without a significant male presence and thereby left "in a very unprotected condition." Her neighbor, Mrs. McMillan, was isolated "on her plantation with over 50 negroes, without a white male member in her family." Another one of Collins's neighbors, Mrs. Mollet, was left on her plantation with "over 100 negroes." Mollet's twelve-year-old son was the only white male on the estate. Collins also expressed concern for her elderly male neighbors. One of them, Mr. William Mollet, owned "three farms" and

> **TAKEN UP**
>
> AND committed to Jail in this place, on the 24th inst. two negro men, who say their names are HENRY and JEF. Henry, complection yellow, 5 feet 9 inches high, weighs 165 lbs., about 25 years old. Jef, dark complection, 5 feet 7 or 8 inches high, about 24 years old, weighs 150 lbs., one upper front tooth out; one says he belongs to Mrs. Sallie Hall, the other to Miss Mary Hall, the daughter of Mrs Sallie Hall. They say their owners now live in or near Fayetteville, that they moved from Brunswick county to Fayetteville this spring, and that they with three other negro men were hired to some man in or near Salisbury. There was a white man with them when they were taken up, who made his escape, who said the owners had sent him to take the negroes home, but after being closely questioned run for life.
>
> G. H. MORRIS, Jailer.
>
> Troy N. C., May 26, 1862. 30*tf

Jailor's notice to Mrs. Sallie Hall and her daughter Miss Mary Hall to reclaim their slaves, *Fayetteville Observer*, June 2, 1862 (Nineteenth-Century U.S. Newspapers database, Cengage/Gale) "over 500 negroes." But Collins did not seem particularly interested in her or her neighbors' personal protection; she did not mention any fear of violence. She was more interested in preventing contact between their slaves and Union forces because federal troops might "place temptations before them," and it was "wrong for negroes to be left as they are." Remarkably, Collins argued that all this potential trouble could be avoided if the governor exempted one white man, James Nunnalee, from military service. Apparently he was a "rigid disciplinarian" who instilled more fear in enslaved people than ten men combined.[27]

Slave-owning women who claimed loyalty to the Union also carped about the alleged or actual confiscation of their slaves and demanded that Union officers return the enslaved people they owned. Even when slave-owning women were unsure of their slaves' whereabouts, they sought assistance from Union officers. Sometimes they asked male friends and kin to write letters to Union military officials on their behalf; at others they communicated with these officials directly. When the Union officer Colonel Wright confiscated Mrs. Robert Wagner Thomas's two male slaves in 1862, her son-in-law, James M. Quarles, a lawyer, Tennessee congressman, and Confederate soldier, wrote a letter to General Grant on her behalf, which noted that she "had two negro-boys—carried off by Col. wright when his command left" her community. He also claimed that "these negroes are all the property she has . . . and they are her sole support." From Quarles's perspective, taking a woman's only property and source of income was "a great injustice," one which he believed "should at once be rectified."[28] Faced with the prospect of destitution, Thomas could think of no other alternative but to try to get her slaves back. Or at least that is how she presented her plight to Quarles and the Union official to whom he wrote.

Mrs. E. Stewart, who lived in the Border State of Missouri, claimed to be in dire straits as well, and she had two daughters to think about. In what seemed to be a last recourse, she directed her appeal for help to President Lincoln himself. In her letter of December 1863, she explained that the seven slaves she owned were all the property that she possessed, and they had left her. Two of the enslaved men had joined a regiment formed in Iowa; another had made his way to Camp Edwards in Massachusetts, where the regiment's colonel issued him freedom papers and told him to remain within the confines of the camp. The four women and girls she owned, learning of this news, fled to Chicago and claimed their freedom based on the enlistment and freedom of the three formerly enslaved men who belonged to their mistress. With all her slaves gone, Mrs. Stewart had no source of income to care for herself or her two daughters. As a Union slave owner, Stewart asked Lincoln to either compensate her for the loss of her slaves or provide some "relief." It is unclear whether he responded.[29]

Women like the Davidson County, Tennessee, slaveholder Mrs. S. F. Baker also sought out assistance and protection from Union officers, even after they found the enslaved people who had run away from them, and some of these men obliged them. In the last months of 1863, Hannah and Becky, two enslaved women Baker owned, ran away from her. Hannah fled to Nashville three months before Christmas, and Becky left to complete an errand for her mistress and never returned. Baker searched for Hannah and Becky until she found them, and at that time applied to Major General Lovell H. Rousseau for permission to take them home without molestation. Rousseau granted her request. He issued a written permit that allowed Baker "to take to her home the following Negro women Hannah and Becky (2)." The permit also warned individuals who might want to obstruct her passage that "the General Commanding directs that she will not be interfered with by any authority either civil or military." Baker was in fact "interfered with"—Major John W. Horner stopped her after he witnessed the "humiliating spectacle" she created as she passed through town with Hannah and Becky in tow—but Rousseau's permit "appeared to bear the sanction of superior Military authority," so Horner allowed her to proceed on her way.[30]

This episode would not have raised ire among Union officers such as Horner had it happened two years earlier, but when he described the incident in a letter to another officer, Horner made it clear that Baker's trek through Nashville with her enslaved fugitives, and Rousseau's approval of her passage, were troubling for another reason. Rousseau's protection permit noted that Baker was a "good loyal lady," and by granting her safe passage he was also accepting Baker's claim that Hannah and Becky were fugitives from her "service or labor." Yet, in deciding on "the validity of the claim of any person to the service or labor of any other person," and by "surrendering up any such person to the claimant," Rousseau was violating the additional article of war which Congress passed in March 1862, the Second Confiscation Act of July 1862, and the Emancipation Proclamation. By the time Rousseau issued Baker's permit, it did not matter whether she was a "good loyal lady" or a secessionist, and it made no difference whether Baker had been Hannah and Becky's lawful owner or not. By issuing Baker a permit granting her passage and protection from interference, Rousseau was countermanding federal laws which he was bound to obey. Perhaps Rousseau, a slaveholder from the Union state of Kentucky, believed that Baker's right to property superseded the new federal laws. But no matter Rousseau's reasons, by his authority Mrs. Baker went home with her slaves, in spite of the increasing threats federal law posed to her property rights.

Mrs. Thomas, Mrs. Stewart, and Mrs. Baker were typical of the majority of slave owners, who generally owned ten slaves or less.[31] They were not large-scale landowners; they may not have owned any land at all. For them, the value ascribed to the people they owned and the labor those people performed constituted their only means of survival. Reclaiming their slaves was, they believed, a matter of life and death, and when Union soldiers "persuaded off" their slaves or when enslaved people ran away, these events marked the beginning of their financial ruin. By pleading with men who held the strongest positions of power, these women sought to stave off such an outcome.

After the United States Congress passed an act which emancipated "all persons held to service or labor within the District of Columbia by reason of African descent" in April 1862 and offered slave owners compensation for their slaves who had been freed, slave-owning women seized the opportunity to submit claims in order to receive some of those funds. The District of Columbia emancipation act required petitioners to "describe the person" they owned, and "state how the claim [to the slave or slaves] was acquired, when, from whom, and for what price or consideration," and "if held under any written evidence of title," to "exhibit [it] thereof, or refer to the public record where the same may be found." Petitioners were also obligated to "state such facts, if any there be, touching the value of" their claim "to the service or labor of the person . . . and also . . . touching the moral, mental, and bodily infirmities or defects of said person, as impair the value of the petitioner's claim to such service or labor." They needed to submit an itemized "schedule" of the enslaved people they were claiming and sign and submit a "Form of the Oath for Verification of the Petition" that attested to their ownership and loyalty to the Union. The commissioners documented their work in daily minutes, which reveal that slave-owning women frequently appeared before them along with their slaves. The commissioners assessed these women's loyalty to the Union and the value of their slaves. Some women, like Mildred Ewell and Fanny Ewell, appeared before the commission more than once because each time they brought only a few of the slaves they claimed. The commission called witnesses to testify on behalf of each petitioner, and in many instances women attested to other women's loyalty and slave ownership.[32]

In response to the act, 1,065 Washington, D.C., slave owners submitted petitions for compensation; 429 were women, totaling about 40 percent of the claimants.[33] Even an order of nuns, the Sisters of the Visitation of Georgetown, submitted a petition for compensation. Slave ownership, in fact, was not unusual among nuns living in the South. Emily Clark notes that the Ursuline nuns of New Orleans "owned enslaved people, bought them, sold them, and used them to work their plantations." And when the District of Columbia emancipation act was passed, the Sisters of the Visitation divested themselves of their property just as other women did.[34] Margaret Miller of Howard County, Maryland, appeared before the commissioners "with two servants" without ever filing the requisite petition for compensation, but she nonetheless hoped "to have them examined and valued." Even though "she had not filed a petition," the commissioners allowed her slaves to be appraised and let her submit a petition for compensation after the fact.[35] Most of these women owned one or two slaves, but others, like Margaret C. Barber, owned more than the average slaveholder. She wrote to the federal government about her thirty-four slaves and included an itemized schedule that identified each by age, name, sex, color, and height; whether they were slaves for life or for specified terms; and the type of labor that they performed. The enslaved people in her holdings ranged from four months to sixty-five years in age and in color from "light mulatto" to "black." They performed a variety of tasks: currying leather, laundering clothes, making shoes, cooking, and fieldwork.[36] The government granted Barber's request and paid her a total amount of $9,351.30 for all but one of her enslaved people, though this was undoubtedly less than the value she ascribed to the people she had once owned.[37] Even so, Margaret Barber could count herself among the more fortunate of slave owners because she did not reside in a Confederate state where the federal government emancipated enslaved people without giving their owners a dime. She cut her losses and capitalized on the government's promise.

Not every slave owner in the district followed Margaret Barber's example. Some neither applied for compensation nor emancipated the enslaved people they held in bondage. So in July 1862, Congress passed another act, which allowed enslaved people to petition for their freedom in cases where their owners did not submit compensation claims. Out of the 108 petitions enslaved people submitted, 42 identified female owners.[38] Many of these women lived in the Union state of Maryland or in Confederate Virginia—although a New Jersey woman named Julia Ten Eyck owned three of the slaves—and had hired out their slaves to residents within the District of Columbia. Upon learning that their slaves had submitted these petitions, the women quickly tried to file their own petitions for recompense before their slaves were granted their freedom. If they failed to do so, they would lose the opportunity to secure any funds associated with their slaves' emancipation.

Similar requests could also be found in the slaveholding states that remained within the Union, especially from women whose male slaves enlisted in federal military forces. In Missouri, for example, around 11 percent of all claimants were women who requested compensation because their former slaves had enlisted in the 4th, 7th, 18th, and 19th U.S. Colored Infantry and the 5th and 6th U.S. Colored Cavalry. They made up about 5 percent of claimants for those whose slaves enlisted in the 1st, 4th, 8th, 12th, and 13th U.S. Colored Heavy Artillery.[39]

At various times during the war, women who were at the other end of the economic spectrum also wrote to military officials in hopes of rectifying wrongs that Union troops perpetrated against them. Mary Duncan, an elite absentee planter and slave owner from Staten Island, New York, took on the role of spokesperson for the Natchez, Tennessee, slave-owning community where her plantations were located. She complained that troops had ransacked property belonging to Unionists and carried off their slaves against the slaves' own will. As a southerner who had remained loyal to the Union, Duncan had been given protection orders that were designed to prevent federal encroachment on her land and seizure of her property. Yet despite these "strong 'protection papers'" Union soldiers had confiscated her property. She further alleged that the officers had forcibly removed and impressed the enslaved and freed men who labored on her plantations. Duncan claimed that her slaves were well treated and cared for, and that until the Union officers appeared, they had been willing to remain on her estate and work for wages. Throughout her letter, she questioned the authority of the men to take her property and demanded swift rectification of the problem, something she saw as her right as a loyal citizen of the Union. The Union official who investigated Duncan's claims and personally interviewed the enslaved people in question told a different story. When he spoke to these allegedly contented laborers, they disputed Duncan's claims, telling the officer that they were poorly treated, badly fed, and hardly cared for. In fact, they had left her estate willingly because they thought they would fare as well or better with the Union Army as they had with her.[40]

The following year, on October 27, 1864, Irene Smith wrote a letter to W. P. Fessenden, the secretary of the treasury, in which she assumed a gentler tone. She declared her unwavering loyalty to the Union and clearly delineated the property and goods she had lost to the officers serving under several Union colonels and captains. She also noted each time that she had made a personal request for protection. Later in her letter, it becomes clear why she so relentlessly petitioned the federal government. She and her daughter's husband, Alexander C. Bullitt, owned four plantations in Mississippi and six hundred slaves. Irene Smith owned the majority of the land (three plantations), and the majority of the slaves who cultivated that land, as well.[41] Irene Smith also had protection orders, and not unlike Mary Duncan's, her orders gave no indication that she was concerned about the military harming *her*; the orders routinely and explicitly referred to her property. In her letter to the secretary, she wanted Fessenden to approve her purchase of supplies to sustain production on her plantations, "to be permitted at the earliest day possible to ship her cotton & produce to market, and return with her winter supplies, and pay all her outstanding Obligations." She was trying to operate her plantation as usual, but the government was obstructing her ability to take care of business.[42]

Smith's letter was written on behalf of the collective financial interest of herself, her daughter, and her son-in-law, and it offers important evidence about the relation of slave-owning women to their property interests. Smith's son-in-law, Alexander Bullitt, was not illiterate; he was a state legislator and member of the New Orleans City Council. He was also a partner in Bullitt, Magne, and Company, the publishers of one of New Orleans's leading newspapers, the *Bee*, and he later served as editor of another, the New Orleans *Picayune*. He was not a military officer; Smith did not need to be his advocate because he was present to witness the destruction of his property. Although he was in his early sixties, nothing suggests that he was incapacitated in any way that would preclude him from writing the letter. While Smith's reason for writing the appeal on Bullitt's behalf is not readily apparent from her correspondence, a comparison of the assets he held in the 1850 and 1860 United States federal censuses and references in his will show that the property Smith attributed to him was actually her daughter's inheritance. In the 1850 census, Bullitt did not claim to own any property. Ten years later, however, he was listed as a member of Irene Smith's household, and his occupation had changed from "editor" to "gentleman." His property value changed, too; in 1860, he valued his real estate at $132,000 and his personal estate, which would have included his slaves, at $191,000. When he requested a presidential pardon from Andrew Johnson on December 15, 1865, he noted his place of residence as Longwood Plantation in Washington County, Mississippi, one of the estates that had belonged to Irene Smith's late husband, Benjamin. Bullitt, who wrote his will in 1861 and died seven years later, bequeathed her two plantations, one of which was Longwood, along with "all the slaves . . . attached" to the plantations. He noted that the entire bequest was "the property formerly owned by my deceased wife," Irene's daughter Fanny L. Smith.[43] All of these facts make it clear that Irene Smith's interest in protecting her own property holdings and those of her daughter served as her motivation for writing her letter personally, rather than leaving it in Bullitt's hands.

Confederate soldiers were equally prone to seize enslaved people who belonged to slave-owning women who were sympathetic to the rebel cause. And these women appealed to the Confederate government and military officials for assistance and recompense when they did. Female slave owners were not immune to Confederate impressment programs, and they were obliged to supply the Confederacy with the laborers it needed.[44] The Confederacy paid slave owners wages for the enslaved people they commandeered, and Confederate officers, who oversaw the work that these enslaved men performed, maintained payroll sheets that recorded the particulars of the transactions. These sheets documented how many enslaved people Confederates took and from whom, any provisions they gave to these laborers, their terms of labor, where they worked, and the wages each laborer earned. Female owners' names, or those of individuals these women appointed to act on their behalf, appear throughout these documents. Scores of enslaved men became ill, died, or disappeared while Confederate soldiers and military officials forced them to work, and in 1864 the Confederate Congress approved an act that provided slave owners with "payment for slaves impressed under State laws, and lost in public service." Women who lost slaves to the Confederacy were among the petitioners who hoped to receive funds devoted to this purpose.[45]

In February 1863, Jacob, a twenty-four-year-old enslaved man owned by Mary Clark of Washington County, Virginia, was forced to work for the Confederacy on fortifications being built in Richmond. During his service, which lasted fifty-one days, he was exposed to inclement weather and deplorable work conditions that made him ill. On his way home, he developed pneumonia and eventually died. Responding to the recently approved Confederate House bill, Mary Clark submitted her request for compensation. She included attestations from neighbors, the physician who attended Jacob during his illness, and an officer who was responsible for transporting the slaves to and from the worksite to support her claim. The CSA Committee on Claims, the body to which her petition was referred, assessed Jacob's value to be around $3,000 and sought permission to send her claim to the state of Virginia for further action.[46] Other states within the Confederacy, such as South Carolina, had local compensation policies as well. According to Jaime Amanda Martinez, petitioners may never have received any of the compensation the Confederacy promised them, but these women's decision to submit their petitions attests to their desire to hold their government accountable for the loss of the people they owned.[47]

Of course, not all women were willing to comply with the Confederacy's impressment policies. Mary A. Tarrant of Perry, Alabama, who possessed an estate worth $93,800 in 1860, refused to give up the slaves requested under the state's impressment policy.[48] She was so averse to relinquishing her slaves that the men appointed to collect them had to return to her plantation with a posse. Once they identified the slaves who had been selected, Tarrant refused to give the soldiers provisions for the enslaved men they took. One of the men, J. W. Harrison, could not understand why Tarrant resisted so resolutely, especially because she was "better able to send hands to work on the defences than many others," including "many widowed women," who sent their slaves "cheerfully without a murmur and who did not own as many slaves as she does."[49] But from Mary Tarrant's perspective, the answer was probably quite simple. These enslaved men were valuable to her as workers and as property, and the labor they would perform on behalf of the government could impair, if not destroy, that value. Mary Tarrant did not want to take the chance.

On neither side of the war did women make up the majority of claimants, but a number of reasons may account for this gender disparity. One may have been slave-owning parents' tendency to give their daughters enslaved women and girls—who did not work on military fortifications and could not be enlisted as soldiers—rather than men and boys. Slave owners who submitted compensation claims to the federal government could only do so for enslaved men who enlisted in the Union forces; those petitioning the CSA government could only do so for enslaved men who died while impressed by the Confederacy. In the latter instances, enslaved male workers were in higher demand, as they were called on to build and maintain fortifications. Although enslaved women served both sides as "cooks, laundresses, officer's servants, and hospital workers," these women were barred from military service involving combat.[50] Another reason for the apparent discrepancy is that the sex of many claimants could not be determined because military officials only noted first and middle initials instead of names in their documents. When accounting for these factors, it is quite possible that the total number of female claimants was higher.

Some women, finding that their letters and requests did not result in the return of their slaves or compensation for those that they lost, took matters into their own hands, traveling to Union encampments to find and repossess their slaves, delegating this task to others, or suing the men who refused to hand them over. As one enslaved man, Louis Jourdan, remembered, "I came with my family to Algiers, [Louisiana,] and was in the Contraband Camp [which accommodated enslaved people who left their Confederate owners] and living here awhile, my wife belonged to Madam Lestree, and she came or sent some one to the Contraband Camp and took my wife and children back to Bayou Lafourche."[51]

Other slave-owning women went in search of the enslaved people they lost as well, frequently delegating this task to the men in their lives, either family members or employees. If, however, their proxies failed to rectify matters, some women pursued the issue themselves. In June 1861, Caroline Noland, a slave owner from Rockville, Maryland, sent her sons to take possession of an enslaved man she owned. She had allegedly "learned through a reliable source" that this enslaved man had crossed the border between Maryland and Virginia and hid himself in Camp Sherman, which was occupied by the 1st and 2nd Ohio Regiments of the Union Army. Noland's sons returned empty-handed, claiming that Union officers had refused them access to the camp. But Assistant Adjutant-General Donn Piatt and Colonel A. McD. McCook, the commanding officer who permitted the search, denied her sons' allegations. The officers had, in fact, granted Noland's sons permission to search the camp for the missing slave, but they had not found him. It was only after their fruitless search that McCook's men escorted her sons out of the camp. This was not the account Noland's sons had given her, and based on their report, Noland took matters into her own hands. She wrote to Winfield Scott, the commanding general of the Union Army, seeking his assistance in the matter. In her letter, Noland asked Scott to "suggest and adopt such course in the premises as may enable me to reclaim my property."[52]

As more enslaved people fled toward Union lines over the course of the war, similar conflicts played out time and again throughout the region. Union officers' responses to slaveholders' requests to reclaim the enslaved people they owned were heavily contingent upon federal and military policy, or, in cases like Caroline Noland's, the absence of formal directives. When Noland submitted her appeal in June 1861, definitive federal policy instructing commanding officers on how to handle property claims like hers did not yet exist. These officers continued to seek out guidance until the U.S. Congress began taking swift action that left little room for doubt.

Some Union officers ignored slave-owning women's letters, and some of those women sued them for refusing to give up their slaves. In 1862, Emily G. Hood, a Union loyalist, brought a civil suit against Colonel Smith D. Atkins in the Fayette County Circuit Court in Kentucky when he refused to allow her to repossess her slave, Henry, from his camp. Atkins would not appear in court or attend to the case until after the war was over. While he claimed that he based his decision upon the urgency and exigencies of war, his letter to a friend offered another reason: as a military commander, he refused to allow his "boys to become slavehounds of Kentuckians" or convert his regiment into "a machine to enforce the slave laws of Kentucky & return slaves to rebel masters."[53] Although he did not make this stance clear to his superiors, they agreed with him and allowed him to attend to his military duties rather than appear in court. As a slave owner in a southern state that remained loyal to the Union, Hood knew that federal policies protected her property rights, and this became even more clear after Lincoln issued his Preliminary Proclamation in September 1862. Although Hood's legal suit was postponed, her decision to file her petition underscores her determination to preserve her investments in the institution of slavery, even if it meant taking a military official to court in the middle of the war to do it.

Quite reasonably, many slave-owning women feared that Union officers would confiscate their slaves, and they were just as concerned that they would lose the enslaved people they owned through flight. To reduce the likelihood of either happening, slave-owning women did what many other slaveholders did; they decided to "refugee." Refugeeing involved relocating from a region threat-ened by Union occupation to an area deemed safer, and it was one way south-erners hoped to protect their families against wartime destruction. But many slave-owning women refugeed specifically to remove their slaves from the Union's reach and preserve their economic investments in the process. Wiley Childress's mistress, Jane Boxley, for example, kept her slaves hidden until the war was over. Childress recalled that "durin' de war may Missis took mah mammy en-us chilluns wid her ter de mountains 'till de war wiz gon." Charlie Pye's mistress, Mary Ealey, owned a number of slaves and "refugeed to Alabama trying to avoid meeting the Yanks." But as Pye recalled, "they came in another direction," so she had to change her plan. Mattie Lee's mistress, Mrs. Baker, took her slaves from Franklin Parish, Louisiana, to Texas because "she was afraid the Union soldiers would take her slaves away from her." At the war's conclusion, however, Union forces infiltrated the area and "told de white peo-ple dat de slaves was free." Lee's mistress was seemingly unafraid of what the Union soldiers might do to her personally. She was more concerned about the financial harm they would cause if they took her slaves. Scores of women echoed these concerns and moved their slaves out of the way of Union forces. Hannah Kelly's mistress Lou Downward also moved her slaves from Louisville, Kentucky, to Texas.[54] Eliza Ripley and her family decided to refugee to Texas because they had "the feeling that the Federals could never get a foothold on its boundless prairies," and "above and beyond all" they could "take refuge in Mexico if the worse came to the worst."[55]

As these slave-owning women knew, refugeeing could be traumatic for enslaved people. Josephine Pugh, the sister of the Confederate general and Louisiana governor Francis T. Nicholls, recognized this in her account of the Civil War. While many families she knew fled encroaching Union forces and relocated to Texas, she and her family stayed put because they recognized "the aversion of the negro to breaking up and moving to a new country." She and her family chose to remain and fight their battles in Assumption Parish, Louisiana, because they believed that their slaves' "demoralization would be less complete at home."[56] Enslaved people had more than an "aversion" to refugeeing. It brought about the same kind of familial and community separation as did compelling them to leave their homes and move to the Deep South, separating families on the death of their owners, and slave sales. Slave-owning refugees often took their most valuable and able-bodied slaves with them and left those who were the least able to care for themselves—the aged, the infirm, and the very young—to fend for themselves. Refugeeing slave owners were frequently taking enslaved people away from the only homes they had ever known. Even when an owner refugeed within her home state, as Sallie Rhett did when she took her slaves from Stirling to Abbeyville, South Carolina, the relocation made it more difficult for long-lost family members to find each other. After the war Silvy Granville and members of her family, Sallie Rhett's former slaves, moved back to Stirling, their home, to try to establish lives as freed people.[57]

Refugeeing was a risky strategy for both slave owners and the people they owned. Confederate soldiers and Union troops could impress able-bodied enslaved men and compel them to work on fortifications or in their encampments. Soldiers on both sides acted in ways that left slave-owning women without their most productive workers. Refugeeing was also difficult because Union officers knew about the practice and its purpose, and they could thwart a slave owner's plans. Henry Miller's mistress packed up about twelve of her slaves and began to trek them to "the woods country." This was a fear-filled excursion, and Miller's mistress became so anxious that she lost her sense of direction. In her confusion, she "done the worst thing she could" and "run right into a Yankee camp." The Union soldiers questioned her slaves about where they came from, eventually freed them, and sent them back home.[58]

Staying put on a plantation, managing the affairs of the estate, and overseeing its cultivation and production, all in the face of military conflict, called for tremendous bravery on the part of white southern women. But gathering together their most valuable property and relocating to uncharted territory where they had never been before required a different kind of courage entirely. Nonetheless, many slave-owning women took the chance and set off, often without a significant white male presence; despite the dangers their decision might bring, they believed that preserving their financial well-being by moving their slaves beyond military and government reach was more important than the possible risks to their physical safety.

The thought of losing the people who embodied their most significant financial investments pushed some women to go beyond refugeeing to hiding their slaves, holding them in captivity, or imprisoning them. Whenever Ike Thomas's mistress got word that the Yankees were approaching, she "would hide her 'little niggers' sometimes in the wardrobe back of her clothes, sometimes between the mattresses, or sometimes in the cane brakes. After the Yankees left, she'd ring a bell and they would know they could come out of hiding."[59] These enslaved children probably thought their mistress was allowing them to play a rare game of hide-and-seek, but there was no element of entertainment in the methods of "hiding" that some white women employed to conceal the whereabouts of the enslaved men and women they owned. Enslaved adults could not fit in the backs of closets or between mattresses, nor would they be likely to try to, so their mistresses held them captive in makeshift and local jails throughout the South.

Unlike the women who posted newspaper advertisements for enslaved people who had already fled, these slave-owning women sought to circumvent enslaved people's escape before they could get the chance to run. During the war, Senator James Grimes of Iowa, who was also chairman of the Committee on the District of Columbia, visited a jail in Washington, D.C., where he came upon an enslaved girl who was sitting "on the floor sewing her apron." When Grimes asked her why she was there, the girl informed the senator that she belonged to Mary Hall, a woman who kept "the largest house of ill fame in Washington." Hall had sent her to the jail "for safe keeping."[60]

In 1863, Colonel William Birney, who acted as the superintendent of Maryland Black Recruitment, confronted a similar situation. He wrote to the headquarters of the Middle Department and 8th Army Corps to notify his superiors that the owners of twenty-four African American men who sought to enlist had imprisoned them in a local jail. The jail record noted the date of each prospective recruit's imprisonment, the length of time he was there, his alleged owner, the individual he identified as his owner—who was often different from those who claimed him—and any other particulars that had led to each man's captivity. Lewis Ayres was one of these prisoners. Although the jailor identified Greenleaf Johnson of Somerset County, Maryland, as his rightful owner, Ayres claimed that "Mrs. Briscoe, a secessionist lady of Georgetown, D.C.," owned him. According to Ayres, Briscoe had brought him to Maryland a little over a year before Birney questioned him, and she did so "for fear he would be freed in the District." This was not the first time she had imprisoned him for this reason. Ayres informed the superintendent that he had also been held in "Campbell's Slave jail," and his mistress had moved him to his current place of captivity because this jail charged her less to keep him. Despite all her efforts to keep him enslaved, Lewis Ayres enlisted and served as a private corporal in Company B of the U.S. Colored Troops, becoming a free man.[61] Catherine

Gardiner imprisoned her slave Augustus Baden in the same jail because he was prone to run away, or, as Baden might see it, for trying to secure his freedom. Nancy Counter imprisoned her slave William Sims for seventeen months in a Baltimore slave pen before Union forces set him free.[62] Faced with the loss of able-bodied laborers who were also their property, many white women elected to lock them up instead of give them up.

Some women held their slaves captive in their homes and on their estates. When Annie Davis's mistress refused to grant her her freedom and allow her to visit her relatives, Davis wrote directly to Abraham Lincoln in the hope that he would clarify whether she had a right to do so. "Mr president" she wrote, "It is my Desire to be free. To go to see my people on the eastern shore," but "My mistress wont let me . . . you will please let me know if we are free. And what I can do. I write to you for advice. please send me word this week. Or as soon as possible and oblidge."[63] Davis did not make clear why her mistress had denied her her freedom and mobility. Perhaps she had observed the war-driven actions of her own or her neighbors' slaves with dismay. Or perhaps she had read about or witnessed slaves leaving and not coming back and imagined the pecuniary loss she would suffer if Annie Davis did the same. She was certainly determined to present that from happening, even if it meant continuing to separate Annie from her family. After Fanny Nelson learned that she was free because of her husband's enlistment in the Union Army, she informed her Kentucky owner's grandchild of this fact. She also told the child that she would have to be paid for her future labor. The child relayed this information to Nelson's mistress, who not only denied her her liberty and refused to pay her; she also "commenced locking her up of nights to keep her from leaving." Nelson found a way to escape despite her mistress's efforts to keep her enslaved.[64]

Other enslaved people did not have an opportunity to make an appeal to the government for their liberty, but they spoke about their troubles after the war was over. Before the war, George King's female owner had built a log cabin on her plantation that she used as a jail for runaways. King's mistress held her reclaimed runaways in this structure until they promised not to flee again. The "old jail was full up during most of the War" since most of the runaways refused to make that promise. When freedom came to the "two-hundred acres of Hell" where King lived, his mistress was still holding three enslaved people captive inside. Union soldiers discovered them chained to the floor.[65]

Slave-owning women often held their slaves captive because they were fearful of Union soldiers carting them off, but sometimes they had to worry about Confederate officers as well. Reflecting upon his mistress's conduct during the war, Milton Hammond said that "during this time Confederate soldiers were known to capture slaves and force them to dig ditches, known as breastworks." Hearing about such activities, his "mistress became frightened, and locked [him] in the closet until late in the evening."[66] As Hammond's recollections illustrate, slave-owning women sometimes ignored politics to stave off the fiscal threats that came from both sides.

Slave-owning women could not always prevent enslaved adults from fleeing to Union lines, but they could hold fast to the children they left behind. Some white women claimed that they did so out of love for enslaved African American children, yet evidence shows that their refusal to reunite the children with their parents was ultimately an economic maneuver. After all, when enslaved parents left, slave-owning women lost part of their wealth, and they had no intention of losing more by giving up the children as well. In 1864, Colonel George H. Hanks appeared before the American Freedmen's Inquiry Commission, a government entity that was charged with evaluating the status of enslaved people who were freed by congressional acts and presidential proclamations. He testified about an unnamed African American soldier whose former mistress refused to give him his children. This soldier approached Hanks and "demanded his children." Hanks responded that the children had a "good home," suggesting that they should be left where they were. The formerly enslaved soldier appealed to Hanks as an officer and a father, apparently hoping that his words would humanize him in Hanks's eyes: "I am in your service; I wear military clothes; I have been in three battles; I was in the assault at Port Hudson; I want those children; they are my flesh and blood." Hanks was apparently moved by this appeal because he sent one of his officers to retrieve the children, but "the mistress refused to deliver them." According to Hanks, "she came with them to the office and acknowledged the facts [related to her refusal]; she affirmed her devotion to them, and denied that the mother cared for them." After an investigation, Hanks discovered that she had bribed the children "to lie about their parents." Hanks delivered the children to their parents.[67] This slave-owning woman went beyond simply refusing to relinquish her economic claim to a formerly enslaved soldier's children; she paid them to tell untruths about the care their parents gave to them and positioned herself as their natural caretaker. And she almost convinced Colonel Hanks that she deserved to keep them.

Many Union officials took the matter of familial reconciliation seriously, and when white owners blocked a freedman's efforts to reclaim his family, soldiers sometimes went to extremes to help him. An enslaved man who belonged to Ida Powell Dulany's husband had escaped prior to the war, and as it raged he traveled back to Dulany's estate accompanied by Union officers to find his family and bring them away. He asked Dulany to give him her assurance that he would be allowed to remove his family unmolested and then return safely to the Union encampment with his wife and children. She refused to grant him this assurance because he and his family no longer belonged to her. He went anyway, but when he did not return to the Union camp, officers arrested Dulany for failing to secure his safe return. She was released shortly afterward.[68]

Freed parents often had less luck in reclaiming their children. The Union Army impressed an enslaved man named Samuel Emery, and he subsequently began working on fortifications. The officials brought Emery's wife to the place where he was employed, but they left their children in the owner's possession. After both Emery and his wife had engaged in an "honest, industrious pursuit of a livelihood" for some time, they attempted to reclaim their children from their former mistress, Eveline Blair. She refused to give them back. When a Union officer, Urbain Ozanne, investigated the Emerys' allegations in the spring of 1865, Blair, with "an utter disregard for the federal government and the earnest solicitations of the oppressed people," as Ozanne put it, "indignantly spurned their united supplication uttering the most opprobrious epithets against the federal government and declaring the children should never be granted their freedom."[69] As other formerly enslaved parents tried to reconstitute their families, they faced similar, formidable odds.

Out of necessity, enslaved children had learned to detect even the slightest changes in their owners' behavior, since such changes could affect their own well-being. Now, with the war threatening slave-owning women's investments in the institution, these women became even more attentive to changes in enslaved children's behavior. Some noticed that enslaved children were acting differently in the presence of Union soldiers. Without their parents or other enslaved adults around, enslaved children were uncertain about what to make of these strange men in their blue suits with shiny gold buttons, and their mistresses capitalized on their fears to discourage the children from flight. Many slave-owning women, such as Caroline Hunter's mistress, resorted to scare tactics to keep enslaved children obedient. Hunter's mistress told her that if she or any other slaves fled to the Yankees, the soldiers would "bore holes in" their arms "an' put wagon staves through the holes" and make them "pull de wagons like hosses." As far-fetched as this threat might seem, it was enough to keep Hunter from running away during the war, and it ensured a steady source of wartime labor for her mistress. Hannah Crasson also feared Union soldiers because her mistress claimed that "the Yankees were going to kill every nigger in the South." In light of such deceptions, some enslaved children and adolescents deemed it safer to remain with the devils they knew than take their chances with heavily armed and unfamiliar ones.[70]

Simply by their presence, African American children imbued both their parents and their female owners with hope. For enslaved parents, their children's very existence offered the prospect of a free future and the promise of a different kind of life, one shaped by liberty rather than bondage. Yet their owners' hopes and financial futures lay in these children's continued enslavement. Their growing, laboring, and potentially childbearing bodies promised white slave-owning women economic stability and continued prosperity. When determined African American parents confronted recalcitrant mistresses to demand their children, their contrasting visions for these young people involved more than conflicts over rights, authority, or custody; they were battles over property, fought on one side to redefine its meaning and on the other to preserve it.

Indeed, no matter how precarious the future of slavery seemed to be, slave-owning women and other southerners continued to buy and sell enslaved people throughout the war. Women bought and sold slaves during the war for the same reasons they had bought them before it, though some of their slave-market activities were intended to address the unique circumstances that the conflict brought about. Euphrasia Tivis, for example, "cheerfully sold" an enslaved female she owned to pay for a substitute who could take her husband's place in the Confederate army.[71]

As the war progressed, many white slave-owning women finally recognized that no strategy could stave off its inevitable outcome. The time was approaching when they would no longer be able to hunt for their escaped slaves, hide them from Union soldiers, or hold them in captivity.[72] They could not reclaim their slaves from Union encampments or seek compensation from either government for them. They had few options left. With their backs against the wall, some slave-owning women divested themselves of their holdings while they still could, selling enslaved people to anyone who would buy them or exchanging them for goods and supplies they needed or deemed more valuable. Henry Kirk Miller's mistress sold his sister for fifteen bales of cotton. He recalled "hearing them tell about the big price she brought because cotton was so high. Old mistress got 15 bales of cotton for sister, and it was only a few days till freedom came and the man who had traded all them bales of cotton lost my sister, but old mistress kept the cotton. She was smart, wasn't she? She knew freedom was right there."[73] Miller does not state precisely when "freedom came." As Susan O'Donovan has shown, when freedom came and what it consisted of were largely contingent upon gender, region, the type of labor enslaved people performed, the presence of and proximity to Union forces, and a host of other factors. It also depended on the dispositions and objectives of the slave owners in question. In the southwestern region of Georgia that O'Donovan explores, she found that "distance . . . kept the war at arm's reach," and it also "kept freedom at bay."[74] Thus Henry Miller, who was born and raised in Fort Valley, Georgia, may have been referring to events that took place toward the end of 1865. Yet despite the delayed freedom that distance created, his mistress was clearly keeping herself abreast of the war's progress, and when she considered whether to keep an enslaved girl who would soon be free or to trade her for cotton, she chose the more stable commodity.

This was a financially savvy decision on her part. Between 1860 and 1865, the price of a pound of cotton in the New York market rose from 11 cents to a high of $1.82 per pound. In 1865, a bale weighed 477 pounds, and each bale could potentially sell for $868. In one swift exchange, Miller's mistress swapped a soon-to-be-free enslaved girl—a commodity without a price—for over 7,000 pounds of another. In theory, the exchange could have brought Henry's mistress a profit of over $13,000.[75] Perhaps the man who bought Miller's sister possessed the same knowledge about the war's impending end and the inevitable unraveling of slavery. But like many southerners who still believed that a Confederate victory was possible, he ignored it and made a very different economic choice, one for which he paid dearly.

As wartime shortages made it harder to care for the basic needs of their own families, slave-owning women could not help but see the once productive and highly valuable people they owned as liabilities and financial burdens, rather than economic investments. Whether for money or bales of cotton, they sold enslaved people away from their families and communities; in many cases, these African American men, women, and children never saw their family and friends again. When a white woman could not sell her slaves, she often got rid of them, particularly the enslaved women and children whom enslaved husbands and fathers left behind as they fled to Union lines. Some owners divested themselves of slaves because they did not want to shoulder the burden of caring for people who no longer held monetary value and they could no longer afford to keep them. Even during brutal weather conditions, white women drove enslaved women and children out of their homes to face an unfamiliar world with no aid.[76] Assistant Superintendent John Seage of the Freedmen's Bureau recorded his observations about some of the refugee women and children he saw: "My heart is made sad every day. . . . Women with families are sent away without House Home Money Clothing or Friends. . . . There are hundreds of women and Children who are destitute of underclothing & who have been driven away from their former homes who have no Husband or Father. . . . The chilly air makes them feel the want of Clothing and shoes. . . . These poor Creatures must starve this winter & are Suffering now."[77] The tragic scenes of slavery's most vulnerable victims thrust out of their homes, frostbitten, starving, and improperly clothed, were repeated across the South.

Although the owners who drove formerly enslaved women and children away from their former homes to freeze and starve remained nameless and sexless in Seage's letter, other people explicitly identified women among the southerners who committed such dire deeds. White southerners such as the Tennessee farmer James Arvent witnessed cruelty by slave-owning women and reported them to the Freedmen's Bureau. Arvent wrote a letter in which he stated that his female neighbor was harshly treating an elderly formerly enslaved woman she once owned. He claimed that "the old lady was *driven* from her former Mistresses premises by this christian mistress some time last February or march, without one particle of compensation for former services, out upon the cold charities of this unfeeling community to seek a home or shelter under which to cover her head." During slavery, the mistress had sold off all this freedwoman's children, but because the mother was feeble and unable to work, she had been left in a state of poverty and destitution without any support. In order to help her, Arvent hired her husband to work for him, paying him twenty dollars per month.[78]

Formerly enslaved people spoke of their mistresses' callousness as well. During the war, one formerly enslaved mother decided that it was time for her to make a break for freedom and take her two daughters with her. When she made her decision, one of her daughters was making clothing for the three of them. Learning of their impending plans, the mistress took the clothing "off the loom" and "took it upstairs and hid it." Without suitable clothing, the enslaved family of three "went away naked."[79]

For some slave-owning women, such as Georgian Sarah H. Maxwell, merely distancing themselves from those who would soon be free was not enough. As emancipation became a near certainty, Maxwell wrote to the Mississippi commander of the Cavalry Corps with an unusual proposition: If the government agreed to buy her land, she would transport all her former slaves to Africa, accompany them there to make sure they settled in, and then establish herself in another part of the world. She does not appear to have asked her *slaves* if they wanted to go. Nor did she express her intention of ever coming back to the United States. Apparently, the idea of emancipation was so troubling that she was willing to cast off her property *and* her country. This idea was equally appealing to Pauline DeCaradeuc Heyward. Upon confirming news of the Confederacy's surrender to the Union, she scribbled in her diary: "All I want is to leave this vile place, to go to some other country. I hate everything here."[80] Women like Eliza Ripley acted upon their wish to go somewhere else. After she refugeed from Louisiana to Texas with her family and their slaves in 1862, she settled briefly in Mexico before finally establishing a sugar plantation in Cuba. There, she and her husband continued to keep their slaves in bondage and worked them alongside Chinese indentured laborers until Cuban law no longer permitted them to do so.[81]

Amid the anguish and privation brought by the war, slave-owning women grappled with the impact the conflict was having upon their wealth. These women fought their own battles for the preservation of slavery. They constructed their own battlefields, scenes of conflict and violence that were often located within the boundaries of their plantations and estates, but also moved beyond them. They took their fight to Union encampments and contraband camps, and into southern courtrooms. Sometimes they won; many times they did not. But even their victories were short-lived. In April 1865, seemingly impossible rumors circulated throughout southern communities that General Robert E. Lee had surrendered to Ulysses S. Grant. Many slave-owning women refused to believe it was true.[82] But after the news sunk in, Lucy Rebecca Buck spoke for them when she lamented, "Our dearest hopes [are] dashed — our fondest dreams [are] dispelled." Slavery was dead, and its destruction compelled slave-owning women to start life anew.[83] With slavery gone, and the bulk of their wealth along with it, slave-owning women found their material and social circumstances profoundly altered. These changes compelled them to confront uncharted terrain upon which to construct new lives without slaves. As Ella Gertrude Clanton Thomas concluded, "The fact is our Negroes are to be made free and a change, a very [great] change will be affected in our mode of living."[84]

For four years, white southern women had fought as vigorously as southern men in their efforts to preserve slavery and the kind of life the institution had sustained. Some women believed that they fought harder than the men on the battlefield. A woman who identified herself only as "N." was "of the opinion that if the men were like the women[,] the villainous Yankees would have been obliged to make a retrograde movement long ago."[85] But despite all their strategies, women like Rebecca Felton "realized that the game had been fully played and all was lost," that "billions of values disappeared," and "nobody but thrifty speculators had a dollar . . . to begin the struggle again . . . with bitter poverty and starvation in front of them."[86] For some, circumstances became so difficult that they found themselves at the mercy of the people they had once held in bondage. And for many who did, this was the bitterest pill of all.

8

"A MOST UNPRECEDENTED ROBBERY"

On June 13, 1865, Eva Jones, a former slave owner from Georgia, penned a letter to her mother-in-law in which she bemoaned emancipation. "I suppose you have learned," she wrote, "even in the more secluded portions of the country that slavery is entirely abolished—a most unprecedented robbery, and most unwise policy." The end of slavery left Jones with the daunting task of reconstructing her life from "a heap of ruins and ashes." For Jones, abolition was nothing short of a criminal act committed on such a grand scale that it would result in a "joyless future of probable ignominy, poverty, and want." She believed that a life without slaves would be "a life robbed of every blessing" for her and similarly situated people living in the South.[1]

Jones was not alone in her thinking. As the Civil War came to a bloody close in the late spring of 1865, Ella Gertrude Thomas reflected deeply upon how she would reckon with the economic impact of the conflict and its aftermath. Initially, she was optimistic: "I am not the person to permit pecuniary loss to afflict me as long as I have health and energy," she wrote in her diary. Thomas recognized that emancipation would hurt her financially, but she also saw slavery as a burden, an encumbrance she was glad to rid herself of. "As to the emancipation of the Negroes, while there is of course a natural dislike to the loss of so much property in my inmost soul I cannot regret it—I always felt that there was a great responsibility—It is in some degree a great relief to have this feeling removed." It only took four weeks for her disposition to change. By June, she had come to "heartily dispise Yankees, Negroes, and everything connected with them."[2] Over the next four months, the reality of Thomas's financial loss and its cataclysmic impact upon her way of life made her bitter, shook her resolve, and weakened her religious faith. Before the war, she and her husband had owned ninety slaves collectively, and she stood to inherit many more from her father's estate. But with abolition, she predicted that her family's "state of affluence" would devolve into one of "comparative poverty."³ Thomas was particularly upset by the personal losses she would inevitably suffer as a consequence of emancipation: "So far as I individually am concerned," she calculated, she was reduced "to utter beggary," for the thirty thousand dollars her father had given her when she married was "invested in Negroes alone—This view of the case I did not at first take, and it is difficult now to realise it. . . . I did not know . . . how intimately my faith in revelations and my faith in the institution of slavery had been woven together. . . . Slavery was done away with and my faith in God's Holy Book was terribly shaken."⁴

Many former slave-owning women found the realization of what a slaveless world would mean for them equally painful. Despite evidence to the contrary, many had been unwilling to believe that the government would simply do away with slavery. In the first two years of the war, the United States Congress had enacted laws that weakened the institution of slavery, and President Lincoln had further compromised slavery with the Emancipation Proclamation. As early as March 1864, slave owners confronted further evidence of slavery's vulnerability when southern states began amending their constitutions to abolish slavery. Before the year ended Arkansas, Louisiana, and Maryland had done so. In January and February of 1865, respectively, Missouri and Tennessee did the same. Perhaps slave-owning women held on to hope of a Confederate victory because the Confederate government continued to act as though the South had a chance of winning the war; only a month before Robert E. Lee surrendered at Appomattox, Virginia, on April 9, 1865, the Confederate Congress passed an act to "increase the military force of the Confederate States." One of the ways the Congress hoped to achieve this was by enlisting enslaved troops. The act further revealed the Confederate government's dogged commitment to the preservation of slavery; it called for the organization of "slaves into companies, battalions, regiments, and brigades," but it explicitly refused to change "the relation which the said slaves shall bear toward their owners," unless their owners or the states in which they lived altered those relationships. These enlistment efforts never came to pass.⁵

Slave-owning women's knowledge of this news was far from complete or consistent across the South, but they soon began to experience the economic effects of abolition upon their lives. While a few were able to hold on to some of their antebellum wealth despite the substantial postbellum devaluation of their assets, many faced poverty and starvation. Some women responded by denying the people they once owned their rights and liberty and sought to coerce them to work as they had under slavery; others adapted old management methods to accommodate new labor arrangements.

Amid the jubilant screams and quick-footed two-steps of enslaved people who had just learned they were free, slave-owning women wept. In April 1865, shortly after the Union forces infiltrated the community where Tiney Shaw was enslaved, she overheard her mistress, Susy Page, crying, because "she wuz a widder 'oman; and her crops wuz jist started ter be planted." As Shaw guessed, the presence of federal troops brought home the economic realities that were to come. When Page laid eyes upon those Union soldiers, "She knowed dat she wuz ruint."[6] Shaw was just guessing about the source of her mistress's distress, but J. W. Terrill's mistress left no doubt about the precise cause of her grief. As her former slaves "jumped up and holler[ed,] and dance[d]" after they learned they were free, she mustered enough resolve through her tears to tell them that she hoped that they would "starve to death and she'[d] be glad, 'cause it ruin[ed] her" to lose them. Although he was only six when the war ended, Tom Haynes remembered the day that his female owner, Becky Franks, approached his mother, Addie, told her, "You is free this morning," and "commenced cryin'."[7] Some women reacted even more strongly. Emma Hurley described the response of her master's mother on learning that the more than two hundred slaves she owned in her own right were free: "She sho' did take on when they wuz all freed. I 'members how she couldn't stay in the house, she just walked up an' down out in the yard a-carrin'-on, talkin' an' a'ravin'."[8]

Enslaved people were as alert as their owners to the economic changes that abolition would bring. On being told that she would soon be freed, Betty Jones's grandmother ran seven miles to her mistress's home, walked up to her, "looked at her real hard," and exclaimed, "I'se free! Yes, I'se free! Ain't got to work fo' you no mo'. You can't put me in yo' pocket now!" Her mistress "started boo-hooin' an' threw her apron over her face an' run in de house." As an enslaved person, Jones's grandmother had lived under the constant threat of sale—of being put in her mistress's pocket. With slavery gone, her mistress would not only lose her investment in human property; she could no longer use the threat of the slave market against her former slaves.[9]

Southern slave-owning women had existed in a world in which slavery and the ownership of human beings constituted core elements of their identities. Faced with the prospect of losing their slaves, some expressed the wish to die. Four days after Lee's surrender, Lucy Rebecca Buck was "almost tempted to envy poor Aunt Bettie lying cold and still in death."[10] Before the war, Polly Brown lived with her daughter and "made her living by taking in sewing," but she was by no means poor. She owned at least eleven slaves, including Annie Wallace, and other property in Eggsbornville, Virginia. Wallace later recalled that her mistress took the news of the Confederacy's surrender and emancipation particularly hard. She "was so hurt that all the negroes was going to be free. . . . She was so mad that she just died."[11] During the course of one slave-owning couple's conversation about the "war to free the niggers," an enslaved woman overheard her mistress declare that she did not "want to live to see the niggers free." When Ella Wilson's mistress laid out her plans for the enslaved people she owned to her husband, he replied, " 'T'aint no use to do all them things" because "the niggers'll soon be free." Wilson's mistress exclaimed, "I'll be dead before that happens, I hope." Both mistresses got their wish: they died before the war ended. The deaths of these women were probably caused by illness or the trauma brought about by the war. But as formerly enslaved people remembered it, their mistresses' deaths were directly linked to the loss of property— that is, enslaved people—that came with abolition.[12]

Death was not a practical option for most women who lost their slaves. But that did not stop them from dwelling on their past situation and lamenting the things they could have done differently had they known that slavery was coming to an end. Failing to seize upon earlier opportunities to sell their slaves ranked high among many women's list of regrets.[13] Three years after the Civil War ended, Ella Gertrude Thomas had a conversation with her former slaves during which she told them that she would have sold them before the close of the war if she had had the opportunity to do so.[14] Liza Jones's mistress refused at least one offer to sell her eight slaves to a speculator and may have refused others. But when the war was over, she bitterly regretted her choice, believing that her former slaves would leave her. Jones recalled her mistress telling them, "Now I could a sold you and had the money, and now you is goin' to leave." Her fears of abandonment were unfounded however; most of her former slaves chose to remain on her estate. Jones's mistress was fortunate in this regard because many other formerly enslaved people walked away from their mistresses without hesitation, at least when they were capable of doing so.[15]

When they were not bewailing their lack of foresight, former slave-owning women actively resisted the implementation of emancipation. Their motives were mixed. Grace Brown Elmore, for example, vehemently opposed emancipation because she did not think that African Americans possessed the intellectual or moral capacity to live on their own as freed people. For Elmore, African Americans were "the most inferior of the human race, far beneath the Indian or Hindu": they were "poor, uneducated, stupid . . . lazy, self indulgent." So deficient did she consider them that she prophesized that they would simply cease to exist once the ties between master and slave were dissolved. As Kay Wright Lewis has shown, the belief that African Americans would disappear after slavery was one of many vicious predictions that circulated among whites in the postbellum South.[16]

Other women felt entitled to formerly enslaved people's unpaid labor and questioned the authority of the federal government to rob them of it. Their resistance to abolition did not surprise Union officials such as Lieutenant Colonel Homer B. Sprague, who expected such recalcitrance. To Sprague the idea that a slave owner could wholeheartedly accept emancipation was preposterous. He considered it equally incredible that people would assume that "a sincere believer in the rightfulness of slavery" would "look with any complacency upon the freemen." They simply would not do it, Sprague argued, because they had made up their minds that "if they cannot have the negroes subject to them," they wished "to have nothing at all to do with them."[17] Using this same logic, white women sought out ways to control the bodies and labor of the people they once owned, even after the federal government declared it illegal to do so. To all outward appearances, their ideological and sentimental ties to the institution of slavery were the key factors influencing their decisions. But the pecuniary losses they had suffered often underlay their responses, emotional or otherwise.

One way former slave-owning women held on to their former slaves was to keep them uninformed about their free status. This proved to be an easier task in some parts of the South than in others. Florida, Texas, "western parts of Arkansas and Louisiana, eastern Mississippi, much of Alabama, southwestern Georgia and the western sections of North and South Carolina" remained relatively untouched by the physical destruction of the war and the presence of Union troops. And within five months of Lee's surrender, the Union forces that occupied the South were drastically reduced. At the war's height, one million Union soldiers occupied and fought in the South; by October 1865 a little over two hundred thousand remained and 36 percent of them were African American. Together, the wartime absence of Union forces and their postwar withdrawal from significant portions of the South made it possible for slave-owning women to hold legally free African Americans in captivity.[18] Violence by whites against blacks also intensified as Union troops evacuated the region. The federal government sought to address these kinds of issues when Congress passed an act that created the Freedmen's Bureau.

The Freedmen's Bureau, or the "bureau of refugees, freedmen, and abandoned lands," was charged with the "supervision and management of all abandoned lands, and the control of all subjects relating to refugees and freedmen from rebel states." As a bureau within the War Department, it was responsible for providing "provisions, clothing, and fuel, as [the secretary of war] may deem needful for the immediate and temporary shelter and supply of destitute and suffering refugees and freedmen and their wives and children." The act that created the Freedmen's Bureau also authorized the president to set aside tracts of land of no more than forty acres "for the use of loyal refugees and freedmen . . . within the insurrectionary states as shall have been abandoned."[19] Two of the Freedmen's Bureau's more important functions after the Civil War were assisting former slave owners and formerly enslaved people in their transition from slave to free labor and helping freed people resolve matters related to employer mistreatment and physical abuse.

The Freedmen's Bureau, however, was designed to be a temporary entity, and it was unfunded and grossly understaffed. These factors made it close to impossible for the bureau to carry out its mandate. When legally free African Americans lived beyond the reach of Union forces or Freedmen's Bureau agents, their female owners might refuse to tell them that they were free and continue to work them as they had before the war. Ben Lawson, for example, was the only slave whom Jane Brazier owned. As a boy Lawson worked 160 acres of Brazier's land alongside her son and the impoverished white laborers she hired. The nearest plantation was at least fifteen or twenty miles away, and Lawson never knew the Civil War was going on. After it ended, Brazier never told him that he was free, so Lawson kept working as he always had.[20] Albert Todd suffered a similar fate. Todd was enslaved in Kentucky, and his mistress took him with her when she refugeed to Texas. Sometime afterward, Todd changed hands from one mistress to another. Though in his later recollection he was not explicit about the details, the transaction he described could have been an apprenticeship, which allowed his new "mistress," Mrs. Gibbs, to keep him in conditions that mimicked slavery for three years after the federal government freed him. She also deprived him of the sustenance he needed to do the work she commanded, and she beat him when he tried to supplement his diet with food pilfered from her. In the end, Todd's sisters found him and took him away.[21]

Trying to keep the news about emancipation from enslaved people was not a foolproof strategy. To the chagrin of many a slave owner, other white southerners, who may have had economic motives, often passed this information along. Fannie Berry said that she "wuz free a long time fo' I knew it," but one day the white woman to whom she had been hired out declared, "Fannie, yo' ar' free an' I don't have to pay your master for you now. You stay with me."[22] Whether the woman told Berry she was free because she believed that keeping this information from her was unjust or whether she did it in order to better position herself to negotiate directly with Berry for her labor is unclear. Notwithstanding, her choice to disclose the news to Berry betrayed the chasms that often existed between those who owned slaves and those who did not.

Under favorable circumstances, women negotiated directly with freed parents when they sought to retain their children and their labor for a while longer. Freed parents persistently and vehemently fought to reconstitute their families in the postwar period, but they struggled financially.[23] Few had the means to care for themselves, and even fewer could care for their children as well. In light of these circumstances, some freed mothers and fathers entrusted their children to their former mistresses in hopes that they would receive proper care. After the war, Martha Orr candidly told James Barber's mother, Caroline, that she was free and advised her to go into the local town and hire herself out for wages. She also suggested that Caroline leave her children behind so that she herself could "take care er 'um." Her reasoning was that without a husband Caroline would not be able to care for the children properly. And after some consideration, Caroline left James and his siblings in her former owner's care.[24] Caroline Barber faced the same formidable circumstances that awaited the majority of newly freed people after the war, but the realities of life for a freed-woman in the South were particularly bleak, especially if she had children. She undoubtedly weighed her options carefully when considering her former owner's proposition and realized that Martha Orr might be able to care for her children in a way that she could not at the time. James's reflections suggest that his mother made a wise choice. He related that Orr treated him and his siblings as though they were her own. They slept on a mattress in her bedroom, and she would tuck them in at night. He even called Orr "mother" well into his teenage years, something that proved so disagreeable to her kin that they called upon the sheriff to banish James from the town. He remained with his mistress for nine years before they were able to persuade the sheriff do so.[25]

Deeming themselves entitled to the bodies and labor of freed children and adolescents, former slave-owning women routinely exploited the chaotic familial circumstances that slavery, antebellum migration, the war, and refugeeing had brought about in order to extend their access to these young people's labor. Women like the mistresses who owned Ben Lawson, Albert Todd, and Fannie Berry often took advantage of parents' absences to coerce children and adolescents into exploitative labor arrangements. One Natchez, Tennessee, woman, for example, called the freed child she still had in her possession her "little Confederate nigger." She proudly told Whitelaw Reid, an Ohio journalist, politician, and diplomat who traveled through the South in the year following the war, that this young girl was "the only one I have been able to keep, and I only have her because her parents haven't yet been able to coax her away."[26] When children were isolated from their parents or other African Americans more generally, it was easier for white women to manipulate and deceive them because they could prevent them from knowing about their changed status. These circumstances also made it possible to bind freed children to them through apprenticeship laws.

After the war, many southern states crafted such laws to contend in part with the large number of allegedly orphaned freed children under the age of eighteen.[27] What often remained unsaid and unrecognized was that many of these children were not orphans at all but had been separated from their parents through their owners' estate divisions, interstate relocations, and sales. Parents tirelessly searched for their children and attempted to reconstruct their families for years after the war, but were often unsuccessful. Even when they could find their children and provide for them, their former mistresses often appealed to courts and military officials to leave the children with them for "maternal" reasons, relying (usually successfully) on these officials' gendered and racist assumptions to help them maintain legal control over freed children. Henry Walton's former mistress, Susan Walton Miller, seized the opportunity to have him bound to her before his father could return from the war. Miller petitioned the court to enforce Walton's apprenticeship and found the judge amenable. The court bound Walton to her until he turned twenty-one. Her legal victory was short-lived, however. When Walton's father returned from the war, he sought nullification of the court's order and won.[28]

Apprenticeship was probably what Annie Huff's owner also had in mind when she "returned from a trip to Macon and called all the children together to tell them that even though they were free, they would have to remain with her until they were twenty-one." Many of the South's apprenticeship laws established periods of indenture that lasted throughout the children's adolescence. Boys served until they were twenty-one years old, while girls served until they were eighteen. Frequently against the wishes of their parents, and often despite a mistress's inability to demonstrate her fitness to care for the children, Freedmen's Bureau agents and southern courts often granted the mistress's requests. Beyond ignoring the often tragic reasons for a freed parent's absence and placing a white southerner's need for labor over a black parent's love, these decisions also dismissed bonds of kinship between children and extended family members who were capable of giving them safe and comfortable homes.[29] To be sure, not all formerly enslaved adults sought to reclaim these children solely because they loved them; they often wanted additional laborers who could contribute to their households. And so the former owners and the formerly owned fought a battle over freed children that was partially economic in scope. Even still, apprenticeship laws and decisions related to them invalidated the fictive and extended kinship ties that the institution of slavery necessitated.[30]

Individuals within southern communities recognized the purpose of these laws and why former slave owners were seizing the opportunities that apprenticeship afforded them. Former slave owners wanted a bound labor force that was legally obligated to submit to their will, and the apprentice laws provided them with one way to secure it. But neighbors who witnessed the injustices they committed against their apprentices and the freed parents of these children might plead with officials "in the Name of Humanity" to stop what they considered the involuntary enslavement of freed children. A southern Unionist, Thomas B. Davis, wrote to the judge of the Baltimore Criminal Court to report a woman who he believed was perpetrating gross violations of the apprenticeship law. The woman, whom Davis referred to as "Yewel," not only forced freedwomen off her land, she also refused to give them their children. Furthermore, Yewel sought to have the freed children bound to her despite her lack of means to care for them or even herself.[31]

Women like Yewel cared little for the rights of African American parents or their desperate attempts to reconstitute their families; they were more concerned about their own financial well-being and stability. They continued to deny freed parents the chance to love and care for their children by claiming those children's labor for decades after slavery ended. But no matter how strongly former slave-owning women held on to African American children after emancipation, the children's kin were equally unwavering in their efforts to reclaim them.

Many freed parents appealed to the Freedmen's Bureau for help when their attempts to take possession of their children failed, but others chose to take matters into their own hands and "steal" their loved ones back. In a period when legal slavery was dead, many freed people had to surreptitiously take their loved ones from women who had no legitimate legal or economic claim to them. When Rebecca Jane Grant was fifteen years old, her uncle Jose Jenkins stole her from her mistress and took her to his home in Savannah, Georgia, approximately fifty miles away. Her father had also been searching for her, but when he finally located her mistress, he learned that the child was no longer there. He consulted with her grandfather Isaac, who finally tracked Rebecca down and took her back to her father. Isaac and Rebecca walked sixty-four miles to the town where their family was finally able to reunite.[32] Annie L. Burton's mother, who had run away during slavery, came back to her mistress's plantation after the war and "demanded that the children be given up to her." Her mistress refused to hand them over and "threatened to set the dogs" on Burton's mother if she did not leave at once. Undaunted, she left, but waited nearby. At dinnertime she asked a boy to call her eldest daughter, Caroline, to the place where she was hiding. When Caroline arrived, she instructed her to go back to the plantation, get Annie and her younger brother Henry, and bring them to a specified location. Once she had done so, Annie's mother carried Henry, and Caroline loaded Annie onto her back. They ran as fast as they could to the small hut that Annie's mother had secured on a plantation some distance away. Discovering their absence, Annie's mistress directed her sons to find them, but when they did, Annie's mother refused to give her children back. She offered to "go with them to the Yankee headquarters to find out if it were really true that all negroes had been made free." Clearly, the young men knew that the government had liberated their mother's slaves because they left, and Annie and her family remained undisturbed.[33]

Jane Turner Censer argues that white southern women harbored fears about the "social disorder" that they believed newly freed people would bring about, and that this and "their longstanding dislike of the isolation of plantations" encouraged them to move away from the countryside. Some women stayed put, however, and adapted to the new order on southern farms and plantations.[34] Reconstructing the South called for the implementation of a free labor system, and white women joined other former slave owners and planters who made contracts with their former slaves and agreed to compensate them for their labor.[35]

Some women adapted poorly to postbellum free labor systems, and they complained that freed people were unwilling to work for them under the same conditions that had existed before the war. But others proved to be well prepared for their new role as employers, particularly in regard to negotiating terms of labor with freed people. Before the war, slave-owning women had routinely negotiated with enslaved people who hoped to hire themselves out so they might purchase their freedom.[36] They had also contracted with other whites who sought to hire their slaves. These were complex transactions that educated both white slave-owning women and the people they owned in the intricacies of labor negotiations. But now that the conditions under which these negotiations were conducted had changed so drastically, white women had to adapt their tactics accordingly.

Before the Civil War, slave-owning women held the upper hand in labor transactions. When slaves wanted to hire themselves out so they could buy their freedom, their female owners could always renege on the agreement or later choose to simply pocket the wages they earned. Additionally, as slave owners, these women held legal title to the men, women, and children that other white people hoped to hire. Their slave ownership granted them extraordinary leverage in prewar hiring arrangements, but this changed when they negotiated with freed laborers after the war. So although former slave-owning women did not lack the skills to negotiate labor agreements with freed people, emancipation required them to modify their prewar strategies to accommodate the constraints which abolition imposed upon their ability to command enslaved people's labor.

It is also important to recognize that while some women might not have been able to own human property before the war, they frequently negotiated with enslaved laborers and others for such labor when they needed it. This may have given them an advantage in the postbellum free labor market, because even though slave-owning women had negotiated with other white southerners for the laborers they sought to hire, they had done so from positions of authority. Their knowledge of the hiring process had been limited, whereas non-slave-owning women had negotiated with slave owners *and* the enslaved people they hired, particularly those whose owners allowed them to hire out their own time and negotiate directly with prospective employers. Thus, non-slave-owning women gained valuable experience in negotiating and working directly with hired laborers, and such knowledge would have been highly advantageous in the free labor market of the postbellum South. The abolition of slavery evened the playing field, creating a market in which hirers and former owners had to negotiate with prospective employees if they hoped to secure the labor that they needed.

A white woman's earlier experiences with enslaved people and her prewar financial circumstances often determined whether she would be successful in her labor negotiations. If she had been able to acquire experience negotiating with free and enslaved laborers, a former slave-owning woman was likely to make an easy transition from owner to employer. Mrs. Sallie Rhett, the woman who owned Silvy Granville, is an example. She told her slaves that they were free at a time when they were "in the middle of a crop." She entered into negotiations with them, and rather than leaving immediately they "agreed to help her make that crop" in exchange for one-third of what they harvested.[37]

On rare occasions, former slave-owning women went beyond negotiating with, employing, and compensating the freed people who cultivated their lands; sometimes they might give their former slaves money and property. Frances Van Zandt gave her former slave Amy Van Zandt Moore two acres of land when she freed her. The woman who owned Mrs. Charles Douthit's mother not only gave her land when slavery ended, she built her former slave a home. Mrs. Douthit's mother gave birth to her in that house, she grew up in it, and she passed the house on to her son, who occupied the home at the time of her interview with a WPA employee.[38]

Most white women, however, hoped to extend their tenure as slave owners, and such women chose a vastly different course when they used exploitative and coercive business practices to maximize their profits and deprive free African Americans of the compensation they deserved. They often embraced the argument Grace Brown Elmore made, that "the negro as a hireling will never answer," and like her scorned paid black labor: "Who would choose black, in any capacity except he be held as a slave, and so bound to be obedient and faithful?"[39] At a Union soldier's mere suggestion that she would "find white labor much cheaper and better," Mary M. Clanton rejected such a notion by proclaiming that she was a "southern woman . . . born and raised at the South, accustomed to the service of Negroes and liked them better." But as enslaved people left her estate and her extended family's households, their absences compelled Mary and the rest of the Clantons to try their luck with white and, eventually, freed African American labor.[40] Much to Grace Elmore's apparent dismay, she found free white laborers a miserable disappointment. When she hired an Irishwoman as a servant, she learned that the woman was incapable of performing any of her assigned tasks efficiently.[41]

It should come as no surprise then, that even as these women pragmatically embraced free labor, they held fast to their sense of entitlement as former slave owners who could command enslaved people to labor tirelessly for them without pay. Former slave-owning women used coercive labor contracts in order to re-create the conditions that had characterized slavery. The labor contract Mary S. Blake devised was so exploitative that Colonel Samuel Thomas, the commander of the 64th U.S. Colored Infantry and provost marshal general of freedmen who was charged with the care and support of formerly enslaved people in Tennessee, objected and refused to allow her to hire laborers under the terms she specified. She complained to a family friend, Adjutant General Lorenzo Thomas, who then wrote to the Freedmen's Bureau on her behalf. Placing all the blame on Colonel Thomas, the adjutant general stated that despite the colonel's objections, the freed people were "perfectly satisfied and desire to remain with her and . . . refuse to go." The colonel, he claimed, was meddling and interfering with a perfectly amicable relationship between an employer and her employees. Colonel Thomas countered that the freed people he had consulted with did not even know the terms of their contracts, but after they had found out they had been upset about the agreements they had signed. When the colonel reviewed the contracts, he discovered that Blake's terms "would not feed and clothe them" and would have given them "less than they received when slaves." In Colonel Thomas's estimation, "Mrs. Blake wished to retain her servants as she always had them," and he refused to approve her contract.[42]

Other female employers contracted with freed people to cultivate and harvest the crops on their lands and then forced their employees off their property without any pay after they completed the work. When the former slave owner and planter Sally V. B. Tabb requested government assistance in forcibly removing her former slaves from her estate, she rationalized her decision by accusing them of failing to perform their required duties. They had refused to work hard, were insolent, and gave her all kinds of trouble; under the circumstances, she could no longer provide for them or pay them for their subpar labor. Yet when W. H. Bergfels, the Freedmen's Bureau assistant superintendent for Mathews County, Virginia, investigated the case, her allegations proved to be false. Furthermore, he discovered that she had not provided her freed workers with the implements they needed for the job. Even her overseer agreed that the tools Tabb expected the workers to use were "more than worn out 2 years ago," yet "she expected these poor people to accomplish wonders" with them. Bergfels concluded that Tabb was "the oppressor and not the oppressed as she would fain make it appear."[43]

The freed people who worked for former slave-owning women did not willingly accept the labor conditions their employers sought to impose. They appealed to Freedmen's Bureau agents and lodged their complaints against their employers in Freedmen's courts. On August 20, 1865, Sealy Banks claimed that Mrs. Estes, her employer and former owner, had refused to give her "any payment, save victuals & clothes, and is not certain about giving her the clothing." Banks further stated that she had "worked for Mrs. Estes all her life," and her former mistress had given her "no clothing for 3 years except one cotton dress, one yarn Dress, Shoes & stockings." The Freedmen's Court ruled in Banks's favor, summoned Mrs. Estes to appear to answer the complaint, and demanded that she pay Banks four dollars for "one month's work" and provide her with summer clothes.[44]

Daniel Baker, Frank Johnson, Lewis Wright, and Timothy Terryl collectively filed a complaint against former slave owner Mary Cowherd on August 28, 1865. She had not only refused to pay them for their work; she demanded that they continue to work for her with no compensation other than "their board & clothing." If they were unwilling to "accept these terms they must leave the plantation & never return." The Freedmen's Bureau directed her to settle with the men or explain why she would not do so.[45]

Beyond denying workers wages, food, and clothing, employers also made threats of violence, and these too led freed people who worked for them to file complaints. On the morning of August 27, 1865, Alfred Goffney approached his employer, Mrs. Strange, for wages she owed him for a month's labor. Strange "got a pistol," pointed the weapon at him, and threatened to "blow his brains out" if he did not leave her land immediately. Escaping with his life but not his wages, Goffney submitted his grievance to the bureau. Strange eventually paid Goffney the $5.20 she owed him, but only after the Freedmen's Bureau ordered her to do so.[46] In a postwar climate characterized by white southerners' unchecked violence against and murder of freed people, it took enormous courage for these formerly enslaved men and women to take such legal actions.

The white women who were in a position to employ freed people on their lands could count themselves among the lucky ones; many others did not share their good fortune. Women who had once owned slaves suddenly found themselves destitute, without property or any means of surviving. A formerly enslaved man named John Smith remembered such women: "Some of de missus had nigger servants to bathe 'em, wash dere feet an' fix dere hair. When one nigger would wash de missus feet dere would be another slave standin' dere wid a towel to dry 'em for her. Some of dese missus atter the war died poor. Before dey died dey went from place to place livin' on de charity of dere friends."[47] Even for women who did not live as extravagantly as this in prewar times, the loss of their economic investment in slaves posed significant financial problems and difficulties.

As many of these women faced poverty and destitution for the first time, they tried to re-create their past lives with the labor of newly freed people. These women assumed that freed people would serve them in the same ways they had before the war. But freed people frequently disappointed them.[48] One former slave owner "came to Beaufort" because "she thought some of her Ma's niggers might come to wait on her," but her mother's former slaves had different plans. Although they refused to work for her, they offered her "food, money, and clothes." In the end, her circumstances compelled her to earn a living with her own hands and "to become a dressmaker for the negroes."[49]

Sometimes life became so difficult for former slave-owning women that they were reduced to beggary among the people they had once owned. Two young women visited their father's former slaves "pleading their poverty" and begging for help. These freed people gave them "grits or potatoes . . . plates and spoons

. . . and money." One enslaved woman even "took the shoes from her own feet and gave them to her former mistresses."[50] The tables had officially turned: former slave owners found themselves at the mercy of those they had once owned. After a lifetime of servitude and abuse, these freed people might have retaliated against their former owners, thereby legitimating slaveholders' concern about "negro rule."[51] Instead, many of them demonstrated their humanity and gave their former mistresses what little they could reasonably spare. To be sure, the racial hostility and violence, as well as the psychological intimidation that characterized the region during and after the war, encouraged many freed people to be magnanimous toward their former owners.[52] But others behaved kindly toward former slave owners because they believed God was inflicting enough punishment upon "white folks." Lillian Clarke used that argument when she spoke to interviewer Susie R. C. Byrd on October 15, 1937: "De way white folks used to treat us," she said, "God has whipped some of 'em worse dan dey beat us."[53]

The spectrum of economic loss among former slave-owning women was broad. A German seamstress whose only slave was emancipated as a consequence of the war lost the equivalent of what would have been a life savings for most: "I worked with my needle, and six months before the war broke out, I bought Jane for twelve hundred dollars in gold, I had earned at the end o' the needle, but now she's free an' I aint a carin' for that, but thar's my hard work gone." The twelve hundred dollars that she paid for Jane would have the purchasing power of approximately $36,500 today.[54] At the other end of the spectrum, Irene Smith, who pleaded with the secretary of the treasury to protect her property during the war, saw her personal estate worth $678,000 in 1860 reduced to $70,000 a decade later.[55] Even women who retained ownership of considerable amounts of land and other property after the Civil War continued to grapple with the pecuniary impact of federal emancipation policies and the financial losses they incurred because of them. For slave-owning women like Irene Smith, the ramifications struck "a blow from which [they] never recovered," and they described those losses in their applications for presidential pardon and amnesty.[56]

When historians write about white southern women's experiences during the Civil War and after, they tend to foreground their human loss, rather than the direct, economic losses that these women suffered. Certainly they grieved for lost family and friends. And they suffered from the loss of slaves their husbands and male kin owned. But the applications of former slave-owning women for pardon and amnesty make it clear that losing the enslaved people they owned in their own right was no small part of the trauma wrought by the war.

On May 29, 1865, President Andrew Johnson issued the first of three procla-mations that granted former Confederates amnesty and pardons if they swore oaths of allegiance to the United States. Abraham Lincoln had issued two such proclamations during the war, but few southerners had heeded his call to rejoin the Union. After all hope for a Confederate victory was lost, however, thousands of southern men and women swore oaths of allegiance to the United States and submitted petitions for pardons and general amnesty. The Johnson administra-tion kept the oath simple. Rebellious southerners simply had to state the follow-ing: "I, _____, do solemnly swear or affirm, in presence of Almighty God, that I will henceforth faithfully support and defend the Constitution of the United States and the Union of the States thereunder. And that I will, in like manner, abide by and faithfully support all laws and proclamations which have been made during the existing rebellion with reference to the emancipation of slaves, so help me God."[57] As straightforward as the oath seemed, saying those words was far from simple for former slave-owning women such as Catherine Ann Edmonston — and meaning them was even more difficult. In Edmonston's opin-ion, the oath of loyalty was an act of humiliation that brought about "hate, con-tempt, & rage" in the breast of "every true Southron." The only reason why so many southerners swore the oath, she surmised, was "to protect themselves against Yankee & negro insolence & to preserve the remnant of [their] property." She made it clear that many who swore the oath did not mean it and had no intention of keeping the promises they made. "Who considers it binding?" she asked. "No one. Not one person whom I have heard speak of it but laughs at and repudiates every obligation it imposes. It binds one no more than a promise at the pistols point to a highwayman!"[58] But white southerners humbled them-selves, swore their oaths, and applied for pardons and amnesty nonetheless.

The federal government concluded that this simple oath was not enough for individuals who engaged in certain kinds of rebellion against the Union or for rebels who owned property valued at twenty thousand dollars or more. Those people had to apply directly to the president for amnesty and pardon, and he would determine whether they could reclaim their property. Over half the peti-tioners who requested special pardons were "excepted" from the general amnesty proclamation because of their large property holdings, and for them the restoration of their citizenship and property rights served as the ultimate goal of their petitions. By 1867, Andrew Johnson had granted special pardons to more than thirteen thousand men and women who sympathized with or aided the rebellion. While men constituted the overwhelming majority of the peti-tioners, more than four hundred married, single, and widowed women were among them.[59]

The smaller representation of women among special pardon requests was probably due to at least two factors. First, their particular acts of rebellion did not render them ineligible for the general pardon. Many of the women who applied for special pardons admitted to actively aiding in the rebellion, primarily by providing food, shelter, and other necessaries to Confederate soldiers. Second, they typically owned more enslaved people than land, and such property held no value after the war, which decreased the likelihood that they would need to request amnesty and pardon directly from Johnson.

Petitioners were not obligated to describe their feelings about the war or to enumerate the financial losses that emancipation brought about. But many former slave-owning women chose to touch on such matters. Though some "cordially accept[ed] . . . the abolition of slavery as a fixed fact," their petitions often focused upon the enslaved people they had owned in their own right. The day that Andrew Johnson issued his proclamation, Carrie Lomax submitted her application for special pardon and amnesty. She wrote that "the largest portion of [her] estate consist[ed] of slaves now free" and, where it had been practicable her former slaves were "employed by petition as freemen under the regulations of the 'Freedmans Bureau' at Montgomery, Ala." Eliza Grey wrote of equally devastating losses. In addition to the loss of "property destroyed by the army of the United States and . . . taken and destroyed by the armies and officials of the so called Confederate states," she owned "one hundred and sixty negro slaves," property that held no value at the war's end. As Mary A. Hood of Meriwether County, Georgia, told the president, "In the beginning of the late rebellion, the most valuable portion of [my] estate consisted in slaves . . . but since that time, in consequence of the emancipation of the slaves, the improvident cultivation of [my] lands," and the inability of her debtors to pay her, it had "greatly diminished in value."[60]

Things were much worse for Sarah J. Firth of Beaufort, South Carolina, who informed the president that she was "utterly destitute of all means of support" because the federal government refused to allow her to "regain possession of her property." Her request for pardon conveyed her sense of double victimization. She and the southern people had lost the war, and now the government had implemented policies that "punish the innocent women of the country as aiders in the rebellion lately quelled." Writing from Longwood plantation in Washington County, Mississippi, Irene Smith claimed that she too was "guiltless." She had only remained in the South during the war because the enslaved people she owned would not have been able to survive without her. Her loyalty was to her slaves, not the Confederacy, she argued, and it was "her duty to protect and defend a large number of persons (then her slaves) who were, for the time, dependent on her for sustenance and support." Punishing women for their benevolence? This could not possibly be what the president intended.[61]

For women like Catharine Fulton, confiscation policies were more than punishment; they were insults. Over the course of 1865 and into 1866, Fulton applied for pardon and amnesty twice and wrote several letters to North Carolina governor Jonathan Worth and to General O. H. Howard, the provost marshal who witnessed her oaths of allegiance. She pled for their assistance in reclaiming property she owned in Charleston, which had been seized and had fallen into "the hands of the 'Freedmen's Bureau.'" It seemed hard, wrote Fulton, that she "should be deprived of it," as she had "already suffered severely by the 'Emancipation Act.'" An acquaintance, Commodore John A. Winslow, supported her application, attaching his own letter of appeal, in which he argued that Fulton had "suffered to great extent by the loss of slaves," and "no good purpose" could be served by "refusal of the only means of livelihood she has." He added that "Mrs. Fulton before the war, was worth more than $20,000 but with the loss of slaves it is doubtful whether her property would reach that amount." With their slaves free, the women who applied for pardons and amnesty could only hope to "obtain assured protection" of their "rights" to their remaining property and "enjoy undisturbed the remnant of [their] estate[s]."[62]

These women's petitions for pardons and amnesty reveal the complex roles former slave-owning women played throughout the South before the war and women's diverse responses to the war's end and abolition. When Caroline Alston of Choctaw County, Alabama, applied for a special pardon, she told the president that she had been "informed that the result of the late war, between the United States and the Confederate States, has been to deprive her of her slaves, and that she has nothing left her, but a little stock and her lands." She was the only property owner in her household: her husband "had no property when she married him" and had "acquired none since" their marriage. Since he entered their marriage without property, the couple "secured all her property to her separate use, by a marriage contract, duly proven and recorded in the Probate Court of Marengo County, Alabama, where the marriage took place." Furthermore, because Alabama law also secured her property "to her separate use," her slaves, stocks, and lands had been "doubly secured." She applied to Johnson for amnesty and pardon so that she could access her livestock and lands. Once she reclaimed her property, she could take care of her family, as she had done before the war. Mary L. Carter also appealed to President Johnson for a pardon because her husband, Jesse Carter, had "little property, and . . . the property and estate owned by her" was "the sole source of income for the support and maintenance of her family." In spite of owning property worth twenty thousand dollars or more, however, she complained that her assets had "been very much diminished by the war," since she had "lost about thirty five slaves."[63]

Alston's and Carter's petitions make it clear that women who possessed the bulk of the slaves in their households and the majority of their families' wealth did not necessarily assume *new* roles during the war or after it was over. Rather, they continued to use their personal estates to help provide for their families, but they, and not their husbands, were the hardest hit economically by abolition. Their wartime losses made that task difficult, if not impossible, to carry out during Reconstruction. Women like Alston and Carter hoped to resume the positions they had held in their households before the war, not as their husbands' submissive dependents but rather as women who took care of their families' material and financial needs as property owners in their own right. For the married women who still possessed property worth at least twenty thousand dollars, pardons and amnesty were all they needed to be restored to their "rights of citizenship and of property." President Johnson routinely approved their requests.[64] Former slave-owning women were thus enabled to restore to their lives some semblance of the familiar. With their landed estates back in their hands, those women began to build their lives anew.

Epilogue: Lost Kindred, Lost Cause

Within months of Lee's surrender to Grant on April 9, 1865, enslaved people began placing advertisements in "Information Wanted" and "Lost Friends" columns of southern newspapers. They were searching for their loved ones. In these ads, they described mothers, fathers, children, siblings, aunts, uncles, and grandparents, many of whom they had not seen for decades: kinfolk who could be alive or dead. The ads were filled with yearning and despair, and the formerly enslaved people who placed them often named the white women responsible for their losses. In the immediate and not so immediate aftermath of slavery, formerly enslaved people traced their lineages through their losses and the separations brought about when their mistresses sold them, when other women bought them, when they were given to women as gifts or bequests, and when their female owners relocated from the Southeast to the Deep South and Southwest.[1]

In the thirty years following abolition, the women who once owned enslaved people and their female descendants also wrote about enslavement and loss, but in a remarkably different way. They laid bare their thoughts about the system and how they perceived the roles they had played within it. Interwoven within their tales of privileged living, these women constructed preposterous narratives about slavery that omitted the trauma of separation, loss of self-determination, and violence that emerged in the "Lost Friends" and "Information Wanted" advertisements. When former slave owners wrote about slavery, their picture showed no brutality, no privation, no agony, no loss, no tears, no sweat, no blood. They portrayed themselves and their female forebears as forever sacrificing women who had played purely benevolent roles within a nurturing system. Enslaved people had only benefited from their mistresses' sacrifices and acts of benevolence, they wrote, and often expressed their recognition and appreciation of that care through their unwavering loyalty and love. This incongruent "reciprocity" led some writers to openly grieve that their female descendants would "never know the tender tie that existed between mistress and servant."[2]

Many of the female authors contended that this tie was bound up in moral obligation; God had ordained that their European ancestors buy, rule over, Christianize, and civilize people of African descent.[3] Letitia Burwell believed that African Americans should be grateful for their enslavement and to show their appreciation might consider creating an "anniversary to celebrate 'the landing of their fathers on the shores of America,' when they were bought and domiciled in American homes." Slavery benefited the enslaved, she and others surmised, but it was a heavy burden for their owners. This was especially the case for white women, whose conduct toward such barbaric people was especially commendable. "What courage, what patience, what perseverance, what long suffering, what Christian forbearance, must it have cost our great-grandmothers to civilize, Christianize, and elevate the naked, savage Africans to the condition of good cooks and respectable maids!" she exclaimed. After all, "They . . . did not enjoy the blessed privilege even of turning their servants off when inefficient or disagreeable, but had to keep them through life."[4]

White women did not have to rely on their imaginations to understand what kind of "savage Africans" their foremothers had had to contend with. In the early decades of the twentieth century, some of these women had firsthand encounters with native-born Africans, and they found it "perfectly appalling" that such people could be human beings. A friend of Nancy Bostick De Saussure visited Africa at the turn of the twentieth century and wrote to her describing her experiences there. Africans, she explained, were devoid of "any humanity" or "affection for anybody or anything." She concluded that it was "an insult to a good dog to compare them to animals." De Saussure, a proud southerner and former slave owner, agreed. In her estimation, the contemporary Africans her friend described resembled "the imported African before he was Christianized and humanized by the people of the South."[5]

In writing these accounts, former slave-owning women offered three primary reasons why they had supported the institution of slavery. First, as noted, it was a positive good for the African savages, whom slavery had civilized. Second, slavery was "God's own plan" for helping these inferior people, and white women were following His divine instructions in furthering it. And finally, they "were born to it, grew up with it, lived with it, and it was [their] daily life"; how could they help supporting it?[6] These women did not express such ideas because they were the views of white men or because white men shielded them from slavery's ugliness. They espoused such views because of their own experiences with the institution of slavery, and they arrived at their conclusions through their own line of reasoning.

As they wrote these reflections about southern life before the war, white women often distorted, obfuscated, and distanced themselves from the fourth reason they supported the system: their direct economic investment in slavery and their pecuniary interest in perpetuating it. Some women claimed that they and their families rarely, if ever, bought enslaved people. Nancy Bostick De Saussure, for example, readily admitted that her "father gave each of his children . . . a plantation with negroes and a house" when they married, but failed to mention that Louis D. De Saussure, the cousin-in-law whose home she occasionally visited, was a major Charleston area slave dealer.[7]

Nancy De Saussure was not the only woman who neglected to acknowledge her economic ties to the slave trade and the people who made their living buying and selling human beings. However, when white women did address the issue, they dismissed such trafficking as a necessary evil and vilified the individuals who traded human beings for profit. As Mary Norcott Bryan wrote, the business of "being bought and sold" was "the only objectionable thing about slavery," and the "class of men . . . who made a business of buying negroes" were "held in horror."[8] Her characterization ignores the many slave-trading men whom southerners held in high regard, not in spite of but *because* of their extraordinary wealth, often accumulated in the slave trade. It also omits mention of the wives, daughters, and granddaughters of these men, whose lives were often sustained by the profits their kin accumulated while buying and selling human beings.

Bryan also claimed that slave-trading men bought slaves only when "an estate became involved" because "owners could not be induced to part with their negroes until . . . everything else had been seized by their creditors." Slave owners, she averred, preferred poverty over profit if it enabled them "to keep and provide for" their slaves. Slave sales could not be avoided, but they took place only as a last resort. Even then, slave owners detested the necessity of selling their human property, and they suffered intense anguish during such sales. None of these female apologists remarked upon the trauma such events caused for enslaved people. Perhaps they, too, drew the conclusion expressed by Letitia Burwell: such sales "turned out best for the negroes."[9]

Other documents that slave-owning women left behind, as well as those maintained by slave traders, southern court officials, and military officers, offer powerful evidence to challenge these fantastical postwar accounts of slavery and the roles their authors had played in sustaining it. In the days, months, and years immediately following abolition, and in the most unlikely of literary media, formerly enslaved people gave the lie to white women's sanitized narratives and revealed former slave-owning women's involvement in marketing them and their families without regard to anything but profit. In the briefest of newspaper ads, freed people like Caroline Mason reported on the loved ones they lost because the white women who owned them had sold them, tearing them away from their families, friends, kin, and homes: "I have a sister, Sallie Summers," Mason wrote, "that was sold out of the Mason family. She was sold from [her] three children, two girls and one boy. . . . She was owned by Betsy Mason and was sold by her at Alexandria, Va."[10] On November 20, 1879, John Colbert Skinner posted an advertisement in the "Lost Friends" column of the *Southwestern Christian Advocate* because he was looking for his brother Edward. The last time John had seen him was on October 12, 1860, in Georgetown, in the District of Columbia. Not long after the brothers crossed paths that day, John and his family were forced to leave Edward behind when their owner refugeed to the Lower South and took them along. One year after John placed his initial "Lost Friends" advertisement, he still had not found Edward, so he placed another, this time offering more detail. Each advertisement made one point clear: Angelica Chew, the woman who owned him and his family, was responsible for their separation. She was the reason he and his family were still searching for Edward.[11]

When African American men served in the United States military during the Civil War, they and their widows and children became eligible for pensions. The applications they later sent to the United States Pension Bureau contained details about their lives as enslaved people. Claimants would identify their female owners and touch upon the significant life changes, losses, and separations these women had brought about. Benjamin B. Manson provided a deposition when his son John White applied for a pension after he served in the 14th U.S. Colored Infantry. Manson stated that he "was born in the State of V[irgini]a as the property of Mrs Nancy Manson of said state," and that when he was eleven years old, she "moved to the State of Tennessee, bringing her slaves with her."[12] Mrs. Manson had died, and Benjamin had been part of the division of her estate and later changed hands twice more as part of Manson family difficulties.

Sometimes the women who had owned the claimants and their family members added their accounts as well. The government would call upon individuals who knew the claimants intimately to provide depositions to support their claims. When Milley Hale submitted her application for a widow's pension, her former owner Olive (Ollie) Queener, her former owner's sister Ann Queener, and the son of Tabitha Hunter, the woman who owned her former husband, provided depositions to support her claim.[13]

Scores of formerly enslaved people provided a different understanding of the institution of slavery, their female owners' knowledge of its workings, the part these women had played in their continued subjugation, and the reasons many white southern women were so adamantly opposed to its abolition. And the white women's economic investments in slavery lay at the heart of such accounts. The formerly enslaved narrators detailed the ways their mistresses' investments colored their actions both within and outside of slave-owning households. They also talked about female owners who procured their slaves from marketplaces and at auctions, not simply through gifts and bequests. They charted the movements of slave-owning women who conducted business with dealers and agents, and took part in economic activities that historians of slavery have either overlooked or alleged never happened. Time and again, with their slaves not far from hearing, white slave-owning women articulated their wish to remain invested in slavery and pass their financial legacies on to their children.[14]

Formerly enslaved people also recalled the marital relations of their owners in ways that challenge current assumptions about the patriarchal order of nineteenth-century households and the influence then-current laws had upon and within them. Married white women contended with husbands, male employees, community members, and officials about their ownership of slaves, as well as about how much control such men could exercise over their property and who else would be afforded the privilege of doing so. Slave auctions, courtrooms, the pages of local newspapers, military correspondence, and even formerly enslaved people's pension applications provided figurative and literal platforms upon which white slave-owning women paraded their economic ties to both the institution of slavery and the people they owned. They conveyed, over and over, the breadth of knowledge they truly possessed about the realities of slavery.

Of course, not all slave-owning women invested in the slave-market economy or exercised control over their own slaves or the slaves of others. Some sought to adhere as closely as possible to the ideals of womanhood that were proffered in the prescriptive literature of their time. They followed precepts that encouraged them to distance themselves from certain dimensions of slavery. But the slave-owning women discussed in this book deviated from these constrained notions of how proper ladies should behave. They fully embraced the institution of slavery and all the economic benefits that came along with it.

These women were not exceptional. They were, in many respects, similar to women in other parts of the world who benefited from the enslavement of

African-descended people. Whether the Englishwomen who invested in the Royal African Company at the height of the Atlantic slave trade, the female slave traders like Madam Efunroye Tinubu of Nigeria who sold captives along the coasts of Africa, the women whom George Pinckard was "shocked to observe" at a West Indian slave auction who had come for "the express purpose of purchasing slaves," or women like the one Richard A. Wyvill saw in a Barbadian market examining enslaved "boys with all possible indelicacy" before she bought them, women who lived in regions that were tied to slavery and the slave trade took an active part in maintaining the institution.[15] The character of slavery and the trade differed from region to region, and women adapted their activities to take full advantage of local and regional market conditions. But despite regional and cultural variations, all these women saw slavery as an economic system from which they could profit.

Former slave-owning women's deeper and more complex investments in slavery help explain why, in the years following the Civil War, they helped construct the South's system of racial segregation, a system premised, as was slavery, upon white supremacy and black oppression. Understanding the direct economic investments white women made in slavery and their stake in its perpetuation, and recognizing the ways they benefited from their whiteness, helps us understand why they and many of their female descendants elected to uphold a white supremacist order after slavery ended. If we acknowledge that white women stood to personally and directly benefit from the commodification and enslavement of African Americans we can better understand their participation in postwar white-supremacist movements and atrocities such as lynching—as well as their membership in organizations like the Ku Klux Klan. Southern white women's roles in upholding and sustaining slavery form part of the much larger history of white supremacy and oppression. And through it all, they were not passive bystanders. They were co-conspirators.

NOTES

INTRODUCTION

1. Redpath, *The Roving Editor*, 183–184.
2. Ibid.
3. Interview with Litt Young, in Rawick, *The American Slave* (hereafter Rawick, AS), Supplement, Series 2, vol. 10, *Texas Narratives, Part 9*, 4301. The interviews in this collection are hereafter cited by the name of the person being interviewed.
4. Ibid.
5. Ibid, 4303.
6. Ibid, 4304–4305.
7. On southern women in general, see, e.g., Anne Firor Scott, *The Southern Lady*; Clinton, *The Plantation Mistress*; Lebsock, *The Free Women of Petersburg*; Fox-Genovese, *Within the Plantation Household*. On southern women, property, and/or the law, see Bynum, *Unruly Women*; Anzilotti, *In the Affairs of the World*; Sturtz, *Within Her Power*; Snyder, *Brabbling Women*; Edwards, *The People and Their Peace*. On southern mothers and motherhood, see McMillen, *Motherhood in the Old South*; Kennedy, *Born Southern*; Katy Simpson Smith, *We Have Raised All of You*. On working, widowed, and single southern women, see Delfino and Gillespie, eds., *Neither Lady nor Slave*; Wood, *Masterful Women*; Carter, *Southern Single Blessedness*. On southern women and the Civil War, see Faust, *Mothers of Invention*; Edwards, *Scarlett Doesn't Live Here Anymore*; Glymph, *Out of the House of Bondage*; Ott, *Confederate Daughters*; McCurry, *Confederate Reckoning*.
8. Wood, *Masterful Women* ("fictive masters"); Bercaw, *Gendered Freedoms*; see, e.g., Fox-Genovese, *Within the Plantation Household*, Faust, *Mothers of Invention*; Glymph, *Out of the House of Bondage*.
9. Fox-Genovese, *Within the Plantation Household*; Cashin, *Our Common Affairs*, 11; Snyder, *Brabbling Women*, 121 ("deputy husbands" and "fictive widows"); Moore, "'Keeping All Hands Moving.'" See also Burke, *On Slavery's Border*, 196; Faust, "'Trying to Do a Man's Business'" ("man's Business").

10. See, e.g., Walter Johnson, *Soul by Soul*, 89–102; Baptist, *The Half Has Never Been Told*, 140; Schermerhorn, *The Business of Slavery*; Gudmestad, *The Troublesome Commerce*, 4; Martin, *Divided Mastery*, 83–85, 114–117; Zaborney, *Slaves for Hire*, 6–7, 98–99.

11. Beckert, "Slavery and Capitalism."

12. Amy Dru Stanley and Ellen Hartigan-O'Connor have recently written compelling essays about this point. See Stanley, "Histories of Capitalism and Sex Difference," and Hartigan-O'Connor, "Gender's Value in the History of Capitalism."

13. Adam Smith, *Lectures on Jurisprudence*, 178.

14. John Quincy Adams to Abigail Adams, August 14, 1790, Abigail Adams to John Quincy Adams, August 20, 1790, and November 7, 1790, in Taylor et al., eds., *The Adams Papers*, 89–92, 92–94, 141–143.

15. John Moore to Mary Moore and Richard Moore, December 10, 1847, Collection of John B. Moore Letters, Gilder Lehrman Collection, 1493–1859, Gilder Lehrman Institute of American History (hereafter GLIAH), GLC04191.16.

16. Gross, "'Good Angels,'" 133–134.

17. Evans, *Born for Liberty*, 35. The historian Laurel Thatcher Ulrich offers a term, the "pretty gentlewoman," which defines what "mistress" has come to mean when historians think of white women's relationship to slavery in the nineteenth century. See Ulrich, *Good Wives*, 113–124.

18. I make the distinction between southern and northern mistresses here because, as the work of Ellen Hartigan-O'Connor, Sarah Damiano, and Amy Dru Stanley has shown, married women in the North, especially those who lived in northern port cities, actively participated in the Atlantic economy. See Hartigan-O'Connor, *Ties That Buy* and "She Said She Did Not Know Money," Damiano, "Agents at Home," and Stanley, "Home Life and the Morality of the Market."

19. Samuel Johnson, *A Dictionary of the English Language*, 52 ("mistress," "mistress-ship"); "master" and "mastery" are defined in identical ways on 470. See also Jane Mills, *Womanwords*, 164, and Erickson, "Mistresses and Marriage," 52.

20. "An Act for the Better Ordering and Governing Negroes and other Slaves," in McCord, *Statutes at Large of South Carolina*, 386.

21. Robert Falls, in Rawick, AS, vol. 16, *Kansas, Kentucky, Maryland, Ohio, Virginia, Tennessee Narratives*, 12.

22. Oakes, *The Ruling Race*, 37–68.

23. O'Donovan, *Becoming Free in the Cotton South*, 4.

24. In 1860, federal census enumerators found that over 500,000 white southerners over the age of twenty were unable to read or write. Of these, white women were almost one and a half times more likely to be unable to read or write than white men. U.S. Bureau of the Census, "Series A 91–104. Population, by Sex and Race: 1790 to 1970," in *The Statistical History of the United States*, 14, and "Persons over Twenty Years of Age Who Cannot Read or Write," in *Statistics of the United States*, 508.

25. For the questions, see U.S. Works Progress Administration, "Supplementary Instructions 9-E to the American Guide Manual," April 22, 1937. Records of the Library of Congress Project, Writers' Unit, National Archives and Records Administration, Washington, D.C. (hereafter NARA).

26. See, e.g., C. Vann Woodward, "History from Slave Sources"; Blassingame, "Using the Testimony of Ex-Slaves"; Soapes, "The Federal Writers' Project Slave Interviews"; Bailey, "A Divided Prism"; Yetman, "Ex-Slave Interviews and the Historiography of Slavery"; Spindel, "Assessing Memory"; Shaw, "Using the WPA Ex-Slave Narratives to Study the Impact of the Great Depression."

27. Interview with Delia Garlic, in *Born in Slavery: Slave Narratives from the Federal Writers' Project, 1936–1938*, Digital Collection, Library of Congress, Manuscript Division, at http://memory.loc.gov/ammem/snhtml/snhome.html (hereafter BS), vol. 1, *Alabama Narratives*, 129; interview with Willis Bennefield, in BS, vol. 4, *Georgia Narratives, Part 4*, 235–236. The interviews in this collection are hereafter cited by the name of the person being interviewed. See also Sarah Hamlin, in Rawick, AS, vol. 2, *South Carolina Narratives, Part 2*, 223 and 226, and Ellen Campbell, in BS, vol. 4, *Georgia Narratives, Part 4*, 222.

28. Margo-Lea Hurwicz et al., "Salient Life Events in Three-Generational Families"; Delicia Patterson, in BS, vol. 10, *Missouri Narratives*, 270; Anne Maddox, in BS, vol. 1, *Alabama Narratives*, 272; Tom McGruder, in BS, vol. 4, *Georgia Narratives, Part 3*, 76.

29. See Berry, *The Price for Their Pound of Flesh*; Schwalm, *Emancipation's Diaspora*, 222.

30. Interview with Mary Harris, in Clayton, *Mother Wit*, 94–95. The interviews in this collection are hereafter cited by the name of the person being interviewed.

1. MISTRESSES IN THE MAKING

1. John A. Burwell, ALS [autograph letter signed], to Elizabeth T. Guy, Lynesville, N.C., April 30, 1847, Burwell-Guy Family Papers, William L. Clements Library, University of Michigan, Ann Arbor (hereafter BGFP-WLCL).

2. Jennifer Morgan, in *Laboring Women*, 144, uses the term "obscene logic" to describe the ways slave owners measured and calculated their intergenerational prosperity and familial well-being by the exploitation, marketing, and possible childbearing uses of their female slaves. I use it here to describe the dis-synchronous coexistence of slave owners' affection for and violence toward enslaved people.

3. See *James Taylor v. State*, January 1848, Georgia Supreme Court, Case Files, 1846–1917, Savannah, Manuscript File No. A-00208, Georgia Archives; *Littleton B. Lewis and Nancy A. Boulware Lewis v. Benjamin Boulware and John G. Barber*, July 1846, Fairfield District, Records of the Equity Court, Bills, South Carolina Department of Archives and History, Columbia (hereafter SCDAH), *Race and Slavery Petitions Project: Race, Slavery, and Free Blacks Series 2: Petitions to Southern County Courts, 1777–1867*, ed. Loren Schweninger, microfilm collection (hereafter RSP-2); Turner, *North Carolina Planters and Their Children*, 105.

4. For more about these kinds of interactions see Wilma King, *African-American Childhoods*, 23–37.

5. See Brewer, *By Birth or Consent*, 39.

6. Keim, "Primogeniture and Entail in Colonial Virginia," 550–551. See Salmon, *Women and the Law of Property in Early America*, 142, 158; Anzilotti, *In the Affairs of the World*,

143, 74; Turner, *North Carolina Planters and Their Children*, 107; Shammas, *The History of Household Government in America*, 72.

7. Rosalie Calvert wrote to her father about her daughter's future inheritance when he lived in Belgium. In her correspondence, Calvert indicated that she and her husband were "presently thinking about giving her what is called here 'real property,' which is to say, lands or houses over which a husband has no power"; Rosalie Calvert to Henri J. Stier, November 9, 1817, in Calvert, *Mistress of Riversdale*, 325. Rosalie's husband, George Calvert, also demanded that his daughter Eugenia devise a marriage contract prior to receiving her inheritance; Calvert, *Mistress of Riversdale*, 378.

8. Interview with Bacchus White, in Perdue et al., *Weevils in the Wheat*, 303 (interviews in this collection hereafter cited by the name of the person being interviewed); Agnes James, in *BS*, vol. 14, *South Carolina Narratives, Part 3*, 8. See also Cornelia Winfield, in *BS*, vol. 4, *Georgia Narratives, Part 4*, 177.

9. *Silas Knight, Robert Knight and Mary Fuller Knight v. Silas M.F. Knight, Robert A. Knight and Mary C.V. Knight*, Docket 457, Petition for Sale of Slave, Filed December 13, 1862, Records of the Equity Court, Petitions, SCDAH, RSP-2. Grimké shared her story, along with a tale about her encounter with a coffle of "twenty children chained together" who were being "driven through the streets of Charleston to be sold in New Orleans," with children who attended an event organized by the Boston Juvenile Anti-Slavery Society. Her aim was to convey what life was like for white girls who were raised in slaveholding households throughout the South. See H. C. Wright, "Boston Juvenile Anti-Slavery Society," *Liberator*, June 16, 1837. An unnamed, formerly enslaved woman told the historian Frederic Bancroft that her owners gave her to their "daughter fer a present [because] [d]ey make *presunts* o' niggahs in *doze* days"; Bancroft, *Slave Trading in the Old South*, 292 (emphasis in original); "Uncle" Fil Hancock, in *BS*, vol. 10, *Missouri Narratives*, 148.

10. Lydia Maria Child, interview with Charity Bowery, 1847–1848, in Blassingame, *Slave Testimony*, 261–267; Amy Perry, in *BS*, vol. 14, *South Carolina Narratives, Part 3*, 251. Apparently, the phrase "daily gift" was endemic to South Carolina and was used by individuals who were raised there to refer to the gifting of slaves from a slave-owning parent to a child. For other examples, see Amos Gadsden, in *BS*, vol. 14, *South Carolina Narratives, Part 2*, 91, and Jane Hollins, ibid., 291.

11. In legal contexts, these acts were referred to as "parol," or oral gifts, and were legitimate in the eyes of the law. However, without more formal documentation to support these gifts, individuals could and often did question their legitimacy. See for example, *Goodwin v. Morgan*, 1 Stewart 278, January 1828, Ala. LEXIS 5, LexisNexis Academic; *Jane Irwin v. Morell*, Dudl. Ga. 72, July 1831, Helen Tunnicliff Catterall, *Judicial Cases Concerning American Slavery and the Negro*, vol. 3, p. 14; *John W. and Esther C. Carter v. George F. Buchannon*, Georgia Supreme Court Records, Milledgeville, Georgia Archives, Manuscript Case File No. A-00253, November 1847.

12. Interview with unidentified enslaved person, in Rawick, *AS*, vol. 18, *Unwritten History of Slavery: Autobiographical Account of Negro Ex-Slaves*, 117. See also Ora M. Flagg, in *BS*, vol. 11, *North Carolina Narratives, Part 1*, 308.

13. The executors of John Devereux referred to the drawing ceremony as a "ballot," but the process unfolded in the same way. See "Division of the Negroes Late the Property

of John Devereux the Older," November 30, 1844, Devereux Family Papers, 1776–1936, *Records of Antebellum Southern Plantations from the Revolution Through the Civil War*, ed. Kenneth M. Stampp, microfilm collection (hereafter *RASP*), Series F: Selections from the Rare Book, Manuscript, and Special Collections Library, Duke University, part 4: North Carolina and Virginia.

14. Sallie Crane, in *BS*, vol. 2, *Arkansas Narratives, Part 2*, 51.
15. Jennie Fitts, in Rawick, *AS*, Supplement, Series 2, vol. 4, *Texas Narratives, Part 3*, 1352.
16. Ibid.
17. Phillips, *Life and Labor in the Old South*, 198–199.
18. Cashin, *Our Common Affairs*, 11.
19. Malone, *Sweet Chariot*, 232; Betty Curlett, in *BS*, vol. 2, *Arkansas Narratives, Part 2*, 73–74.
20. Octave Lilly, Jr., Interview with Louisa Sidney Martin, February 17, 1938, WPA Federal Writers' Project, Ex-Slave Studies, Marcus Christian Collection, Accession 11, Historical Source Material, Slave Narratives, Box 4 of 16, Earl K. Long Library, University of New Orleans; interview with unidentified formerly enslaved person, in *Unwritten History of Slavery*, 150. See also interview with Savilla Burrell, in Hurmence, *Before Freedom, When I Just Can Remember*, 133 (interviews in this volume hereafter cited by the name of the person being interviewed).
21. George Womble, in *BS*, vol. 4, *Georgia Narratives, Part 4*, 191.
22. Rebecca Jane Grant, in Hurmence, *Before Freedom, When I Just Can Remember*, 57.
23. Interview with unidentified former slave, "Mistreatment of Slaves," in *BS*, vol. 4, *Georgia Narratives, Part 4*, 303.
24. Ibid.
25. Kemble, *Journal of a Residence on a Georgian Plantation*, 22.
26. Betty Cofer, in *BS*, vol. 11, *North Carolina Narratives, Part 1*, 168.
27. Burwell, *A Girl's Life in Virginia Before the War*, 2–3; *Thomas Gorsuch, Hannah J. (Onion) Gorsuch, Alexander Kennand and Agness Maria (Onion) Kennard v. John W. Onion*, Schweninger Collection, Maryland State Archives, Annapolis, Maryland, July 1839, *RSP-2*.
28. Ella Washington, in Rawick, *AS*, Supplement, Series 2, vol. 10, *Texas Narratives, Part 9*, 3969, 3971–3972.
29. Melinda, in Clayton, *Mother Wit*, 167–168.
30. American Freedmen's Inquiry Commission interview with Solomon Bradley, South Carolina, 1863, in Blassingame, *Slave Testimony*, 372.
31. *Green Martin v. the State*, Georgia Supreme Court Records, Savannah, Georgia Archives, Manuscript Case File No. A-02450, decided June 22, 1858.
32. Ibid.
33. Ibid.
34. Ibid.
35. "Narrative of James Curry," in Blassingame, *Slave Testimony*, 132–133.
36. Tines Kendricks, in *BS*, vol. 2, *Arkansas Narratives, Part 4*, 178–179; J. L. Smith, in *BS*, vol. 2, *Arkansas Narratives, Part 6*, 199.
37. Henrietta King in Perdue et al., *Weevils in the Wheat*, 190–192.

38. Ibid.
39. Henry Gibbs, in Rawick, AS, Supplement, Series 1, vol. 8, *Mississippi Narratives, Part 3*, 15.
40. Mary Armstrong, in BS, vol. 16, *Texas Narratives, Part 1*, 25–27. Some young southern white women chose not to embrace slavery at all. Sarah and Angelina Grimké hailed from one of the wealthiest and most politically prominent slaveholding families in South Carolina. Both women rejected the life which slavery afforded them. At different times, they left their family behind and moved to the northern United States, where they became staunch abolitionists. See Lerner, *The Grimké Sisters from South Carolina*.
41. Elizabeth Sparks, in BS, vol. 17, *Virginia Narratives*, 50–52.
42. Kenny, "Mastering Childhood," 68–69, 73; letter to the editor from Julia, *The Rose Bud; or, Youth's Gazette*, vol. 1, no. 32, April 6, 1832.
43. See "Religious Privileges of the Negroes in Charleston," *Southern Rose*, vol. 4, no. 6, November 14, 1835, 41; "Recollections of a Southern Matron," chapter 9, *Southern Rose*, vol. 4, no. 4, October 17, 1835, 25; "Recollections of a Southern Matron," chapter 20, *Southern Rose*, vol. 4, no. 16, April 2, 1836, 121. *The Rose Bud* was renamed *The Southern Rose*.
44. Sedgwick, *The Linwoods*, vol. 2, pp. 222–224.
45. "The Editor's Boudoir: Miss Sedgwick Ignorant of Negro Character," *Southern Rose*, vol. 4, no. 5, October 31, 1835, 38–39.
46. Ibid. Sedgwick also drafted Elizabeth Freeman's biography, *Mum Bett*, in 1853. Freeman's experience as described in *Mum Bett* and Rose's ordeal in *The Linwoods* are nearly identical. See Sedgwick, *The Linwoods*, vol. 2, pp. 222–224, and *Mum Bett*, manuscript draft, 1853, Massachusetts Historical Society. Both northern and southern children could also have learned about slavery from other books aimed specifically at young readers, such as *The Child's Book on Slavery; or, Slavery Made Plain*, a remarkable abolitionist text that included chapters on the realities of slavery, the relationship between race and enslavement, slave law, slave population data, and the impact slavery had upon bondspeople as well as on their enslavers. See Horace C. Grosvenor, *The Child's Book on Slavery; or, Slavery Made Plain* (Cincinnati: American Reform Tract and Book Society, 1857). I am indebted to Daina Ramey Berry for bringing this source to my attention.
47. Ellen Thomas, in BS, vol. 1, *Alabama Narratives*, 376–377.
48. Nancy Thomas, in Rawick, AS, Supplement, Series 2, vol. 9, *Texas Narratives, Part 8*, 3810. According to Angelina Grimké, this three-legged stool conferred inferior position. During her visit with a slave-owning woman, she noticed that all the enslaved seamstresses, no matter how "delicate might be [their] circumstances, were forced to sit upon low stools, without backs, that they might be constantly reminded of their inferiority." "Testimony of Angelina Grimké," in Theodore Dwight Weld, *American Slavery as It Is*, 54.
49. For a similar account, see Delicia Patterson, in BS, vol. 10, *Missouri Narratives*, 270.
50. Olmsted, *A Journey in the Back Country*, 443–445.
51. Berry, *The Price for Their Pound of Flesh*, 39.

52. Interview with unidentified formerly enslaved woman, in *Unwritten History of Slavery*, 279–280.
53. On recollections of being given as gifts, see, e.g., Martha Mays, in Rawick, AS, Supplement, Series 1, vol. 9, *Mississippi Narratives, Part 4*, 1467; James Baker, in BS, vol. 2, *Arkansas Narratives, Part 1*, 92–93; Hannah Crosson, in BS, vol. 11, *North Carolina Narratives, Part 1*, 189; Emma Knight, in BS, vol. 10, *Missouri Narratives*, 218; Laura Stewart, in BS, vol. 4, "Excerpts from Slave Interviews," *Georgia Narratives, Part 4*, 216. For a case that corroborates such remembrances, see *Littleton B. Lewis and Nancy A. Boulware Lewis v. Benjamin Boulware and John G. Barber*, Filed May 18, 1842, Records of the Equity Court, Bills, SCDAH, RSP-2.
54. Julia Casey, in BS, vol. 15, *Tennessee Narratives*, 3; Louisa Davidson et al. from the WPA History of Copiah County, "Antebellum Negroes Section," in Rawick, AS, Supplement, Series 1, vol. 7, *Mississippi Narratives, Part 2*, 573.
55. Adeline Blakely, in BS, vol. 2, *Arkansas Narratives, Part 1*, 12.
56. Ibid. A considerable amount of time could elapse between the moment when relatives gave women gifts consisting of enslaved people and the women's decisions to get rid of them. See *Emily J. Moore and Hansel Batton v. William B. Harwood*, Records of the Chancery Court, University of South Alabama Archives, Mobile, Alabama, RSP-2.
57. James Winchester to Maria Breedlove, November 3, 1814, Nashville, Tennessee, Gilder Lehrman Collection, 1493–1945, GLIAH, GLC06997.41, available at http://www.americanhistory.amdigital.co.uk/Documents/Details/GLC06997.41 (accessed December 3, 2015). For a similar instance, see Martha Mays, in Rawick, AS, Supplement, Series 1, vol. 9, *Mississippi Narratives, Part 4*, 1467.
58. Bill Homer, in BS, vol. 16, *Texas Narratives, Part 2*, 154; Ben Johnson, in BS, vol. 2, *Arkansas Narratives, Part 4*, 9.
59. Kittie Stanford, in BS, vol. 2, *Arkansas Narratives, Part 6*, 214.
60. *Catharine B. Jones, James P. Trezerant, Mary A. E. Trezerant v. William C. Hicks and William Murrah*, Records of the Chancery Court, Second District, Suits, Old Series, Hinds County Courthouse, Raymond, Mississippi, RSP-2.
61. Deed of Gift, Theodorick Bland to Frances Bland Tucker, June 1, 1787, item 1411, Tucker-Coleman Papers, Special Collections Research Center, Earl Gregg Swem Library, College of William and Mary, Williamsburg, Virginia (hereafter TCP-EGSL).
62. *Catharine V. Phillips by Nathaniel H. Clanton her Next Friend v. John W. Bridges, Samuel G. Phillips, and Martin Stetson*, Docket 3083, Filed June 8, 1853, Macon County, Alabama (1851–53), Alabama Supreme Court Cases, RSP-2.
63. Ibid.
64. See Berry, *The Price for Their Pound of Flesh*, 10–57.
65. Mary Lindsay, in BS, vol. 13, *Oklahoma Narratives*, 179.
66. See, e.g., Hening, *Statutes at Large*, 170. For one such exception, see Mollie Williams, in BS, vol. 9, *Mississippi Narratives*, 158.
67. Enslaved people knew that the children born from marriages between enslaved people who were owned by different masters and lived apart "always went with their mammies," and they recognized the legal importance of this. Charlotte Stephens, for

example, told her interviewer Beulah Sherwood Hagg that "the children belonged to the master who owned the mother. This was according to law." Charlotte E. Stephens, in *BS*, vol. 2, *Arkansas Narratives, Part 6*, 226. See also Mary Colbert, in *BS*, vol. 4, *Georgia Narratives, Part 1*, 207, and Minnie Folkes, in Perdue et al., *Weevils in the Wheat*, 94.

68. Daina Ramey Berry shows that this was especially true for enslaved men between the ages of twenty-three and thirty-nine; Berry, *The Price for Their Pound of Flesh*, 95.

69. Ibid., 81.

70. Henrietta Butler, in Clayton, *Mother Wit*, 38.

71. Emma Chapman, in *BS*, vol. 1, *Alabama Narratives*, 62–64. Francis Hudson Haynie's first name is spelled with an "i" on the documents.

72. Even as white southerners developed a keen interest in enslaved women of reproductive age and the children they bore, they refrained from putting a value on enslaved infants until after they survived their first year. Once that milestone was passed, they would record the enslaved children's valuations in their account books, and those appraisals increased incrementally as the enslaved children grew older. See Berry, *The Price for Their Pound of Flesh*, 33–57.

73. See O'Connor, *Mistress of Evergreen Plantation*, 185 and 190 especially. The historian Avery O. Craven surmised the same. When analyzing O'Connor's discussions of the enslaved children born on her sister's plantation and on her own, Craven saw her reaction as "that of a planter viewing the increase of Negro babies as she might have viewed an unusual litter in the barnyard"; Craven, *Rachel of Old Louisiana*, 31.

74. Craven, *Rachel of Old Louisiana*, 115–122; Jane Kemp, "Negroes on Plassy Plantation, May 23, 1854," Bass-Farrar Family Papers, Mss. 4907, Louisiana and Lower Mississippi Valley Collections, Louisiana State University Libraries, Baton Rouge.

75. Mom Ryer Emmanuel, in *BS*, vol. 14, *South Carolina Narratives, Part 2*, 11–12. Sallie Paul remembered the language referring to enslaved children as crops in her interview with Annie Ruth Davis; Sallie Paul, in *BS*, vol. 14, *South Carolina Narratives, Part 3*, 238–239.

76. Interview with unidentified formerly enslaved woman, in *Unwritten History of Slavery*, 77.

77. Cited in Weld, *American Slavery as It Is*, 68–69.

78. Jennifer Morgan, *Laboring Women*, 79, 82; Richard Follett, "'Lives of Living Death'"; Kemble, *Journal of a Residence on a Georgian Plantation*, 190–191, 199–200, 204.

79. Baptist, *The Half Has Never Been Told*, 126; Walter Johnson, *River of Dark Dreams*, 178–180, 198.

80. See Thomas, *The Secret Eye*, 149.

81. Sallie Paul, in *BS*, vol. 14, *South Carolina Narratives, Part 3*, 238–239.

82. John Brown, *Slave Life in Georgia*, 3.

2. "I BELONG TO DE MISTIS"

Chapter title: Mary Overton, in *BS*, vol. 16, *Texas Narratives, Part 3*, 162–163.

1. Blackstone, *Commentaries on the Laws of England*, vol. 1, p. 442.

2. Will Typescript of Francis Davis of Marion District (Mss Will: Book 1, Page 291; Estate Packet: Roll 223) (1 Frame) and Will Typescript of Elizabeth McWhite of Marion District (Mss Will: Book 2, Page 90; Estate Packet: Roll 598), SCDAH. According to Schedule 2 of the 1850 and 1860 United States Federal Census taken in 1860 (which enumerated the number of slaves each southerner owned), Sarah still owned some of those slaves; see Seventh and Eighth Censuses of the United States, Marion, South Carolina, Schedule 1 (free inhabitants). These documents also support much of the demographic information below that Hester Hunter details in her testimony, as does W. W. Sellers's extensive history of Marion County, A *History of Marion County, South Carolina*, 452–453, 898.

3. Kerber, *No Constitutional Right to Be Ladies*, 15.

4. Hester Hunter, in *BS*, vol. 14, *South Carolina Narratives, Part 2*, 342–343.

5. Ibid. Formerly enslaved people routinely remarked upon the inferior diets their own ers provided for them, and often cited the scarce amounts of meat, or the complete lack of it, in their reflections about this aspect of their lives in bondage. See Benny Dillard, in Rawick, *AS*, vol. 12, *Georgia Narratives, Part 1*, 291, and Bill Austin, in *BS*, vol. 3, *Florida Narratives*, 23. For a more recent discussion of planters' tendency to limit or omit meat from the diets of their slaves see Walter Johnson, *River of Dark Dreams*, 178–179, 185–188.

6. Hester Hunter, in *BS*, vol. 14, *South Carolina Narratives, Part 2*, 342–343.

7. Ibid.

8. Women's quarrels over their men's actions and claims was so common, in fact, that colonial Virginia and other regions tried to curtail their "brabbling" by legislating against it. See Snyder, *Brabbling Women*.

9. See Cashin, *Our Common Affairs*, 1–41.

10. See Schwarz, *Twice Condemned*, 323–335; Killens, *The Trial Records of Denmark Vesey*, 140–146. For women's requests for compensation after their slaves were executed see Petition of Sarah Martin for Compensation for a Slave Executed, Document Number ND 1816, Petition of Martha R. Garner for Compensation for a Slave Executed, Document Number ND 234, and Petition of Duncan McRae et al. Praying Compensation for Slaves Executed, Document Number ND 1661, all in Records of the General Assembly, SCDAH. See Summons issued by Judge Terence Le Blanc ordering Mrs. Antoine Vichner to have her slaves Charles, David, and Madelaine in court on the twelfth day of the month to testify, 1820 July 10, Folder 49, Receipt for funds due [Mrs.] Eliza Farrell by the Second Municipality of New Orleans for the labor of her slave Rose, 1843 Sept. 4, Folder 78, and Receipt to Sanitte Joublan for taxes on slaves by A. Cruzat, Treasurer, Orleans Parish, 1820 Apr. 10 [*sic*], Folder 80, all in the Slavery in Louisiana Collection, MSS 44, Williams Research Center, Historic New Orleans Collection, New Orleans.

11. Salmon, *Women and the Law of Property in Early America*, 15. See also Hartog, *Man and Wife in America*, 93–166.

12. Hartog, *Man and Wife in America*, 169; Baptist, "Toxic Debt, Liar Loans, and Securitized Human Beings"; Lepler, *The Many Panics of 1837*; Woody Holton, "Equality as Unintended Consequence," 313–340.

13. Salmon, *Women and the Law of Property in Early America*, 13 (quotation); Shammas, Salmon, and Dahlin, *Inheritance in America*, 57, 112; Shammas, *The History of Household Government in America*, 60, 76, 96–97.

14. See Lebsock, *The Free Women of Petersburg*, 63–75.

15. Emily Camster Green, in *BS*, vol. 10, *Missouri Narratives*, 139. For young people's western movement see Cashin, *A Family Venture*.

16. *Mary Snodgrass Hall v. Alexander Hall*, Records of the Chancery Court, Case Files, 7, Feb. 1847, Case 344B [or 8], Reel 63, Frames 2659–2674, Tennessee State Library and Archives, Nashville (hereafter TSLA), *RSP-2*.

17. For women who talked of the financial risks associated with friends' and family members' marital choices see Anderson, *Brokenburn*, 176.

18. Will Typescript of Nancy Boulware, Proved January 23, 1837, Fairfield District Estate Record Book I, Will Book 11, pp. 255–259, and Will Typescript of Thomas Boulware, Fairfield District Estate Record Book Q, Will Book 18, pp. 153–162, SCDAH. See also *Penelope Gums, William Gums, Elizabeth Gums, and Delia Gums v. Alexander Nelson and Alanson Capehart*, 1855, Records of the North Carolina Supreme Court, North Carolina Department of Archives and History, Raleigh (hereafter NCDAH), *RSP-2*.

19. Letters from Mrs. Sarah E. Devereux to Thomas Devereux, May 27, 1839, July 9, 1839, and December 10, 1839, Devereux Family Papers, 1776–1936, *RASP*, Series F.

20. Dougan, "The Arkansas Married Women's Property Law," 12; Holton, "Equality as Unintended Consequence," 324.

21. See, e.g., *Petition of R. H. Goodwyn and John Goodwyn*, January 30, 1847, Records of the Equity Court, Petitions, SCDAH, *RSP-2*.

22. In a letter to her brother-in-law, Sarah Devereux described how a protective clause such as this was included in a family acquaintance's will. Letter from Mrs. Sarah E. Devereux to Thomas Devereux, September 3, 1839, Devereux Family Papers, 1776–1936, *RASP*, Series F.

23. Mary Jane Jones, in Rawick, *AS*, Supplement, Series 1, vol. 8, *Mississippi Narratives, Part 3*, 1243; Walter Johnson, *River of Dark Dreams*, 195; F. H. Brown, in *BS*, vol. 2, *Arkansas Narratives, Part 1*, 276. See also *Elizabeth Harrison and Edmund Harrison v. John Foote, et al.*, Records of the Circuit Court, Final Records, Lowndes County Courthouse, Hayneville, Alabama, *RSP-2*, *Maria L. Bailey by her Next Friend Henry Bailey v. Benjamin Martin and Algernon Bailey*, Filed March 7, 1855, Records of the Circuit Court, "Old Circuit Court Papers from 1830 to 1860," Bradley County Courthouse, Warren, Arkansas, *RSP-2*.

24. Indenture [Marital Agreement], Sarah Barncs and Dennis Welsh, November 22, 1836, Recorded with William Taylor, Clerk of the County Court of Mobile County, appearing in "Deed Book R, pages 372, 513–514 & 515," included in *Sarah Welsh by her next friend David White v. Dennis Welsh and Richard Redwood*, Filed July 23, 1839, Records of the Chancery Court, Divorce Cases, University of Southern Alabama Archives, Mobile, *RSP-2*.

25. *Mary Williams v. William B. Williams*, Filed June 2, 1849, Knox County, Records of the Chancery Court, Loose Records, TSLA, *RSP-2*. See also *Elizabeth Long Oliver v.*

John Oliver, Filed September 5, 1825, Ended Chancery Court Causes, 1825–1832, Library of Virginia, Richmond, *RSP-2*.

26. See Dougan, "The Arkansas Married Women's Property Law," 12.

27. *Eliza A. Strickland v. Barnabas Strickland et al.*, Filed February 4, 1853, Records of the Circuit Court, Chancery Records, 1852–1854, Dallas County Courthouse, Selma, Alabama, *RSP-2*.

28. See, e.g., *Ann Spain by her next friend and trustee Dela Thompson v. William Henry Spain, Robert Spain, James K. Spain, John W. Spain, Sarah S. Spain, Ephraim F. Spain, Susan M. Shelton, John F. Shelton,* Case 1489, Filed October 20, 1855, Box 13, Records of the Chancery Court, Case Files, Metropolitan Nashville–Davidson County Archives, TSLA, *RSP-2*, and *Elizabeth Little by next friend Jefferson B. Allgood v. Blake Little and James Hair*, Filed May 24, 1848, Records of the Circuit Court, Estates, Sumter County Courthouse, Livingston, Alabama, *RSP-2*.

29. "An act to amend an act for giving further time for probate and registration of bills of sale for slaves and marriage settlements" and "An act declaring what gifts of slaves shall be valid, For the prevention of frauds," in Potter, Taylor, and Yancey, *Laws of the State of North-Carolina*, vol. 2, pp. 908–909, 1068–1069.

30. See, e.g., *Mary R. Massie Leake by her Next Friend Charles A. Leake v. John A. Dailey and Joseph Leake*, April 1849, Records of the Chancery Court, Record of District Chancery Court, 1848–1850, Noxubee County Courthouse, Noxubee County, Mississippi, *RSP-2*.

31. *Susan Hunter by Will A. Bridges her Next Friend v. Dr. James Hunter*, 1846, Records of the Circuit Court, Equity/Chancery Cases, Kentucky Division of Libraries and Archives, Frankfort, Kentucky, *RSP-2*. See also *Jane Hunter by James Harlan her Next Friend v. John Hunter*, 1846, Records of the Circuit Court, Equity/Chancery Cases, Kentucky Division of Libraries and Archives, Frankfort, *RSP-2*.

32. *Victoria Le Sassier v. Pedro de Alba Sr.*, Filed 1831, Records of Probate Court, Escambia County Courthouse, Pensacola, Florida (Superior Court of West Florida), *RSP-2*. For a more expansive discussion of how this process of transferal affected women's property rights see Laurel A. Clark, "The Rights of a Florida Wife."

33. Sara Sundberg's work on women and property in colonial Louisiana is instructive on this point. See Sundberg, "Women and Property in Early Louisiana," and "Women and the Law of Property Under Louisiana Civil Law."

34. *Louisiana Digest of 1808*, Book III, Title V, Chapter III, Article 86–87. Women's rights to control movable and immovable property are discussed ibid., Book II, Title I, Chapter II, Article 19, and Book III, Title V, Chapter III, Article 97.

35. Ibid., Book III, Title V, Chapter III, Article 89.

36. *Turnbull v. Davis et al.*, Docket 227, Western District, September, 1823, Historical Archives of the Louisiana Supreme Court, Earl K. Long Library, University of New Orleans (hereafter HALSC-UNO).

37. *Jane Rowley v. Charles N. Rowley*, 2 La. Ann. 208, Docket 204, February 1847, HALSC-UNO; "The Recent Murder of Judge Tenney," *Pennsylvania Inquirer and Daily Courier*, October 25, 1841; "Result of the Duel," *Weekly Herald*, September 25, 1841; "The Late Judge Tenney," *Vermont Chronicle*, October 13, 1841; "Progress of Duelling,"

New York Herald, September 20, 1841; "An Affair of Honor," *North American and Daily Advertiser*, September 20, 1841.

38. Morris Sheppard, in *BS*, vol. 13, *Oklahoma Narratives*, 285.

39. *Winney v. Heirs at law of William Whitehead and Heirs at law of Elizabeth Whitehead*, Filed February 19, 1844, Records of the Circuit Court, Case Files, Kentucky Division of Libraries and Archives, Frankfort, Kentucky, *RSP-2*.

40. See, for example, *Josiah Price et al. v. James Maddox*, Filed June 4, 1860, Schweninger Collection, Maryland State Archives, Annapolis, *RSP-2*.

41. See Penningroth, *The Claims of Kinfolk*, 79–109.

42. *Pensacola Gazette*, March 7–8, 1846. Elizabeth Humphreyville petitioned the Mobile County, Alabama, court for a divorce from her husband, Joseph, and in her suit claimed that he was not only a "very unthrifty shiftless man who can hardly support himself," he was also engaging in adulterous relations with Ann. Presumably this is why she accused him of stealing her slave. See *Elizabeth Humphreyville v. Joseph Humphreyville*, December 9, 1846, Records of the Chancery Court, Divorce Cases, University of South Alabama Archives, Mobile, *RSP-2*.

43. See, e.g., Parker, *Stealing a Little Freedom*, 316, 331, 377, 382.

44. "Committed to Jail" notice, *Daily National Intelligencer*, March 4, 1825.

45. *James C. Norris v. H. W. Schroder, Ann E. Chitty Schroder, Ann Bell, John W. Chitty, John C. Lozier*, Bill of Interpleading, Filed June 21, 1841, Records of the Equity Court, Bills, SCDAH, *RSP-2*.

46. Ibid.

47. Ibid.; Bill of Sale from Catherine Roulain to Charles C. Chitty for Ann E. Chitty Schroder, March 30, 1830, SCDAH; Fifth Census of the United States, 1830, Charleston, South Carolina, Ward 4, Schedule 1 (free inhabitants).

48. Edwards, *The People and Their Peace*, 155–156.

49. For an example of a man who sued a slave-owning woman for compensation he was due, see, e.g., *William T. Wragg v. Nathaniel G. Cleary, Susan M. McPherson Cleary, Henry A. DeSaussure and James R. Pringle*, Filed December 1, 1837, Records of the Equity Court, Petitions, SCDAH, *RSP-2*.

50. See Salmon, *Women and the Law of Property in Early America*, 11; Alfred Henry Marsh, *History of the Court of Chancery and of the Rise and Development of the Doctrines of Equity*, 14, 32, 47.

51. See Basch, "Invisible Women," 348–349.

52. See Story, *Commentaries on Equity Jurisprudence as Administered in England and America*, 619–691.

53. Hartog, *Man and Wife in America*, 169.

54. See, e.g., Bynum, *Unruly Women*, 88–110, and Grossberg, *Governing the Hearth*.

55. Dayton, *Women Before the Bar*, 4.

56. See Snyder, *Brabbling Women*, 87.

57. Katie Rowe, in *BS*, vol. 13, *Oklahoma Narratives*, 277–278.

58. Ibid.

59. See, e.g., *Eliza A. Strickland v. Barnabas Strickland et al.*, Filed February 4, 1853, Records of the Circuit Court, Chancery Records, 1852–1854, Dallas County Courthouse,

Selma, Alabama, RSP-2; *Ruth Balderee by her next friend Nathan Nelson v. Sterling Balderee*, September 1845, Records of the Circuit Court, Final Record Chancery Court, Lowndes County Courthouse, Hayneville, Alabama, RSP-2; and *Ellen Lanier by her Brother in Law and Next Friend Edward J. Lanier v. Thomas J. Lanier and Thomas Ellis*, Adams County, Mississippi, 1846–1848, Records of the Chancery Court, Adams County Courthouse, Natchez, Mississippi, RSP-2.

60. Alice Marshall in Perdue et al., *Weevils in the Wheat*, 201.

61. *Mary Massie Leake v. John A. Dailey and Joseph Leake*, April 1849, Records of the Chancery Court, Noxubee County, RSP-2.

62. Uncle Shade, in Armstrong, *Old Massa's People*, 258.

63. See, e.g., *Mary Massie Leake v. John A. Dailey and Joseph Leake*, April 1849, Records of the Chancery Court, Noxubee County, RSP-2.

64. See Joel Prentiss Bishop, *Commentaries on the Law of Married Women*, 600–601, 604; *Mary Ann Spears by her next friend John J. Goldsmith v. Townsend, Crane & Co. et al.*, November Term 1857, Records of the Circuit Court, Minutes and Decrees Chancery Court 1855–1867, County Courthouse, Dadeville, Alabama, RSP-2.

65. *Mary Ann Spears v. Townsend, Crane & Co. et al.*

66. Ibid.

67. *Mary Jane Taylor, Thomas Taylor, her husband, and Warren D. Wood*, April Term 1859, Records of the Superior Court, Minutes Book, 1848–1860, Pulaski County Courthouse, Hawkinsville, Georgia, RSP-2.

68. *Elizabeth Duncan by her next friend Noah L. Chapman v. William Duncan*, Docket 469, Filed May 3, 1851, Records of the Chancery Court, Noxubee County Courthouse, Mississippi, RSP-2.

69. Ibid.

70. *Samuel B. Thompson and Rachel Thompson v. John Hannon*, Filed June 17, 1842, Records of the Chancery Court, Noxubee County Courthouse, Mississippi, RSP-2.

71. George Bishop's *Every Woman Her Own Lawyer* was specifically designed to meet the legal needs of women. It contained 374 pages of advice and boilerplate templates for legal actions such as wills and marital contracts. The full title conveys the wide scope of the guidance: *Every Woman Her Own Lawyer: A Private Guide in All Matters of Law, of Essential Interest to Women, and by the Aid of Which Every Female May, in Whatever Situation, Understand Her Legal Course and Redress, and Be Her Own Legal Adviser; Containing the Laws of Different States Relative to Marriage and Divorce, Property in Marriage, Guardians and Wards, Rights in Property of a Wife, Rights of Widows, Arrests of Females for Debt, Alimony, Bigamy, Voluntary Separations, Discarded Wives, Suits by and Against Married Women, Breach of Promise, Deserted Wives, Clandestine Marriages, Adultery, Dower, Illegitimate Children, Step-fathers and Step-children, Seduction, Slander, Minors, Medical Maltreatment, Just Causes for Leaving a Husband, a Wife's Support, Property in Trust, Transfers of Property, Deeds of Gift, Annuities, Articles of Separation, False Pretenses in Courtship, &c., &c., &c.* (New York: Dick and Fitzgerald, 1858).

72. *Margaret M. Witherspoon by her next friend William Cannon v. Edwin Mason et al.*, Filed July 27, 1847, Lowndes County, Mississippi, Records of the Chancery Court, Noxubee County Courthouse, Noxubee County, Mississippi, RSP-2.

73. See, for example, *Puryear v. Puryear*, 12 Ala. 13, June Term, 1847, in *Reports of Cases Argued and Determined in the Supreme Court of Alabama*, 2–4. According to Joel Prentiss Bishop, even an oral agreement established upon marriage would be considered legally binding if the agreement was fulfilled and carried out during the marriage. See Bishop, *Commentaries on the Law of Married Women*, 605–606.

74. Sundberg, *Women and the Law of Property Under Louisiana Civil Law*, 34–35; see, for example, these petitions: *Elizabeth C. Atkins Boozer by George Duncan her Next Friend v. David Atkins, George Boozer, and Philip H. Crolwell*, Filed May 12, 1845, Newberry District, South Carolina, Records of the Equity Court, Bills, SCDAH, RSP-2, *Deborah Houston v. William Houston*, Filed August 5, 1844, Washington County Court Records, Chancery Court, Subseries C-III-A, Archives of Appalachia, East Tennessee State University, Johnson City, Box 169 F/4-ACC18, RSP-2, *Mary A. Neil [no named defendants]*, March 1827, Records of the Equity Court, Petitions, SCDAH, *Rebecca Turner v. Matthias Turner*, May 21, 1818, Pinckney District, South Carolina, Records of the Equity Court, Bills, Spartanburg County, SCDAH, RSP-2, *Elizabeth Jones v. Samuel G. Berry*, Northern Chancery Division of the State of Alabama, April 21, 1853, Records of the Chancery Court, Chancery Record 1851–[1854], Madison County Public Library Archives, Huntsville, Alabama, RSP-2. For women who signed with a mark, see *Mary Williams by her next friend William B. Williams v. Henry W. Williams et al.*, June 2, 1849, Knox County, Records of the Chancery Court, Loose Records, TSLA, RSP-2, and *Martha R. W. Booth by George Hodges her Next Friend v. John P. Booth*, Records of the Circuit Court, Record Book, Circuit Court Clerk's Office, Clayton, Alabama, RSP-2.

75. For an example of creditors accusing a wife with a separate estate of committing fraud, see *Marguerite Landry et al. v. P. Marchais*, 6 La. Ann. 87, 1851 WL 3541 (La.) February 1851.

76. See, e.g., *Mary Ann Spears v. Townsend, Crane & Co. et al., Elizabeth Harrison and Edmund Harrison v. John Foote et al.*, Records of the Circuit Court, Final Records, Lowndes County Courthouse, Hayneville, Alabama, RSP-2, and *Maria Betts by her next friend John Wellborn v. Elisha Betts, et al.*, November 1846, Records of the Circuit Court, Barbour County Clerk's Office, Clayton, Alabama, RSP-2.

77. See, for example, *Electa B. Bertie v. John C. Walker, Sheriff*, Docket 4764, March 1842, HALSC-UNO, and *Levistones v. Brady* 11 La. Ann. 696, 1856 WL 4815 (La.).

78. See, e.g., *Turnbull v. Davis et al.*, Docket 227, Western District, September, 1823, HALSC-UNO.

79. *Martin M. Crews v. Charlotte Goodwin and James M. Goodwin, William C. Patrick v. Charlotte Goodwin and James M. Goodwin*, both in Montgomery County, Alabama, Records of the Circuit Court, [Records 1845–1846], Montgomery County Courthouse, Montgomery, RSP-2. See also *Sarah A. Berry per pro ami v. John H. Berry et al.*, Filed March 30, 1847, Records of the Equity Court, Petitions, SCDAH, RSP-2, *William T. Wragg v. Nathaniel G. Cleary, Susan M. McPherson Cleary, Henry A. DeSaussure, and James R. Pringle*, Records of the Equity Court, Petitions, SCDAH, RSP-2, and *William W. Boyce v. Thomas McDowell, Martha E. Sutton McDowell, and James C. Neil*, Records of the Equity Court, Petitions, SCDAH, RSP-2.

80. Honoré, "Ownership," 113–116.
81. Charles W. Dickens, in *BS*, vol. 11, *North Carolina Narratives, Part 1*, 256.'

3. "MISSUS DONE HER OWN BOSSING"

Chapter title: Charles W. Dickens, in *BS*, vol. 11, *North Carolina Narratives, Part 1*, 256.
1. *Maria Betts by her next friend John Wellborn v. Elisha Betts, et al.*, November 1846, Records of the Circuit Court, Barbour County Clerk's Office, Clayton, Alabama, *RSP-2*.
2. Charles C. Mills, a neighbor who attended the wedding and reception, "heard Capt. Betts say his wife told him before marriage her negroes were secured to her and her heirs by her father" and that "Mr. Betts spoke of his wife's good sense in making the fact known before marriage, least it might produce difficulty afterwards." Deposition of C. Mills, November 7, 1846, ibid.
3. Ibid.
4. Ibid.
5. *Maria Betts v. Elisha Betts, et al.*
6. Deposition of Abram Greeson, October 10, 1846, ibid.
7. Seventh and Eighth Censuses of the United States, Barbour County, Alabama, Division 23, Schedule 1 (free inhabitants) and Schedule 2 (slave inhabitants) and Alabama, Secretary of State. *U.S. Census Non-population Schedules, Alabama, 1850–1880*. Alabama Department of Archives and History, Montgomery (Provo, Utah: Ancestry.com Operations, Inc., 2010), online database.
8. Harriet Collins, in *BS*, vol. 16, *Texas Narratives, Part 1*, 243; Addy Gill, in *BS*, vol. 11, *North Carolina Narratives, Part 1*, 326.
9. Fox-Genovese, *Within the Plantation Household*, 97, 205–206, 61.
10. See, e.g., Glymph, *Out of the House of Bondage*, 18–32.
11. William Henry Foster, *Gender, Mastery, and Slavery*, 8, 15. On this point see also Walter Johnson, *River of Dark Dreams*, 192–198, and Ariela Gross, *Double Character*, 105.
12. William Henry Foster, *Gender, Mastery, and Slavery*, 8.
13. For an elaboration of this point see Ariela Gross, *Double Character*, 105.
14. See, for example, Aiken, *Digest of the Laws of the State of Alabama*, 392; "Respecting Crimes Committed by, and in Relation to Slaves, in the District of Columbia," in District of Columbia, *Code of Laws for the District of Columbia*, 289–297; Littell, *Statute Law of Kentucky*, 114, 264; Morehead and Brown, *Digest of the Statute Laws of Kentucky*, 1511–1512; *Revised Statutes of the State of Missouri*, 585.
15. Robinson, *Digest of the Penal Law of the State of Louisiana*, 12–13.
16. "An Act for the Better Ordering and Governing Negroes and other Slaves," in McCord, *Statutes at Large of South Carolina*, 359–360.
17. Rosalie Calvert to Isabelle van Havre, April 26, 1818, January 11, 1819, in Calvert, *Mistress of Riversdale*, 340.
18. Bill Homer, in *BS*, vol. 16, *Texas Narratives, Part 2*, 154–155.

19. Lucy Galloway, in Rawick, *AS*, Supplement, Series 1, vol. 7, *Mississippi Narratives, Part 2*, 802; Austin Pen Parnell [son of Henry and Priscilla], in *BS*, vol. 2, *Arkansas Narratives, Part 5*, 269–270. For other examples see Henry Gibbs, in Rawick, *AS*, Supplement, Series 1, vol. 8, *Mississippi Narratives, Part 3*, 820, Kittie Stanford, in Rawick, *AS*, vol. 10, *Arkansas Narratives, Parts 5 and 6*, 214, Lizzie Williams, in *BS*, vol. 11, *North Carolina Narratives, Part 2*, 397, and Emma Lowran, in *BS*, vol. 14, *South Carolina Narratives, Part 3*, 125.

20. Ben Horry, in "Uncle Ben and Visitors," in *BS*, vol. 14, *South Carolina Narratives, Part 2*, 317; Rebecca Brown Hill, in *BS*, vol. 2, *Arkansas Narratives, Part 3*, 269. See also Gus Johnson, in *BS*, vol. 16, *Texas Narratives, Part 2*, 210.

21. See, e.g., Lucretia Alexander, in *BS*, vol. 2, *Arkansas Narratives, Part 1*, 36; Roberta Manson, in *BS*, vol. 11, *North Carolina Narratives, Part 2*, 101.

22. *Lucy Perrie v. James A. Williams, et al.*, Docket 1444, Eastern District, May 1827, 5 Mart. (N.S.) 694, HALSC-UNO.

23. Interview with unidentified formerly enslaved man, in *Unwritten History of Slavery*, 44; Edwards, *The People and Their Peace*, 15.

24. F. H. Brown, in *BS*, vol. 2, *Arkansas Narratives, Part 1*, 276; Arrie Binns, in *BS*, vol. 4, *Georgia Narratives, Part 1*, 74–75.

25. Ellen Campbell, in *BS*, vol. 4, *Georgia Narratives, Part 4*, 315–316.

26. See, e.g., *The State v. John Mann from Chowan*. Supreme Court of North Carolina, 13 N.C. 263; 1829 N.C. LEXIS 62, December, 1829.

27. Joe High, in *BS*, vol. 11, *North Carolina Narratives, Part 1*, 411–412.

28. Henry Watson, *Narrative of Henry Watson*, 22, 23; Cecelia Chappel, in *BS*, vol. 15, *Tennessee Narratives*, 6; P. C. Weston, "Management of a Southern Plantation," *DeBow's Review* 22 (January 1857): 38–44; A Mississippi Planter, "Management of Negroes upon Southern Estates," *DeBow's Review* 10 (June 1851): 621–627; "The Duties of an Overseer," *Farmer and Planter* 8 (June 1857): 139–140; Henry Watson, *Narrative of Henry Watson*, 23.

29. Ariela Gross, *Double Character*, 106; W. W. Hazzard, "On the General Management of a Plantation," *Southern Agriculturalist* 4 (July 1831): 350–354. See also "Mistreatment of Slaves," in *BS*, vol. 4, *Georgia Narratives, Part 4*, 298.

30. *Lettie Luke by H. H. Kinard, her next friend v. William J. Luke and John P. Kinard*, Filed July 2, 1850, Records of the Equity Court, Petitions, SCDAH, RSP-2.

31. See Faust, "Trying to Do a Man's Business," 197–214.

32. Pauline Howell, in *BS*, vol. 2, *Arkansas Narratives, Part 3*, 342.

33. Analiza Foster, in *BS*, vol. 11, *North Carolina Narratives, Part 1*, 312; Claiborne Moss, in *BS*, vol. 2, *Arkansas Narratives, Part 5*, 160.

34. See Crumley, "Heterarchy and the Analysis of Complex Societies."

35. Millie Evans, in *BS*, vol. 2, *Arkansas Narratives, Part 2*, 240; Cecelia Chappel, in *BS*, vol. 15, *Tennessee Narratives*, 6.

36. Anna Miller, in *BS*, vol. 16, *Texas Narratives, Part 3*, 82–83; see "Stinging nettle," Milton S. Hershey Medical Center, Penn State University, Hershey, http://pennstate hershey.adam.com/content.aspx?productId=107&pid=33&gid=000275.

37. Julia Blanks, in *BS*, vol. 16, *Texas Narratives, Part 1*, 96.

38. Penny Thompson, in *BS*, vol. 16, *Texas Narratives, Part 4*, 103; George C. King, in Rawick, *AS*, vol. 7, *Oklahoma and Mississippi Narratives*, 165–166; interview with unidentified formerly enslaved woman, *Unwritten History of Slavery*, 3.

39. Interview with unidentified formerly enslaved woman, *Unwritten History of Slavery*, 140; Ria Sorrell, in *BS*, vol. 11, *North Carolina Narratives, Part 2*, 300–301.

40. Silas Glenn, in *BS*, vol. 14, *South Carolina Narratives, Part 2*, 136; Susan Merritt, in *BS*, vol. 16, *Texas Narratives, Part 3*, 77–78.

41. "Mistreatment of Slaves," in *BS*, vol. 4, *Georgia Narratives, Part 4*, 298–299.

42. Hartman, *Scenes of Subjection*, 17–48.

43. See, e.g., Tattler, "Management of Negroes," *Southern Cultivator* 8 (November 1850): 162–164. "On the Management of Slaves," *Southern Agriculturalist* 6 (June 1833): 281–287; "A Planter," "Notions on the Management of Negroes, &c.," *Farmers' Register* 4 (December 1836 and January 1837): 494–495 and 574–575.

44. Cecilia, "Management of Servants," *Southern Planter* 3 (1843): 175.

45. Although a man could have written the article and simply posed as a woman, a woman might also have written it. In either case, it was written *for* female readers. John F. Kvach found at least two women among the subscribers to *DeBow's Review*, but there could have been many more. Many subscribers used only their first and middle initials; in addition women could have read copies procured by their spouses or male kin. See Kvach, *De Bow's Review*, 183–184. In *Southern Womanhood and Slavery* (122), Leigh Fought describes how Louisa McCord, who published numerous pieces in *DeBow's Review*, identified herself using initials rather than her full name.

46. *Walker v. Cucullu*, Docket 326, *249 18 La. Ann., March 1866, HALSC-UNO.

47. McCord, "An Act for the Better Ordering and Governing Negroes and Other Slaves," in *Statutes at Large of South Carolina*, 353.

48. Hutchinson, *Code of Mississippi*, 957.

49. They could also be exonerated if two white witnesses could not be found to attest to the crime. Other southern states had similar laws. See Phillips, *Life and Labor in the Old South*, 162.

50. "Trial of Mrs. Eliza Rowand," *Southern Patriot*, May 7, 1847; "An Extraordinary Trial," *Emancipator*, June 16, 1847; "The Charleston Case: A Trial for Murder," *Pennsylvania Freeman*, January 28, 1847; "From the London Standard of Freedom," *North Star*, October 5, 1849. Individuals involved in the case were unclear about who owned Maria. They identify Maria as the property of Eliza's husband. But the physicians who performed the autopsy on Maria noted that she belonged to Frances C. Bee, Eliza Rowand's aunt. See Peter Porcher and A. P. Hayne, Petition Asking Payment for Performing an Autopsy on a Slave Named Maria Belonging to Mrs. Frances C. Bee, January 12, 1847, Records of the General Assembly, Petitions, SCDAH. For a recent analysis of this case see Fede, *Homicide Justified*.

51. Thomas Morris discusses legal prohibitions against enslaved people's testimony in cases involving white defendants in *Southern Slavery and the Law*, 193.

52. *Mann v. Trabue* 1 Mo. 709, 1827 WL 1987 (Mo.). On Marshall Mann's murder trial, see Fede, *Homicide Justified*, 212. A detailed account, which centers Mann's wife in Fanny's murder and includes the quotation, can be found in Weld, *American Slavery*

as It Is, 71. For mistresses whose crimes remained confined within their households see Rankin, *Letters on American Slavery*, 54–55, Stowe, *A Key to Uncle Tom's Cabin*, 49, and Parsons, *An Inside View of Slavery*, 206–209.

53. For slave owners who hid their cruelty, see Jordon Smith, in *BS*, vol. 16, *Texas Narratives, Part 4*, 37, Interview with unidentified formerly enslaved person, *Unwritten History of Slavery*, 99, Testimony of Angelina Grimké Weld, Joseph Ide, and Theodore Dwight Weld, in Weld, *American Slavery as It Is*, 53–55, 101–102, and 129–130, and "A Star Chamber in New Orleans," *Frederick Douglass' Paper*, November 17, 1854. On selling cadavers, see Berry, *The Price for Their Pound of Flesh*, 148–193.

54. See Sprankling, "The Right to Destroy," 294.

55. Strahilevitz, "The Right to Destroy," 785, 794, 824.

56. On the public display of rebels' heads see Rasmussen, *American Uprising*, 140, 150, 157. On white southerners' right to kill runaways, see "Acts Relating to Slaves," in McCord, *Statutes at Large of South Carolina*, 353, 372, 386.

57. "Acts Relating to Slaves," 346–347, 363.

58. See Strahilevitz, "The Right to Destroy," 823.

59. See *Petition of Craven County residents William Galtin, Calvin Burch, Nathan Whitford, Levin Gaskins, and Daniel Gaskins to the Honourable the General Assembly of the State of North Carolina*, December 1831, General Assembly, Session Records, NCDAH, and *Petition of thirty-seven residents of Marion County, South Carolina to the Senate and House of Representatives of Said State*, 1858, Document Number ND 2894, Records of the General Assembly, SCDAH.

60. Alan Watson, "Roman Slave Law," 591, 596. On this point also see Sprankling, "The Right to Destroy," 294, 302, and Strahilevitz, "The Right to Destroy," 796.

4. "SHE THOUGHT SHE COULD FIND A BETTER MARKET"

Chapter title: Lydia M. Child, "Selections: Charity Bowery," in *North Star*, March 3, 1848.

1. Martha J. Jones, in *BS*, vol. 7, *Kentucky Narratives*, 48. Although Jones never actually identified herself as white, census data and facts mentioned in her interview such as that her father owned three slaves and was in the legislature in West Virginia, and that her brothers fought for the Confederacy, make it clear that she was.

2. On the business of slave trading, see Walter Johnson, "Masters and Slaves in the Market," 110.

3. Walter Johnson, for example, chose not to use the testimony of formerly enslaved people documented by the FWP in the 1930s; see his *Soul by Soul*, 9–10, 226n24. More recently, however, historians such as Edward Baptist, Calvin Schermerhorn, and Daina Ramey Berry have centered such testimony in their studies of southern slave markets and the trade; see Baptist, *The Half Has Never Been Told*, Schermerhorn, *The Business of Slavery*, and Berry, *The Price for Their Pound of Flesh*.

4. Walter Johnson, "Masters and Slaves in the Market," 117; Johnson, *Soul by Soul*, 52. See also Gudmestad, *The Troublesome Commerce*, 4, Martin, *Divided Mastery* (esp. 83–85, 114–117), and Zaborney, *Slaves for Hire*, 6–7 and 98–99.

5. Johnson, *Soul by Soul*, 90. The recent work of women's historians, such as Amy Dru Stanley, belies these assumptions in relation to the markets of the North and the South. Stanley, "Home Life and the Morality of the Market," 86.

6. Quotes are taken from *Lucy P. Burwell by etc. v. John A. Burwell*, Petition for Divorce, September Term, 1856, Chancery Court Cases, Library of Virginia, Richmond, Virginia, *RSP*-2. Although John denied the allegations, letters between his and Lucy's sons corroborated her account of domestic abuse and adultery; John E. Burwell to Thomas E. Burwell, November 7, 1856, Burwell-Guy Family Papers, Virginia Historical Society, *RASP*, John E. Burwell to Thomas E. Burwell, March 27, 1857, BGFP-WLCL.

7. See Glymph, *Out of the House of Bondage*, 3, 20–21.

8. Walter Johnson, "Masters and Slaves in the Market," 110.

9. In *Soul by Soul* (48), Walter Johnson mentions "private sales on a slaveholder's land," but he does not say that these sales brought the slave market and the household together, nor does he consider the significance of these sales for the enslaved people who were sold or the white women who may have benefited from them.

10. For men who asked male relatives and friends to conduct slave market business on their behalf see J. A. Burwell to Thomas G. Burwell, Lynesville, N.C., April 27, 1854, BGFP-WLCL, and Sir Peyton Skipwith at Prestwould to St. George Tucker, August 26, 1797, TCP-EGSL. For men asking for men to accompany them to southern slave markets see Walter Johnson, *Soul by Soul*, 136–137.

11. Damiano, "Agents at Home," 835.

12. Woodman, *King Cotton and His Retainers*, 43.

13. Letter from Sarah E. Devereux to Thomas P. Devereux, New Haven, [Connecticut], December 4, 1840, Devereux Family Papers, Raleigh, Wake County, North Carolina, Correspondence, 1791–1841, *RASP*, Series F.

14. Elizabeth T. Guy to Lucy Penn Burwell, [Middletown, Kentucky], December 17, 1846, BGFP-WLCL.

15. John A. Burwell ALS to Elizabeth T. Guy, Lynesville, N.C., June 8, 1848, BGFP-WLCL.

16. See, for example, "Burke, Watt and Company Account of Sales of Fifty Bales Cotton recd pr Steamer Columbia for account Mrs. Eliza Bowman," October 14, 1836, Turnbull-Bowman-Lyons Family Papers, 4026, 1835–1848, "Financial Papers Eliza B. Lyons-Factors Statements-Burke, Watt and Co.," *RASP*, Series I: Selections from the Louisiana and Lower Mississippi Valley Collections, Louisiana State University Libraries, Part 4: Barrow, Bisland, Bowman, and Other Collections. See also Transcribed Bill of Sale, *Eliza Bowman v. John Davis Ware*, Docket 3929, Eastern District, June 1841, 18 La. 597, HALSC-UNO, and Lewis deSaulles to Mrs. Eliza B. Lyons (Near Bayou Sarah), New Orleans, November 15, 1843, Turnbull-Bowman-Lyons Family Papers, 4026, 1826–1851, Correspondence to Eliza B. Lyons from Misc. Lyons Family, *RASP*, Series I: Selections from the Louisiana and Lower Mississippi Valley Collections, Louisiana State University Libraries, Part 4: Barrow, Bisland, Bowman, and Other Collections.

17. Lallande to Mrs. Eliza B. Lyons, December 17, 1850, Turnbull-Bowman-Lyons Family Papers, 4026, 1826–1851, Correspondence to Eliza B. Lyons from Misc. Lyons Family,

RASP, Series I: Selections from the Louisiana and Lower Mississippi Valley Collections, Louisiana State University Libraries, Part 4: Barrow, Bisland, Bowman, and Other Collections.

18. Hartigan-O'Connor, *The Ties That Buy*, 130–131.

19. Ibid., 130. On the "collaborative and mediated nature of shopping," see pages 7, 129–160.

20. Lelia (Skipwith) Carter Tucker at Williamsburg to St. George Tucker, circa 1809 Nov. 13, Item #5227, TCP-EGSL.

21. Stanley, "Home Life and the Morality of the Market," 83.

22. See, e.g., C. B. McRay, in *BS*, vol. 16, *Texas Narratives, Part 3*, 40; William Byrd, in *BS*, vol. 16, *Texas Narratives, Part 1*, 182; Joseph Mosley, Amy Elizabeth Patterson, in *BS*, vol. 5, *Indiana Narratives*, 147, 150; Charlotte Mitchell Martin, in *BS*, vol. 3, *Florida Narratives*, 167.

23. Entry for June 21, 1859, in Raska and Hill, *The Uncompromising Diary of Sallie McNeill*, 45.

24. Entry for October 5, 1860, ibid., 87.

25. Historians are just beginning to explore the subject of slave traders' families, particularly the ways in which female kin fit into the larger scheme of the slave trade. See, for example, Finley, "Blood Money."

26. On Issac Franklin, see Schermerhorn, *The Business of Slavery*, 126; on a slave trader who was married while engaged in buying and selling enslaved people, see interview with unidentified former slave, in *Unwritten History of Slavery*, 253.

27. Isaac Jarratt to Harriet Jarratt, December 7, 1834, Jarratt-Puryear Family Papers, 1807–1865, Surry and Yadkin Counties, North Carolina, also Alabama and Arkansas, *RASP*, Series F, part 3, North Carolina, Maryland, and Virginia, reels 11–15.

28. Isaac Jarratt to Harriet Jarratt, December 7, 1834; Harriet Jarratt to Isaac Jarratt, October 29, 1835, Jarratt-Puryear Family Papers, 1807–1865, Surry and Yadkin Counties, North Carolina, also Alabama and Arkansas, *RASP*, Series F, part 3, North Carolina, Maryland, and Virginia, reels 11–15. See also Isaac Jarratt to Harriet Jarratt, November 9, 1835, ibid.

29. Samuel Scomp in Blassingame, *Slave Testimony*, 180–181; Jesse Green to Joseph Watson, February 28, 1826, quoted in Eric Ledell Smith, "Rescuing African American Kidnapping Victims in Philadelphia as Documented in the Joseph Watson Papers at the Historical Society of Pennsylvania," 328; Joseph Watson to J. W. Hamilton and John Henderson, March 10, 1826, reprinted ibid., 334. For a close examination of Patty Cannon's career, see Bell, "'Thence to Patty Cannon's.'"

30. *Piety Tisdale v. William Tisdale*, Petition for Divorce and Alimony, Filed April 10, 1832, Nash County Court Divorce Records, NCDAH, *RSP-2*.

31. *Mary Crosby by her Next Friend Solomon Coleman v. William Crosby, Alfred H. Colvin, Stephen Crosby, and John R. Buchanan*, Bill for Alimony and Relief, Filed May 18, 1844, Records of the Equity Court, Bills, SCDAH, *RSP-2*.

32. Armstead Barrett, in Rawick, *AS*, Supplement, Series 2, vol. 2, *Texas Narratives, Part 1*, 196; Mattie Logan, in *BS*, vol. 13, *Oklahoma Narratives*, 189.

33. Harriet Jarratt to Isaac Jarratt, October 29, 1835; Isaac Jarratt to Harriet Jarratt, November 9, 1835, Jarratt-Puryear Family Papers, 1807–1865, Surry and Yadkin

Counties, North Carolina, also Alabama and Arkansas, *RASP*, Series F, part 3, North Carolina, Maryland, and Virginia, reels 11–15.

34. *Vinot v. Hite et al.* Unreported Case, Docket 3251, New Orleans, January 1855, HALSC-UNO.

35. See, for example, Act of Sale for Slave Julia, Adelaide Hite to Antonio Rodi, Recorded before Theodore Guyol, June 2, 1859, and Act of Sale for Slave Charles, Joseph Cohn to Adelaide Hite, Recorded before John Connolly, July 30, 1862 Annual Conveyance Vendor and Vendee Indexes, New Orleans Notarial Archives, New Orleans, Louisiana.

36. Susan Merritt, in BS, vol. 16, *Texas Narratives, Part 3*, 77; Wade Dudley, in BS, vol. 2, *Arkansas Narratives, Part 2*, 212; Alex Woods, in BS, vol. 11, *North Carolina Narratives, Part 2*, 417; W. L. Bost, in BS, vol. 11, *North Carolina Narratives, Part 1*, 139; Robert Glenn, in *BS*, vol. 11, *North Carolina Narratives, Part 1*, 329–332.

37. See interviews with George Patterson, in BS, vol. 14, *South Carolina Narratives, Part 3*, 230, and Amy Else, in Rawick, AS, Supplement, Series 2, vol. 4, *Texas Narratives, Part 3*, 1300.

38. Caleb Craig, in BS, vol. 14, *South Carolina Narratives, Part 1*, 231.

39. Deposition of Mary Craig[e], York District, S.C. [photocopy], 1804, in PC.1629.1/ folder 22, Slave Collection, State Archives of North Carolina, Raleigh.

40. Liza (Cookie) Jones, in BS, vol. 2, *Arkansas Narratives, Part 4*, 156.

41. Parsons, *An Inside View of Slavery*, 313–314.

42. See Uncle George Scruggs, in BS, vol. 7, *Kentucky Narratives*, 30; Rev. Silas Jackson, in BS, vol. 8, *Maryland Narratives*, 31; Mary Moriah Anne Susanna James, in BS, vol. 8, *Maryland Narratives*, 39; Calvin Moye, in Rawick, AS, Supplement, Series 2, vol. 7, *Texas Narratives, Part 6*, 2836, Lou Smith, in BS, vol. 13, *Oklahoma Narratives*, 304; Pick Gladdeny, in BS, vol. 14, *South Carolina Narratives, Part 2*, 125.

43. S. E. Spicer, Interview with Nancy Bell, Kentucky, 1923, in Blassingame, *Slave Testimony*, 555–557; Lydia M. Child, "Selections: Charity Bowery," *North Star*, March 3, 1848.

44. Hartman, *Scenes of Subjection*, 37.

45. Katie Rowe, in BS, vol. 13, *Oklahoma Narratives*, 277–279. See also Charlie Richardson, in BS, vol. 10, *Missouri Narratives*, 294, and Dicey Thomas, in BS, vol. 2, *Arkansas Narratives, Part 6*, 288. For a discussion of similar scenes, see McKittrick, *Demonic Grounds*, 65–90.

46. Joe High, in BS, vol. 11, *North Carolina Narratives, Part 1*, 413.

47. Tom Hawkins, in BS, vol. 4, *Georgia Narratives, Part 2*, 130.

48. Angelina Grimké Weld, "Testimony of Angelina Grimké Weld," in Theodore Dwight Weld, *American Slavery as It Is*, 52–57.

49. George Womble, in BS, vol. 4, *Georgia Narratives, Part 4*, 180.

50. Martha Organ, in BS, vol. 11, *North Carolina Narratives, Part 2*, 154.

51. Smoky Eulenberg, in BS, vol. 10, *Missouri Narratives*, 112.

52. Sir Peyton Skipwith at Prestwould to St. George Tucker, August 26, 1797, TCP-EGSL.

53. See, for example, Wood, *Masterful Women*.

54. Spear, *Race, Sex, and Social Order in Early New Orleans*, 13. On the laws, see Nicholls, "Strangers Setting Among Us," Hanger, *Bounded Lives, Bounded Places*, 25–26,

Schafer, *Becoming Free, Remaining Free*, 45–58, and French, *Historical Collections of Louisiana*.

55. Lane, *The Narrative of Lunsford Lane*, 16n, 16.

56. Walter Johnson, *Soul by Soul*, 182. For discussions about enslaved women's values see Berry, "'We'm Fus' Rate Bargain.'" Also see Berry, *The Price for Their Pound of Flesh*, Bancroft, *Slave Trading in the Old South*, Tadman, *Speculators and Slaves*, and Steven Deyle, *Carry Me Back*.

57. Fortunately, individuals who were sympathetic to Henry's plight intervened and helped free him: *The North Star*, March 3, 1848. See also Grandy, *Narrative of the Life of Moses Grandy*, 17–24; "The Original Dred Scott a Resident of St. Louis—Sketch of His History," *Newark* (Ohio) *Advocate*, April 22, 1857. Many years later, Scott's former mistress denied ever being directly involved in any part of these negotiations, the Scott family's continued enslavement, or the court cases *Scott v. Emerson* and *Scott v. Sanford* that followed her rejection of Scott's proposition. See "Famous Dred Scott Case: Mrs. Chafee, Owner of Old Slave, Still Living in Springfield. Why Her Husband Bought Him. For Many Years He Was in Their Service and Finally Was Given His Time, if Not His Freedom," *New York Times*, December 22, 1895.

58. Child, "Selections: Charity Bowery."

5. "WET NURSE FOR SALE OR HIRE"

Chapter title: "Wet Nurse for Sale or Hire," *Daily Picayune*, August 22, 1839.

1. Alicia Middleton to Anne M. Dehon, Undated Letter, Dehon Family Papers, South Carolina Historical Society, Charleston.

2. Walter Johnson, *River of Dark Dreams*, 197–198.

3. See, e.g., McMillen, *Motherhood in the Old South*, 5–6, 111–112, Turner, *North Carolina Planters and Their Children*, 34–38, and Kennedy, *Born Southern*, 100, 103. However, Valerie Fildes, Geraldine Youcha, and Maria Helena Pereira Toledo Machado, who study infant nursing through the ages in a global context, have found that cross-class or cross-racial wet nursing was commonplace. See Fildes, *Breasts, Bottles, and Babies*, 138–143, Youcha, *Minding the Children*, 60–66, and Machado, "Between Two Beneditos."

4. McMillen, *Motherhood in the Old South*, 118, 124–125; McMillen, "Breastfeeding and Elite White Motherhood," 251; Rachel Sullivan, in *BS*, vol. 4, *Georgia Narratives, Part 4*, 226.

5. "Supplementary Instructions #9-E to the American Guide Manual," April 22, 1937, Records of the Library of Congress Project, Writers' Unit, NARA.

6. Yetman, "The Background of the Slave Narrative Collection," 535n2.

7. See Molloy, *Single, White, Slaveholding Women in the Nineteenth-Century American South*, and Spruill, *Women's Life and Work in the Southern Colonies*, 55–57.

8. See Fildes, *Breasts, Bottles, and Babies*, 188–210, and Youcha, *Minding the Children*, 61.

9. Salmon, "The Cultural Significance of Breastfeeding and Infant Care in Early Modern England and America," 250.

10. Ibid., 255.

11. On the long history of wet nursing see Fildes, *Wet Nursing*. On American ideas about wet nursing and the role of medical and scientific professionals in shaping women's understanding of it see Golden, *A Social History of Wet Nursing in America*, 51–57, McMillen, "Mothers' Sacred Duty," 333–356, and McMillen, *Motherhood in the Old South*, 4–5.

12. John Van Hook, in *BS*, vol. 4, *Georgia Narratives, Part 4*, 74–75.

13. Peggy Sloan, in *BS*, vol. 2, *Arkansas Narratives, Part 6*, 168.

14. See Doyle, "'The Highest Pleasure of Which Woman's Nature Is Capable.'"

15. The *Ripley Advertiser*, March 31, 1858, 2. That such advertisements were appearing in widely circulating journals is evidence that many mothers struggled with ailments that affected their ability to nurse their children.

16. Mrs. Esther Cox to Mrs. Mary Chesnut, March 25, 1800, Folder 9, March 7, 1801, Folder 10, April 21, 1805, Folder 16, August 16, 1805, Folder 17, October 3, 1805, Folder 18, and April 5, 1806, Folder 19, Cox and Chesnut Family Papers, South Caroliniana Library, University of South Carolina, Columbia.

17. See Salmon, "The Cultural Significance of Breastfeeding and Infant Care in Early Modern England and America," 261–262.

18. Machado, "Between Two Beneditos," 320.

19. See, e.g., Louise Pettis, in *BS*, vol. 2, *Arkansas Narratives, Part 5*, 334.

20. See Mary Kincheon Edwards, in *BS*, vol. 16, *Texas Narratives, Part 2*, 15, Jeff Calhoun, in *BS*, vol. 16, *Texas Narratives, Part 1*, 188, and Esther Cox to Mary Chesnut, October 3, 1805, Folder 18, Cox and Chesnut Family Papers, South Caroliniana Library.

21. Rachel Sullivan, in *BS*, vol. 4, *Georgia Narratives, Part 4*, 226; Betty Curlett, in *BS*, vol. 2, *Arkansas Narratives, Part 2*, 76–77; Jane Amelia Petigru to Adele Petigru Allston, December 20, 1833, Robert F. W. Alston Papers, South Carolina Historical Society, Charleston, quoted in Pease and Pease, *A Family of Women*, 28.

22. McMillen, *Motherhood in the Old South*, 32–33; Steckel, "Antebellum Southern White Fertility," 338.

23. Mary Jane Jones, in Rawick, *AS*, Supplement, Series 1, vol. 8, *Mississippi Narratives, Part 3*, 1243; Eugenia Woodberry, in *BS*, vol. 14, *South Carolina Narratives, Part 4*, 218. See also Cynthia Jones, in *BS*, vol. 2, *Arkansas Narratives, Part 4*, 139, and Sarah Louise Augustus, in *BS*, vol. 11, *North Carolina Narratives, Part 1*, 54.

24. Mattie Logan, in *BS*, vol. 13, *Oklahoma Narratives*, 187–188.

25. See entry for Tuesday, July 16, 1861, in Thomas, *The Secret Eye*, 186–187.

26. Warren Taylor, in *BS*, vol. 2, *Arkansas Narratives, Part 6*, 274; Mary Kincheon Edwards, in *BS*, vol. 16, *Texas Narratives, Part 2*, 15.

27. Amy Elizabeth Patterson, in *BS*, vol. 5, *Indiana Narratives*, 151.

28. Henrietta Butler, in Clayton, *Mother Wit*, 38.

29. Ellen Vaden, in *BS*, vol. 2, *Arkansas Narratives, Part 7*, 3.

30. Rachel Sullivan, in *BS*, vol. 2, *Arkansas Narratives, Part 2*, 226.

31. T. W. Cotton, in *BS*, vol. 2, *Arkansas Narratives, Part 2*, 40–41. On the dangers of bottle-feeding in this period see Marie Jenkins Schwartz, "At Noon, Oh How I Ran: Breastfeeding and Weaning on Plantation and Farm in Antebellum Virginia and Alabama," in *Discovering the Women in Slavery*, 249. Although technological innova-

tions and scientific breakthroughs had made artificial feeding safer by the mid-nineteenth century, historians of the South have found that southern women rarely employed artificial nursing practices, though they were becoming widely available and acceptable. Those who did, as Maria Machado argues in "Between Two Beneditos," frequently ignored physicians' advice or had limited access to the prescriptive literature they published and continued to rely upon unsanitary bottle-feeding practices, such as those T. W. Cotton's grandmother was forced to use. See also McMillen, *Motherhood in the Old South*, 115, 123.

32. See, e.g., Rhodes, "Domestic Vulnerabilities"; Golden, *A Social History of Wet Nursing in America*, 72.

33. Golden, *A Social History of Wet Nursing in America*, 95, 27, 70.

34. Doyle, "'The Highest Pleasure of Which Woman's Nature Is Capable,'" 960.

35. See Boydston, *Home and Work*.

36. See, e.g., entry for Tuesday, July 16, 1861, in Thomas, *The Secret Eye*, 187.

37. *Federal Gazette & Baltimore Daily Advertiser*, June 2, 1801. See also Ulrich, *A Midwife's Tale*.

38. *Elizabeth Patterson, wife of Robert Rogers v. George Jackson*, Docket #2093, Filed May 12, 1834, Records of the Fifth Judicial District Court, Saint Landry Parish Courthouse, Opelousas, Louisiana.

39. Bancroft, *Slave Trading in the Old South*, 154, 155n27.

40. See, e.g., Martin, *Divided Mastery*, esp. 83–85, 114–117, and Zaborney, *Slaves for Hire*, 6–7, 98–99.

41. Venable, *Down South Before the War*, 488–489. During the time of Venable's visit, Mount Sterling, Kentucky, was a very small town. Even in 1860, there were only 754 residents: see Kleber et al., *The Kentucky Encyclopedia*, 658.

42. Venable, *Down South Before the War*, 488–489.

43. "Wanted to Purchase," *Orleans Gazette, and Commercial Advertiser*, August 24, 1819; "Private Sales. Healthy Young Wet Nurse," *Charleston Mercury*, June 7, 1856; "Wanted," *Macon Daily Telegraph*, February 17, 1864. On other offers to hire or sell see "To Hire as a Wet Nurse or to be Disposed of," *Federal Intelligencer, & Baltimore Daily Gazette*, August 10, 1795, "Wanted—A Wet Nurse," *The Daily Dispatch* (Richmond, Va.), July 13, 1852, "Wanted—To Purchase," *The Daily Picayune*, July 8, 1854, and *City Gazette and Commercial Daily Advertiser* (hereafter CGCDA), April 16, 1792, April 17, 1798.

44. "For Sale—A Wet Nurse," *Daily Crescent*, December 21, 1850; "Private Sales," *Charleston Mercury*, June 7, 1856. In 1837, S. Bennet offered a "healthy young woman and child, suitable for a wet nurse" for sale: "Negroes for Sale," *Daily Picayune*, June 2, 1837. See also the New Orleans slave trader Thomas Foster's advertisement "Valuable Girl for Sale," *Daily Picayune*, January 26, 1859.

45. Advertisement, *Louisville Public Advertiser*, April 20, 1830.

46. See Walter Johnson, *Soul by Soul*, 123–127, 144–147.

47. *Charleston Mercury*, August 3, 1857; *Daily Dispatch*, March 28, 1855; *Mississippi Free Trader and Natchez Gazette*, August 14, 1845. See also *Daily South Carolinian*, January 16, 1858.

48. See Berry, "'In Pressing Need of Cash,'" 25.

49. "Wet Nurse to Hire," *CGCDA*, June 12, 1823, 3; "A Wet Nurse," *CGCDA*, June 21, 1816; "A Wet Nurse to Hire," *CGCDA*, November 3, 1800; "To Be Hired, as a Wet Nurse," *CGCDA*, June 23, 1795. See also "Wet Nurse for Hire," *The Daily Dispatch*, May 3, 1854, and "To Be Sold, Before the Vendue Store of Laurence Campbell, this Day, Between the Hours of 11 and 12 o'clock, a Negro Wench, with Her Child," April 17, 1798, both in the *CGCDA*. See also Brian Cape's ad in the *CGCDA*, April 17, 1798.

50. See, e.g., "A Wet Nurse to Hire," *CGCDA*, July 19, 1808, "To Be Hired," *CGCDA*, September 3, 1806, "To Be Hired," *CGCDA*, February 13, 1805, "A Wet Nurse to Be Hired," *CGCDA*, December 13, 1804, and "A Wet Nurse to Hire," *CGCDA*, November 3, 1800.

51. "Wet Nurse Wanted," *Daily Morning News*, January 6, 1855.

52. "To Be Hired, as a Wet Nurse," *CGCDA*, June 23, 1795, 2.

53. Entry for Tuesday, July 16, 1861, in Thomas, *Secret Eye*, 187.

54. Beckert, *Empire of Cotton*, 209–212.

55. See, e.g., advertisements in the *Daily Dispatch*, March 22, 1862, and August 1, 1863, and the *Daily South Carolinian*, July 31, 1856.

56. "Valuable Negroes," *CGCDA*, May 22, 1820; "A Wet Nurse," *CGCDA*, June 21, 1816; "For Sale," *CGCDA*, February 7, 1820.

57. "Wet Nurse, Seamstress, Washer, Ironer, and House Servant to Hire," *Southern Patriot*, May 10, 1842. See also the slave trader Thomas J. Bagby's advertisement in the *Daily Dispatch*, August 1, 1863.

58. "To Hire," *South-Carolina State Gazette, and Timothy's Daily Advertiser*, November 19, 1800.

59. "For Private Sale," *CGCDA*, February 23, 1803; "For Sale," *CGCDA*, November 12, 1808.

60. "A Wet Nurse to be Hired," *CGCDA*, December 13, 1804; "A Wet Nurse to Hire," *CCCDA*, April 8, 1812.

61. Esther Cox to Mary Chesnut, October 3, 1805, Folder 18, Cox and Chesnut Family Papers, South Caroliniana Library, University of South Carolina, Columbia.

62. *The Liberator*, Saturday, March 26, 1831.

63. Emancipation Petition of Raphaël Toledano, Records of the Parish Court, Emancipation Petitions, 1813–1843, New Orleans Public Library (hereafter NOPL); Emancipation Petition of Samuel Street, April 26, 1823, Records of the County Court, Slaves and Free Negroes, 1775–1861, NCDAH. See also Petition of John Martin and other Residents of Scott County, Virginia, December 1832, Legislative Petitions, Virginia State Archives, Richmond, *RSP-2*.

64. Joseph Gladney and James Wilson request to sell slaves, July 10, 1837, Records of the Equity Court, Petitions, SCDAH, *RSP-2*.

65. "A Wet Nurse to Be Hired," *CGCDA*, June 17, 1813; "To Be Hired," *CGCDA*, November 17, 1813, 1. See "A Wet Nurse," *Richmond Enquirer*, August 18, 1804, "To Be Let," *CGCDA*, January 13, 1794, "To Be Hired as a Wet Nurse," *CGCDA*, January 9, 1810, "A Wet Nurse," *CGCDA*, May 11, 1810, "A Wet Nurse," *CGCDA*, December 22, 1810.

66. See, e.g., "Wet Nurse and House Servant," *Charleston Mercury*, July 2, 1858. Conversely, advertisements like the one J. P. Boiffeuillet placed in the Savannah, Georgia, *Daily Morning News* on June 17, 1862 ("Wet Nurse Wanted"), sought a wet nurse for a "motherless child."

67. See, e.g., "Nurse Wanted," *New-Orleans Commercial Bulletin*, February 15, 1836, "A Wet Nurse Wanted," CGCDA, May 4, 1797, and "A Wet Nurse," *Enquirer*, August 8, 1804.

68. "To Be Hired," CGCDA, November 14, 1795; "Wanted, a Wet Nurse," CGCDA, February 20, 1796. See also "Wanted, a Wet Nurse for a Very Young Child," *Daily Dispatch*, November 23, 1864, "For Hire—A Wet Nurse," *Daily Dispatch*, January 2, 1855, "Wanted," *Daily Picayune*, January 7, 1854, "Wet Nurse to Hire," *Daily Picayune*, February 11, 1854, "To Be Hired," CGCDA, October 28, 1795, "Wet Nurse," *Louisiana Advertiser*, July 11, 1827, "Nurse Wanted," *New-Orleans Commercial Bulletin*, February 15, 1836, "Wanted to Hire," *Daily National Intelligencer*, May 4, 1842, "Wet Nurse for Hire," *Daily National Intelligencer*, March 16, 1829.

69. Machado, "Between Two Beneditos," 324.

70. "A Wet Nurse to Be Hired," CGCDA, December 13, 1804.

71. "A Wet Nurse," CGCDA, May 9, 1821; Advertisement, *Augusta Chronicle and Georgia Advertiser*, October 14, 1826.

72. Historians of slavery and the domestic slave trade, as well as those who explore dimensions of slave families and community formation, have established the centrality of the slave market in the traumatic separation of mothers and children as well as the dissolution of extended kinship networks. But rarely do these studies conceive of the mother-child separation by sale as an act of maternal violence, nor do they consider how the process of commodification made specific kinds of maternal violence possible.

73. Such was the case for William McWhorter's aunt Mary, who belonged to John Craddock, whose wife died some time after giving birth to their daughter Lucy. McWhorter's aunt was nursing a son at the time of Mrs. Craddock's death, and John Craddock forced her to suckle his infant daughter along with her own child. If Mary was feeding her son and Craddock's daughter began to cry, he would snatch Mary's baby from her, spank him, and place his infant daughter at Mary's breast instead. Mary would feed Lucy Craddock without opposition, but all the while she would "cry 'til de tears met under her chin." William McWhorter, in *BS*, vol. 4, *Georgia Narratives, Part 3*, 96–97; on physical violence, ibid., 99.

74. Entries of Tuesday, July 16, 1861, and Friday, July 31, 1863, in Thomas, *The Secret Eye*, 186–187, 218.

75. Entry of Tuesday, July 16, 1861, ibid.

76. Testimony of Richard Miles, Esq., May 28, 1789, *House of Commons Sessional Papers of the Eighteenth Century*, 112.

77. Entry of Friday, July 31, 1863, in Thomas, *The Secret Eye*.

78. Cheng, *Melancholy of Race*, 99.

79. "A Wet Nurse to Hire," CGCDA, November 3, 1800; "A Wet Nurse," CGCDA, July 5, 1813.

80. McMahon, "'So Truly Afflicting and Distressing to Me His Sorrowing Mother,'" 49, 46–47, 49. In the colonial period and the eighteenth century, Anglo-Americans encouraged each other to accept the loss of loved ones as God's will, but as Lucia McMahon has adeptly shown, such religious resignation was not easy for many, especially those who lost children. See also Steele, "The Gender and Racial Politics of Mourning in Antebellum America," 92. Steele makes it clear that such grief was integral to abolitionist writing, even as the abolitionists' emotional appeals used that pain for their own purposes (98).

81. See Treckel, "Breastfeeding and Maternal Sexuality in Colonial America," 34–35.

82. Deborah Kuhn McGregor argues that James Marion Sims, who is known as the "father of obstetrics and gynecology," "operated openly and publicly on nude African American women, when to do so with white middle- and upper-class women patients would have caused severe repercussions." McGregor, *From Midwives to Medicine*, 61, 48.

6. "THAT 'OMAN TOOK DELIGHT IN SELLIN' SLAVES"

Chapter title: "Ah Always Had a Hard Time," interview with Julia Brown (Aunt Sally), in BS, vol. 4, *Georgia Narratives, Part 1*, 142.

1. *Elizabeth Childress by her Next Friend James Sneed v. William L. Boyd, William Whitworth and J. K. Taylor*, Filed March 1, 1859, Chancery Court at Nashville, Davidson County, Tennessee, Metropolitan Government Archives of Nashville and Davidson County. In property-related matters, the law declared individuals under the age of twenty-one to be minors in all but four states—Ohio, Illinois, Iowa, and Vermont. In these places, minors were defined as eighteen years of age or younger. See Bishop, *Every Woman Her Own Lawyer*, 268–269. For slave traders' advertising see Schermerhorn, *The Business of Slavery*, 33–68.

2. *Elizabeth Childress by her Next Friend James Sneed v. William L. Boyd, William Whitworth and J. K. Taylor*.

3. Ibid.

4. Ibid.

5. Ibid. Guardians or parents typically bought and sold property on behalf of minors. Therefore, since Elizabeth Childress had not reached her majority when she initiated and executed the sale, Boyd was correct in arguing that it should have never taken place. However, the law still upheld such transactions; see Bishop, *Every Woman Her Own Lawyer*, 269–270.

6. *Elizabeth Childress by her Next Friend James Sneed v. William L. Boyd, William Whitworth and J. K. Taylor*.

7. The historian Lester C. Lamon called Nashville "a significant slave trading center," and another historian, Bobby L. Lovett, noted that the Nashville slave market was second only to the Memphis market; see Lamon, *Blacks in Tennessee*, 23, and Lovett, *The African-American History of Nashville*, 18.

8. Walter Johnson, *Soul by Soul*, 89; Robert Gudmestad, *The Troublesome Commerce*, 4; Anzilotti, *In the Affairs of the World*, 54, 60.

9. Stanley L. Engerman and Robert W. Fogel, *New Orleans Slave Sale Sample, 1804–1862.* Compiled by Robert W. Fogel and Stanley L. Engerman, University of Rochester, ICPSR07423-v2, Ann Arbor, Michigan: Inter-university Consortium for Political and Social Research [producer and distributor], 2008-08-04 [August 4, 2008], http://doi.org/10.3886/ICPSR07423.v2.

10. Exceptions to this masculinization are Pargas, *Slavery and Forced Migration in the Antebellum South*, Burke, *On Slavery's Border*, 17–51, and Billingsley, *Communities of Kinship.* On how slavery transformed the political and global economies, see Adam Rothman, *Slave Country*, Joshua D. Rothman, *Flush Times and Fever Dreams*, Walter Johnson, *River of Dark Dreams*, 156, Baptist, *The Half Has Never Been Told*, 140, and Schermerhorn, *The Business of Slavery.*

11. On these points see Schermerhorn, *The Business of Slavery.*

12. "Fredrika Bremer," Encyclopaedia Britannica Online, http://www.britannica.com/EBchecked/topic/78770/Fredrika-Bremer (accessed November 18, 2013). Bremer, *Homes of the New World*, vol. 2, p. 198; Kramer, *The Slave-Auction*, 6.

13. Kramer, *The Slave-Auction*, 11, 42–43.

14. On the Saint Louis Hotel see Edward King, *The Great South*, 37, and Daniel E. Walker, *No More, No More*, 36.

15. A person known only as "J.Y.S." wrote about a visit to a slave auction in Columbia, South Carolina, and suggested that class affected a prospective buyer's selection processes and bidding behavior. Perhaps class also determined the kinds of slave auctions "ladies" and "gentlemen" might attend as well. See J.Y.S., "A Slave Market," *The National Era*, June 25, 1857.

16. Ingraham, *The South-West*, vol. 2, pp. 200–201.

17. Bremer, *Homes of the New World*, vol. 1, p. 373.

18. Interview with Joseph Peterson, in Armstrong, *Old Massa's People*, 263–264.

19. Bremer, *Homes of the New World*, vol. 2, p. 535.

20. Bancroft, *Slave Trading in the Old South*, 53.

21. Bremer, *Homes of the New World*, vol. 1, p. 493.

22. Bancroft, *Slave Trading in the Old South*, 165, 170.

23. Martineau, *Retrospect of Western Travel*, vol. 1, pp. 234–235.

24. For a comprehensive examination of these ideas, see Tise, *Proslavery.*

25. Sometimes slave markets even ended up in residential neighborhoods, but this might lead to protests from homeowners who preferred to keep commerce out of their backyards. In 1856, property holders petitioned the Common Council and Board of Assistant Aldermen of New Orleans to remove a slave market and depot on "the lower side of Esplanade street, at the corner of Chartres . . . together with all slave markets and depots that may be on, or near Esplanade street, within six months" because the slave market had "become a nuisance to the neighborhood." *New Orleans Daily Creole*, August 21, 1856, and November 27, 1856.

26. On the ubiquitous nature of southern slave markets, see Charles Weld, *A Vacation Tour in the United States and Canada*, Chesnut, *Mary Chesnut's Civil War*, 15, and "Mary Boykin Miller Chesnut, 1823–1886," in Wilson et al., *Encyclopedia of Southern Culture.*

27. Ann Maria Davison, Diary entries for January 16 and January 28, 1854, Ann Maria Davison Papers, 1814–1861. Diary entries, May 1853–November 1854, MC 234, folder 3, Schlesinger Library, Radcliffe Institute, Harvard University, Cambridge, Massachusetts.

28. Bremer, *Homes of the New World*, vol. 2, pp. 202–204.

29. New Orleans Street Commissioner's Office, *Census of Merchants and Persons Following Professions Requiring Licenses, 1855–1856*, Louisiana Research Collection, NOPL.

30. John Adams Paxton, *The New-Orleans Directory and Register*, and H. & A. Cohen, *Cohen's New Orleans and Lafayette City Directory*, Louisiana Research Collection, NOPL.

31. *New Orleans (La.) Treasurer's Office. Census of Merchants, 1854, volumes, 1, 2, and 3, First, Second, and Third Districts*, NOPL. In the opening pages of the census, a list of professions with corresponding license fees appears. It includes only a few of the trades women engaged in, namely operating retail and grocery stores.

32. "Susan Boggs, Interviewed, 1863, Canada," in Blassingame, *Slave Testimony*, 419–420.

33. A. J. McElveen to Ziba B. Oakes, Sumterville, S.C., August 10, 1853, Folder 195, Ziba B. Oakes Papers, MS Am. 322, Rare Books and Manuscripts Department, Boston Public Library.

34. A. J. McElveen to Ziba B. Oakes, Darlington Court House, S.C., August 29, 1853, Folder 182, Ziba B. Oakes Papers, MS Am. 322, Rare Books and Manuscripts Department, Boston Public Library.

35. A. J. McElveen to Z. B. Oakes, Sumterville, S.C., January 13, 1855, Folder 259, and A. J. McElveen to Z. B. Oakes, Sumterville, S.C., January 16, 1855, Folder 270, Ziba B. Oakes Papers, MS Am. 322, Rare Books and Manuscripts Department, Boston Public Library.

36. Bill of sale from Ziba Oakes to Harriet A. Heath, December 16, 1845, vol.: 006A, Page: 00515, and July 8, 1846, vol.: 006B, Page: 00082, Series: S213050, SCDAH.

37. Act of Sale, Marie Aimee Carraby to Elihu Creswell, Recorded before Theodore Stark, July 25, 1850, Act of Sale, George Ann Botts to Miss Eleanor Hainline, Recorded before Stuart Lewis, November 11, 1850, Act of Sale, John Hagan to Mrs. Mathilda Mascey, Recorded before Theodore Guyol, February 19, 1850, Act of Sale, Margaret Flood to John Rucker White, Recorded before Theodore Stark, May 17, 1850, Act of Sale, William Talbott to Mrs. Louise Marie Eugenie Bailly Blachard, Recorded before Adolphe Boudousquie, November 28, 1850, *Annual Conveyance Vendor and Vendee Indexes*, New Orleans Conveyance Records Office, New Orleans Notarial Archives, New Orleans, Louisiana. Hereafter cited as NONA.

38. Tyre Glen Slave Trade Account Books for January 1, 1830–December 31, 1833, and January 1, 1834–December 31, 1853, Tyre Glen Papers, Manuscript Department, Duke University Library, Duke University, Durham, North Carolina, *RASP*; Isaac Jarratt Slave Trade Account Book for January 1, 1832–December 31, 1881, Jarratt-Puryear Family Papers, 1807–1865, Manuscript Department, Duke University Library, Duke University, *RASP*; John White Account Book, R.B. Chinn Collection, Missouri History Museum Archives, Saint Louis.

39. Interview with unidentified formerly enslaved person in *Unwritten History of Slavery*,

139. For more on the "fancy trade" see Baptist, "'Cuffy,' 'Fancy Maids,' and 'One-Eyed Men,'" and Green, "'Mr Ballard, I am compelled to write again.'" For women who knew that their husbands bought enslaved women for sexual purposes see *Sarah Oneel v. William Oneel*, County Court Divorce Records, NCDAH, *RSP-2*.

40. B. E. Rogers, in Rawick, *AS*, Supplement, Series 1, vol. 11, *North Carolina and South Carolina Narratives*, 55.

41. Ank Bishop, in *BS*, vol. 1, *Alabama Narratives*, 35.

42. Ike Thomas, in *BS*, vol. 4, *Georgia Narratives, Part 4*, 25.

43. Rose Russell, in Rawick, *AS*, Supplement, Series 1, vol. 9, *Mississippi Narratives, Part 4*, 1903.

44. Thomas Jefferson to Jared Sparks, February 4, 1824, in Jefferson, *The Works of Thomas Jefferson*, vol. 7, p. 333; Richard G. Morris et al., Petition to the Legislature of Virginia, Buckingham County, Virginia, December 1831, Legislative Petitions, 1820–1832, Virginia State Archives, Richmond, *RSP-2*.

45. H. B. Holloway, in *BS*, vol. 2, *Arkansas Narratives, Part 3*, 289.

46. William Wells Brown, *The Narrative of William W. Brown*, 49.

47. See Act of Sale, Charles Alexis LeBean represented by Mrs. Marie Dorothee Morel his attorney in fact, to Elihu Cresswell, Recorded before Alphonse Barnett, September 4, 1850, NONA, and Act of Sale, Miss Alice Martin, represented by Mrs. Mary Jane Williams, her attorney in fact, to Caleb Pruel, Recorded before Michael Geruon, June 29, 1850, NONA.

48. *Elias and Mary Gumaer v. Peter Hevener*, Records of the United States Circuit Court, Chancery Dockets and Rule Case Files, NARA, Record Group 21, Document Number 885, Box: 76, Folder 20, Book: Rules #5, *RSP-2*.

49. *Ruth Williams by her next friend William A. B. Faulkner v. William Williams et al.*, Filed August 13, 1856, Alabama Supreme Court Cases, Supreme Court Record [1861], Alabama Department of Archives and History, Montgomery, *RSP-2*.

50. *Jane Buie v. John Kelly*, Filed December 1844, Docket #3328, North Carolina Supreme Court, Raleigh, North Carolina State Archives, *RSP-2*.

51. Armstrong, *Old Massa's People*, 130–132.

52. Walter Johnson and Daina Ramey Berry have examined exchanges between enslaved people and prospective buyers at slave sales, and the questions this woman posed to Sarah were common. See Johnson, *Soul by Soul*, 162–188, and Berry, "We'm Fus' Rate Bargain," 55–71.

53. "Black Code: An Act Prescribing the Rules and Conduct to Be Observed with Respect to Negroes and Other Slaves of This Territory," in Territory of Orleans, *Acts Passed at the First Session of the First Legislature of the Territory of Orleans*, 154. See also Schafer, *Slavery, the Civil Law, and the Supreme Court of Louisiana*, 134.

54. See "Kidnapping," in Lewis, *The African Observer*, 37–50.

55. Elliott, *The Bible and Slavery*, 83; Norman, *Norman's New Orleans and Environs*, 156–157.

56. Walter Johnson, *Soul by Soul*, 55; Bancroft, *Slave Trading in the Old South*, 324–325.

57. *Bedilia Gaynor Kellar v. John Fink, Syndic and A. Boas (Emily Boyer)*, Docket #598, Filed July 27, 1846, 3 La. Ann. 17, HALSC-UNO.

58. "Furniture at Auction—Housekeepers Attention!" *Memphis Daily Appeal*, December 12, 1861; "Ladies' Auction at 185 Camp Street, L. A. Levy, Jr. Auctioneer," *New Orleans Daily Crescent*, November 24, 1857; "All the Ladies should attend Hanna's Great Auction Sale Every Morning and Evening," *Memphis Daily Appeal*, April 15, 1858; Barind's "Ladies' Auction! Great Chance!" *Memphis Daily Appeal*, December 1, 1857. Ellen Hartigan-O'Connor's work in progress examines these auctions as well as what were called "ladies' auction rooms" in greater detail. I am indebted to her for bringing these events to my attention.

59. A hundred women attended a ladies' auction that M. C. Cayce & Son held in Memphis on September 27, 1858, and the auctioneers induced women to attend their next ladies' auction. See *Memphis Daily Appeal*, September 28, 1858. For women standing on chairs, see "A Ladies Auction," *The Daily Picayune*, April 18, 1852. L. A. Levy, untitled ad, *New Orleans Daily Crescent*, November 24, 1857 ("for the sale of real estate"). Levy advertised his Ladies' Auction on the same page in the same edition.

60. "Positive Sale by Rapelye, Bennett and Company" and "Ladies' Auction," *CGCDA*, March 18, 1823. "Negro Boy at Auction by A.S. Levy & Co." and "Ladies' Auction. Fancy Dry Goods by A.S. Levy," *Memphis Daily Appeal*, August 10, 1861.

61. See "Ladies' Auction," *The South-Western*, December 5, 1855.

62. See, e.g., Susan Myrick, Interview with Catherine Beale, 1929, in Blassingame, *Slave Testimony*, 574–575.

63. *Charity Ramsey, Administratrix v. Zadock Blalock, et al.*, Docket #A-03500, Filed August 29, 1860, Judgment delivered: April 3, 1861, Georgia Supreme Court, Atlanta, Georgia, Division of Archives and History.

64. Depositions of Sarah Smith, Milly Stuart, Elizabeth King, and Martha Morris, taken August 1860, ibid.

65. George White in Purdue, et al., *Weevils in the Wheat*, 309. Depositions of Sarah Smith, Milly Stuart, Elizabeth King, and Martha Morris, taken August 1860, *Charity Ramsey, Administratrix v. Zadock Blalock*.

66. See, e.g., *Catharine Munro v. Duke Goodman and his agent Thomas Cochran*, Bill for Injunction and Relief, Filed March 14, 1823, Charleston, S.C., Record of the Equity Court, Bills, SCDAH, *RSP-2*, Millie Simpkins, in *BS*, vol. 15, *Tennessee Narratives*, 66, and letter from Frances Marvin Smith Webster to Frances Kirby Smith, August 10, 1851, in Baker, *The Websters*, 266–268.

67. *Leah Woods v. John McFall*, Bill for Relief, Injunction, etc., Docket #456, Filed February 1862, Record of the Equity Court, Bills, SCDAH, *RSP-2*.

68. Elvira Boles, in *BS*, vol. 16, *Texas Narratives, Part 1*, 106.

69. *Margaret J. Mason v. Willie Mason*, Giles County, Chancery Court Cases, Filed August 31, 1857, Docket #1450, TSLA, *RSP-2*; *Mrs. Sarah Hill v. James White*, Docket #7584, Second District Court of New Orleans, Filed March 21, 1854, *RSP-2*.

70. Interview with unidentified woman, "Mistreatment of Slaves," in *BS*, vol. 4, *Georgia Narratives, Part 4*, 293–294.

71. Court Brief, *Catharine Megrath v. Administrators of John Robertson and Ann Robertson*, March, 1795, 1 Des. 445, 1 S.C.Eq. 445 (S.C.), 1795, Court of Appeals of South Carolina, SCDAH.

72. Although buying and caring for sickly slaves might be interpreted as "maternal" or "womanly," it was an economically grounded practice that slave buyers engaged in on a regular basis, especially before the abolition of the African Slave Trade to British North America in 1808. Slave ships often sold "refuse slaves," who were elderly, injured, or severely ill for low prices and people like Ann Robertson bought them in the hope of turning a profit.

73. Inventory and Appraisement of the Goods and Chattels, Rights and Credits of Ann Robertson, Later of Charleston, June 23, 1794, SCDAH.

74. Mathilda Bushy was widowed sometime in the late 1840s. She married her husband, Jacob, in 1840 and by 1850 she was living with her nephew Bernard among other members of his household, which did not include Jacob.

75. In the 1860 census, Bernard Kendig was the third-wealthiest slave trader in New Orleans. See Tansey, "Bernard Kendig and the New Orleans Slave Trade," 177.

76. Walter Johnson, *Soul by Soul*, 52–53.

77. Testimony of J. W. Boazman, *Folger v. Kendig* Docket #5337, Unreported Case, June 1858, HALSC-UNO. See "Document 'D' Filed 28 Nov 1856," *Folger v. Kendig* Docket #5337, Unreported Case, June 1858, HALSC-UNO. Boazman was not the only one to accuse Kendig of using Bushy's name to conduct business during his insolvency. But in the cases when individuals did call the legitimacy of their partnership into question, such witnesses were testifying against Bushy or Kendig in matters pertaining to slave sales. It is best to interpret these dismissals within the broader tendency for those engaged in commerce to challenge women's claims to separate property. For others who dismissed Kendig and Bushy's partnership see John Kellar's answer to Mathilda's charges and Testimony of J. D. Mix, in *Bushy v. Kellar*, Docket #3615, Jan 1856, Unreported Case 11 La. Ann. xvi.

78. U.S. Bureau of the Census, *Seventh Census of the United States, 1850* and *Eighth Census of the United States, 1860*; testimony of Bernard Kendig, *Nixon v. Bozeman et al.*, Docket #3485, November 1856, 11 La. Ann. 750, HALSC-UNO.

79. Testimony of Bernard Kendig, *Nixon v. Bozeman et al.*, 1856, HALSC-UNO. The "et al." in the case name happens to be referring to Mathilda Bushy. For a case in which Bushy was sued for selling an afflicted slave, see *Couch v. Bushey*, Records of the Fifth Judicial District Court, Suit Records, New Orleans Public Library, New Orleans, Louisiana, RSP-2. J. W. Boazman's name was spelled incorrectly in the court records, but he was the defendant named in this case. Additionally, Mathilda Bushy's name is spelled a variety of ways (Matilda, Mathilda, Bushey, Bushy). In the court transcripts and in the notarial records, clerks and notaries referred to Bushy as "Widow Jacob Bushey," "Mrs. Matilda Bushey." Bernard is identified as Barnard and Barney in court records as well as notarial acts.

80. Testimony of Bernard Kendig, *Nixon v. Bozeman et al.*, 1856, HALSC-UNO. For lawyers' confirmation of slave trading partnership between Boazman and Bushy see "Answer and Call in Warranty and Plea in Reconvention filed 23 April 1853," *Nixon v. Bozeman et al.*, 1856. First quote from plaintiff's petition and second quote from Testimony of Bernard Kendig, both in *Nixon v. Bozeman et al.* For testimony related to Boazman's business relationship with Bushy see *Bushey v. Kellar*, Docket #3615,

Jan 1856, Unreported Case 11 La. Ann. xvi, and Testimony of J. W. Boazman, *Kendig v. Cutler,* Docket #3978, Unreported Case, Delay Docket, November 1856, HALSC-UNO. In *Bushey v. Kellar,* Boazman's name is spelled "Brazman." Emile Beauregard testified that he was "agent of Mrs. Kendig," while R. P. Willmot stated that "Brazman carry on the negro trading business in the same house [as Kendig] on Gravier St." Testimony of Emile Beauregard and R. P. Willmot, *Bushey v. Kellar.*

81. *Moore v. Bushey,* Unreported Louisiana Supreme Court case Docket #4544, 1857, HALSC-UNO.

82. Ibid.; Tansey, "Bernard Kendig and the New Orleans Slave Trade," 162n8; Notarial Act passed before P. W. Robert, Power of Attorney, August 14, 1852, NONA. For sales in which the notary public identifies Mathilda Bushy without any proxy or agent involved see Act of Sale, William Barnes to Mathilda Kendig, Widow Jacob Bushey, Recorded before S. H. Lewis, May 28, 1849, NONA; Act of Sale, George Ann Botts to Mathilda Kendig, Widow Jacob Bushey, Recorded before Joseph Beard, June 15, 1849, NONA; Act of Sale, Mathilda Kendig, Widow Jacob Bushey to William Carroll, Recorded before Antoine Abat, May 31, 1851, NONA; Act of Sale, Mathilda Kendig, Widow Jacob Bushey to William Jackson Maynard, Recorded before William Woods, July 2, 1851, NONA; Semmes and Edwards, Attorneys for Matilda Bushy to John Kellar, November 23, 1853, "Letter to Deft: Marked A," *Bushey v. Kellar,* Docket #3615, Jan 1856, Unreported Case 11 La. Ann. xvi. R. P. Wilmott witnessed the act of sale at the heart of this suit and testified to the fact that William, the "faulty" slave Bushy was accused of selling, was in "the plaintiff's yard part of the time." He also claimed to have taken the enslaved man to "Kendig's yard," but Bushy's lawyers stated that it was hers. Adding further evidence of her ownership, Augustus Davezac, a physician who examined William on Kellar's behalf, attested to doing so at the "plaintiff's yard." Testimony of R. P. Wilmott and Augustus Davezac, *Bushey v. Kellar.* Court records similarly reveal that Catharine Hyams, another widow, who struggled with some form of illiteracy, owned a slave yard in New Orleans, the country's largest slave market; see *Hyams v. Smith,* 6 La. Ann. 362, 1851, HALSC-UNO.

83. See Tansey, "Bernard Kendig and the New Orleans Slave Trade," Schafer, *Slavery, the Civil Law, and the Supreme Court of Louisiana,* 140–142, Morris, *Southern Slavery and the Law,* 111, and Deyle, *Carry Me Back,* 122.

84. Testimony of W. B. Koontz, *Boazman v. Cannon,* Docket #2466, Unreported Case, Delay Docket, November 1853, HALSC-UNO.

85. On the Woolfolks, see Schermerhorn, *The Business of Slavery,* 69–94. On partnerships that resembled that of Bushy and Kendig and alternative arrangements see *William H. Simmonds v. James Sneed,* Filed February 4, 1824, Supreme Court Cases, Middle Tennessee, TSLA, RSP-2, and *James and Wiley Carothers v. Patrick A. Erskine and William H. Crutcher,* Filed October 2, 1851, Records of the Chancery Court, Williamson County Courthouse, Franklin, Tennessee, RSP-2.

86. On such arrangements see *William B. March v. John Hall,* Records of the County Court, Miscellaneous Records–1869, NCDAH. See also *Taswell Alderson and James M. Mitchell v. Thomas Ridley,* Docket #418, Filed February 12, 1839, Records of the Chancery Court, Case Files, Maury County Historical Society Loose Records Project,

Columbia, Tennessee, *Samuel Stone v. William Worsham*, Filed May 22, 1841, Records of the Equity Court, Bill, SCDAH, *William Pertut v. Amaziah Cobb*, September 13, 1825, Records of the Superior Court, Proceedings 1852–1854, Greene County Courthouse, Greensboro, Georgia, *William A. Todd and John Fleming [Flemming] v. Toliver Lindsey [Lindsay]*, August 27, 1842, Records of the Equity Court, Bills, SCDAH, *William A. Smith v. Thomas N. Gadsden*, 1843, Records of the Equity Court, Bills, SCDAH, *RSP-2*, *Larkin Lynch v. Joseph A. Bitting*, Docket #8654, Fall Term 1859, Court of Equity, Yadkin County, North Carolina, NCDAH, and *Thomas Hundley v. Benjamin W. Walker*, Filed September 9, 1843, Records of the Circuit Superior Court of Chancery, Final Repository: Halifax Circuit Court Building, Halifax, Virginia, all in *RSP-2*.

87. Bynum, *Unruly Women*, 79–80; Baptist, "'Cuffy,' 'Fancy Maids,' and 'One-Eyed Men.'"
88. See Walter Johnson, *River of Dark Dreams*, 84, 86, and Schafer, *Brothels, Depravity, and Abandoned Women*.
89. See Tansey, "Prostitution and Politics in Antebellum New Orleans."
90. *Daily Picayune*, August 13, 1847; *State v. Mathilda Raymond*, no. 2,495, June 17, 1848, and *State v. Mathilda Raymond*, no. 2,868, November 14, 1848, First District Court of New Orleans, Louisiana Collection, NOPL.
91. *The Daily Picayune*, July 6, 1855, 2, September 14, 1858, 5, and July 17, 1862, 2. On estimated purchasing power, Samuel H. Williamson, "Seven Ways to Compute the Relative Value of a U.S. Dollar Amount, 1774 to Present," Measuring Worth, www.measuringworth.com/uscompare/ (accessed July 13, 2018).
92. See, e.g., *New Orleans Bee*, March 29, 1849, and *The Daily Picayune*, July 21, 1852, November 18, 1852, June 24, 1856, December 23, 1856, June 30, 1857, and September 2, 1857. Article 179 of the Civil Code of Louisiana stated that slave owners were "bound by the acts of their slaves done by their command." Morgan, *Civil Code of the State of Louisiana*, 28–29.
93. "Police Matters," *Times-Picayune*, August 17, 1857, 4.
94. In a recent article, Brenda Stevenson argues that enslaved women who had relationships with white men (outside of brothels and within slaveholding communities) were "concubines." Stevenson, "What's Love Got to Do with It?" The enslaved women who left the bulk of the testimony collected by the Federal Writers' Project describe these relationships as nonconsensual.
95. Block, *Rape and Sexual Power in Early America*. See also my "Rethinking Sexual Violence and the Marketplace of Slavery."

7. "HER SLAVES HAVE BEEN LIBERATED AND LOST TO HER"

Chapter title: Elizabeth A. Bailey, by her Next Friend Hawkey F. Harris v. Richard C. Bailey, October 1866, Ended Chancery Court Causes, Library of Virginia, Richmond, *RSP-2*.

1. "A Barbarous Relic of Slavery," *Liberator*, October 9, 1863.
2. Convention of the People of South Carolina, *Declaration of the Immediate Causes Which Induce and Justify the Secession of South Carolina from the Federal Union*.

3. United States Congressional House of Delegates, "Joint Resolution to Amend the Constitution of the United States," in Sanger, *The Statutes at Large, Treaties, and Proclamations, of the United States of America from December 5, 1859, to March 3, 1863*, 251.

4. Abraham Lincoln, "Proclamation Calling 75,000 Militia, and Convening Congress in Extra Session," April 5, 1861, in Nicolay and Hay, *Abraham Lincoln*, 34.

5. See Penningroth, *The Claims of Kinfolk*, Feimster, "General Benjamin Butler and the Threat of Sexual Violence During the American Civil War," Downs, *Sick from Freedom*, Downs, "The Other Side of Freedom," and Long, *Doctoring Freedom*. For more on the Civil War–era domestic slave trade see Martinez, "The Slave Market in Civil War Virginia."

6. "First Inaugural Address, Delivered at Washington, D.C., March 4, 1861," in Miller, *Life and Works of Abraham Lincoln*, 134–135.

7. Major-General Benjamin F. Butler to Lieutenant General Winfield Scott, May 24, 1861, and May 27, 1861, in U.S. War Department, *The War of the Rebellion*, series 2, vol. 1, pp. 752, 754.

8. Benjamin F. Butler, General of the Third Brigade, to His Excellency Thomas H. Hicks, Governor of the State of Maryland, April 23, 1861, ibid., 750.

9. "An Act to Confiscate Property Used for Insurrectionary Purposes," August 6, 1861; "An Act to Make an Additional Article of War," March 13, 1862, Chapter 40; "An Act for the Release of Certain Persons Held to Service or Labor in the District of Columbia," April 16, 1862, Chapter 54; "An Act to Secure Freedom to All Persons Within the Territories of the United States," June 19, 1862, Chapter 111; "An Act to Suppress Insurrection, to Punish Treason and Rebellion, to Seize and Confiscate the Property of Rebels, and for Other Purposes," July 17, 1862, Chapter 195; "An Act to Amend the Act Calling Forth the Militia to Execute the Laws of the Union, Suppress Insurrections, and Repel Invasion, Approved February Twenty-Eight, Seventeen Hundred and Ninety-Five, and the Acts Amendatory Thereof, and for Other Purposes," July 17, 1862, Chapter 201, all in Sanger, *The Statutes at Large, Treaties, and Proclamations, of the United States of America from December 5, 1859, to March 3, 1863*, 319, 354, 376–378, 432, 590–592, 597–600.

10. Abraham Lincoln, "Declaring Order of General Hunter Emancipating Slaves Void," in U.S. House of Representatives, Executive Documents Printed by Order of the House of Representatives, during the First Session of the Thirty Ninth Congress, 1865–'66, 212–214. For Frémont's proclamation see "Marshal Law in Missouri," *Daily National Intelligencer*, September 4, 1861, and for Lincoln's personal letter to Frémont asking him to rescind it, see "Gen. Fremont's Proclamation—The President's Letter," *Lowell Daily Citizen and News*, September 16, 1861.

11. Proclamation Nos. 16 and 17, in Sanger, *The Statutes at Large, Treaties, and Proclamations, of the United States of America from December 5, 1859, to March 3, 1863*, 1267–1269.

12. See, e.g., Faust, *Mothers of Invention*, Ott, *Confederate Daughters*, Edwards, *Scarlett Doesn't Live Here Anymore*, Clinton, *Southern Families at War*, Bercaw, *Gendered*

Freedoms, Kirsten Wood, *Masterful Women,* 159–191, and Glymph, *Out of the House of Bondage,* 97–166.

13. See McCurry, "The Soldier's Wife" and *Confederate Reckoning.*

14. Interviews with unidentified formerly enslaved person, in *Unwritten History of Slavery,* 147.

15. Ripley, *From Flag to Flag,* 58.

16. Sarah Johnson Berliner, in Rawick, *AS,* Supplement, Series 2, vol. 10, *Texas Narratives, Part 9, Appendix,* 4333.

17. Interview with unidentified formerly enslaved man, in *Unwritten History of Slavery,* 129. On changes in enslaved people's behavior and owners' responses to it see Hunter, *To 'Joy My Freedom,* 4–20, Hahn, *A Nation Under Our Feet,* part 1, Heather Andrea Williams, *Self-Taught,* 7–29, and Glymph, *Out of the House of Bondage,* 97–136.

18. Entry for August 23, 1861, in Chesnut, *A Diary from Dixie,* 109; Catherine McRae to "James," February 24, 1862, Colin J. McRae Papers, LPR264, Box 1, Folder 5, Alabama Department of Archives and History, Montgomery.

19. Affidavit of Eldred Satterwhite, given before Robert B. Tunstall, Justice of the Peace, October 3, 1862, Woolfolk Family (of Carolina County, Virginia) Papers, 1780–1936, MSS #1W8844a 388–390, Section 32, *RASP,* Series M: Selections from the Virginia Historical Society, Part 3: Other Tidewater Virginia. See also Affidavits of Jourdan Woolfolk, John W. Woolfolk, and William Woolfolk with regard to the enslaved people owned by Mary Elizabeth Woolfolk, given before Robert B. Tunstall, Justice of the Peace, October 3, 1862, ibid.

20. Confederate States of America, "An Act to Perpetuate Testimony in Cases of Slaves Abducted or Harbored by the Enemy and of Other Property Seized Wasted or Destroyed by them," August 30, 1861, in U.S. War Department, *The War of the Rebellion,* series 4, vol. 1, p. 593. The act was clear about one thing, though; the Confederate government had no intention of providing slaveholders with any form of recompense for the losses they claimed. Affidavits of Eldred Satterwhite, Jourdan Woolfolk, John W. Woolfolk, and William Woolfolk with regard to the enslaved people owned by Mary Elizabeth Woolfolk, given before Robert B. Tunstall, Justice of the Peace, October 3, 1862, in Woolfolk Family (of Carolina County, Virginia) Papers, 1780–1936, MSS #1W8844a 388–390, Section 32, *RASP.* All of the affidavits on Mary Woolfolk's behalf attested to her ownership of these runaways. On October 3, 1862, Jourdan Woolfolk filed his own claim and appeared along with his son John and neighbor Filman Carual to provide affidavits related to the flight of his own slaves to Union forces stationed in Fredericksburg. See Affidavits of John W. Woolfolk, Filman Carual, and Jourdan Woolfolk with regard to the enslaved people owned by Jourdan Woolfolk, given before Robert B. Tunstall, Justice of the Peace, October 3, 1862, ibid.

21. Receipt of Payment to Robert Y. Henley, November 15, 1864, and Sworn statement of Eldred Satterwhite, June 11, 1866, Woolfolk Family Papers, 1780–1936, MSS #1W8844a 388–390, Section 31, Folder 2, 1860–1873, and Section 32, respectively, *RASP.*

22. Advertisements, *Sun*, December 27, 1861, *Macon Daily Telegraph*, September 28, 1861, *Augusta Chronicle*, August 27, 1862.

23. Advertisement, *Charleston Courier*, October 28, 1861.

24. See, e.g., Advertisements, *Fayetteville Observer*, June 2, 1862, and *Charleston Mercury*, January 25, 1861.

25. McCurry, *Confederate Reckoning*, 94.

26. Ibid, 88.

27. Letter from Mrs. P. E. Collins in Cahaba, Alabama, to Governor John Gill Shorter, April 5, 1862, Box #RSG00252, Folder 2, Alabama Governor (1861–1863: Shorter) Administrative Files, 1861–1863, Government Records Collections, Alabama Department of Archives and History, Montgomery.

28. P. B. Fouke to General, March 30, 1862, enclosing Jas. M. Quarles to Major Genl. Grant, March 27, 1862, in Berlin et al., *The Destruction of Slavery*, 272–274. Entry for James Minor Quarles, United States, *Biographical Directory of the United States Congress 1774–Present*, http://bioguide.congress.gov/scripts/biodisplay.pl?index=Q000002. Amy E. Murrell found that women constituted the majority of petitioners who wrote directly to state leaders. See Murrell, "'Of Necessity and Public Benefit.'"

29. Mrs. E. Stewart to the President of the U. States, December 1863, in Berlin et al., *The Destruction of Slavery*, 476.

30. Major John W. Horner to Maj. W. R. Rowley, February 27, 1864, ibid., 318–319.

31. J. D. B. DeBow, "Table XC.—Classification of Slave Holders in the United States," in DeBow, *Statistical View of the United States*, 95.

32. "An Act for the Release of certain Persons held to Service or Labor in the District of Columbia," available at https://www.archives.gov/exhibits/featured-documents/dc-emancipation-act/transcription.html; notations for Mildred Ewell, Fanny Ewell, Mary Moore, Louisa Kearney, M[argaret] A. Goddard, Ann E. Robertson, Ann Robertson, Mary Kraft, Margaret Miller, Minutes of Meetings, April 28, 1862–January 14, 1863, Entry for Friday, June 13, 1862, 38–39, and Saturday, June 14, 1862, 40, Records of the Board of Commissioners for the Emancipation of Slaves in the District of Columbia, 1862–1863, NARA Microfilm Publication M520, 6 rolls, Records of the United States General Accounting Office, Record Group 217, NARA.

33. Emancipation Papers, 1862, Records of the U.S. District Court for the District of Columbia Relating to Slaves, 1851–1863, NARA Microfilm Publication M433, roll 1, Records of District Courts of the United States, RG 21.

34. Petition of the Sisters of the Visitation, #569, submitted June 2, 1862, "Petitions Filed Under the Act of July 12, 1862," Records of the Board of Commissioners for the Emancipation of Slaves in the District of Columbia, 1862–1863, NARA Microfilm Publication M520, 6 rolls, Records of the United States General Accounting Office, Record Group 217 (hereafter "NARA-Petitions"); Emily Clark, *Masterless Mistresses*, 161.

35. Notation for Margaret Miller, Minutes of Meetings, April 28, 1862–January 14, 1863, Entry for Friday, June 3, 1862, 39, Records of the Board of Commissioners, NARA.

36. M. C. Barber to Jno A. Smith, Esq., May 14, 1862, in Berlin et al., *The Destruction of Slavery*, 179–181.

37. Eight of Barber's slaves were under ten years old, thirteen fell between the ages of ten and thirty, seven were between the ages of thirty-one and forty, and six were over forty. Most of them were in the prime of their working lives and would have been at their highest value.

38. Supplemental Act of July 12, 1862, available at https://www.archives.gov/exhibits/featured-documents/dc-emancipation-act/supplemental-act.html; NARA-Petitions.

39. Civil War Slave Compensation Claims in Compiled Military Service Records of U.S. Colored Troops, Saint Louis County Library, https://www.slcl.org/content/civil-war-slave-compensation-claims-compiled-military-service-records-us-colored-troops.

40. Mary Duncan to General Thomas, June 2, 1863, in Berlin et al., *The Black Military Experience*, 146–148; Brazy, *An American Planter*, 154–155.

41. Irene Smith to Hon. W. P. Fessenden, October 27, 1864, in Berlin et al., *The Wartime Genesis of Free Labor: The Lower South*, 853–856.

42. In the United States Federal Census for 1860, Irene Smith valued her real estate at $275,000, and she estimated the value of her personal property, which included her slaves, at $403,000. See U.S. Bureau of the Census, *Eighth Census of the United States, 1860*.

43. Seventh and Eighth Census of the United States and Case Files of Applications from Former Confederates for Presidential Pardons, 1865–1867, NARA Microfilm Publication M1003, 73 rolls, Records of the Adjutant General's Office, 1780's–1917, Record Group 94, NARA (hereafter NARA-Amnesty Papers); Will of Alexander C. Bullitt, October 22, 1861, Mississippi County, District and Probate Courts. Bullitt died in 1868. Succession of Alexander C. Bullitt, Successions, 32175–32220, 1846–1880, Case #32215, Second District Court of New Orleans, Louisiana County, District and Probate Courts, NOPL.

44. See Martinez, *Confederate Impressment in the Upper South*, Colin Edward Woodward, *Marching Masters*, 55–79, McCurry, *Confederate Reckoning*, and Nelson, "Confederate Slave Impressment Legislation, 1861–1865."

45. Confederate States of America, Congress, House of Representatives, *A Bill to Be Entitled "An Act to Provide Payment for Slaves Impressed Under State Laws, and Lost in the Public Service."* James A. Seddon, the Confederacy's secretary of war, believed that "the sum of three millions one hundred and eight thousand dollars [would] be necessary to pay such claims." A. L. Rives, a lieutenant colonel and the acting chief of the Engineer[ing] Bureau, estimated that over $700,000 would be necessary to compensate slave owners in the state of Virginia alone. See Confederate States of America, Engineer Department, *Estimate*.

46. Confederate States of America, Congress, House of Representatives, *A Bill to Be Entitled "An Act to Provide Payment for Slaves Impressed Under State Laws, and Lost in the Public Service,"* and House of Representatives, Committee on Claims, *Report of Committee on Claims in the Case of Mary Clark*.

47. For South Carolina laws contemplated and enacted to compensate slave owners, see South Carolina, General Assembly, "Resolution to Establish a Process by Which the State Auditor Would Hear All Claims for Slaves Lost in Public Service" (1862 c.), ND-1326-01, "Resolution to Direct the State to Pay Owners for Slaves Lost in Co[a]stal

Defense and Fortification" (1862 c.), ND-1327-01, "Resolution to Have the Judiciary Committee Report on Establishing a Court to Hear Claims for Slaves Killed or Injured in State Service" (1862 c.), ND-1328-01, "Resolutions to Establish the Principle and Process of State Compensation for Slave Deaths Caused by Disease Contracted While in Public Service" (1863), 1863-53-01, and "Resolution to Authorize the Committee on Claims to Allow All Claims for Slaves Lost in Public Service Suspention [*sic*] by the State Auditor Because They Were Impressed by the Confederate Government" (12/19/1864), 1864-29-01, Resolutions of the General Assembly, Series S165018, SCDAH. For compensation claims submitted in South Carolina see Tupper, *Report of the Auditor of South Carolina on Claims Against the State for Slaves Lost in the Public Service*, Tupper, *Report, Office of State Auditor, South Carolina: Claims Against the State for Slaves Lost in the Public Service*, and Tupper, *Report Listing Eight Additional Claims for Slaves Lost in Public Service;* Martinez, *Confederate Impressment in the Upper South*, 43.

48. U.S. Bureau of the Census, *Eighth Census of the United States, 1860*.

49. J. W. Harrison (Selma, Alabama) to Governor John Gill Shorter, March 14, 1863, Alabama Governor (1861–1863: Shorter), Administrative files, SG24882, Reels 6–14, and SG006472, Reels 5–6, Administrative files, Box Number: RSG00204, Folder Number 9, Alabama Department of Archives and History, Montgomery.

50. See Dunaway, *The African American Family in Slavery and Emancipation*, 187.

51. Deposition of Louis Jourdan, May 27, 1915, quoted in Regosin and Shaffer, *Voices of Emancipation*, 166–168. After his family was taken away, Jourdan remained inside the camp, but when he went to visit his family, Confederate forces seized him, impressed him into service, and made him "dig trenches and breastworks." He escaped, and on September 1, 1864, he enlisted in Company F of the 77th Regiment of the United States Colored Infantry. As soon as he was discharged, he went to Bayou Lafourche and took his wife and children away from Madam Lestree.

52. Brigadier General Robert C. Schenck to Captain James B. Fry, July 6, 1861, enclosing Assistant Adjutant-General Donn Piatt to Brigadier General Robert C. Schenck, July 6, 1861, Col. A. McD. McCook to Capt. Donn Piatt, July 5, 1861, and Caroline Noland to Lieutenant-General Winfield Scott, June 27, 1861, in U.S. War Department, *The War of the Rebellion*, series 2, vol. 1, pp. 755–759.

53. Clipping from an unidentified Cleveland, Ohio, newspaper, [November? 1862], enclosed in Brig. Genl. Q. A. Gillmore to Major Gen. Gordon Granger, December 11, 1862, and S. D. Atkins to Miller, November 2, 1862, in Berlin et al., *The Destruction of Slavery*, 531–534, 528–529.

54. Wiley Childress, in Rawick, *AS*, vol. 16, *Kansas, Kentucky, Maryland, Ohio, Virginia, and Tennessee Narratives*, 9; Charlie Pye, in *BS*, vol. 4, *Georgia Narratives, Part 3*, 187–188; Mattie Lee, in *BS*, vol. 10, *Missouri Narratives*, 224; Hannah Kelly, in Clayton, *Mother Wit*, 147.

55. Ripley, *From Flag to Flag*, 66.

56. Josephine Pugh, "Dark Days: A Woman's Record," page 3, in Pugh Civil War Account Mss #2618, Colonel W. W. Pugh Family Papers, Mss. 2052, Louisiana and Lower Mississippi Valley Collections, Louisiana State University Libraries, Baton Rouge,

Louisiana, *RASP*, Series B: Selections from the Louisiana and Lower Mississippi Valley Collections, Louisiana State University Libraries, Part 3: Louisiana Sugar Plantations (Bayou Lafourche and Bayou Teche).

57. Deposition of Silvy Granville, November 21, 1901, in Regosin and Shaffer, *Voices of Emancipation*, 44. On the practice of refugeeing and its impact on enslaved people see Jacqueline Jones, *Saving Savannah*, 145–146.

58. Henry Kirk Miller, in *BS*, vol. 2, *Arkansas Narratives, Part 5*, 79.

59. Ike Thomas, in *BS*, vol. 4, *Georgia Narratives, Part 4*, 25–26.

60. "A Visit to Washington Jail," *Chicago Tribune*, December 5, 1861. The following year, on May 7, 1862, a woman named Mary Ann Hall, who could have been the person mentioned here, submitted a petition for compensation for four slaves, two of them women, under the April 1862 District of Columbia emancipation act. This woman owned an estate worth over eighteen thousand dollars in 1860. Mary Ann Hall, May 7, 1862, NARA-Petitions, and U.S. Bureau of the Census, *Eighth Census of the United States, 1860*.

61. Colonel William Birney to Assistant Adj. General, July 13, 1863, in Berlin et al., *The Destruction of Slavery*, 372–376. A woman named Ann Biscoe who lived in Washington, D.C., and operated a boardinghouse also filed a petition for compensation under the District of Columbia emancipation act on May 13, 1862. One of the slaves she claimed was a fifty-two-year-old woman named Mary Ayres. It is possible that this Ann Biscoe is the same woman Lewis Ayres was referring to. See Petition #430, filed May 26, 1862, NARA-Petitions. More details of Ayres's story appear in Lewis Ayres, U.S. Colored Troops Muster Roll Card, #53, Compiled Military Service Records of Volunteer Union Soldiers Who Served with the United States Colored Troops: Infantry Organizations, 36th through 40th Microfilm Serial: M1993, Microfilm Roll: 79, NARA.

62. Colonel William Birney to Lt. Col. Wm. H. Chesebrough, July 27, 1863, in Berlin et al., *The Black Military Experience*, 198–199.

63. Annie Davis to Mr. president, August 25, 1864, in Berlin et al., *The Destruction of Slavery*, 384.

64. Affidavit of a Kentucky Freedwoman, Affidavit of Fanny Nelson, April 12, 1867, in Berlin et al., *The Wartime Genesis of Free Labor: The Upper South*, 710–712.

65. George G. King, in *BS*, vol. 13, *Oklahoma Narratives*, 166.

66. Milton Hammond, in *BS*, vol. 4, *Georgia Narratives, Part 2*, 95.

67. "Deposition of Colonel George H. Hanks before the American Freedmen's Inquiry Commission," February 2, 1864, in Berlin et al., *The Wartime Genesis of Free Labor: The Lower South*, 517–521.

68. Entry for December 1, 1864, in Dulany, *In the Shadow of the Enemy*, 178–183.

69. Tennessee Brewer to the Governor of Tennessee, Urbain Ozanne to his Excellency William G. Brownlow, April 10, 1865, in Berlin et al., *The Wartime Genesis of Free Labor: The Upper South*, 462–463.

70. Caroline Hunter, in Perdue et al., *Weevils in the Wheat*, 149; Hannah Crasson, in *BS*, vol. 11, *North Carolina Narratives, Part 1*, 192.

71. *Euphrasia Tivis v. Benjamin Franklin Tivis*, File #434, Filed September 13, 1864, Reel 6, Records of the District Court, Jefferson County Courthouse, Beaumont, Texas, *RSP-2*.

72. One formerly enslaved woman, Rhody Holsell, believed that slave-owning women hated emancipation because it denied them the right to do as they wished to enslaved people. They "thought it was awful dat dey could not whip de slaves any longer," Rhody surmised. See Aunt Rhody Holsell, in *BS*, vol. 10, *Missouri Narratives*, 192.
73. Henry Kirk Miller, in *BS*, vol. 2, *Arkansas Narratives, Part 5*, 79.
74. O'Donovan, *Becoming Free in the Cotton South*, 113.
75. For the prices of cotton in 1860 and 1865, see Watkins, *Production and Price of Cotton for One Hundred Years*, 10–11, and Dattel, *Cotton and Race in the Making of America*, 203.
76. See Downs, "The Other Side of Freedom," 78–103.
77. John Seage to Brig Genl Fisk, October 4, 1865, in Hahn et al., *Land and Labor, 1865*, 641.
78. James M. Arvent to Brig. Gen. C. B. Fisk, July 27, 1865, ibid., 623–624.
79. Interview with formerly enslaved woman, in *Unwritten History of Slavery*, 139.
80. Sarah H. Maxwell to Genl Wilson, May 21, 1865, in Hahn et al., *Land and Labor*, 86; entry for May 15, 1865, in Heyward, *A Confederate Lady Comes of Age*, 76.
81. Ripley, *From Flag to Flag*.
82. See entry for April 10, 1865, in Judith White Brockenbrough McGuire, "Diary of a Southern Refugee, During the War," 351–353, and entry for April 11, 1865, in Emma Mordecai, "Diary of Emma Mordecai, April, 1865," both in Marcus, *Memoirs of American Jews, 1775–1865*, vol. 3, p. 338.
83. Entry for April 13, 1865, in Buck, *Shadows on My Heart*, 319. For how slave owners adapted in postwar Virginia, see Morseman, *The Big House After Slavery*, 158–192.
84. Entry for May 8, 1865, in Thomas, *The Secret Eye*, 264.
85. "N." made this comment in a letter to Fanny James, who was charged with treason for smuggling supplies to Confederate soldiers. See "Charged with Treason," *Sun*, May 12, 1863, 1.
86. Felton, *Country Life in Georgia in the Days of My Youth*, 92.

8. "A MOST UNPRECEDENTED ROBBERY"

1. Eva Jones to Mary Jones, June 13, 1865, in Myers, *Children of Pride*, 1273–1274.
2. Entries for Monday, May 8, 1865, and Monday, June 12, 1865, in Thomas, *The Secret Eye*, 265, 275–276.
3. Entry for Sunday, October 8, 1865, ibid., 276.
4. Ibid., 276–277.
5. Congress of the Confederate States of America, "An Act to Increase the Military Force of the Confederate States," in U.S. War Department, *The War of the Rebellion*, series 4, vol. 3, pp. 1161–1162.
6. Tiney Shaw, in *BS*, vol. 11, *North Carolina Narratives, Part 2*, 266–267.
7. J. W. Terrill, in *BS*, vol. 16, *Texas Narratives, Part 4*, 82; Tom Haynes, in *BS*, vol. 2, *Arkansas Narratives, Part 3*, 227.
8. Emma Hurley, in *BS*, vol. 4, *Georgia Narratives, Part 2*, 278.
9. Betty Jones, in Perdue et al., *Weevils in the Wheat*, 180.

10. Entry for April 13, 1865, in Buck, *Shadows on My Heart*, 319.
11. Annie Wallace, in Perdue et al., *Weevils in the Wheat*, 294.
12. Interview with an unidentified formerly enslaved woman, *Unwritten History of Slavery*, 113; Ella Wilson, in *BS*, vol. 2, *Arkansas Narratives, Part 7*, 203.
13. Slave-owning men engaged in similar self-recriminations. See Heather Andrea Williams, *Help Me to Find My People*, 140–141.
14. Entry for November 1, 1868, in Thomas, *The Secret Eye*, 293–296.
15. Interview with Liza Jones (Cookie), in *BS*, vol. 2, *Arkansas Narratives, Part 4*, 156.
16. Entries for March 1, 1865, and May 24, 1865, in Elmore, *A Heritage of Woe*, 106–107, 121; Kay Wright Lewis, *A Curse Upon the Nation*.
17. Lt. Col. H. B. Sprague to Brig General Davis Tillson, January 10, 1866, in Hahn et al., *Land and Labor, 1865*, 905.
18. Hahn et al., *Land and Labor, 1865*, 5, 16. For a more extensive discussion of this process, see O'Donovan, *Becoming Free in the Cotton South*.
19. U.S. Congress, "An Act to Establish a Bureau for the Relief of Freedmen and Refugees," in Sanger, *The Statutes at Large, Treaties, and Proclamations of the United States of America from December 1863, to December 1865*, 507–509.
20. Ben Lawson, in *BS*, vol. 13, *Oklahoma Narratives*, 177.
21. Albert Todd, in *BS*, vol. 16, *Texas Narratives, Part 4*, 106–107.
22. Fannie Berry, in Perdue et al., *Weevils in the Wheat*, 36–37.
23. For an eloquent discussion of these efforts see Schwalm, *A Hard Fight for We*.
24. James Barber, in Rawick, *AS*, Supplement, Series 2, vol. 2, *Texas Narratives, Part 1*, 151.
25. Ibid.
26. Reid, *After the War*, 568. On Reid, see Michael P. Riccard, "Whitelaw Reid," American National Biography Online, http://www.anb.org/articles/05/05-00653.html (accessed February 2000).
27. For an example of such a law see "Mississippi Apprentice Law," *New-Orleans Times*, December 10, 1865, 14. Tera Hunter discusses the impact of Georgia's Apprentice Act of 1866, which placed freed children alleged to be orphans in the homes of southern whites until they reached the age of twenty-one. Through Hunter's research in the American Missionary Association's (AMA) papers, she demonstrates how "benevolent" organizations ignored, dismissed, and overlooked family members in order to avoid placing the children with their kin. The AMA also operated "orphan holding stations" where black orphans were held until apprenticed. See Hunter, *To 'Joy My Freedom*, 21–43.
28. Interview with Henry Walton, in Rawick, *AS*, Supplement, Series 1, vol. 10, *Mississippi Narratives, Part 5*, 2168–2169.
29. See, e.g., Heather Andrea Williams, *Help Me to Find My People*, Wilma King, *Stolen Childhood*, 314–360, Fields, *Slavery and Freedom on the Middle Ground*, 140, and Litwack, *Been in the Storm So Long*, esp. 229–247.
30. Mary Niall Mitchell discusses white northerners' and southerners' abuses of the apprenticeship laws at length in her *Raising Freedom's Child*. See also interview with Annie Huff, in *BS*, vol. 4, *Georgia Narratives, Part 2*, 236, "Mississippi Apprentice

Law," *New Orleans Times*, December 10, 1865, 14, Scott, "The Battle over the Child," and Catherine Jones, "Ties That Bind, Bonds That Break."

31. Thos. B. Davis to Hon. J. Lanox Bond, November 6, 1864, in Berlin et al., *The Wartime Genesis of Free Labor: The Lower South*, 512.

32. "Ninety Two Year Old Negro Tells of Early Life as Slave," in *BS*, vol. 14, *South Carolina Narratives, Part 2*, 179–180.

33. Burton, *Memories of Childhood's Slavery Days*, 8, 11–12.

34. Censer, *The Reconstruction of White Southern Womanhood*, 128. For a comprehensive discussion of the postwar adaptations to a free labor system see Glymph, "Freedpeople and Ex-Masters."

35. See Glymph, *Out of the House of Bondage*, 139.

36. See Hunter, *To 'Joy My Freedom*, 4–20.

37. Deposition of Silvy Granville, November 21, 1901, in Regosin and Shaffer, *Voices of Emancipation*, 44.

38. Jerry Moore, in *BS*, vol. 16, *Texas Narratives, Part 3*, 122; Mrs. Charles Douthit, in *BS*, vol. 10, *Missouri Narratives*, 107.

39. Entry for May 30, 1865, in Elmore, *A Heritage of Woe*, 122–123.

40. Entry for Monday, May 29, 1865, in Thomas, *The Secret Eye*, 274.

41. Entry for July or August 14, 1865, in Elmore, *A Heritage of Woe*, 126–127.

42. Adjt Genl L. Thomas to Major Genl O. O. Howard, July 19, 1865, in Hahn et al., *Land and Labor, 1865*, 373–374. As the number of enslaved people who sought protection behind the Union's Tennessee lines grew, Major General N. J. T. Dana appointed Colonel Samuel Thomas, then commander of the 64th U.S. Colored Infantry, as the provost marshal general of Freedmen. He was charged with the care and support of the freedmen who would be resident on the "whole peninsula known as Davis Bend, including the three islands known as 'Hurricane,' 'Palmyra,' and 'Big Black' in Tennessee." See Eaton, *Report of the General Superintendent of Freedmen*, 40–41.

43. Miss. Sally V. B. Tabb to Major General Howard, August 15, 1865, and W. H. Bergfels to Capt. C. B. Wilder, September 7, 1865, in Hahn et al., *Land and Labor, 1865*, 517–521. Sally was the eldest daughter remaining in the household of Dr. Henry Wylie Tabb, a prominent Virginia physician. In his will he bequeathed to Sally his "woman Isabel and all of her children [along with] all of the children of [his] woman Sue who ha[d] lately died." He left the bulk of his estate to his sons, yet by the close of the war, Sally had 101 of her father's former slaves in her charge. See U.S. Bureau of the Census, *Eighth Census of the United States*, 1860, and last will and testament of Henry W. Tabb, May 16, 1860, Gilder Lehrman Collection, 1493–1859, GLIAH, Middlesex County, Virginia, documents, GLC03434.22.

44. *Sealy Banks v. Mrs Estes*, August 20, 1865, in Hahn et al., *Land and Labor, 1865*, 524.

45. *Daniel Baker, Frank Johnson, Lewis Wright, and Timothy Terryl v. Miss Mary Cowherd*, August 28, 1865, ibid., 525. At the 1850 U.S. Federal Census Slave Schedule, Mary S. Cowherd owned thirty-six slaves ranging in age from one year to seventy-five years. U.S. Bureau of the Census, *Seventh Census of the United States*, 1850.

46. *Alfred Goffney v. Widow Strange*, August 27, 1865, in Hahn et al., *Land and Labor, 1865*, 525. See also *Lucy Ann Johnson and Patsy Gordon v. Widow Ham*, August 29, 1865, ibid.

47. Interview with John Smith, in *BS*, vol. 11, *North Carolina Narratives, Part 2*, 278.

48. See Glymph, *Out of the House of Bondage*, 167–203, Schwalm, *A Hard Fight for We*, 187–233, and Hunter, *To 'Joy My Freedom*, 27–43.

49. W. E. Towne to Brvt. Major General Saxton, August 17, 1865, in Hahn et al., *Land and Labor, 1865*, 159.

50. Ibid.

51. Thomas Dixon dwelt on this idea in his novels *The Leopard's Spots* and *The Clansman*.

52. For discussions of Reconstruction-era racial violence see Kidada E. Williams, *They Left Great Marks on Me*, 17–54, Rosen, *Terror in the Heart of Freedom*, and Blight, *Race and Reunion*, 110.

53. Lillian Clarke, in Perdue et al., *Weevils in the Wheat*, 73.

54. Quoted in Waterbury, *Seven Years Among the Freedmen*, 28. Calculation from Samuel H. Williamson, "Seven Ways to Compute the Relative Value of a U.S. Dollar Amount, 1774 to Present," Measuring Worth, www.measuringworth.com/uscompare/ (accessed July 13, 2018).

55. U.S. Bureau of the Census, *Eighth Census of the United States, 1860* and *Ninth Census of the United States, 1870*.

56. See Kearney, *A Slaveholder's Daughter*, 23.

57. "President Johnson's Amnesty Proclamation. Restoration to Rights of Property Except in Slaves. An Oath of Loyalty as a Condition Precedent. Legality of Confiscation Proceedings Recognized. Exception of Certain Offenders from This Amnesty. By These Special Applications for Pardon May Be Made. Reorganization in North Carolina. Appointment of a Provisional Governor. A State Convention to Be Chosen by Loyal Citizens. The Machinery of the Federal Government to Be Put in Operation. AMNESTY PROCLAMATION," *New York Times*, May 30, 1865, available at http://www.nytimes.com/1865/05/30/news/president-johnson-s-amnesty-proclamation-restoration-rights-property-except.html.

58. Entry for July 28, 1865, in Edmondston, *Journal of a Secesh Lady*, 716.

59. NARA-Amnesty Papers. Bradley R. Clampitt examines a sample of women's applications for pardon and amnesty, and he finds that the overwhelming majority of women made their applications to regain their property rights. He does not discuss the fact that coverture should have precluded these applications, nor does he consider the profound implications these losses had for married, single, and widowed women. See Clampitt, "'Not Intended to Dispossess Females.'" See also McCurry, *Confederate Reckoning*, 214–215.

60. Louisa M. Harris, Application for Pardon and Amnesty, Huntsville, Alabama, Submitted October 4, 1865, Carrie Lomax, Application for Pardon and Amnesty, Submitted May 29, 1865, Mrs. Eliza Grey, Dallas County, Alabama, Application for Pardon and Amnesty, Submitted August 4, 1865, Sworn and subscribed August 21, 1865, Mary A. Hood, Meriwether County, Georgia, Submitted August 1865, all in NARA-Amnesty Papers.

61. Sarah J. Firth, Submitted July 13, 1865, Barnwell District, South Carolina, and Irene Smith, Washington County, Mississippi, Submitted December 15, 1865, NARA-Amnesty Papers.

62. Catharine Fulton to His Excellency, Governor Jonathan Worth, Wilmington, NC, Submitted January 16, 1866, Catharine Fulton to General O. H. Howard, Wilmington, NC, Submitted March 7, 1866, and John A. Winslow to Andrew Johnson, Roxbury, Submitted April 7, 1866, Catharine Fulton, Submitted November 16, 1865, Julie P. Henderson, Submitted August 16, 1865, Natchez, Mississippi, Annie L. Davis, Submitted September 11, 1865, Richmond, Virginia, NARA-Amnesty Papers.

63. Mrs. Caroline Alston, Application for Pardon and Amnesty, Choctaw County, Alabama, Submitted August 4, 1865, and Mrs. Mary L. Carter, Application for Pardon and Amnesty, Mobile County, Alabama, October 30, 1865, both in NARA-Amnesty Papers.

64. Mrs. Eliza Grey, Dallas County, Alabama, Application for Pardon and Amnesty, Submitted August 4, 1865, Sworn and subscribed August 21, 1865, NARA-Amnesty Papers.

EPILOGUE

1. See Heather Andrea Williams, *Help Me to Find My People*, 139–168, Michael P. Johnson, "Looking for Lost Kin," and Litwack, *Been in the Storm So Long*, 229–247.

2. Bryan, *A Grandmother's Recollection of Dixie*, 3. This kind of mythologizing was not the work of older white southern women alone. According to the historian Victoria E. Ott, young women also recognized their "responsibility in promoting this return to white supremacy, and their postwar reminiscences became the vehicle for articulating their vision of the New South's racial order." Ott, *Confederate Daughters*, 130.

3. Diane N. Captiani explores how this logic operated in white women's writing at length in *Truthful Pictures*.

4. Burwell, *A Girl's Life in Virginia Before the War*, 44.

5. De Saussure, *Old Plantation Days*, 19.

6. Ripley, *Social Life in Old New Orleans*, 192. See also Burwell, *A Girl's Life in Virginia Before the War*, 44–46.

7. De Saussure, *Old Plantation Days*, 80. An example of Louis's advertisements as a slave broker can be found in the *Charleston Courier*, January 4, 1848. Nancy mentions her visit to Louis's home in *Old Plantation Days*, 65.

8. Bryan, *A Grandmother's Recollection of Dixie*, 23.

9. Burwell, *A Girl's Life in Virginia Before the War*, 28–29.

10. Advertisement, *Southwestern Christian Advocate*, December 25, 1879.

11. Advertisements, *Southwestern Christian Advocate*, November 20, 1879, and June 10, 1880.

12. Excerpt from the Deposition of Benjamin B. Manson, July 1909, Civil War Pension File of John White, 14th USCI, RG 15, in Regosin and Shaffer, *Voices of Emancipation*, 21. See also Regosin, *Freedom's Promise*, Shaffer, *After the Glory*, and Kaye, *Joining Places*.

13. Excerpt from the Deposition of Milley Hale, June 28, 1898, Excerpt from the Deposition of Sarah Clotfelter, July 1, 1898, Excerpt from the Deposition of Ollie [Olive] Queener, July 1, 1898, and Excerpt from the Deposition of J[ames]. C. Hunter,

July 16, 1898, Civil War Pension File of Joseph Hale, 1st USCHA, RG 15, in Regosin and Shaffer, *Voices of Emancipation*, 127–129. Tabitha Marcum Hunter, James's mother, owned three enslaved females, aged forty-one, twelve, and ten, in 1850. See Entry for Sampson D. Queener and Tabitha Marcum Hunter, U.S. Bureau of the Census, *Seventh Census of the United States, 1850*, Campbell, Tennessee, Schedule 2 (slave inhabitants).

14. For an example of an enslaved person who witnessed white women at a slave auction, see B. E. Rogers, in Rawick, *AS*, Supplement, Series 1, vol. 11, *North Carolina and South Carolina Narratives*, 55.

15. Carlos, Maguire, and Neal, "Financial Acumen, Women Speculators, and the Royal African Company During the South Sea Bubble"; Biobaku, "Madame Tinubu"; Pinckard, *Notes on the West Indies*, vol. 2, pp. 327–328. Pinckard even remarked upon the children who "were brought [to the auction] to point the lucky finger, and the boy or girl, thus chosen, was bought by papa at the request of superstitious mama, to give to young massa or missy!" (328). Richard A. Wyvill, *Memoirs of an Old Army Officer*, 24.

BIBLIOGRAPHY

ARCHIVAL AND MICROFILM COLLECTIONS

Listed here are the collections most often cited. Other archival collections appear in the notes as appropriate.

BGFP-WLCL   Burwell-Guy Family Papers, 1820–1873, William L. Clements Library, University of Michigan, Ann Arbor

BS   *Born in Slavery: Slave Narratives from the Federal Writers' Project, 1936–1938.* Digital Collection, Library of Congress, Manuscript Division, http://memory.loc.gov/ammem/snhtml/snhome.html

GLIAH   The Gilder Lehrman Institute of American History, New York The Gilder Lehrman Collection, 1493–1859

HALSC-UNO   Historical Archives of the Louisiana Supreme Court, Earl K. Long Library, University of New Orleans

NARA   National Archives and Records Administration, Washington, D.C. Amnesty Papers: Case Files of Applications From Former Confederates for Presidential Pardons, 1865–1867. NARA Microfilm Publication M1003, 73 rolls. Records of the Adjutant General's Office, 1780's–1917, Record Group 94.
Records of the United States Circuit Court, Chancery Dockets and Rule Case Files, Record Group 21
Petitions: "Petitions Filed Under the Act of July 12, 1862," Records of the Board of Commissioners for the Emancipation of Slaves in the District of Columbia, 1862–1863. NARA Microfilm Publication M520, 6 rolls. Records of the United States General Accounting Office, Record Group 217.

NCDAH   North Carolina Department of Archives and History, Raleigh General Assembly, Session Records
Records of the County Court
Records of the North Carolina Supreme Court

NONA New Orleans Notarial Archives, New Orleans, Louisiana
NOPL New Orleans Public Library
  Louisiana Research Collection
  Records of the Parish Court, Emancipation Petitions, 1813–1843
RASP *Records of Antebellum Southern Plantations from the Revolution*
  Through the Civil War, ed. Kenneth M. Stampp, microfilm collection
RSP-2 *Race and Slavery Petitions Project: Race, Slavery, and Free Blacks*
  Series 2: Petitions to Southern County Courts, 1777–1867, ed. Loren
  Schweninger, microfilm collection
SCDAH South Carolina Department of Archives and History, Columbia
  Records of the Equity Court
  Records of the General Assembly
  Resolutions of the General Assembly
TCP-EGSL Tucker-Coleman Papers, Special Collections Research Center, Earl
  Gregg Swem Library, College of William and Mary, Williamsburg,
  Virginia
TSLA Tennessee State Library and Archives, Nashville
  Records of the Chancery Court

NEWSPAPERS

Augusta Chronicle
Augusta Chronicle and Georgia Advertiser
Charleston Courier
Charleston Mercury
Chicago Tribune
City Gazette and Commercial Daily Advertiser (Charleston, S.C.; CGCDA)
Daily Crescent (New Orleans, La.)
Daily Dispatch (Richmond, Va.)
Daily Morning News (Savannah, Ga.)
Daily National Intelligencer (Washington, D.C.)
Daily Picayune (New Orleans, La.)
Daily South Carolinian
DeBow's Review
Emancipator
Enquirer
Farmer and Planter
Farmers' Register
Federal Gazette & Baltimore Daily Advertiser
Federal Intelligencer, and Baltimore Daily Gazette
Frederick Douglass' Paper
Liberator
Louisiana Advertiser
Louisville Public Advertiser

Lowell Daily Citizen and News (Lowell, Mass.)
Macon Daily Telegraph
Memphis Daily Appeal
Mississippi Free Trader and Natchez Gazette
National Era
Newark Advocate (Ohio)
New Orleans Bee
New-Orleans Commercial Bulletin
New Orleans Daily Creole
New Orleans Daily Crescent
New-Orleans Times
New York Herald
New York Times
North American and Daily Advertiser
North Star (Rochester, N.Y.)
Orleans Gazette, and Commercial Advertiser
Pennsylvania Freeman
Pennsylvania Inquirer and Daily Courier
Pensacola Gazette
Ripley Advertiser
Rosebud; or, Youth's Gazette
South-Carolina State Gazette, and Timothy's Daily Advertiser
Southern Agriculturalist
Southern Cultivator
Southern Patriot
Southern Planter
Southern Rose
South-Western
Southwestern Christian Advocate
Sun (Baltimore, Md.)
Times-Picayune (New Orleans, La.)
Vermont Chronicle
Weekly Herald (New York, N.Y.)

PUBLISHED PRIMARY AND SECONDARY SOURCES

Aikin, John G. *Digest of the Laws of the State of Alabama: Containing All the Statutes of a Public and General Nature, in Force at the Close of the Session of the General Assembly, in January 1833.* Tuscaloosa, Ala.: Woodruff, 1836.

Alabama, Secretary of State. *U.S. Census Non-population Schedules, Alabama, 1850–1880.* Alabama Department of Archives and History, Montgomery, Alabama. Online database. Provo, Utah: Ancestry.com Operations, 2010.

Anderson, John Q., ed. *Brokenburn: The Journal of Kate Stone, 1861–1868.* Baton Rouge: Louisiana State University Press, 1955.

Anzilotti, Cara, *In the Affairs of the World: Women, Patriarchy, and Power in Colonial South Carolina*. Westport, Conn.: Greenwood, 2002.

Armstrong, Orland Kay. *Old Massa's People: The Old Slaves Tell Their Story*. Indianapolis: Bobbs-Merrill, 1931.

Bailey, David Thomas. "A Divided Prism: Two Sources of Black Testimony on Slavery." *Journal of Southern History* 46, no. 3 (1980): 381–404.

Baker, Van R., ed. *The Websters: Letters of an Army Family in Peace and War, 1836–1853*. Kent, Ohio: Kent State University Press, 2000.

Bancroft, Frederic. *Slave Trading in the Old South*. Columbia: University of South Carolina Press, 1996.

Baptist, Edward. "'Cuffy,' 'Fancy Maids,' and 'One-Eyed Men': Rape, Commodification, and the Domestic Slave Trade in the United States." *American Historical Review* 106, no. 5 (December 2001): 1619–1650.

———. *The Half Has Never Been Told: Slavery and the Making of American Capitalism*. New York: Basic, 2014.

———. "Toxic Debt, Liar Loans, and Securitized Human Beings: The Panic of 1837 and the Fate of Slavery." *Common-Place* 10, no. 3 (April 2010), available at http://www.common-place-archives.org/vol-10/no-03/baptist/.

Basch, Norma, "Invisible Women: The Legal Fiction of Marital Unity in Nineteenth-Century America." *Feminist Studies* 5, no. 2 (Summer 1979): 346–366.

Beckert, Sven. *Empire of Cotton: A Global History*. New York: Knopf, 2014.

———. "Slavery and Capitalism." *Chronicle Review*, December 12, 2014, available at http://www.chronicle.com/article/SlaveryCapitalism/150787/.o.

Bell, Richard. "'Thence to Patty Cannon's': Gender, Family, and the Reverse Underground Railroad." *Slavery and Abolition* 37, no. 1 (April 2016): 661–679.

Bercaw, Nancy. *Gendered Freedoms: Race, Rights and the Politics of Household in the Delta, 1861–1875*. Gainesville: University Press of Florida, 2003.

Berlin, Ira, Barbara Fields, Thavolia Glymph, Joseph P. Reidy, and Leslie Rowland, eds. *The Destruction of Slavery*. Series 1, vol. 1 of *Freedom: A Documentary History of Emancipation, 1861–1867*. London: Cambridge University Press, 1985.

Berlin, Ira, Barbara Fields, Thavolia Glymph, Joseph P. Reidy, and Leslie Rowland, eds. *The Wartime Genesis of Free Labor: The Lower South*. Series 1, vol. 3 of *Freedom: A Documentary History of Emancipation, 1861–1867*. New York: Cambridge University Press, 1990.

Berlin, Ira, Steven F. Miller, Joseph P. Reidy, and Leslie S. Rowland, eds. *The Wartime Genesis of Free Labor: The Upper South*. Series 1, vol. 2 of *Freedom: A Documentary History of Emancipation, 1861–1867*. Cambridge: Cambridge University Press, 1993.

Berlin, Ira, Joseph P. Reidy, and Leslie S. Rowland, eds. *The Black Military Experience*. Cambridge: Cambridge University Press, 1982.

Berry, Daina Ramey. "'In Pressing Need of Cash': Gender, Skill, and Family Persistence in the Domestic Slave Trade." *Journal of African American History* 92, no. 1 (Winter 2007): 22–36.

———. *The Price for Their Pound of Flesh: The Value of the Enslaved, from Womb to Grave, in the Building of a Nation*. New York: Beacon, 2017.

———. "'We'm Fus' Rate Bargain': Value, Labor, and Price in a Georgia Slave Community." In *The Chattel Principle: Internal Slave Trades in the Americas, 1808–1888*, ed. Walter Johnson, 55–71. New Haven: Yale University Press, 2004.

Billingsley, Carolyn Earle. *Communities of Kinship: Antebellum Families and the Settlement of the Cotton Frontier.* Athens: University of Georgia Press, 2004.

Biobaku, S. O. "Madame Tinubu." In *Eminent Nigerians of the Nineteenth Century: A Series of Studies Originally Broadcast by the Nigerian Broadcasting Corporation*, ed. Nigerian Broadcasting Corporation, 33–41. Cambridge: Cambridge University Press, 1960.

Bishop, George. *Every Woman Her Own Lawyer: A Private Guide in All Matters of Law, of Essential Interest to Women, and by the Aid of Which Every Female May, in Whatever Situation, Understand Her Legal Course and Redress, and Be Her Own Legal Adviser; Containing the Laws of Different States Relative to Marriage and Divorce, Property in Marriage, Guardians and Wards, Rights in Property of a Wife, Rights of Widows, Arrests of Females for Debt, Alimony, Bigamy, Voluntary Separations, Discarded Wives, Suits by and Against Married Women, Breach of Promise, Deserted Wives, Clandestine Marriages, Adultery, Dower, Illegitimate Children, Step-fathers and Step-children, Seduction, Slander, Minors, Medical Maltreatment, Just Causes for Leaving a Husband, a Wife's Support, Property in Trust, Transfers of Property, Deeds of Gift, Annuities, Articles of Separation, False Pretenses in Courtship, &c., &c., &c.* New York: Dick and Fitzgerald, 1858.

Bishop, Joel Prentiss. *Commentaries on the Law of Married Women: Under the Statutes of the Several States, and at Common Law and in Equity.* Vol. 1. Boston: Little, Brown, 1878.

Blackstone, William. *Commentaries on the Laws of England.* 4 vols. Oxford: Clarendon Press, 1765–1769.

Blassingame, John W. "Using the Testimony of Ex-Slaves: Approaches and Problems." *Journal of Southern History* 41, no. 4 (1975): 473–492.

Blassingame, John W., ed. *Slave Testimony: Two Centuries of Letters, Speeches, Interviews, and Autobiographies.* Baton Rouge: Louisiana State University Press, 1977.

Blight, David. *Race and Reunion: The Civil War in American Memory.* Cambridge: Harvard University Press, 2001.

Block, Sharon. *Rape and Sexual Power in Early America.* Chapel Hill: University of North Carolina Press, 2006.

Boydston, Jeanne. *Home and Work: Housework, Wages and the Ideology of Labor in the Early Republic.* New York: Oxford University Press, 1994.

———. "The Woman Who Wasn't There: Women's Market Labor and the Transition to Capitalism in the United Sates." *Journal of the Early Republic* 16, no. 2 (Summer 1996): 183–206.

Brazy, Martha Jane. *An American Planter: Stephen Duncan of Antebellum Natchez and New York.* Baton Rouge: Louisiana State University Press, 2006.

Bremer, Fredrika. *Homes of the New World: Impressions of America.* 2 vols. New York: Harper and Brothers, 1858.

Brewer, Holly. *By Birth or Consent: Children, Law, and the Anglo-American Revolution in Authority.* Chapel Hill: University of North Carolina Press, 2012.

Brown, John. *Slave Life in Georgia: A Narrative of the Life, Sufferings, and Escape of John Brown, a Fugitive Slave, Now in England.* Ed. Louis Alexis Chamerovzow. London: W. M. Watts, 1855.

Brown, William Wells. *The Narrative of William W. Brown, a Fugitive Slave, Written by Himself.* Boston: Anti-Slavery Office, 1847.

Bryan, Mary Norcott. *A Grandmother's Recollection of Dixie.* New Bern: Owen G. Dunn, n.d.

Buck, Lucy Rebecca. *Shadows on My Heart: The Civil War Diary of Lucy Rebecca Buck of Virginia.* Ed. Elizabeth R. Baer. Athens: University of Georgia Press, 1997.

Burke, Diane Mutti. *On Slavery's Border: Missouri's Small Slaveholding Households, 1815–1865.* Athens: University of Georgia Press, 2010.

Burton, Annie L. *Memories of Childhood's Slavery Days.* Boston: Ross Publishing, 1909.

Burwell, Letitia M. *A Girl's Life in Virginia Before the War.* New York: Frederick A. Stokes, 1895.

Bynum, Victoria. *Unruly Women: The Politics of Social and Sexual Control in the Old South.* Chapel Hill: University of North Carolina Press, 1992.

Calvert, Rosalie. *Mistress of Riversdale: The Plantation Letters of Rosalie Stier Calvert, 1795–1821.* Ed. Margaret Law Callcott. Baltimore: Johns Hopkins University Press, 1991.

Captiani, Diane N. *Truthful Pictures: Slavery Ordained by God in the Domestic, Sentimental Novel of the Nineteenth-Century South.* Lanham, Md.: Lexington, 2009.

Carlos, Ann M., Karen Maguire, and Larry Neal. "Financial Acumen, Women Speculators, and the Royal African Company During the South Sea Bubble." *Accounting, Business & Financial History* 16, no. 2 (2006): 219–243.

Carter, Christine Jacobson. *Southern Single Blessedness: Unmarried Women in the Urban South, 1800–1865.* Urbana: University of Illinois Press, 2006.

Cashin, Joan E. *Our Common Affairs: Texts from Women in the Old South.* Baltimore: Johns Hopkins University Press, 1996.

Catterall, Helen Tunnicliff, ed. *Judicial Cases Concerning American Slavery and the Negro.* Vol. 3: *Cases from the Courts of Georgia, Florida, Alabama, Mississippi, and Louisiana.* Washington, D.C.: Carnegie Institute of Washington, 1932; New York: Octagon, 1968.

Censer, Jane Turner. *North Carolina Planters and Their Children, 1800–1860.* Baton Rouge: Louisiana State University Press, 1984.

Cheng, Ann Anlin. *Melancholy of Race: Psychoanalysis, Assimilation, and Hidden Grief.* Oxford: Oxford University Press, 2000.

Chesnut, Mary Boykin. *A Diary from Dixie, as Written by Mary Boykin Chesnut, Wife of James Chesnut, Jr., United States Senator from South Carolina, 1859–1861, and Afterward an Aide to Jefferson Davis and a Brigadier-General in the Confederate Army.* Ed. Isabella D. Martin and Myrta Lockett Avary. New York: Appleton, 1905. Available at http://doc south.unc.edu/southlit/chesnut/maryches.html.

———. *Mary Chesnut's Civil War.* Ed. C. Vann Woodward. New Haven: Yale University Press, 1981.

Clampitt, Bradley R. "'Not Intended to Dispossess Females': Southern Women and Civil War Amnesty." *Civil War History* 56, no. 4 (December 2010): 325–349.

Clark, Emily. *Masterless Mistresses: The New Orleans Ursulines and the Development of a New World Society, 1727–1834*. Chapel Hill: University of North Carolina Press, 2007.

Clark, Laurel A. "The Rights of a Florida Wife: Slavery, U.S. Expansion, and Married Women's Property Law." *Journal of Women's History* 22, no. 4 (Winter 2010): 39–63.

Clayton, Ronnie W. *Mother Wit: The Ex-Slave Narratives of the Louisiana Writers' Project*. New York: Peter Lang, 1990.

Clinton, Catherine. *The Plantation Mistress: Woman's World in the Old South*. New York: Pantheon, 1982.

Clinton, Catherine, ed. *Southern Families at War: Loyalty and Conflict in the Civil War South*. Oxford: Oxford University Press, 2000.

Cohen, H. & A. *Cohen's New Orleans and Lafayette City Directory, including Carrollton, Freeport, Algiers, Gretna and M'Donogh for 1850*. New Orleans: Printed at the Job Office of the Delta, 112 Poydras Street, 1849.

Confederate States of America. *A Digest of the Military and Naval Laws of the Confederate States, from the Commencement of the Provisional Congress to the End of the First Congress Under the Permanent Constitution*. Columbia, S.C.: Evans and Cogswell, 1864.

——. Congress. House of Representatives. *A Bill to Be Entitled "An Act to Provide Payment for Slaves Impressed Under State Laws, And Lost In the Public Service."* Richmond, Va.: C.S.A., 1864.

——. Congress. House of Representatives. Committee on Claims. *Report of Committee in Claims in the Case of Mary Clark*. Richmond, Va.: s.n., 1863.

——. Engineer Department. *Estimate of Five Hundred Thousand Dollars Required to Meet the Just Claims Presented: Or to Be Presented Hereafter, for the Loss of Slaves Who Have Been Impressed In the State of Virginia*. Richmond, Va.: C.S.A., 1864.

——. *Act to Perpetuate Testimony in Cases of Slaves Abducted or Harbored by the Enemy and of Other Property Seized, Wasted, or Destroyed by Them*. No. 270. Approved August 30, 1861. Richmond, Va.? : s.n., 1861?.

Convention of the People of South Carolina. *Declaration of the Immediate Causes Which Induce and Justify the Secession of South Carolina from the Federal Union*. Charleston: Printers to the Convention, 1860.

Cott, Nancy. "Marriage and Women's Citizenship in the United States, 1830–1934." *American Historical Review* 103, no. 5 (December 1998): 1440–1474.

Craven, Avery O. *Rachel of Old Louisiana*. Baton Rouge: Louisiana State University Press, 1975.

Crumley, Carole. "Heterarchy and the Analysis of Complex Societies." *Archeological Papers of the American Anthropological Association* 6, no. 1 (January 1999): 1–5.

Damiano, Sara T. "Agents at Home: Wives, Lawyers, and Financial Competence in Eighteenth-Century New England Port Cities." *Early American Studies* (Fall 2015): 808–835.

Dattel, Gene. *Cotton and Race in the Making of America: The Human Costs of Economic Power*. Lanham, Md.: Ivan R. Dee, 2009.

Dayton, Cornelia Hughes. *Women Before the Bar: Gender, Law, and Society in Connecticut, 1639–1789*. Chapel Hill: University of North Carolina Press, 1995.

DeBow, J. D. B. *Statistical View of the United States, Embracing Its Territory, Population—White, Free Colored, and Slave—Moral and Social Condition, Industry, Property, and Revenue: The Detailed Statistics of Cities, Towns, and Counties; Being a Compendium of the Seventh Census.* Washington, D.C.: Beverley Tucker, Senate Printer, 1854.

Delaware General Assembly. *Laws of the State of Delaware, to the Year of Our Lord, One Thousand Eight Hundred and Twenty Nine, Inclusive.* Wilmington: R. Porter and Son, 1829.

Delfino, Susanna, and Michele Gillespie, eds. *Neither Lady nor Slave: Working Women of the Old South.* Chapel Hill: University of North Carolina Press, 2002.

De Saussure, Nancy Bostick. *Old Plantation Days: Being Recollections of Southern Life Before the Civil War.* New York: Duffield, 1909.

Deyle, Steven. *Carry Me Back: The Domestic Slave Trade in American Life.* Oxford: Oxford University Press, 2005.

District of Columbia. *An Act for the Release of Certain Persons Held to Service or Labor in the District of Columbia.* Available at http://www.archives.gov/exhibits/featured_documents/dc_emancipation_act/transcription.html.

———. *Code of Laws for the District of Columbia: Prepared Under the Authority of the Act of Congress of the 29th of April 1816.* Washington, D.C.: David and Force, 1819.

———. *Supplemental Act of July 12, 1862.* Available at https://www.archives.gov/exhibits/featured-documents/dc-emancipation-act/supplemental-act.html.

Dixon, Thomas. *The Clansman: An Historical Romance of the Ku Klux Klan.* New York: Doubleday, Page, 1905.

———. *The Leopard's Spots: A Romance of the White Man's Burden, 1865–1900.* New York: Doubleday, Page, 1902.

Dougan, Michael B. "The Arkansas Married Women's Property Law." *Arkansas Historical Quarterly* 46, no. 1 (Spring 1987): 3–26.

Downs, Jim. "The Other Side of Freedom: Destitution, Disease, and Dependency Among Freedwomen and Their Children During and After the Civil War." In *Battle Scars: Gender and Sexuality in the American Civil War,* ed. Catherine Clinton and Nina Silber, 78–103. New York: Oxford University Press, 2006.

———. *Sick from Freedom: African-American Illness and Suffering During the Civil War and Reconstruction.* New York: Oxford University Press, 2012.

Doyle, Nora. "'The Highest Pleasure of Which Woman's Nature Is Capable': Breast-Feeding and the Sentimental Maternal Ideal in America, 1750–1860." *Journal of American History* 97, no. 4 (March 2011): 958–973.

Dulany, Ida Powell. *In the Shadow of the Enemy: The Civil War Journal of Ida Powell Dulany.* Ed. Mary L. Mackall, Stevan F. Meserve, and Anne Mackall Sasscer. Knoxville: University of Tennessee Press, 2009.

Dunaway, Wilma A. *The African-American Family in Slavery and Emancipation.* New York: Cambridge University Press, 2003.

Eaton, John, Jr. *Report of the General Superintendent of Freedmen, Department of the Tennessee and State of Arkansas for 1864.* Memphis: Published by Permission, 1865.

Edmondston, Catherine Ann Devereux. *Journal of a Secesh Lady: The Diary of Catherine Ann Devereux Edmondston, 1860–1866.* Ed. Beth G. Crabtree and James W. Patton. Raleigh: North Carolina Division of Archives and History, 1979.

Edwards, Laura F. *The People and Their Peace: Legal Culture and the Transformation of Inequality in the Post-Revolutionary South*. Chapel Hill: University of North Carolina Press, 2009.

———. *Scarlett Doesn't Live Here Anymore: Southern Women in the Civil War Era*. Urbana: University of Illinois Press, 2000.

Elliott, Charles. *The Bible and Slavery: In Which the Abrahamic and Mosaic Discipline Is Considered in Connection with the Most Ancient Forms of Slavery and the Pauline Code on Slavery as Related to Roman Slavery and the Discipline of the Apostolic Churches*. Cincinnati: Poe and Hitchcock, 1863.

Elmore, Grace Brown. *A Heritage of Woe: The Civil War Diary of Grace Brown Elmore, 1861–1868*. Ed. Marli Weiner. Athens: University of Georgia Press, 1997.

Engerman, Stanley L. and Robert W. Fogel. *New Orleans Slave Sale Sample, 1804–1862*. University of Rochester. ICPSR07423-v2. Ann Arbor, Mich.: Inter-university Consortium for Political and Social Research [producer and distributor], 2008-08-04. http://doi.org/10.3886/ICPSR07423.v2.

Erickson, Amy Louise. "Mistresses and Marriage; or, A Short History of the Mrs." *History Workshop Journal* 78 (Autumn 2014): 39–57.

Evans, Sarah. *Born for Liberty: A History of Women in America*. New York: Free Press, 1989.

Faust, Drew Gilpin. *Mothers of Invention: Women of the Slaveholding South in the American Civil War*. Chapel Hill: University of North Carolina Press, 1996.

———. "'Trying to Do a Man's Business': Slavery, Violence and Gender in the American Civil War." *Gender and History* 4, no. 2. (1992): 197–214.

Fede, Andrew T. *Homicide Justified: The Legality of Killing Slaves in the United States and the Atlantic World*. Athens: University of Georgia Press, 2017.

Feimster, Crystal N. "General Benjamin Butler and the Threat of Sexual Violence During the American Civil War." *Daedalus* 138, no. 2 (Spring 2009): 126–134.

Felton, Rebecca Latimer. *Country Life in Georgia in the Days of My Youth*. Atlanta: Index Printing, 1919.

Fields, Barbara Jeanne. *Slavery and Freedom on the Middle Ground: Maryland During the Nineteenth Century*. New Haven: Yale University Press, 1985.

Fildes, Valerie. *Breasts, Bottles, and Babies: A History of Infant Feeding*. Edinburgh: Edinburgh University Press, 1986.

———. *Wet Nursing: A History from Antiquity to the Present*. New York: Blackwell, 1988.

Finley, Alexandra. "Blood Money: Sex, Family, and Finance in the Antebellum Slave Trade." Ph.D. Diss. College of William and Mary, 2017.

Follett, Richard. "'Lives of Living Death': The Reproductive Lives of Slave Women in the Cane World of Louisiana." *Slavery and Abolition* 26, no. 2 (August 2005): 289–304.

Foster, Craig L. "Tarnished Angels: Prostitution in Storyville, New Orleans, 1900–1910." *Louisiana History* 31, no. 4 (Winter 1990): 387–397.

Foster, William Henry. *Gender, Mastery, and Slavery: From European to Atlantic Frontiers*. New York: Palgrave Macmillan, 2010.

Fought, Leigh. *Southern Womanhood and Slavery: A Biography of Louisa S. McCord, 1810–1879*. Columbia: University of Missouri Press, 2003.

Fox-Genovese, Elizabeth. *Within the Plantation Household: Black and White Women of the Old Plantation South.* Chapel Hill: University of North Carolina Press, 1988.

French, B. F. *Historical Collections of Louisiana: Embracing Translations of Many Rare and Valuable Documents Relating to the Natural, Civil, and Political History of That State.* New York: Appleton, 1851.

Glymph, Thavolia. "Freedpeople and Ex-Masters: Shaping a New Order in the Postbellum South, 1865–1868." In *Essays on the Postbellum Southern Economy,* ed. Thavolia Glymph and John J. Kushma, 48–72. College Station: Texas A&M University Press, 1985.

———. *Out of the House of Bondage: The Transformation of the Plantation Household.* New York: Cambridge University Press, 2008.

Golden, Janet Lynne. *A Social History of Wet Nursing in America: From Breast to Bottle.* Cambridge: Cambridge University Press, 1996.

Grandy, Moses. *Narrative of the Life of Moses Grandy: Late a Slave in the United States of America.* London: Gilpin, 1843.

Great Britain. Parliament. *House of Commons Sessional Papers of the Eighteenth Century.* Vol. 68. Ed. Sheila Lambert. Wilmington, Del.: Scholarly Resources, 1975.

Green, Sharony. "'Mr Ballard, I Am Compelled to Write Again': Beyond Bedrooms and Brothels, a Fancy Girl Speaks." *Black Women, Gender & Families* 5, no. 1 (Spring 2011): 17–40.

Gross, Ariela. *Double Character: Slavery and Mastery in the Antebellum Southern Courtroom.* Athens: University of Georgia Press, 2006.

Gross, Jennifer Lynn. "'Good Angels': Confederate Widowhood in Virginia." In *Southern Families at War: Loyalty and Conflict in the Civil War South,* ed. Catherine Clinton, 133–148. Oxford: Oxford University Press, 2000.

Grossberg, Michael. *Governing the Hearth: Law and the Family in Nineteenth-Century America.* Chapel Hill: University of North Carolina Press, 1985.

Grosvenor, Horace C. *The Child's Book on Slavery; or, Slavery Made Plain.* Cincinnati: American Reform Tract and Book Society, 1857.

Gudmestad, Robert. *The Troublesome Commerce: The Transformation of the Interstate Slave Trade.* Baton Rouge: Louisiana State University Press, 2003.

Gutman, Herbert. *The Black Family in Slavery and Freedom, 1750–1925.* New York: Vintage, 1977.

Hahn, Steven. *A Nation Under Our Feet: Black Political Struggle in the Rural South from Slavery to the Great Migration.* Cambridge, Mass.: Belknap, 2003.

Hahn, Steven, Steven F. Miller, Susan E. O'Donovan, John C. Rodrigue, and Leslie S. Rowland, eds. *Land and Labor, 1865.* Series 3, vol. 1 of *Freedom: A Documentary History of Emancipation, 1861–1867.* Chapel Hill: University of North Carolina Press, 2008.

Hanger, Kimberly. *Bounded Lives, Bounded Places: Free Black Society in Colonial New Orleans, 1769–1803.* Durham, N.C.: Duke University Press, 1997.

Hartigan-O'Connor, Ellen. "Gender's Value in the History of Capitalism." *Journal of the Early Republic* 36, no. 4 (Winter 2016): 613–635.

———. "She Said She Did Not Know Money: Urban Women and Atlantic Markets in the Revolutionary Era." *Early American Studies* 4, no. 2 (Fall 2006): 322–352.

———. *The Ties That Buy: Women and Commerce in Revolutionary America.* Philadelphia: University of Pennsylvania Press, 2011.

Hartman, Saidiya V. *Scenes of Subjection: Terror, Slavery and Self-Making in Nineteenth-Century America.* New York: Oxford University Press, 1997.

Hartog, Hendrik. *Man and Wife in America: A History.* Cambridge: Harvard University Press, 2000.

Hening, William Waller. *Statutes at Large; Being a Collection of All the Laws of Virginia.* Vol. 2. New York: R. & W. & G. Bartow, 1823.

Heyward, Pauline DeCaradeuc. *A Confederate Lady Comes of Age: The Journal of Pauline DeCaradeuc Heyward, 1863–1888.* Ed. Mary D. Robertson. Columbia: University of South Carolina Press, 1992.

Holton, Woody. "Equality as Unintended Consequence: The Contracts Clause and the Married Women's Property Acts." *Journal of Southern History* 81, no. 2 (May 2015): 313–340.

Honoré, A. M. "Ownership." In *Oxford Essays in Jurisprudence,* ed. Anthony G. Guest, 107–147. Oxford: Oxford University Press, 1961.

Hunter, Tera. *To 'Joy My Freedom: Southern Black Women's Lives and Labors After the Civil War.* Cambridge: Harvard University Press, 1998.

Hurmence, Belinda, ed. *Before Freedom, When I Just Can Remember: Twenty-Seven Oral Histories of South Carolina Slaves.* Winston-Salem, N.C.: John F. Blair, 1989.

Hurwicz, Margo-Lea, et al. "Salient Life Events in Three-Generational Families." *Journal of Gerontology* 47 (1992): 11–13.

Hutchinson, A. *Code of Mississippi: Being an Analytical Compilation of the Public and General Statutes of the Territory and State, with Tabular References to the Local and Private Acts, from 1798 to 1848.* Jackson: Price and Fall, 1848.

Ingraham, Joseph Holt. *The South-West: By a Yankee.* 2 vols. New York: Harper and Brothers, 1835.

Jefferson, Thomas. *The Works of Thomas Jefferson: Published by Order of Congress from the Original Manuscripts Deposited in the Department of State.* Ed. H. A. Washington. 9 vols. New York: Townsend MacCoun, 1853–1856.

Johnson, Michael P. "Looking for Lost Kin: Efforts to Reunite Freed Families After Emancipation." In *Southern Families at War: Loyalty and Conflict in the Civil War South,* ed. Catherine Clinton, 15–34. Oxford: Oxford University Press, 2000.

Johnson, Samuel. *A Dictionary of the English Language: In Which the Words Are Deduced from Their Originals, Explained in Their Different Meanings, and Authorized by the Names of the Writers in Whose Works They Are Found.* London: Longman, Brown, 1853.

Johnson, Walter. "Masters and Slaves in the Market: Slavery and the New Orleans Trade, 1804–1864." Ph.D. Diss. Princeton University, 1995.

———. *River of Dark Dreams: Slavery and Empire in the Cotton Kingdom.* Cambridge, Mass.: Belknap, 2013.

———. *Soul by Soul: Life Inside the Antebellum Slave Market.* Cambridge: Harvard University Press, 1999.

Jones, Catherine. "Ties That Bind, Bonds That Break: Children in the Reorganization of Households in Postemancipation Virginia." *Journal of Southern History* 76, no. 1 (February 2010): 71–106.

Jones, Jacqueline. *Saving Savannah: The City and the Civil War.* New York: Vintage, 2008.

Jones, Norese. *Born a Child of Freedom, Yet a Slave: Mechanisms of Control and Strategies of Resistance in Antebellum South Carolina.* Middletown, Conn.: Wesleyan University Press; Hanover, N.H.: University Press of New England, 1990.

Jones-Rogers, Stephanie. "Rethinking Sexual Violence and the Marketplace of Slavery." In *Sexuality and Slavery*, ed. Leslie M. Harris and Daina Ramey Berry. Athens: University of Georgia Press, 2018.

Kaye, Anthony E. *Joining Places: Slave Neighborhoods in the Old South.* Chapel Hill: University of North Carolina Press, 2007.

Kearney, Belle. *A Slaveholder's Daughter.* New York: Abbey, 1900.

Keim, C. Ray. "Primogeniture and Entail in Colonial Virginia." *William and Mary Quarterly* 25, no. 4 (October 1968): 545–586.

Kemble, Frances Anne. *Journal of a Residence on a Georgian Plantation, 1838–1839.* New York: Harper and Brothers, 1864.

Kennedy, V. Lynn. *Born Southern: Childbirth, Motherhood, and Social Networks in the Old South.* Baltimore: Johns Hopkins University Press, 2010.

Kenny, Gale L. "Mastering Childhood: Paternalism, Slavery, and the Southern Domestic in Caroline Howard Gilman's Antebellum Children's Literature." *Southern Quarterly* 44, no.1 (Fall 2006): 65–87.

Kerber, Linda. *No Constitutional Right to Be Ladies: Women and the Obligations of Citizenship.* New York: Hill and Wang, 1999.

Killens, John Oliver. *The Trial Records of Denmark Vesey.* Boston: Beacon, 1970.

King, Edward. *The Great South: A Record of Journeys in Louisiana, Texas, the Indian Territory, Missouri, Arkansas, Mississippi, Alabama, Georgia, Florida, South Carolina, North Carolina, Kentucky, Tennessee, Virginia, West Virginia, and Maryland.* Hartford, Conn.: American Publishing, 1875.

King, Wilma. *African-American Childhoods.* New York: Palgrave Macmillan, 2005.

———. *Stolen Childhood: Slave Youth in Nineteenth-Century America.* Bloomington: Indiana University Press, 2011.

Kleber, John E., Thomas D. Clark, Lowell H. Harrison, and James C. Klotter, eds. *The Kentucky Encyclopedia.* Lexington: University Press of Kentucky, 1992.

Kramer, John Theophilus. *The Slave-Auction.* Boston: Robert F. Wallcut, 1859.

Kvach, John F. *De Bow's Review: The Antebellum Vision of a New South.* Lexington: University Press of Kentucky, 2013.

Lamon, Lester C. *Blacks in Tennessee, 1791–1970.* Knoxville: University of Tennessee Press, 1981.

Lane, Lunsford. *The Narrative of Lunsford Lane, Formerly of Raleigh, N.C., Embracing an Account of His Early Life, the Redemption by Purchase of Himself and Family from Slavery, and His Banishment from the Place of His Birth for the Crime of Wearing a Colored Skin.* Boston: Hewes and Watson's Print, 1848.

Lebsock, Suzanne. *The Free Women of Petersburg: Status and Culture in a Southern Town, 1784–1860.* New York: Norton, 1985.

Lepler, Jessica. *The Many Panics of 1837: People, Politics, and the Creation of a Transatlantic Financial Crisis.* New York: Cambridge University Press, 2013.

Lerner, Gerda. *The Grimké Sisters from South Carolina: Pioneers for Woman's Rights and Abolition*. New York: Oxford University Press, 1998.

Lewis, Enoch, ed. *The African Observer: A Monthly Journal Containing Essays and Documents Illustrative of the General Character and Moral and Political Effects, of Negro Slavery*. Philadelphia: Published by the Editor, 1828.

Lewis, Kay Wright. *A Curse upon the Nation: Race, Freedom, and Extermination in America and the Atlantic World*. Athens: University of Georgia Press, 2017.

Littell, William. *Statute Law of Kentucky; with Notes, Praelections, and Observations on the Public Acts*. Vol. 2. Frankfort: Johnston and Pleasants, 1810.

Litwack, Leon. *Been in the Storm So Long: The Aftermath of Slavery*. New York: Knopf, 1979.

Long, Gretchen. *Doctoring Freedom: The Politics of African American Medical Care in Slavery and Emancipation*. Chapel Hill: University of North Carolina Press, 2012.

Louisiana Digest of 1808, http://digestof1808.law.lsu.edu/.

Lovett, Bobby L. *The African-American History of Nashville, Tennessee, 1780–1930: Elites and Dilemmas*. Fayetteville: University of Arkansas Press, 1999.

Machado, Maria Helena Pereira Toledo. "Between Two Beneditos: Slave Wet-Nurses amid Slavery's Decline in Southeast Brazil." *Slavery and Abolition* 38, no. 2 (April 2017): 320–336.

Malone, Ann Paton. *Sweet Chariot: Slave Family and Household Structure in Nineteenth-Century Louisiana*. Chapel Hill: University of North Carolina Press, 2000.

Marcus, Jacob Rader, ed. *Memoirs of American Jews, 1775–1865*. 3 vols. Philadelphia: Jewish Publication Society of America, 1955–1956.

Marsh, Alfred Henry. *History of the Court of Chancery and of the Rise and Development of the Doctrines of Equity*. Toronto: Carswell, 1890.

Martin, Jonathan D. *Divided Mastery: Slave Hiring in the American South*. Cambridge: Harvard University Press, 2004.

Martineau, Harriet. *Retrospect of Western Travel*. 2 vols. London: Saunders and Otley, 1838.

Martinez, Jaime Amanda. *Confederate Impressment in the Upper South*. Chapel Hill: University of North Carolina Press, 2013.

———. "The Slave Market in Civil War Virginia." In *Crucible of the Civil War: Virginia from Secession to Commemoration*, ed. Edward L. Ayers, Gary W. Gallagher, and Andrew J. Torget, 106–135. Charlottesville: University of Virginia Press, 2006.

McClurken, Jeffrey W. *Take Care of the Living: Reconstructing Confederate Veteran Families in Virginia*. Charlottesville: University of Virginia Press, 2009.

McCord, David J., ed. *Statutes at Large of South Carolina*. Columbia: A. S. Johnston, 1840.

McCurry, Stephanie. *Confederate Reckoning: Power and Politics in the Civil War South*. Cambridge: Harvard University Press, 2010.

———. "The Soldier's Wife: White Women, the State and the Politics of Protection in the Confederacy." In *Women and the Unstable State in Nineteenth-Century America*, ed. Alison M. Parker and Stephanie Cole, 15–36. College Station: Texas A&M University Press, 2000.

McGregor, Deborah Kuhn. *From Midwives to Medicine: The Birth of American Gynecology*. New Brunswick, N.J.: Rutgers University Press, 1998.

McInnis, Maurie. *Slaves Waiting for Sale: Abolitionist Art and the American Slave Trade*. Chicago: University of Chicago Press, 2011.

McKittrick, Katherine. *Demonic Grounds: Black Women and the Cartographies of Struggle*. Minneapolis: University of Minnesota Press, 2006.

McMahon, Lucia. "'So Truly Afflicting and Distressing to Me His Sorrowing Mother': Expressions of Maternal Grief in Eighteenth-Century Philadelphia." *Journal of the Early Republic* 32, no. 1 (2012): 27–60.

McMillen, Sally G. "Breastfeeding and Elite White Motherhood." In *The Old South*, ed. Mark Smith, 249–265. Malden: Blackwell, 2001.

———. *Motherhood in the Old South: Pregnancy, Childbirth and Infant Rearing*. Baton Rouge: Louisiana State University Press, 1990.

———. "Mothers' Sacred Duty: Breast-Feeding Patterns Among Middle- and Upper-Class Women in the Antebellum South." *Journal of Southern History* 51, no. 3 (August 1985): 333–356.

Miller, Marion Mills, ed. *Life and Works of Abraham Lincoln: Speeches and Presidential Addresses, 1859–1865*. Vol. 5. New York: Permanent Literature Company, 1907.

Mills, Jane. *Womanwords: A Dictionary of Words About Women*. New York: Free Press, 1992.

Mitchell, Mary Niall. *Raising Freedom's Child: Black Children and Visions of the Future After Slavery*. New York: New York University Press, 2008.

Molloy, Marie S. *Single, White, Slaveholding Women in the Nineteenth-Century American South*. Columbia: University of South Carolina Press, 2018.

Moore, Jessica Parker. "Keeping All Hands Moving": A Plantation Mistress in Antebellum Arkansas." *Arkansas Historical Quarterly* 74, no. 3 (2015): 257–276.

Morehead, C. S., and Mason Brown. *Digest of the Statute Laws of Kentucky, of a Public and Permanent Nature, from the Commencement of the Government to the Session of the Legislature, Ending on the 24th February, 1834, with References to Judicial Decisions*. Frankfort: A. G. Hodges, 1834.

Morgan, Jennifer. *Laboring Women: Reproduction and Gender in New World Slavery*. Philadelphia: University of Pennsylvania Press, 2004.

Morgan, Thomas Gibbes. *Civil Code of the State of Louisiana: With Statutory Amendments, from 1825 to 1853*. New Orleans: Bloomfield and Steel, 1861.

Morris, Thomas. *Southern Slavery and the Law, 1619–1860*. Chapel Hill: University of North Carolina Press, 1999.

Morseman, Amy Feely. *The Big House After Slavery: Virginia Plantation Families and Their Postbellum Domestic Experiment*. Charlottesville: University of Virginia Press, 2010.

Murrell, Amy. "'Of Necessity and Public Benefit': Southern Families and Their Appeals for Protection." In *Southern Families at War: Loyalty and Conflict in the Civil War South*, ed. Catherine Clinton, 77–100. Oxford: Oxford University Press, 2000.

Myers, Robert Manson. *Children of Pride: A True Story of Georgia and the Civil War*. New Haven: Yale University Press, 1972.

Nelson, Bernard H. "Confederate Slave Impressment Legislation, 1861–1865." *Journal of Negro History* 31, no. 4 (October 1946): 392–410.

Nicholls, Michael L. "Strangers Setting Among Us." *Virginia Magazine of History & Biography* 108, no. 2 (2000): 155–180.

Nicolay, John G., and John Hay, eds. *Abraham Lincoln: Complete Works, Comprising His Speeches, Letters, State Papers, and Miscellaneous Writings.* Vol. 2. New York: Century, 1902.

Norman, Benjamin Moore. *Norman's New Orleans and Environs: Containing a Brief Historical Sketch of the Territory and State of Louisiana, and the City of New Orleans from the Earliest Period to the Present Time.* New Orleans: B. M. Norman, 1845.

Oakes, James. *The Ruling Race: A History of American Slaveholders.* New York: Norton, 1982.

O'Connor, Rachel. *Mistress of Evergreen Plantation: Rachel O'Connor's Legacy of Letters, 1823–1845.* Ed. Allie Bayne Windham Webb. Albany: State University of New York Press, 1983.

O'Donovan, Susan. *Becoming Free in the Cotton South.* Cambridge: Harvard University Press, 2007.

Olmsted, Frederick Law. *A Journey in the Back Country.* New York: Mason Brothers, 1860.

Ott, Victoria E. *Confederate Daughters: Coming of Age During the Civil War.* Carbondale: Southern Illinois University Press, 2008.

Painter, Nell Irvin. "Soul Murder and Slavery: Toward a Full Loaded Cost Accounting." In Painter, *Southern History Across the Color Line,* 15–39. Chapel Hill: University of North Carolina Press, 2002.

Pargas, Damian Alan. *Slavery and Forced Migration in the Antebellum South.* New York: Cambridge University Press, 2014.

Parker, Freddie L., ed. *Stealing a Little Freedom: Advertisements for Slave Runaways in North Carolina, 1791–1840.* New York: Garland, 1994.

Parsons, C. G., M.D. *An Inside View of Slavery; or, A Tour Among the Planters.* Boston: John Jewett, 1855.

Paxton, John Adams. *The New-Orleans Directory and Register: Containing the Names, Professions, & Residences, of All the Heads of Families, and Persons in Business, of the City and Suburbs; Notes on New-Orleans; with Other Useful Information.* New Orleans: Benj. Levy, 1830.

Pease, Jane, and William Pease. *A Family of Women: The Carolina Petigrus in Peace and War.* Chapel Hill: University of North Carolina Press, 1999.

Penningroth, Dylan C. *The Claims of Kinfolk: African American Property and Community in the Nineteenth-Century South.* Chapel Hill: University of North Carolina Press, 2003.

Perdue, Charles L., Thomas E. Barden, and Robert K. Phillips, eds. *Weevils in the Wheat: Interviews with Virginia Ex-Slaves.* Charlottesville: University of Virginia Press, 1976.

Phillips, Ulrich B. *Life and Labor in the Old South.* Boston: Little, Brown, 1929.

Pinckard, George. *Notes on the West Indies: Written During the Expedition Under the Command of the Late General Sir Ralph Abercromby: Including Observations on the Island of Barbadoes, and the Settlements Captured by the British Troops, upon the Coast of Guiana; Likewise Remarks Relating to the Creoles and Slaves of the Western Colonies, and the Indians of South America: With Occasional Hints, Regarding the Seasoning, or Yellow Fever of Hot Climates.* 3 vols. London: Longman, Hurst, Rees, and Orme, 1806.

Potter, Henry, J. L. Taylor, and Bartholomew Yancey, Esq. *Laws of the State of North-Carolina.* Vol. 2. Raleigh: J. Gales, 1821.

Rankin, Thomas. *Letters on American Slavery: Addressed to Thomas Rankin, Merchant at Middlebrook, Augusta Co., Va.* 5th ed. Boston: Isaac Knapp, 1838.

Raska, Ginny McNeill, and Mary Lynne Gasaway Hill, eds. *The Uncompromising Diary of Sallie McNeill, 1858–1867.* College Station: Texas A&M University Press, 2009.

Rasmussen, Daniel. *American Uprising: The Untold Story of America's Largest Slave Revolt.* New York: Harper-Collins, 2011.

Rawick, George P., gen. ed. *The American Slave: A Composite Autobiography.* 19 vols., 2 suppl. series (series 1, 12 vols.; series 2, 10 vols.). Westport: Greenwood, 1972–1979.

Redpath, James. *The Roving Editor; or, Talks with Slaves in the Southern States.* New York: A. B. Burdick, 1859.

Regosin, Elizabeth. *Freedom's Promise: Ex-Slave Families and Citizenship in the Age of Emancipation.* Charlottesville: University of Virginia Press, 2002.

Regosin, Elizabeth, and Donald Shaffer, eds. *Voices of Emancipation: Understanding Slavery, the Civil War, and Reconstruction Through the U.S. Pension Bureau Files.* New York: New York University Press, 2008.

Reid, Whitelaw. *After the War: A Southern Tour, May 1, 1865, to May 1, 1866.* New York: Moore, Wilstach and Baldwin; London: Sampson Low, Son, 1866.

Reports of Cases Argued and Determined in the Supreme Court of Alabama During June Term, 1847 and Part of January Term, 1848. Vol. 12. Tuscaloosa, Ala.: M. D. J. Slade, 1848.

Revised Statutes of the State of Missouri, Revised and Digested by the Eighth General Assembly During the Years One Thousand Eight Hundred and Thirty-Four, and One Thousand Eight Hundred and Thirty-Five. Saint Louis: Argus Office, 1835.

Rhodes, Marissa C. "Domestic Vulnerabilities: Reading Families and Bodies into Eighteenth-Century Anglo-Atlantic Wet Nurse Advertisements." *Journal of Family History* 40, no. 1 (2015): 39–63.

Ripley, Eliza. *From Flag to Flag: A Woman's Adventures and Experiences in the South During the War, in Mexico, and in Cuba.* New York: Appleton, 1889.

———. *Social Life in Old New Orleans.* New York: Appleton, 1912.

Robinson, M. M. *Digest of the Penal Law of the State of Louisiana, Analytically Arranged.* New Orleans: Published for the author, 1841.

Rosen, Hannah. *Terror in the Heart of Freedom: Citizenship, Sexual Violence, and the Meaning of Race in the Postemancipation South.* Chapel Hill: University of North Carolina Press, 2009.

Rothman, Adam. *Slave Country: American Expansion and the Origins of the Deep South.* Cambridge: Harvard University Press, 2005.

Rothman, Joshua D. *Flush Times and Fever Dreams: A Story of Capitalism and Slavery in the Age of Jackson.* Athens: University of Georgia Press, 2012.

Ryan, Mary. *Women in Public: Between Banners and Ballots, 1825–1880.* Baltimore: Johns Hopkins University Press, 1990.

Salmon, Marylynn. "The Cultural Significance of Breastfeeding and Infant Care in Early Modern England and America." *Journal of Social History* 28, no. 2 (Winter 1994): 247–269.

——. *Women and the Law of Property in Early America*. Chapel Hill: University of North Carolina Press, 1986.

Sanger, George P., ed. *The Statutes at Large, Treaties, and Proclamations, of the United States of America from December 5, 1859, to March 3, 1863*. Vol. 12. Boston: Little, Brown, 1863.

——. *The Statutes at Large, Treaties, and Proclamations, of the United States of America from December 1863, to December 1865*. Vol. 13. Boston: Little, Brown, 1866.

Schafer, Judith. *Becoming Free, Remaining Free: Manumission and Enslavement in New Orleans, 1846–1862*. Baton Rouge: Louisiana State University Press, 2003.

——. *Brothels, Depravity, and Abandoned Women: Illegal Sex in Antebellum New Orleans*. Baton Rouge: Louisiana State University Press, 2011.

——. *Slavery, the Civil Law, and the Supreme Court of Louisiana*. Baton Rouge: Louisiana State University Press, 1997.

Schermerhorn, Calvin. *The Business of Slavery and the Rise of American Capitalism, 1815–1860*. New Haven: Yale University Press, 2015.

Schwalm, Leslie. *Emancipation's Diaspora: Race and Reconstruction in the Upper Midwest*. Chapel Hill: University of North Carolina Press, 2009.

——. *A Hard Fight for We: Women's Transition from Slavery to Freedom in South Carolina*. Bloomington: University of Illinois Press, 1997.

Schwartz, Marie Jenkins. "At Noon, Oh How I Ran: Breastfeeding and Weaning on Plantation and Farm in Antebellum Virginia and Alabama." In *Discovering the Women in Slavery: Emancipating Perspectives of the American Past*, ed. Patricia Morton, 241–259. Athens: University of Georgia Press, 1996.

Schwarz, Philip J. *Twice Condemned: Slaves and Criminal Laws of Virginia*. Baton Rouge: Louisiana State University Press, 1988.

Scott, Anne Firor. *The Southern Lady: From Pedestal to Politics, 1830–1930*. Chicago: University of Chicago Press, 1970.

Scott, Rebecca. "The Battle over the Child: Child Apprenticeship and the Freedmen's Bureau in North Carolina." *Prologue: The Journal of the National Archives* 10, no. 2 (Summer 1978): 101–113.

Sedgwick, Catharine. *The Linwoods; or, "Sixty Years Since" in America*. 2 vols. New York: Harper and Brothers, 1836.

Sellers, W. W. *A History of Marion County, South Carolina, from its Earliest Times to the Present, 1901*. Columbia: R. L. Bryan, 1902.

Shaffer, Donald. *After the Glory: The Struggles of Black Civil War Veterans*. Lawrence: University Press of Kansas, 2004.

Shammas, Carol. *The History of Household Government in America*. Charlottesville: University of Virginia Press, 2002.

Shammas, Carol, Marylynn Salmon, and Michel Dahlin. *Inheritance in America*. New Brunswick, N.J.: Rutgers University Press, 1987.

Shaw, Stephanie J. "Using the WPA Ex-Slave Narratives to Study the Impact of the Great Depression." *Journal of Southern History* 69, no. 3 (2003): 623–658.

Smith, Adam. *Lectures on Jurisprudence*. Ed. R. L. Meek, D. D. Raphael, and P. G. Stein. Oxford: Oxford University Press, 1978.

Smith, Eric Ledell. "Rescuing African American Kidnapping Victims in Philadelphia as Documented in the Joseph Watson Papers at the Historical Society of Pennsylvania." *Pennsylvania Magazine of History and Biography* 129, no. 3 (July 2005): 317–345.

Smith, Katy Simpson. *We Have Raised All of You: Motherhood in the South, 1750–1835*. Baton Rouge: Louisiana State University Press, 2013.

Snyder, Terri L. *Brabbling Women: Disorderly Speech and the Law in Early Virginia*. Ithaca: Cornell University Press, 2003.

Soapes, Thomas F. "The Federal Writers' Project Slave Interviews: Useful Data or Misleading Source." *Oral History Review* 5 (1977): 33–38.

Spear, Jennifer. *Race, Sex, and Social Order in Early New Orleans*. Baltimore: Johns Hopkins University Press, 2009.

Spindel, Donna J. "Assessing Memory: Twentieth-Century Slave Narratives Reconsidered." *Journal of Interdisciplinary History* 27, no. 2 (1996): 247–261.

Sprankling, John G. "The Right to Destroy." In *The International Law of Property*, ed. John G. Sprankling. Oxford: Oxford University Press, 2014.

Spruill, Julia Cherry. *Women's Life and Work in the Southern Colonies*. New York: Norton, 1972.

Stanley, Amy Dru. "Histories of Capitalism and Sex Difference." *Journal of the Early Republic* 36, no. 2 (Summer 2016): 343–350.

——. "Home Life and the Morality of the Market." In *The Market Revolution in America: Social, Political, and Religious Expressions, 1800–1880*, ed. Melvyn Stokes and Stephen Conway, 76–81. Charlottesville: University of Virginia Press, 1996.

Steckel, Richard H. "Antebellum Southern White Fertility: A Demographic and Economic Analysis." *Journal of Economic History* 40, no. 2 (June 1980): 331–350.

Steele, Jeffrey. "The Gender and Racial Politics of Mourning in Antebellum America." In *An Emotional History of the United States*, ed. Peter N. Stearns and Jan Lewis, 91–106. New York: New York University Press, 1998.

Stevenson, Brenda. "What's Love Got to Do with It? Concubinage and Enslaved Women and Girls in the Antebellum South." *Journal of African American History* 98, no. 1 (Winter 2013): 99–125.

Story, Joseph. *Commentaries on Equity Jurisprudence as Administered in England and America*. 10th ed. Ed. Rev. Isaac F. Redfield. Boston: Little, Brown, 1870.

Stowe, Harriet Beecher. *A Key to "Uncle Tom's Cabin": Presenting the Original Facts and Documents upon Which the Story Is Founded. Together with Corroborative Statements Verifying the Truth of the Work*. Boston: John P. Jewett, 1853.

Strahilevitz, Lior Jacob. "The Right to Destroy." *Yale Law Journal* 114, no. 4 (January 2005): 781–854.

Sturtz, Linda L. *Within Her Power: Propertied Women in Colonial Virginia*. New York: Routledge, 2002.

Sundberg, Sara. "Women and Property in Early Louisiana: Legal Systems at Odds." *Journal of the Early Republic* 32 (Winter 2012): 633–665.

———. "Women and the Law of Property Under Louisiana Civil Law, 1782–1835." Ph.D. Diss. Louisiana State University, 2001.

Tadman, Michael. *Speculators and Slaves: Masters, Traders, and Slaves in the Old South.* Madison: University of Wisconsin Press, 1989.

Tansey, Richard. "Bernard Kendig and the New Orleans Slave Trade." *Louisiana History* 23, no. 2 (Spring 1982): 159–178.

———. "Prostitution and Politics in Antebellum New Orleans." *Southern Studies* 18 (1980): 449–479.

Taylor, C. James, Margaret A. Hogan, Karen N. Barzilay, Gregg L. Lint, Hobson Woodward, Mary T. Claffey, Robert F. Karachuk, and Sara B. Sikes, eds. *The Adams Papers, Adams Family Correspondence.* Vol. 9: *January 1790–December 1793.* Cambridge: Harvard University Press, 2009.

Taylor, David. *Soul of a People: The WPA Writers' Project Uncovers Depression America.* Hoboken, N.J.: Wiley, 2009.

Territory of Orleans. *Acts Passed at the First Session of the First Legislature of the Territory of Orleans.* New Orleans: Bradford and Anderson, Printers to the Territory, 1807.

Thomas, Ella Gertrude Clanton. *The Secret Eye: The Journal of Ella Gertrude Clanton Thomas, 1848–1889.* Ed. Virginia Ingraham Burr. Chapel Hill: University of North Carolina Press, 1990.

Tise, Larry E. *Proslavery: A History of the Defense of Slavery in America, 1701–1840.* Athens: University of Georgia Press, 1987.

Treckel, Paula A. "Breastfeeding and Maternal Sexuality in Colonial America." *Journal of Interdisciplinary History* 20, no. 1 (1989): 25–51.

Tupper, James. *Report, Office of State Auditor, South Carolina: Claims Against the State for Slaves Lost in the Public Service.* Columbia: November 28, 1863.

———. *Report Listing Eight Additional Claims for Slaves Lost in Public Service.* Columbia, 1863.

———. *Report of the Auditor of South Carolina on Claims Against the State for Slaves Lost in the Public Service.* Columbia: Charles P. Pelham, State Printer, 1864.

Ulrich, Laurel Thatcher. *Good Wives: Image and Reality in the Lives of Women in Northern New England.* New York: Knopf, 1982.

———. *A Midwife's Tale: The Life of Martha Ballard, Based on Her Diary, 1785–1812.* New York: Vintage, 1991.

Unwritten History of Slavery: Autobiographical Accounts of Negro Ex-Slaves. Nashville: Fisk University Social Science Institute, 1968.

U.S. Bureau of the Census. *Fifth Census of the United States.* Washington, D.C.: National Archives and Records Administration, 1830.

———. *Seventh Census of the United States.* Washington, D.C.: National Archives and Records Administration, 1850.

———. *Eighth Census of the United States, 1860.* Washington, D.C.: National Archives and Records Administration, 1860.

———. *Ninth Census of the United States, 1870.* Washington, D.C.: National Archives and Records Administration, 1870.

———. *The Statistical History of the United States, from Colonial Times to the Present: Historical Statistics of the United States, Colonial Times to 1970*. New York: Basic, 1976.

———. *Statistics of the United States, Including Mortality, Property, etc. in 1860*. Washington, D.C.: Government Printing Office, 1866.

U.S. House of Representatives. Executive Documents Printed by Order of the House of Representatives, During the First Session of the Thirty Ninth Congress, 1865–'66. Washington, D.C.: Government Printing Office, 1866.

U.S. War Department. *The War of the Rebellion: A Compilation of the Official Records of the Union and Confederate Armies*. 69 vols. (series 1, 53 vols.; series 2, 8 vols.; series 3, 5 vols.; series 4, 3 vols.). Washington, D.C.: Government Printing Office, 1880–1901.

Venable, William Henry. *Down South Before the War: Record of a Ramble to New Orleans in 1858*. Reprinted in *Ohio Archaeological and Historical Quarterly* 2, no. 4. Columbus: Ohio State Archaeological and Historical Society, 1888, n.p.

Walker, Daniel E. *No More, No More: Slavery and Cultural Resistance in Havana and New Orleans*. Minneapolis: University of Minnesota Press, 2004.

Waterbury, Maria. *Seven Years Among the Freedmen*. Chicago: T. B. Arnold, 1890.

Watkins, James L., Special Agent. U.S. Department of Agriculture. Division of Statistics. *Production and Price of Cotton for One Hundred Years*. Washington, D.C.: Government Printing Office, 1895.

Watson, Alan. "Roman Slave Law: An Anglo-American Perspective." *Cardozo Law Review* 18 (1996): 591–598.

Watson, Henry. *Narrative of Henry Watson, a Fugitive Slave, Written by Himself*. Boston: Published by Bela Marsh, 25 Cornhill, 1848.

Weld, Charles. *A Vacation Tour in the United States and Canada*. London: Longman, Brown, Green, and Longmans, 1855.

Weld, Theodore Dwight. *American Slavery as It Is: Testimony of a Thousand Witnesses*. New York: American Anti-Slavery Society, 1839.

Williams, Heather Andrea. *Help Me to Find My People: The African-American Search for Family Lost in Slavery*. Chapel Hill: University of North Carolina Press, 2012.

———. *Self-Taught: African American Education in Slavery and Freedom*. Chapel Hill: University of North Carolina Press, 2005.

Williams, Kidada E. *They Left Great Marks on Me: African American Testimonies of Racial Violence from Emancipation to World War I*. New York: New York University Press, 2012.

Wilson, Charles Reagan, William Ferris, and Ann J. Adadie, eds. *Encyclopedia of Southern Culture*. Chapel Hill: University of North Carolina Press, 1989.

Wood, Kirsten E. *Masterful Women: Slaveholding Widows from the American Revolution Through the Civil War*. Chapel Hill: University of North Carolina Press, 2004.

Woodman, Harold. *King Cotton and His Retainers: Financing and Marketing the Cotton Crop of the South, 1800–1925*. Washington, D.C.: Beard Books, 1999.

Woodward, Colin Edward. *Marching Masters: Slavery, Race, and the Confederate Army During the Civil War*. Charlottesville: University of Virginia Press, 2014.

Woodward, C. Vann. "History from Slave Sources." *American Historical Review* 79, no. 2 (1974): 470–481.

Wyvill, Richard A. *Memoirs of an Old Army Officer: Richard A. Wyvill's Visits to Barbadoes in 1796 and 1806–7*, ed. Jerome S. Handler, as quoted in *Journal of the Barbados Museum and Historical Society* 35, no. 1 (March 1975): 21–30.

Yetman, Norman R. "The Background of the Slave Narrative Collection." *American Quarterly* 19, no. 3 (Fall 1967): 534–553.

——. "Ex-Slave Interviews and the Historiography of Slavery." *American Quarterly* 36, no. 2 (1984): 181–210.

Youcha, Geraldine. *Minding the Children: Child Care in America from Colonial Times to the Present*. New York: Scribner's, 1995.

Zabin, Serena. "Women's Trading Networks and Dangerous Economies in Eighteenth-Century New York City." *Early American Studies* 4, no. 2 (Fall 2006): 291–321.

Zaborney, John J. *Slaves for Hire: Renting Enslaved Laborers in Antebellum Virginia*. Baton Rouge: Louisiana State University Press, 2012.

ACKNOWLEDGMENTS

I rarely read other authors' acknowledgments because they make me cry. They not only lay bare the extraordinary networks of family, friends, and peers who make books possible; they also reveal the profound love that helps sustain each author on his or her journey to completion. That's what gets me every time. Now that I am writing my own, I find it to be a momentous task, one that is far more difficult to complete than I ever imagined.

I am a statistic in almost every way, and no one, including myself, could have guessed that I would become a professor of history or write a book. My grandparents were North Carolina sharecroppers who never attended high school. I am the daughter of a single mother who finished high school while she was pregnant with my sister. I was raised in Newark, New Jersey, which, until recently, claimed the highest homicide rate in the state. I was a teenage mother. I received welfare benefits and food stamps and was even evicted from my apartment because I could not pay my rent. And despite, or perhaps because of, this past, I am here. Many people guided me along the way.

My mother was the first historian I ever knew. When I was a teenager, we drank coffee and tea while she told me stories of her childhood as a sharecropper's daughter. She wrote dates and locations on the backs of every historical object we kept in our apartment, and she recounted the events that made each object worth keeping. She taught me the importance of remembering and of truths that should never be forgotten. She was like a magician to me because she always seemed to know how to make the apparently impossible possible. Even more than this, she never placed constraints on what I could become, and she never doubted that I could be all that I am today. Her boundless love has sustained me through the darkest and brightest times. She continues to be my biggest and most enthusiastic fan, and for that I owe her my greatest debt.

At nineteen, I met one of the most extraordinary human beings to walk the earth, my husband, Tyshon. He has been the glue that has held me together all these years. We have been dirt-poor together, barely making it together, and semi-comfortable together. He's been an exceptional father to our son, Ramess. He's also been my friend, my therapist, my at-home colleague, my editor, and a bit of my agent, too. More vitally, he has always respected me and treated me as his equal. He is a rare bird indeed, and I'm so fortunate to have him in my life.

I have to thank my sister Stacy for supporting me through a tough phase of my life and opening her home to me while I was writing the final chapters of my dissertation.

I would not be a historian today if it were not for Deborah Gray White and Kim Butler. As an undergraduate psychology major, I was convinced that I'd become a psychologist. But the course of my life changed when I met Deborah and Kim. In word and deed, Deborah personified the historian I hoped to become. She was candid about her humble beginnings, and she talked about the discrimination she'd experienced over the course of her career. As my intellectual mother, she never dismissed my hopes or my ideas. She introduced me to a world I had never known as a young girl living in Newark. She was gracious enough to allow me to bring my infant son to class when I was an undergraduate, and as my mentor and dissertation chair, she continued to support me in ways that could never be reciprocated.

Kim Butler, whose passion for history made it exciting for me, was the first professor to talk to me about graduate school, something I had never considered. It was her encouragement that ultimately led to my pursuit of a doctoral degree. For all of this, I owe Deborah and Kim my deep gratitude.

No amount of thanks could possibly convey my appreciation for the support that Daina Ramey Berry, Ellen Hartigan-O'Connor, Cornelia Dayton Hughes, Leslie Schwalm, and Kathryn Kish Sklar have given to me. They have been gracious and extraordinarily generous with their time and their wisdom as I completed this project. I have grown immensely because of them.

Thavolia Glymph and Jennifer Morgan, as well as the late Stephanie M. H. Camp and the late Judith Kelleher Shafer, whose work proved to be, and continues to be, fundamental to my training and intellectual development as a scholar of slavery, read my work in progress and offered invaluable feedback. Linda Kerber and Emily West provided me with my first opportunities to publish my work. I am forever grateful to them for recognizing the importance and value of my research.

I extend special thanks to my friend Alix Genter, whose questions during Nancy Hewitt's women's and gender history research seminar served as the catalyst for the research that began as my dissertation and forms the basis of this book. When other graduate students made me feel invisible, she made it clear that she saw me. Her acknowledgment of my presence, her support, and her conversation made all the difference during particularly isolating times.

Leigh-Anne Francis became my dear friend and intellectual big sister. I remember the first time I met her. When she came into the room her presence was immediately felt. She did not shrink in the ways that I initially did. She recognized my potential, taught me about the importance of self-care, and encouraged me to take a seat at the proverbial table. She always treated me with kindness and honored my humanity. I could never repay her in kind.

Professors in the Rutgers-Newark Federated History Department, especially Beryl Satter, Susan Carruthers, Karen Caplan, James Goodman, Eva Giloi, and Stephen Pemberton were critical to my training, and they helped me become the historian I am today. They all pushed me out of my intellectual comfort zone. They were tough but always supportive. A heartfelt thanks to them. Christina Strasburger always brightened my day with her kindness and her smiles. I owe them all, and the Rutgers-Newark History Department, a great debt.

From the moment I met her, Nancy Hewitt exuded an indescribable kind of light. From the time I was completing my doctoral work, she has offered me nothing but support, smiles, and encouragement. Thank you for sharing your light with me, Nancy. Michael Adas, Mia Bay, Ruth Feldstein, Seth Koven, James Livingston, Donna Murch, and Camilla Townsend taught me to think about history in nuanced ways and helped me to further polish and refine my skills as a historian both in and out of their classrooms.

My Berkeley colleagues have supported me in innumerable ways since my arrival in fall 2014. I am especially indebted to Rebecca McLennan, Thomas Laqueur, Waldo Martin, David Henkin, Dylan Penningroth, Margaret Chowning, Tabitha Konogo, Mark Peterson, Robin Einhorn, Mark Brilliant, and Victoria Frede, who read multiple drafts of this book and helped me work through most of the kinks. The advice, support, and friendship of my colleagues Sandra Eder, Caitlin Rosenthal, and Elena Schneider have made my time at Berkeley enjoyable. A warm thanks must go to Marianne Bartholomew-Couts, Janet Flores, and Jan Haase, who helped me maximize my research funds and figure out how to afford to do the research while paying off a six-figure student debt and caring for my family.

Edward Baptist, Rick Bell, Steven Deyle, Walter Johnson, Adam Rothman, and many peers have read and offered helpful feedback about this book. Yvonne Pitts proposed the term "double mastery" in her commentary about my conference paper "'Her Title to Said Negroes Is Perfect & Complete': Slavery, Marriage, and Women's Challenges to Coverture in the Nineteenth-Century South," which was presented during the American Society for Legal History's 2015 Annual Meeting. I thank them all for their generative comments and feedback.

Heartfelt thanks must be extended to the undergraduate students who enrolled in my classes and assisted me with my research via Berkeley's Undergraduate Research Apprenticeship Program over the years. They routinely posed provocative questions about women and slavery for which I had no answer, and their questions compelled me to search for answers, searches that helped shape the content that appears in this book.

The University of Iowa School of Letters and Sciences, the Newcomb College Institute of Tulane University (with warm thanks to Sally Kenney and Laura Wolford), the Institute of International Studies, and the Board of Regents at the University of California, Berkeley, offered generous funding that helped support this project.

Thank you to archivists on staff who meticulously care for the invaluable special collections housed in the New Orleans Public Library, the Earl K. Long Library at the University of New Orleans, the Historical New Orleans Collection, and the New Orleans Historical Notarial Archives. I especially thank Jennifer Dorner, the former history librarian at Berkeley, who fought to acquire access to archival collections that proved vital to my research for this book.

And last, but certainly not least, I send my deepest thanks to my editors, William Frucht, Karen Olson, Susan Laity, and Cecelia Cancellaro. I extend special thanks to Laura Duvalis and Chuck Grench, who worked with me on earlier versions of this project.

Portions of chapter 1 first appeared as "Mistresses in the Making," in *Women's America: Refocusing the Past*, 8th ed. (Oxford: Oxford University Press, 2015). Linda Kerber, Jane Sherron De Hart, Cornelia Hughes Dayton, and Judy Wu served as editors, and the content is reproduced by permission of Oxford University Press, https://global.oup.com/ushe/product/womens-america-9780199349340?cc=us&lang=en&. An abbreviated version of Chapter 5 appeared as "'[S]he could . . . spare one ample breast for the profit of her owner': White Mothers and Enslaved Wet Nurses' Invisible Labor in American Slave Markets," in *Slavery & Abolition* 38, no. 2 (April 2017), and is republished by permission of Taylor and Francis Ltd.

INDEX

Page numbers in italics refer to illustrations.

279